CONSTRUCTING COMMUNITY

Constructing Community

URBAN GOVERNANCE,
DEVELOPMENT, AND
INEQUALITY IN BOSTON

Jeremy R. Levine

PRINCETON UNIVERSITY PRESS
PRINCETON & OXFORD

Copyright © 2021 by Princeton University Press

Princeton University Press is committed to the protection of copyright and the intellectual property our authors entrust to us. Copyright promotes the progress and integrity of knowledge. Thank you for supporting free speech and the global exchange of ideas by purchasing an authorized edition of this book. If you wish to reproduce or distribute any part of it in any form, please obtain permission.

Requests for permission to reproduce material from this work should be sent to permissions@press.princeton.edu

Published by Princeton University Press
41 William Street, Princeton, New Jersey 08540
6 Oxford Street, Woodstock, Oxfordshire OX20 1TR

press.princeton.edu

All Rights Reserved
ISBN 9780691193656
ISBN (pbk.) 9780691193649
ISBN (e-book) 9780691205885

Library of Congress Control Number: 2021932711

British Library Cataloging-in-Publication Data is available

Editorial: Meagan Levinson and Jacqueline Delaney
Production Editorial: Karen Carter
Jacket/Cover Design: Lauren Smith
Production: Brigid Ackerman
Publicity: Kate Hensley and Kathryn Stevens
Copyeditor: Karen Verde

This book has been composed in Miller

Printed on acid-free paper. ∞

Printed in the United States of America

10 9 8 7 6 5 4 3 2 1

CONTENTS

Acknowledgments · vii

Introduction   1

PART I

CHAPTER 1	Slow Train Coming	31
CHAPTER 2	A Seat at the Table	55
CHAPTER 3	In Search of Spatial Legibility	83

PART II

CHAPTER 4	Representing the Community	109
CHAPTER 5	Following the Money	137
CHAPTER 6	Community Power	163
	Conclusion	192

Methodological Appendix · 205
Notes · 219
Bibliography · 239
Index · 257

ACKNOWLEDGMENTS

BEFORE THIS BOOK WAS A BOOK, it was a dissertation completed under the guidance of four brilliant Harvard sociologists. Bill Wilson was my advisor—a statement that frankly is surreal to put in writing. Bill is an intellectual giant and it was an incredible privilege to be part of his most recent generation of advisees. We co-authored an article (my first publication) and co-taught a seminar (my first teaching experience). But Bill's mentorship extended far beyond research and teaching. We talked about urban policy over meals at some of Cambridge's best restaurants. Knowing that I was a Celtics fan, he even treated me to tenth-row, half-court seats at a playoff game. Bill showed me how to do sociology, but also how to live a fulfilling life as a sociologist.

Chris Winship was my dissertation co-chair and, like Bill, has advised an extensive list of urban sociologists. Chris is best known as an expert in quantitative methodology, but he is no less skilled in ethnography. He also has a deep interest in Boston politics with plenty of stories to share. All told, Chris helped make every aspect of this project better.

Compared to Bill and Chris, Rob Sampson was much more guarded with his time—a useful lesson in its own right as I move forward on the tenure track. His comments were always worth the wait though, and he went above and beyond the call of duty whenever I could nail him down. Rob took my work seriously and believed in my ability to make important contributions to knowledge. Perhaps most important, he had an uncanny ability to find all of the loose threads in my writing and give each and every one of them a good, hearty tug. One thing that always puzzled me was his fixation on certain phrases or small points that were unrelated to a paper's core thesis. I didn't understand what the big deal was until I started submitting my work to the peer review process. When it finally clicked and I could see what Rob saw, I knew I was starting to see like a sociologist.

Jocelyn Viterna rounded out my dissertation committee. One of the best compliments I can give Jocelyn is that she was an absolutely indispensable committee member even though she is not an urban sociologist. That speaks to both her generosity as a mentor and her intellectual breadth as a scholar. We shared similar perspectives about the discipline, and she supported the substantive focus of my research, even when others advised against it. I simply could not have completed this work without her.

I can't say enough about my peers in the Department of Sociology at Harvard and the Multidisciplinary Program in Inequality and Social Policy at the Kennedy School. It was daunting, intimidating, and a little bit exhilarating to be surrounded by so many smart, dedicated, and even helpful social scientists. I learned that I work best when I'm a little fish in a big pond—and Harvard was a massive ocean. I oscillated between imposter syndrome, unearned arrogance, and a little fake-it-til-you-make-it perseverance. Ultimately, I left graduate school with more perspective than I came in with, and far more humility (if you can believe it).

While in graduate school, a number of friends, colleagues, and faculty members provided feedback on various aspects of this research. Some read full drafts, others served as sounding boards for me to work out ideas. All were invaluable. I thank Monica Bell, Bart Bonikowski, Sarah Brayne, Steven Brown, Tony Chen, Carl Gershenson, David Hureau, Jackie Hwang, Carly Knight, Michéle Lamont, Caroline Lee, Theo Leenman, Paul Lichterman, David Luberoff, Michael McQuarrie, Alex Murphy, Rourke O'Brien, Ann Owens, David Pedulla, Kristin Perkins, Kim Pernell, Jim Quane, Eva Rosen, Jasmin Sandelson, Tracey Shollenberger, Mario Small, Ben Sosnaud, Mo Torres, and Rob Vargas. If I left out anyone who helped push this project forward, I'm sorry, it wasn't intentional. It has just taken a really (really!) long time to get this book out.

My colleagues at Michigan—both past and present—have been overwhelmingly supportive. Elizabeth Armstrong, Beth Popp Berman, Nick Camp, Steve Garcia, Ashley Harrell, Arnold Ho, Sandy Levitsky, Mark Mizruchi, Steve Samford, Sara Soderstrom, and Al Young helped make this book possible by making all other aspects of life as an assistant professor painless.

I benefited tremendously from two writing groups as a faculty member at Michigan. Karyn Lacy, Jacob Lederman, Sanyu Mojola, and Alex Murphy were instrumental during the initial stages of writing. Alex, Jacob, Neil Gong, and Dan Hirschman offered big-picture insights on a near-complete draft. Both groups pulled me out of the weeds and helped me see the forest for the trees.

I was also fortunate enough to organize a book conference with four outside readers. Nicole Marwell, Andy Papachristos, Pat Sharkey, and Ed Walker read an early draft and provided excellent—if a bit overwhelming—feedback that made this a stronger, more cohesive book.

I presented this research at Stanford University, UC Riverside, the University of Chicago, the University of Michigan, UCLA, NYU, Drexel University, the University of Pittsburgh, and the Annual Meetings of the American Sociological Association. Thanks to everyone who attended these presentations and asked incisive questions, pushing me to clarify or refine my arguments.

Portions of chapters 4 and 6 are reproduced from articles published in the *American Sociological Review* and *Social Forces*, respectively. I thank the editors and reviewers from both journals for helping me develop these ideas.

I also thank the anonymous reviewers for helping make this book the best it could be.

Lindsay Hiser and Zoe Mankes provided crucial research assistance.

Letta Page made the prose crisper and clearer than I ever could have on my own.

The team at Princeton University Press has been first-class all the way. My editor, Meagan Levinson, skillfully ushered the manuscript through an unusually long and complicated review process. She's a real mensch. Karen Carter was an awesome production editor, and Jackie Delaney did excellent project management work behind the scenes. Theresa Liu was an exceptional copywriter. Each of the teams handling the different stages of production and promotion have been an absolute pleasure to work with. My only complaint is that they did not honor my wish to use a photo taken when I was three years old, "reading" Bill Wilson's classic *The Truly Disadvantaged* on my mother's lap while she prepared to teach a class on social stratification, as my professional headshot. They sided with my wife, who thought it was a ridiculous request. I'll concede that they probably made the right decision.

Of course, I cannot leave out the people who allowed me to attend their meetings and observe their work. To everyone trying to make the Fairmount Corridor a better place for its residents: Thank you.

We now come to the friends and family section—the people who helped me complete my research and writing mostly by doing things that had nothing to do with research and writing. Thank you for all of the skills, lessons, and privileges that informed who I am and what I have been able to accomplish. Allie Levine deserves special recognition—the most recognition, in fact. More than anyone else, Allie has supported me from the beginning of my fieldwork to the final production of this book. She is, without question, the most important person in my life. She is also responsible for our kids' best traits. Abram is the kindest, sweetest, most empathetic person I have ever known. In just one year of life, Zara has proven to be remarkably determined, decisive, and adventurous. I write these words in the fall of 2020, as the COVID-19 pandemic continues to take a toll on our lives and the lives of those we care about. We are living in a moment of great uncertainty and unrest. At the same time—or perhaps because of it—we have grown closer than I ever could have imagined. While I wish the circumstances were different, I am forever grateful for the time we were able to spend together and the incredible bond we forged as a result.

I want to close by dedicating this book to my late grandmother, Rae Levine. When I chose to study the Fairmount Corridor, I knew there were connections to my family history. The Corridor includes the neighborhoods of Roxbury, Dorchester, and Mattapan—formerly Jewish neighborhoods where my maternal family resided between the 1890s and 1970s. But I didn't initially appreciate how closely the stories intertwined. As it turned out, the building where Rae spent part of her adolescence was redeveloped during my fieldwork. And not only that: The project was part of a major federal grant, awarded to a partnership between city government and four Corridor nonprofits, with supplemental funding provided by a number of philanthropic foundations. In other words, the story of Rae's childhood apartment symbolizes many of the tensions and themes that animate my work. The intersection of fieldwork and family history was always in the back of my mind, and it made writing this book especially meaningful.

CONSTRUCTING COMMUNITY

Introduction

ON A SWEATY June afternoon in 2011, fifty professionally dressed men and women gathered at a construction site in Codman Square, a low-income neighborhood in Boston. Two events were on the day's agenda. The first was a groundbreaking for a new transit station on a 9-mile commuter rail line known as the Fairmount Line. The tracks bisected some of the city's poorest neighborhoods, yet no train had stopped in Codman Square in more than sixty years. Local nonprofit leaders considered this an injustice, and in the early 2000s, they urged the state to expand access to the transit line. In 2005, state officials committed to four new stations, including the one in Codman Square.

The second event was a ribbon cutting for an affordable housing development located two blocks from the new transit station. The proximity was no coincidence. Nonprofit developers and city government officials saw the new stations as an opportunity to concentrate housing and commercial development within walking distance to public transit, all with an eye toward environmental sustainability—a form of urban planning generally referred to as "community development." The project was one of dozens developed by a coalition of nonprofit organizations in neighborhoods adjacent to the rail line. By the late 2000s, these nonprofit leaders and their funders began calling the area "the Fairmount Corridor" as a way to organize their collective efforts. Together, the two events represented their vision for the Corridor, a vision at the forefront of US urban policy.

Notable figures from Boston's redevelopment community were in attendance that day. Highly visible state representatives and city councilors mingled with lesser-known bureaucrats from city, state, and federal departments. Program officers from philanthropic foundations chatted with community organizers and consultants who had offered technical or strategic expertise. A slight majority were white—an inversion of the neighborhood's majority nonwhite demographics. Most people knew each other; others introduced themselves by listing their current and previous affiliations.

[2] INTRODUCTION

The star of the show was Gail Latimore, executive director of the Codman Square Neighborhood Development Corporation (CSNDC). Gail and her staff had advocated strongly for the new train station and developed the new housing alongside a coalition of additional nonprofits. She may not have been recognizable to most Bostonians, but Gail, a prominent Black nonprofit director, was as well-known as anyone in Codman Square that day.

The site in Codman Square was perfectly prepared for a photo op. A podium bearing the state seal was placed in front of a large construction vehicle. A line of speakers—elected representatives, appointed government bureaucrats, and nonprofit leaders—stood side by side behind the podium. To their left, fifteen bright silver shovels had been planted in a pile of light brown dirt. To their right, passenger trains slowly rumbled down the Fairmount Line tracks.

As the sun beat down, the formal speaking program began. "We are here to celebrate the revitalization of the Fairmount Corridor," a state transportation official began, "and continued good progress on an important project that we committed to many years ago and are delivering on today." Deval Patrick, the state's first Black governor, followed. "This is an exciting project," he beamed. "A long time coming."

Mayor Thomas Menino, serving his fifth term in office, spoke next. Not known for his way with words, the mayor nevertheless captured the occasion well. "What a great day in the neighborhood, right?" he observed with pride. "Long awaited, and today we have the day." He singled out Gail and her organization for "bringing economic opportunity to the people who live in our neighborhoods." He also extolled the virtue of intergovernmental collaboration, thanking "the team at the state . . . [and] the folks in the federal government. All of us working together, with your legislators and City Council." But ultimate credit went to Gail, who "kept our feet to the fire on this project. And today that reality is here."

Word of these accomplishments would spread beyond Boston. As the regional administrator for the Environmental Protection Agency (EPA) later told the crowd, federal officials would "keep talking about this wherever we go throughout the country so this becomes the model of how we do environmental policy, housing policy, and transit policy in America."

Once the formal speaking portion ended, it was time to "break ground" on the new station. The speakers lined up behind the shovels, scooped up small piles of dirt, and, on the count of three, tossed the dirt in the air. Everyone smiled as photographers snapped photos and TV cameras rolled. Afterward, the group walked down the street to the site of the new housing development. Gail and five representatives from private funding organizations posed for pictures alongside the mayor as he cut a large red ribbon.

Celebrations like the ones in Codman Square typically occur at the end of a project's life cycle. Yet before any celebration—before the smiles and photos and collective back patting—officials first host a series of public meetings in which residents vet plans for their neighborhoods. These meetings see more contestation than celebration as the public learns the details of a proposed project and expresses any reservations about its impact.

One such meeting occurred six days before the events in Codman Square. About thirty people gathered at a public library in the low-income neighborhood of Mattapan. A mix of white and Latino state officials moderated, while a handful of Black nonprofit organizers and residents sat in the audience. The topic was the placement of another proposed station on the Fairmount Line—this one not yet under construction.

State officials had intended to present a construction schedule and, if necessary, alleviate any concerns about noise or other minor inconveniences. But residents had a different agenda. A small group of older, middle-class Black women whose homes abutted the proposed construction area bitterly contested the new station. One, Barbara, had come to the meeting not to discuss particulars of construction, but to resist the station altogether. "I just want it to be publicly known that [we are] opposed to it, as we were from the beginning," she announced. "So that people don't get the impression that you are moving forward with our approval. We still feel the same way and we will still continue to oppose it any way we can." Barbara and her neighbors were not opposed to the train that traveled behind their backyards, but they feared that the new station would negatively impact their property values and disrupt their quality of life.

Barbara's comments were a blow to the nonprofit community organizers who had advocated for better public transit access along the Fairmount Corridor. To them, the proposed station represented an important opportunity for low-income, carless Mattapan residents to quickly and cheaply reach jobs and other resources located in downtown Boston. More practically, they knew that "community consensus" was necessary for the project to move forward. Barbara's firm opposition posed a significant threat to their advocacy.

After the meeting, the organizers huddled in the back of the room. They dismissed the opposition as a product of insufficient community organizing, vowing to do a better job "organizing for a 'yes' on the station in Mattapan," as one Black nonprofit director later put it. The idea was to stack future meetings with supporters and convince state officials that the community did, in fact, approve of the new station—even though Barbara and her neighbors were the only community members who had collectively expressed any opinion, one way or another. Private conversations with state bureaucrats, they added, could help solidify support outside the bounds of public meetings.

Barbara and her neighbors strategized, too. Instead of targeting state bureaucrats, they met privately with two elected officials—a white city councilor and a white state senator—who, in turn, advocated against the station on their behalf. They had limited options to align with nonprofit organizations in the neighborhood; the sole community development nonprofit was barely keeping its lights on and would formally file for Chapter 11 bankruptcy protection the following year.

Initially, it appeared as though the residents would be successful in blocking the station. Years passed and plans for the station languished. But their elected advocates soon left office. The state senator, who had served on the Ways and Means Committee, became partner at a downtown law firm. And after a failed bid for mayor, the city councilor took a job in gas sales for a utility company.

Meanwhile, the nonprofit organizers continued their behind-the-scenes advocacy. Their persistence paid off. In public follow-up meetings, state officials explained that they had considered, but ultimately rejected, alternative sites. During a public event in October 2014, Governor Patrick formally announced the new station's construction schedule. Barbara attended the celebration and held strong in her opposition. The local press acknowledged her disapproval, but nevertheless concluded that "[c]ommunity members . . . praised the news."[1]

Residents attend public meetings expecting to influence plans for their neighborhoods. But before any idea or proposal is presented in public, plans are created and debated in private. Consider another meeting, held two months before the scenes in Codman Square and Mattapan. No television cameras or reporters were on hand to document the discussion. No members of the general public were invited to voice concerns. No representatives from government departments or agencies provided public oversight. Indeed, the only people who knew about the meeting were the nonprofit employees, foundation funders, and ethnographer in attendance.

Even if members of the public somehow found out about it, they would not have gained entry; the site of the meeting, a nondescript office building in downtown Boston, was a labyrinth of security barriers. Participants first lined up at a large wooden desk inside a ground floor atrium. A security guard collected their driver's licenses and crosschecked their names against a predetermined visitor list. Each was issued a small paper pass, which they showed to a second security guard in order to gain access to the building's elevators. Upon reaching the tenth floor, they approached a third checkpoint, where smiling staff from The Boston Foundation provided clip-on name badges and folders filled with colorful maps of the Fairmount Corridor.

About forty middle-aged men and women of varying ethnic backgrounds, all dressed in plain, unremarkable business-casual attire, filed into a large conference room. Robert, the fifty-something Black vice president of the foundation, welcomed the crowd. Grant-making is not a vehicle to solve problems, he said; it is a process. And, he added, that process depends on the leaders—the men and women gathered in the conference room—who represent their organizations and their communities. The purpose of the day's convening was to channel that leadership into policies and program proposals for residents of the Fairmount Corridor. Geeta, an Indian American immigrant and the foundation's associate vice president of programs, added that it is not grants that end poverty, but the collective wisdom and energy of nonprofit leaders. Put simply, this meeting was an opportunity to "come up with solutions to problems."

The group met behind closed doors for three hours. They pored over maps shaded by income, race, and other demographic characteristics. They discussed one another's development projects and social service programs. And they proposed metrics to define "impact" and strategized ways to increase it. After the meeting ended, they slowly trickled out of the conference room, returning to their own offices to make follow-up phone calls, send emails, and schedule more meetings. Later, concrete proposals in hand, they would meet with public officials who, in turn, would share their own plans with the nonprofit leaders.

Before any ceremonial ribbon could be cut, before any resident could hear about a plan for a development project, dozens of these discussions played out in conference rooms throughout the city.

These scenes reflect the current moment in cities—a moment that has many names. Some describe urban policymaking as increasingly collaborative and networked. Others critique what they see as neoliberal or austerity urbanism: public budget cuts coinciding with the privatization of public responsibilities. Still others portray a hollow state shored up by a system of third-party service providers. And for others, it is an era characterized by new models of consensus planning and collective impact.[2]

Despite disconnected intellectual histories, scholarship from sociology, political science, urban planning, nonprofit studies, public administration, and geography nevertheless shares a set of core empirical observations: A wide range of organizations and institutions make and implement the policies that matter for city residents. Horizontal collaboration replaced top-down hierarchical authority. Boundaries separating the public, for-profit, and nonprofit sectors blurred to the point of imperceptibility. In theory, everyone is seen as a potential partner, not an adversary, and the goal is consensus, not political conflict.[3] In short, urban policy is no longer exclusively a *government* affair, but more accurately described as urban *governance*.[4]

The present moment is defined as much by what it is as what it is not. And what it is not, quite simply, is urban renewal. Between the late 1940s and early 1970s, the federal government provided funds for city governments and newly established Redevelopment Authorities to "revitalize" and "renew" so-called slums located near central business districts. Urban renewal essentially entailed the systematic demolition of homes that had fallen into disrepair and the displacement of poor urban residents who had little power to contest government decisions. Entire neighborhoods, such as Boston's West End, were wiped out. Urban renewal was especially devastating for poor Black neighborhoods. In 1963, James Baldwin famously equated it with "moving the Negroes out. It means Negro removal, that is what it means."[5]

Subsequent changes in American politics and civil society created a very different urban policy environment. Today, Americans across all income levels are currently in the midst of a "participatory revolution." Formal government regulations and informal political norms institutionalized public meetings and other forms of engagement so that participation is now common in domains ranging from public budgeting to education policy. It is especially common in community development politics. Opportunities for residents like Barbara and her neighbors to "have a say" and play a role in public decision-making seem endless, and urban policymaking appears—at least on the surface—more democratic than ever before.[6]

New norms of participation rely on nonprofit organizations to mobilize citizens and facilitate public engagement. This relates to a second important change: the rapid expansion of the nonprofit sector. Between the 1980s and 2000s, the number of community-based organizations (CBOs) like CSNDC grew 130 percent, and the number of foundations like The Boston Foundation grew 64 percent.[7] Figure I.1 depicts the annual growth rate of CBOs across 264 US cities. Since 1995, cities have consistently gained an average of 1.5 to 2 CBOs per 1,000 urban residents each year. These organizations engage in a range of activities, from public art installations to prisoner reentry programs. They are also responsible for a sizable share of the country's affordable housing development. According to the National Alliance of Community Economic Development Associations, as of 2008, nonprofits had developed, rehabbed, or acquired 1.61 million units of low- and moderate-income housing— approximately one-third of all federally subsidized housing.[8]

Foundations and other private funders are devoting more and more resources to these various projects. Between 2002 and 2015, total foundation grants grew 58 percent, from $39.8 billion to just under $63 billion in inflation-adjusted dollars. Grants from community foundations, a subset of foundations that distribute grants locally rather than nationally, grew 110 percent during this same time period.[9] Their presence in cities also expanded; the number of community foundations grew 20 percent, reaching nearly 800 in operation in 2015 (see figure I.2).

Foundation grants are largely *competitive*, and competition contributed to sector-wide professionalization. Both philanthropic and community-based organizations became more managerial, bureaucratic, and market-driven. Paid professionals and management consultants replaced volunteers and activists; market logics replaced radical agendas.[10] To a greater extent than ever before, a highly professionalized nonprofit sector finances and implements community development projects in poor neighborhoods.

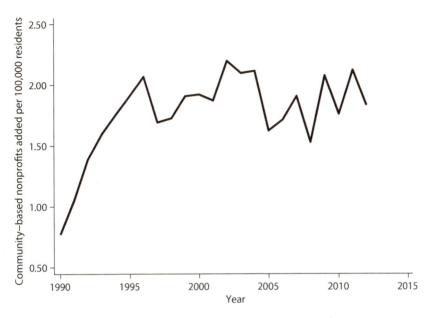

FIGURE I.1. Annual Growth Rate for Community-Based Nonprofits, 1990–2013
Notes: Based on a sample of 264 US cities. Includes organizations focused on crime prevention, neighborhood development, substance abuse, workforce development, and youth programs.
Source: National Center for Charitable Statistics (https://web.archive.org/web/20200409084628/https://nccs-data.urban.org/index.php).
I thank Patrick Sharkey, Gerard Torrats-Espinosa, and Delaram Takyar for sharing data and code. See Sharkey et al. (2017).

Over time, governments became increasingly reliant on these and other private organizations to take on the responsibilities of public governance. Massive government funding in the 1960s helped the community development field grow; subsequent funding cuts left government dependent on the field. One major source of federal funding, the Community Development Block Grant (CDBG), declined 79 percent in inflation-adjusted dollars at precisely the same time community development nonprofits grew in number and assets (see figure I.3). Escalating responsibilities allowed nonprofit leaders to become active co-producers of urban policy, working alongside government executives like Mayor Menino and Governor Patrick. Indeed, collaboration between public agencies (from various levels of government) and private organizations (from various sectors) is now ubiquitous.

Through a case study of the Fairmount Corridor, *Constructing Community* asks how these major institutional changes affect democratic representation and neighborhood inequality. Over the course of four years, I gained unique access to the agencies and organizations that planned community development projects in the Corridor. I observed local nonprofit leaders' and consultants'

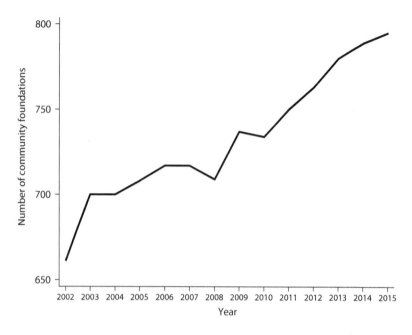
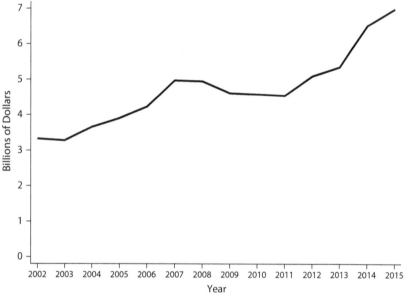

FIGURE I.2. Growth of Community Foundations in Number and Funding, 2002–2015
Notes: All figures in inflation-adjusted 2015 dollars. Not *all* community foundation funding supports the activities depicted in this book, but all activities depicted in this book can be supported by community foundations. The chart is therefore a rough approximation of increased private funding for community development.
Source: Author's tabulations. Community foundation data come from the Foundation Center (https://web.archive.org/web/20200503035432/ http://data.foundationcenter.org/).

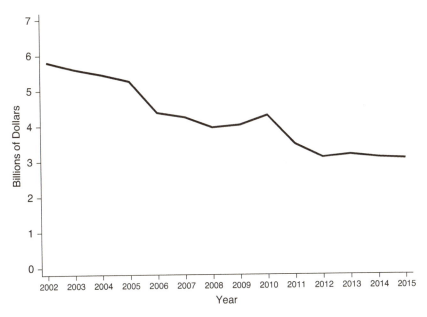

FIGURE I.3. CDBG Allocations, 2002–2015

Notes: All figures in inflation-adjusted 2015 dollars. Not *all* CDBG appropriations support the activities depicted in this book, but many of the activities depicted in this book can be supported by CDBG grants. The chart is therefore a rough approximation of decreased public funding for community development. *Sources:* Author's tabulations. CDBG appropriations come from HUD (https://web.archive.org/web/20190618110215/https://www.hud.gov/program_offices/comm_planning/about/budget).

private strategy sessions, worked inside Boston City Hall, served as a consultant for a local foundation, and attended dozens of public meetings in which residents heard and reacted to plans for their neighborhoods. My research questions focused on understanding how urban governance unfolds on the ground in poor neighborhoods. Who governs? What does it mean for democratic representation? And to what extent do these political dynamics reverse, reinforce, or simply reconfigure familiar patterns of urban inequality?

In this book, I make two arguments. The first is that the growing presence of private nonprofits in urban governance—including community organizations, foundations, funding intermediaries, and their many consultants—fundamentally altered local democracy. In earlier decades, local government officials and district politicians controlled local development projects from start to finish. But declines in public funding reduced local politicians' influence, while government bureaucracies' reliance on the private sector elevated the political status of nonprofit CBOs and their private funders. As a result, CBO leaders are now seen as more authentic neighborhood representatives than democratically elected politicians.

While CBOs help bring resources to poor neighborhoods, the privatization of political representation is not without significant costs. For one, professionalization in the nonprofit sector means that neighborhood *representatives* are not always neighborhood *residents*; Gail, for example, remained director of CSNDC even after she moved out of Codman Square. More generally, when private organizations supersede elected politicians, residents of poor neighborhoods sacrifice the ability to elect, appoint, or impeach their representatives in politics—a significant challenge to the tenets of representative democracy.

My second contention is that these institutional arrangements introduced new, unintended mechanisms of inequality. Social scientists typically attribute the urban poor's lack of political power to their limited economic, social, and cultural capital: Poor residents are denied access to the money, social network ties, and cultural know-how necessary to successfully contest powerful elites. Government reforms seemed to level the playing field, incorporating community organizations into decision-making and institutionalizing public participation. But participation can fail to empower poor residents if government decision-makers deploy strategies to undermine it. And nonprofits can't transfer power to poor residents if they don't exist. Neighborhoods without CBOs, or neighborhoods in which CBOs lack sufficient capacity, will be at a structural disadvantage as they compete for scarce resources. The fact that these are finite resources distributed on a competitive basis further complicates matters. Because CBOs are private organizations competing for organizational survival, CBO leaders and their funders will tend to focus their efforts in neighborhoods most likely to show success—ignoring, at times, the people and places in greatest need.

Together, these insights point to a more diverse yet still stubbornly unequal system of urban governance. Public participation has not replaced private gatherings like the one described at the beginning of this chapter. Similarly, community organizations may be key decision-makers, but there is no stipulation requiring directors to live in the neighborhoods they represent. And so, the players around the table now look different—pushing us to rethink scholarly assumptions about who governs—yet both the lack of public transparency and limited empowerment of urban residents remain.

Private Organizations and Public Governance

In 1961, political scientist Robert Dahl asked a simple yet profound question about US cities: Who governs? At the time, sociologists argued that a small group of economic elites controlled city policy. In his groundbreaking study of New Haven, Dahl agreed that direct political decision-making power was once, and continued to be, concentrated among a few important people. But to say that big business runs cities was to downplay the constraints of democratic politics. Organized stakeholders can *indirectly* influence decisions through elections, Dahl reasoned, even if *direct* influence ultimately rests in the hands of a few key players.[11] Rather than one group pulling the levers of city policy, the particular people with decision-making power will vary depending on the issue area and relative electoral power of interest groups. In the "community power debate" that followed, Dahl and his students pushed their theory of pluralist urban governance, while other social scientists countered with continued evidence of a ruling power elite.[12]

Subsequent research proposed new names for city power brokers and developed new typologies of urban governance. For sociologists John Logan and Harvey Molotch, cities are "growth machines" controlled by "growth coalitions" of politicians, developers, and other ancillary actors like labor unions and sports franchises. Growth coalitions dominate urban politics and steer urban policy toward growth, enriching developers and filling city coffers but ignoring the needs of the urban poor.[13] Clarence Stone's regime theory takes a more general view, depicting city governance as a productive accomplishment of coordination and cooperation between public agencies and private interests. Scholars working in the growth machine and regime traditions classify entire cities based on who seems to make important governance decisions.[14]

These perspectives generally fall into what sociologists Hillary Angelo and David Wachsmuth call "methodological cityism": Scholars equate "urban governance" with "local government," conflating the political *process* of governance with a *place* where governance unfolds.[15] But "urban" policies do not necessarily begin or even end in City Hall. As political scientist Paul Peterson argues, city governments do not control urban policy alone; macroeconomic forces limit available policy options, and the United States' political system of federalism prevents cities from functioning as independent nation-states.[16] Offering complementary arguments, legal scholars show how constitutional law limits city governments' formal control over many of the resources and policies that matter to city residents. City government is, in short, "bound" by legal powers vested in state and federal government.[17]

Scholars of the nonprofit sector extend this line of thinking a step further.[18] It is impossible to fully capture the structure of urban governance without considering multiple levels of government. It is also impossible to ignore *nongovernmental* institutions and organizational fields. Tax law restricts nonprofits' engagement in politics; in order to maintain tax-exempt status, community-based organizations cannot endorse particular candidates for office and must limit lobbying to "an insubstantial part" of their activities. Philanthropic foundations face additional restrictions that prohibit lobbying altogether.[19] The purpose of these laws is to limit public subsidies for partisan politics, and more abstractly, to maintain a nonpartisan civil society. But formal restrictions have not impeded deeper, more consequential involvement in everyday governance decisions. Understanding how nonprofits engage in politics *on the ground* matters just as much as understanding what the law formally restricts.

Americans have in fact debated the appropriate role of nonprofit organizations in democratic politics since the founding of the republic. Influential thinkers such as James Madison and George Washington worried that private associations, which flourished around the time of the American Revolution, "made some citizens 'more equal' than others and threatened to undermine the egalitarian foundation of the new governmental order."[20] As wealth grew in the late nineteenth and early twentieth centuries, private philanthropy received special scrutiny. Business titans like Andrew Carnegie and John D. Rockefeller may have established charitable foundations and pledged to "promote the well-being of mankind," but some worried that those foundations were little more than publicly subsidized vehicles for personal political influence. In 1915, a blistering report by the United States Commission on Industrial Relations concluded that distributing personal wealth through foundations created a "hereditary aristocracy, which is foreign to every conception of American Government and menacing to the welfare of the people and the existence of the Nation as a democracy."[21]

These debates persist today. In the early 2000s, a new generation of "philanthro-capitalists" ushered in a model of giving driven by "returns" on "social investment."[22] The movement reinvigorated questions about whether private wealth can truly serve a broader public good. Billionaire philanthropists such as Bill Gates, Warren Buffet, and Mark Zuckerberg face criticisms echoing those from a century ago. In 2015, when Zuckerberg and his wife Priscilla Chan announced plans to devote 99 percent of their Facebook shares to charity, a journalist lamented America's transformation into "a society of oligarchs" in which billionaires set public priorities without any form of democratic accountability.[23]

The behavior of nonprofit leaders and philanthropists is only one side of the issue; the state has also taken actions to blur the distinction between private organizations and public governance. In the 1960s, Lyndon Johnson's War on Poverty programs helped build a private welfare state, shifting the burden of service provision to the nonprofit sector. Federal funding cuts in the 1970s and 1980s deepened government's reliance on nonprofit service organizations.[24] Contracting for services became common. At its most basic level, contracting reconfigured the relationship between nonprofits and government into a system of mutual dependence: Government needs nonprofits to deliver services, and nonprofits need government for funding. While contracting is more common among social service providers than community development organizations, the symbiotic relationship is notably similar. Across the board, it is increasingly unclear where the state ends and private service providers begin.[25]

And this is not happening only in the United States. Concerns about private interests and the public good extend to large international nongovernmental organizations (INGOs), such as Oxfam and Amnesty International. These groups claim to represent marginalized populations across the globe and negotiate with governments on their behalf. But as *The Economist* pointedly asked in 2000, "Who elected Oxfam?" The rhetorical question underscores a fundamental tension: While nonprofits represent the public, the public did not elect them to do so, and the public lacks traditional democratic mechanisms to hold these groups accountable if they fail to accurately reflect the public interest.[26]

[margin note: hard to hold nonprofit accountable]

These dilemmas spilled over into the Fairmount Corridor, where nonprofit CBOs were central players in urban governance. Government policymakers expected CBOs to speak on behalf of urban neighborhoods. CBOs, in turn, superseded elected politicians and acted as the de facto representatives of Corridor neighborhoods. I refer to these organizations as *nonelected neighborhood representatives*: CBO leaders adopted the language of political representation while eschewing electoral politics; claimed to represent neighborhoods' interests and were legitimated by funders and government officials; and negotiated directly with government executives rather than through elected intermediaries.[27]

Philanthropic foundations were central political players, as well. These and other private funders collaborated extensively with government officials and supported CBOs through grants. Like government officials, they deferred to CBO leaders as neighborhood representatives. The reason was structural: Funders neither implement community development projects nor have the ability to fund neighborhoods directly. Instead, they need *CBOs* to accept the money and manage the funds. As such, funders' success *depended on the accomplishments of their grantees*. These conditions put nonprofit CBOs, funders, and government agencies into a system of mutual dependence, reorganizing the structure of urban governance.

None of this is to suggest *mayors* lack power, particularly in a strong-mayor city like Boston. My argument instead focuses on the diminished role of district-based state and local politicians. Nonprofit leaders can now come close to resembling a co-equal branch of government alongside mayors, governors, and public agency staff—assuming positions we might otherwise expect to be occupied by elected city councilors and state legislators. In this new equation, the legislative side governs less, and nonprofits govern more.[28]

The particulars no doubt vary across cities. In Chicago, for instance, city councilors, called aldermen, can veto development projects in their districts, a special power known as aldermanic prerogative. Yet even in Chicago's context of strong city council power, urban planning scholar John Betancur and colleagues argue that "aldermanic prerogative is not absolute" because "city government is often not where neighborhood policy is conceived" and "the civic arena has become more important" than ever before. Ward politics still affects neighborhood development in cities like Chicago. But it is "a blended model of neighborhood policymaking" including foundations and other nonprofit groups as well.[29]

Returning to Dahl's famous question, I argue that the relationship between public agencies and nonprofit organizations has a profound effect on local democracy and representation. My argument is not simply "nonprofits matter"—though this is a reasonable top-line takeaway. More precisely, I show *how* community organizations and philanthropic foundations matter, use the tools of ethnography to make sense of their place in urban governance, and grapple with the unique tensions and tradeoffs that emerge when private nonprofits assume important public responsibilities.

Politics, Organizations, and Urban Inequality

In *The Truly Disadvantaged,* William Julius Wilson laid out an ambitious theory of urban inequality, inspiring generations of sociologists. For Wilson, urban inequality had both structural and cultural roots. On the structural side, government policies, economic shifts, and racial discrimination facilitated the flight of jobs and middle-class residents away from cities. The result was a concentration of poverty in urban neighborhoods and the urban poor's social isolation from mainstream institutions and middle-class social networks. Structural and cultural forces combine to restrict the kinds of resources available to the urban poor as well as their opportunities for upward mobility.[30]

Wilson's theory is largely at the macro level, documenting major changes over time and revealing their effects on social organization in poor neighborhoods. Another, more recent body of work takes a meso-level approach to illustrate how formal organizations mediate the conditions of urban poverty. Childcare centers, for instance, can reduce social isolation by connecting poor mothers to other organizational resources.[31] Organizations can also offset *neighborhood*-level isolation by facilitating collective action and helping residents solve neighborhood problems.[32] Beyond the presence of organizations in a neighborhood and the opportunities for social interaction they provide, their political actions also affect inequality. For instance, sociologists Nicole Marwell and Robert Vargas each show how community organizations strategically align with local elected officials in order to influence public resource distribution and give poor residents a stronger voice in politics.[33]

This book brings together Wilson's macro structural approach with the recent focus on organizations in urban poverty research. I make the case for considering *organizations' place in macro governance structures* as an important but underexplored mechanism of urban inequality. We can think of governance structures as a field, or "a set of interorganizational relationships, sometimes collaborative, sometimes antagonistic, in a particular area of action."[34] Organizations' structural position in the field affords certain powers and opens up particular roles in politics. Most important, the structure of the field affects how resources are distributed and which neighborhoods benefit as a result.

Over the last three decades, public funding declines opened the door for private funders to fill budget gaps and initiate new relationships with government officials. And political reforms created new relationships of mutual dependence between government and community-based organizations. The community development field grew into a sprawling network of government agencies, community-based nonprofits, development professionals, philanthropic foundations, consultants, and other intermediaries linking funders with developers.

Mutual dependence facilitated the political ascent of CBOs—something that was both a blessing and a curse for poor neighborhoods in the Fairmount Corridor. The system benefited neighborhoods like Codman Square, where Gail and CSNDC converted public and private funding into new housing and environmentally sustainable commercial development. At the same time, it disadvantaged neighborhoods like Mattapan, where CSNDC's counterpart, the Mattapan Community Development Corporation (MCDC), confronted severe fundraising challenges. Facing budget shortfalls in the fall of 2011, the organization's interim director met with three private funders in a failed attempt to prevent insolvency. The funders explained in no uncertain terms that supporting a low-capacity organization would make *them* appear weak and ineffectual as funders. They are in the business of funding successful projects, they said, not keeping a struggling organization afloat. MCDC filed for Chapter 11 bankruptcy protection six months later. Without a local nonprofit willing and able to accept and manage grants, progress on community development projects in Mattapan ground to a halt.

The rise of public participation was another institutional change intended to reduce inequality and provide poor residents with greater decision-making power. Here, too, nonprofits affected power and resource distribution in unexpected ways. Recall Barbara and her Mattapan neighbors, who aligned with local elected officials but failed to block the construction of a new train station in their backyards. By contrast, at the northern end of the Corridor, in Upham's Corner, poor residents aligned with local nonprofit leaders rather than politicians. They successfully blocked city government's plans to convert an abandoned factory into a Public Works storage facility, ultimately persuading officials to pursue an alternative development project in their neighborhood. In both cases, residents participated. But because the current institutional context favors nonprofits over elected politicians, organizational allies were more effective at translating their participation into actual political influence.

On the surface, political reforms leveled the playing field. Yet rather than eliminate unequal access to resources, new institutional arrangements *reconfigured* mechanisms of neighborhood inequality. The structure of urban governance increased government's reliance on nonprofit community-based organizations, such that nonprofit leaders could assume some of the responsibilities of political representation. Neighborhoods lacking CBOs (or lacking CBOs with sufficient capacity) were at a competitive disadvantage for grants and failed to have their needs accurately reflected in political decision-making. Because CBOs and their private funders *compete* for grants, there was less incentive to support the neighborhoods in greatest need. Norms of participation were no panacea, because here, too, the presence and behavior of local organizations affected which participating residents were empowered. This is a fuzzier depiction of urban inequality than Wilson's canonical depiction, but the effects are no less consequential.

Constructing Community

The idea of community has long motivated sociologists. Classical theorists worried that industrialization and urbanization would dissolve personal associations and undermine traditional family life. Not surprisingly, *community* emerged as an especially important topic in urban sociology. As cities grew and became more diverse, urban sociologists debated the degree of community organization in poor neighborhoods. Are poor neighborhoods disadvantaged because they lack community? Or are poor neighborhoods rich in communal bonds despite poverty, ethnic heterogeneity, and other supposedly "disorganizing" features?[35]

Research on life in urban communities sidestepped the more basic question: What *is* community? Sociologist George Hillery identified ninety-four distinct definitions of the concept in 1955.[36] Is it a spatial territory? When we study "social organization in an urban community," we mean relationships between people living in a spatially bounded place. Is it a group linked by a shared identity? When we speak of cultural traditions in "the Black community," we mean a diasporic ethnic group, unbound by any specific territory.[37] Or does it mean intimate social bonds? When we speak of religion providing a "sense of community," we mean feelings of social solidarity and cohesion, transcending both time and space. And what does community mean when it is used as an adjective in phrases like "community policing" or "community development"? Community policing refers to strategic partnerships between police officers and citizens, but community development refers to housing, commercial, and economic development in urban neighborhoods. The objects of reference are distinct: In the former, people matter more than the place; in the latter, places matter more than the people.

To make things even more complicated, objects of reference can change over time and across contexts. "Community development" offers a case in point. In the 1960s, advocates and policymakers defined community development in racial terms: Rooted in the Black Power Movement's ideas of community control, community development was understood as a project of racial uplift and Black empowerment.[38] By the 1990s, a more mundane definition emerged: Community development became a catchall term for place-based urban policy. The "community" in community development shifted from a reference to a specific racial group (Black residents) to a deracialized place (urban neighborhoods).

What unites all of these definitions is that community invariably means something good. Community is something positive and valued, a goal to be achieved and a moral state to which we can aspire. The multiple definitions of community are consistent only with respect to the normative belief that community represents the common good, that collectivity and communal benefits are superior to individual interests or elite domination. Community is *significant* without signifying a singular group or place, *meaningful* without a stable meaning.

"But if community has come to mean everything good," sociologist Robert Sampson worries, "as a concept it loses its analytical bite and therefore means nothing."[39] The issue is that ambiguity makes it difficult to pinpoint the specific benefits of community and harder still to improve community through social policy. In this book, I take a different approach. It is *precisely* because community "has come to mean everything good" that the concept is so important. A parsimonious definition is beside the point. As the book's title implies, community is a *political construct*, a symbolic vehicle of meaning used to pursue certain political ends.[40] I am less concerned with describing what community is, analyzing levels of community organization, or arguing whether some nonprofit organizations are more "community-based" than others. I am more interested in understanding how particular people marshal the idea and rhetoric of community—and for what political purposes.

When viewed through this lens, the symbolic boundaries that determine membership in "the community" become especially important. Symbolic boundaries are cultural processes of categorization that reinforce the unequal distribution of resources, value, and status. With respect to the symbolic boundary surrounding "the community," varying definitions of the concept make the boundary unstable; it can shift based on who is speaking, who is listening, and for what purpose the concept is invoked.

Thinking about community in these terms helps us better understand how urban governance unfolds and why nonprofit leaders have achieved special status. Everyone involved in Corridor development in some way appealed to community, whether it was CBO leaders claiming to represent the community or government officials claiming to value the needs of the community. The *performance* of community—"doing" community, as it were—gave actors legitimacy. And it legitimized this particular *system* of urban governance, answering not only the question of who governs, but also how they came to govern and who got to speak for the urban poor.

Government reforms designed to reduce urban inequality are predicated on a very different understanding of community. Relying on community-based organizations and public participation to elevate the community's voice assumes that there is such a thing as *a* community voice. According to this perspective, the challenge is to find the right organization to advocate on the community's behalf or the best method to solicit community input. Community development professionals make similar assumptions: Community-based organizations are organizations based in *a* community, community organizers organize *a* community, and the ideal outcome is to incorporate *a* community's vision into a particular project or issue area. Because they assume unified, self-contained communities, they also assume that community-based organizations can be more or less tied to communities.

An overarching goal of this book is to show how no organization or participatory process can accurately reflect the community's voice, no matter how accountable or well run. There will never be a definitive answer to the question of true, authentic community representation, because *there is no such thing as a single, cohesive community voice.* Challenging that implicit assumption will help us better understand inequality in neighborhood politics, and moreover, explain why some reforms consistently fail to meet lofty expectations.

A Note on Race and Gentrification

Two issues of vital importance to cities are noticeably absent from my discussion so far: race (and racism) and gentrification. Racism is an omnipresent backdrop to everything discussed in this book. The entire system I describe—the important role of nonprofit leaders and the consequences for democratic representation and inequality—is a feature of poor, segregated neighborhoods for a reason. Generations of political neglect and disinvestment created intersecting inequalities of race, class, and space. There would be no calls for "community development policy" without racial segregation and the concentration of poverty in urban centers. Race affects urban governance and debates over community development today as well, albeit in complex ways. Some practitioners attempt to deracialize community development as "place-based" urban policy, while others push back by pointing out how this approach ignores racialized power differentials between white neighborhoods and neighborhoods of color. All of which is to say: Race continues to matter in cities generally and community development policy specifically.

In terms of my specific arguments about representation and inequality, I did not observe consistent patterns with respect to race. If anything, funders and government officials generally preferred working with organizations that looked like their vision of "the community." And that meant, all else equal, Black CBO leaders in predominantly Black neighborhoods were considered more authentic and worthier of resources than their white peers—though the number in my study is too small to make strong claims. I do not assume residents and/or people of color are necessarily better representatives of "the community," nor do I assume white and Black middle-class CBO leaders are, by virtue of their race and/or class, worse representatives of "the community." Indeed, I argue such claims are specious: This thinking homogenizes poor neighborhoods and, in effect, reifies the misguided idea that an individual nonprofit leader can singularly represent an entire neighborhood. And so, while my main arguments described above do not explicitly reference race or racism, I analyze these dynamics as important contextual factors throughout the book.

Similarly, gentrification was a constant subtext during discussions of community development in the Corridor. Nearly everyone depicted in this book saw their work as resisting gentrification and doing a different kind of urban renewal. The extent to which they succeeded is very much up for debate. Some advocates and scholars argue nonprofit developers materially benefit from gentrification; others worry that community development projects merely facilitate gentrification by inadvertently making poor neighborhoods attractive to speculators and for-profit interests. A deep tension between people and place animates concerns around gentrification: What does it mean for higher-income, typically white people to move into a lower-income, typically Black or Latino neighborhood? A parallel tension animates debates over community development policy and the meaning of community: How do community development resources for the community as a *place* affect the community as *current residents*? The threat of gentrification loomed large in the Fairmount Corridor, even when it went unmentioned. In what follows, I show how a particular group of community development professionals confronted neighborhood change and understood the resulting tension between supporting poor people and improving poor neighborhoods.

The Fairmount Corridor

This book shows how the rise of nonprofit organizations in urban governance affects representation and inequality through a case study of the Fairmount Corridor. The Corridor gets its name from the Fairmount Commuter Rail Line, sometimes referred to as the Fairmount-Indigo Line (a reference to Boston's color-coded transit lines) or the Fairmount Line, for short. Commuter rail is typically designed to bring workers from the suburbs, where they live, to the city, where they work. And so, unlike Boston's rapid rail lines, the Fairmount Line was more expensive to ride and offered little to no service during off-peak times. Today, however, the fare for most of the line is the same as the city's subway system, a result of events described in chapter 4.[41] It is the only commuter rail line located entirely within Boston city limits, and it runs directly through an impoverished area of the city underserved by alternative rapid rail options.

The idea of a redevelopment "corridor" derives from urban planning practices. Planners and policymakers believe that poor urban residents benefit most when housing, jobs, and social services are coordinated and sited in close

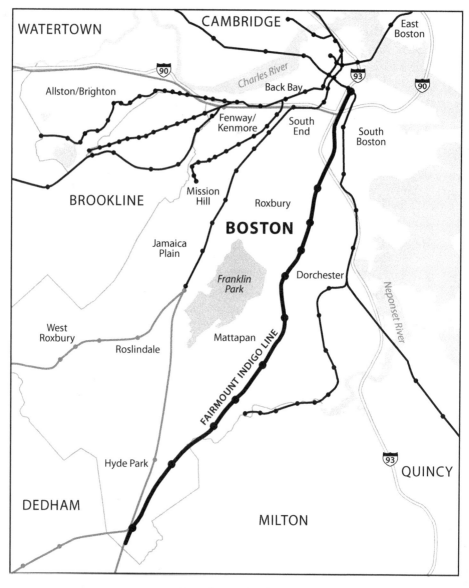

FIGURE I.4. Map of Boston's Public Transit Lines
Notes: Includes rapid rail and select commuter rail lines. Neighborhood names are also labeled.

proximity to public transit stations. In general terms, then, the "Corridor" is the area within a half-mile radius of the rail line—the standard definition of residential "walking distance" to public transit.

The Corridor includes sections of eight neighborhoods. Significant portions of the endpoints—Newmarket and Readville—are industrial.[42] A large suburban-style shopping center is located steps from the Newmarket stop, featuring Target, Marshals, Home Depot, and Panera Bread, among other stores. The six remaining neighborhoods—Upham's Corner, Grove Hall, Four Corners, Codman Square, Mattapan, and Logan Square—are primarily residential, and are the focus of community development efforts.

A note on neighborhoods: "Neighborhood" is an inherently tricky concept. Commonly evoked, it lacks a standardized definition.[43] In Boston, like many other cities, one's neighborhood is like a Russian nesting doll of increasingly large, overlapping geographical areas. In this book, I refer to eight "neighborhoods," but these areas are nested within the larger, more familiar districts of Roxbury, Dorchester, Mattapan, and Hyde Park. Newmarket, Upham's Corner, and Grove Hall straddle Boston's Dorchester and Roxbury districts. Four Corners and Codman Square are within the Dorchester district, and Logan Square and Readville fall within Hyde Park.

When I began this research in 2010, the 88,698 Corridor residents were 61 percent Black, 21 percent Latino, 9 percent white, and 1 percent Asian. Thirty-five percent were foreign-born. The Corridor included 14 percent of Boston's total population, 39 percent of the city's Black population, and 50 percent of the city's population with Caribbean ancestry. Nearly half of all households earned less than $40,000 annually, and according to 2006–2010 American Community Survey estimates, the Corridor's 14.9 percent unemployment rate was significantly higher than the citywide rate of 9.3 percent.[44]

A central organizing feature of the Fairmount Corridor was a $200 million state investment in new rail stations. In 1999, Marvin Martin, executive director of a CBO in Four Corners, raised concerns about the neighborhood's limited access to public transportation. Together with other nonprofit advocates, Marvin persuaded the state transportation authority to study the feasibility of new stations along the Fairmount Line. In 2005, the state committed financing for four new stations, and between November 2012 and July 2013, three new stations opened in Four Corners, Codman Square, and Newmarket, respectively. A fourth station, located in Mattapan, opened in 2019.

During my fieldwork, nine CBOs in the Corridor were the key actors planning development projects. Between 2000 and 2008, these organizations formed three overlapping coalitions: a development coalition focused on affordable housing and economic development; a transit coalition focused on improving the Fairmount Line transit service; and an environmental coalition focused on planning a "greenway"—a collection of parks, bike paths, and community gardens alongside the rail line.

Institutional support came from both the public and philanthropic sectors. Nonprofit organizations in the Corridor received significant funding from foundations and other funding intermediaries, including The Boston Foundation. In 2009, The Boston Foundation reorganized its internal strategic framework to include a focus on community development in the Corridor.

The Corridor caught the attention of federal policymakers that same year, when the Department of Housing and Urban Development (HUD), Department of Transportation (DOT), and Environmental Protection Agency (EPA) named it a "pilot project" for a newly created interagency partnership. Two years later, the official White House blog featured a four-minute YouTube video and accompanying text cataloguing federal support for the Corridor and plans for future development—support that included Promise and Choice Neighborhoods grants ($26 million in total), two of the Obama administration's highly publicized urban policy programs. Following the federal attention, city officials placed their own mark on community development in the area. In early 2012, the Boston Redevelopment Authority formally announced a Corridor planning initiative. The Boston Foundation supplied $100,000 for the $350,000 initiative.

Public agencies and nonprofit organizations planned fifty-one projects in the Fairmount Corridor and managed eleven urban planning processes during my fieldwork.[45] These projects ranged from new transit stations to affordable housing development, public art to community gardens. In total, the projects included 1,077 new apartments or townhouses, 105,965 square feet of commercial development, and 523,058 square feet of vacant land development.

The Study

From January 2010 to May 2014, I immersed myself in the politics of community development along the Fairmount Corridor. Decentralized urban policy poses challenges for traditional ethnographic approaches, which often focus on single neighborhoods, street corners, social groups, or organizations. The interconnected web of agencies and organizations in the Fairmount Corridor required a nimbler technique.[46] All told, my fieldwork took me to foundation offices, nonprofit conference rooms, community centers, government departments, and nearly every other imaginable meeting place in between. I observed private nonprofit coalition meetings, received two fellowships to work inside Boston City Hall, and was part of a team hired by The Boston Foundation to evaluate its role in the Corridor. The core of my fieldwork consisted of sitting in on private meetings (nearly 200), listening in on conference calls (nearly 70), and attending forums open to the public (nearly 100).

Outside of meetings, I engaged in informal interactions, like going out to lunch with a consultant or getting coffee with a government official. I used the fact that I didn't own a car as an excuse to get rides before and after meetings. During these trips, I asked follow-up questions and tested out hunches as my fieldwork progressed. I collected additional supplemental data, including approximately 900 news articles; more than 2,000 emails between nonprofit directors, consultants, and government officials;[47] and all reports, agendas, and presentations focused on the Fairmount Corridor.

This approach to fieldwork forced me to bounce between multiple research settings. After observing a meeting between nonprofit developers and government officials in City Hall, I would walk out of the building with the developers—observing their post-meeting debrief—only to circle back to City Hall and return to my cubicle next to the Mayor's Advisor to Housing. I viewed drafts of grant applications as nonprofits tweaked their progress reports, and I reviewed internal strategy memos from grant providers. I attended meetings where nonprofits asked foundations for grants, meetings where they were granted funding, and meetings where they were unceremoniously denied support. I would catch a ride with city officials to an event, then ask a nonprofit director for a ride to the train station when it ended. Above all, access to these various groups depended on a relatively simple, but nevertheless time-consuming act: showing up to meeting after meeting, even if I was not formally invited. If I was invited to a meeting, I showed up. If during a meeting someone happened to mention another meeting, I showed up to that one, too. And I kept showing up for four years, until I reached saturation.[48]

Ingratiating myself into a complex web of actors—and justifying my presence in their closed-door meetings—required an ever-shifting researcher identity. Throughout my fieldwork, I was variously confused for a state official, a member of the press, a community organizer, a nonprofit employee, and (twice) a resident of Dorchester. Perhaps most telling were the affiliations assigned to me during private "stakeholder meetings" convened by The Boston Foundation. Name tags were distributed for easy introductions, and my affiliation on them changed from being associated with a nonprofit coalition in 2011, to my university affiliation in 2012, to a blank space near the end of my fieldwork when assigning a single affiliation proved too complicated. Mike, executive director of a Hyde Park nonprofit, compared me to the chameleon-like title character in the 1983 film *Zelig*. "It's about a guy who is *everywhere*," Mike told me. "And I think that's what I'm going to start calling you." Around the same time, a consultant referred to me as "Dr. Shadow" in an email to a city government official.[49] Both nicknames signaled my constant presence as a "fly on the wall"—noticeable to anyone paying attention, but more as a voyeur than active participant-observer.

Why choose to study urban community development, and why the Fairmount Corridor? I was initially drawn to community development policy because it encompasses a wide range of substantively consequential projects—activities that affect the quality of housing, availability of jobs, presence of social services, and quality of life in poor neighborhoods. As sociologist Harvey Molotch argues, the politics of urban development "determines who, *in material terms*, gets what, where, and how."[50]

Studying a corridor (as opposed to a single neighborhood) was analytically useful. While much of my analysis treats the Corridor as a single case, the fact that it is actually composed of eight distinct neighborhoods allowed me to conduct within-case caparisons. When possible, I exploit variation across Corridor neighborhoods in order to reveal how particular structures or processes produced divergent outcomes.

Above all else, I chose this case because, when I began this project, the Corridor was emerging as an exemplar of US urban policy. CBO leaders presented their accomplishments at national urban planning conferences coast to coast, from North Carolina to California. Local foundations hosted out-of-town funders from Pittsburgh to pass on grant-making lessons. And federal officials brought grantees from eleven Connecticut cities to take a bus tour of the Corridor and meet with local CBO leaders. The ideas and organizational structures present in the Corridor were being actively promoted across the country and legitimated by institutions as powerful as the federal government and presidential administration. The Corridor's outsized policy significance made it an especially attractive research site.

This raises the question of generalizability. As an ethnographic study, my observations are limited by both time and space. Yet there are reasons to believe that the processes I discuss in this book are not unique to Boston—or even the Fairmount Corridor, for that matter. The local government officials I studied, for example, work on similar projects in other Boston neighborhoods. State officials work on similar projects in other Massachusetts cities, and federal officials work on similar projects throughout the country. The same logic holds for local, regional, and national funders; I have no reason to believe these agencies and organizations approached community development differently in the Fairmount Corridor than in other US cities and neighborhoods.

Nor is each aspect of the Corridor necessarily unique. The specific projects—like a twenty-seven-unit apartment complex, a community garden, or a public mural—are remarkably unremarkable. Community-based organizations and philanthropic foundations play important roles in urban development throughout North America. Development near transit is common—in fact, it is a priority in US urban policy. Transit corridors can be found throughout the world. One could point to research based in a number of cities—Baltimore, Chicago, Cleveland, Denver, Detroit, Flint, Houston, Johannesburg, Los Angeles, Miami, New Orleans, New York City, Philadelphia, Phoenix, Pittsburgh, San Francisco, and Toronto, to name just a few—and find some similarities with the Fairmount Corridor.[51]

Yet the *combination* of these elements in a single case may seem unusual relative to existing scholarship. That may be because the political processes I discuss are unique to Boston, to community development, to transit corridors, or to some other element of the study. Or it may be because scholars haven't known what to look for. I can't say for certain, and so I will do my best to flag certain findings or arguments that may not be generalizable and let the reader decide how much it matters for the story I want to tell.

The Fairmount Corridor reflects broader historical changes to urban governance—changes that at least partially affected poor neighborhoods throughout the United States. If the particulars of community development politics vary across cities or neighborhoods, I would argue that it is a matter of degree, not kind.

Plan of the Book

This book analyzes the role of private nonprofits in urban governance and the unintended consequences for democratic representation and inequality. Part I sets the stage—the who, what, where, and when. Chapter 1 situates the Fairmount Corridor within the context of national, state, and local urban policy changes. The social and political failure of urban renewal in the postwar period gave way to new community-based approaches to urban policy in the 1960s. These institutional reforms empowered local nonprofit organizations and carved out novel political roles for private foundations. Community-based organizations grew substantially following federal retrenchment in the 1980s and 1990s, further cementing their place in the community development field. The Obama administration's emphasis on public-private partnerships would become the capstone to a trend that was decades in the making, providing grants directly to nonprofits and developing policy ideas hand in hand with private foundations. It is impossible to understand urban governance today without understanding how it has changed over time.

Chapter 2 moves to contemporary processes of urban governance in the Fairmount Corridor: Who governs, and how did they get a seat at the table? I introduce each of the players in the community development field, from government agencies to consultants and foundations. Taking a top-down view, one might characterize these public and private organizations as a powerful coalition that collectively decided what got built and where. And one might assume those with power and influence were the ones who had the most money, political connections, or elite network ties. Getting closer to the ground revealed quite different dynamics. This was an urban policy context that privileged collaboration, partnership, and that oft-used concept: *community*. As a result, influence over plans for the Corridor depended on one's ability to negotiate a role as a partner with or on behalf of the community. That did not mean one's status as a partner was a fixed identity. People *performed* their partner bona fides for others in the field—sometimes successfully, other times less so. Thus, I observed a fairly fluid and loosely connected policy network, one in which private nonprofit leaders who represented or funded "the community" were just as involved as public officials.

Chapter 3 asks how, once at the table, individuals and organizations defined "the Fairmount Corridor" and puzzled over its malleable spatial boundaries. Like any neighborhood or region, the Corridor's boundaries were subjectively demarcated. Still, "the Fairmount Corridor" had political salience as a place. I show how private actors like consultants and nonprofit leaders defined and redefined the Corridor's spatial boundaries to fit their particular political objectives. The seemingly banal practice of rationalizing the Corridor's geography nevertheless had important consequences for resource allocation: Making the Corridor legible—defining what is (and what is not) "in" the Corridor—ultimately created neighborhood winners and losers.

Part II dives deeper into the central argument of the book: the unintended consequences of this public-private governance arrangement for democratic representation and neighborhood inequality. In chapter 4, I show how CBOs in the Corridor superseded elected politicians as de facto neighborhood representatives. Local elected officials were, at best, marginal players in the broader community development field. It was not necessarily the case that *residents* viewed CBOs as more authentic than elected representatives; in fact, *regardless of resident perceptions*, government officials and foundation funders viewed nonprofit CBOs as the legitimate representatives of poor neighborhoods. The privatization of political representation is a double-edged sword for the urban poor: CBOs can bring much needed resources to poor neighborhoods but are not subject to the same systems of accountability as democratically elected politicians.

Chapter 5 follows the money. Consistent with a burgeoning body of research on philanthropy and public policy, funders in the Corridor saw themselves as strategic political actors who successfully influenced urban policymaking. But their power had limits. Because large grants were hard to come by, funders often pooled and repackaged grants from *other* funders before providing a grant to a local nonprofit or city agency. The dense network of grant distributions and redistributions reduced individual funders' leverage and created a system whereby grantees could, surprisingly, push back against funder priorities. It also incentivized funders to embellish grantee accomplishments because their own fulfillment of grant requirements was tied to grantees' successes. Funders prioritized neighborhoods with high-capacity organizations—those most likely to show success—over neighborhoods lacking a strong local organizational presence. Taken-for-granted funding practices, as a result, inadvertently contributed to neighborhood inequality.

The voices of the urban poor are almost entirely absent in the preceding chapters. Chapter 6 offers an explanation. In the Fairmount Corridor, resident involvement in community development was limited to "the community process," a series of public meetings that ostensibly democratized public decision-making. But these meetings were held long after plans had already been created, and as such, functioned less like a vehicle for influence and more like a bureaucratic box to check at the end of a long to-do list. Coming full circle, I show how poor residents were most effective in exercising their political voice *when they aligned with local nonprofit organizations* during these meetings.

Channeling their interests through legitimated nonprofits was more effective than threats of collective mobilization or alliances with elected politicians. Put more critically, community control was realized to the extent that residents' interests aligned with the interests of local community organizations.

{⸺⁂⸺}

The pages that follow tell a specific story about community development and inequality in one part of one city. But *Constructing Community* is also a larger account of the structure of urban governance and the dilemmas associated with the inclusion of private nonprofits in public policy. It is about the people who make policy decisions and set policy priorities—and all the messiness their interdependent relationships and organizational incentives entail. At its core, this is a book about the unintended consequences of (mostly) well-intentioned efforts: how attempts to empower the urban poor can inadvertently create more inequality, not less.

Housing, transportation, environmental protection, social welfare, private foundation, and public charity policies are deeply interconnected in the United States. Collectively, these and other policy arenas circumscribe opportunities for the urban poor. Yet policies are only as good as they work on the ground. This book, then, tells a story about *urban policy in practice*: the tensions in current approaches, unanticipated shortcomings, and most important, opportunities for change. If urban policy is to be an engine for equity and make life better for people living in poverty, we must first understand how, and why, it sometimes falls short.

Part I

CHAPTER ONE

Slow Train Coming

IN 1958, THE FEDERAL GOVERNMENT approved the demolition of Boston's West End, a "slum" neighborhood filled mostly with low-income European immigrants. Seven years earlier, city officials had applied for a federal urban renewal grant to replace the West End's "blighted" buildings with new development projects. It was a government-controlled and -funded process from beginning to end: The federal government paid two-thirds and city government paid one-third toward the cost of purchasing properties, relocating residents, demolishing existing structures, and contracting a developer to, essentially, construct a new community. State government officials provided additional oversight. By 1960, "only rubble remained where two years ago had lived more than 7,000 people."[1]

West End residents were mostly oblivious to the implications of redevelopment when city officials first announced their plans. They received "poor information," and "official announcements were vague."[2] According to sociologist Herbert Gans, who happened to be living in the neighborhood as part of an ethnographic study of community life, there was "relatively little concern about the redevelopment, and even less public discussion of it."[3] When the final announcement came, residents "did not understand that this was the last step in the process . . . Thus, they felt certain that there would be more meetings, and more decisions, and that twenty-five years later, the West End would still be there."[4]

Nor were local organizations privy to city officials' preliminary discussions or funding applications. After the plans became public, a "Save the West End Committee" formed, but "the Committee, in effect, had no political influence."[5] West Enders found it difficult to organize. Even though some were upset about the proposed destruction of their neighborhood, "the act of joining with neighbors to work together for halting the redevelopment was inconceivable."[6] "The truth was," Gans observed, "that for a group unaccustomed to organizational activity, saving the West End was an overwhelming, and perhaps impossible, task."[7]

Fifty-five years later, as I conducted my fieldwork in the Fairmount Corridor, redevelopment projects remained a constant presence in Boston's poorest neighborhoods. Yet none followed the same script that led to the wholesale destruction of the West End. The 2013 ribbon cutting for one project, a new Fairmount Line station in Four Corners, provides a useful contrast. There, on a scorching hot July day, about fifty people gathered. A large tent offered only modest protection from a bright sun in a cloudless sky. Two photographers positioned themselves in front of a podium flanked by large black loudspeakers. A dozen residents sat in folding chairs while the rest formed a semicircle facing the podium.

Governor Deval Patrick approached the podium at 10:15. He thanked each government official in attendance, then paused for dramatic effect before thanking "the community, that insisted, for a long time, that an investment in *you*, would make for a better, stronger, community."

"Amen!" a nonprofit organizer in the audience shouted out gleefully.

Governor Patrick acknowledged "the visionary leaders" in city and state government, "but the members of the community—"

"Alright now!" a woman in the audience erupted.

"—who stepped up and said, 'This. Is something. We. *Deserve*.'" The governor thanked everyone again before leaving the podium to resounding applause.

Speaking next, Mayor Thomas Menino emphasized that it was "a *community* victory, the opening of this station." He linked the train station to another project, an affordable housing development across the street on what was once vacant land. His "friends" from the Codman Square Neighborhood Development Corporation (CSNDC), a private nonprofit, managed that project. "I just want to make sure," he said, "that we continue to work together. That's how we get things done: The state, the city, and the neighborhoods."

State Senator Linda Dorcena Forry followed, and after acknowledging various government officials and "the community," she thanked The Boston Foundation and "other nonprofits." She additionally noted that the public in attendance deserved credit for "going to meetings in the evenings . . . [and] holding us accountable."

After two more elected officials spoke, a Black community organizer took to the stage. A former resident of the neighborhood, she thanked, in order, seventeen city and state officials, "residents of Four Corners," eight nonprofit leaders, nine private foundations, and once more, "the people of the Four Corners community." She also singled out the director of her "small nonprofit," an important figure "who started all of this."

Finally, the CEO of The Boston Foundation spoke. His remarks were short, but to the point: He announced $10 million in grants to support community development planning in the Corridor. A federal housing official in the audience yelped in approval. "Whoa!" she exclaimed. She turned to Geeta, associate vice president of programs at the Foundation, standing to her right. "Did you know about this?!?" she whispered excitedly. Geeta just laughed and clapped her hands, reveling in the surprise.

{~~~}W{~~~}

This chapter documents how community development policy transformed from the government-directed destruction of entire neighborhoods to extensive collaboration between public agencies and the private, predominantly nonprofit sector. These public-private partnerships, funded by both government and nongovernmental sources, spanned multiple levels of government and several institutional arenas. Whereas neighborhood groups in the 1950s "in effect, had no political influence," by the 2000s, many nonprofit leaders in the Fairmount Corridor found themselves in key decision-making positions.

This shift represents a victory in battles fought throughout the 1960s, when the federal government adopted community-based approaches to urban policy in response to public outcry following the sorts of "urban renewal" projects that destroyed the West End. Grassroots organizations received direct federal funding, and resident participation became the norm. Foundations helped fund various initiatives and developed policies in conjunction with government agencies. As public funding for community development declined, these newly empowered organizations became fundamental to the functioning of urban governance.

We can think of the shift toward private nonprofits in urban policy as a "slow train coming," a reference to a scene in the HBO drama *The Wire*. In the scene, two men overlook the remnants of a demolished public housing project in Baltimore. As the camera pans over the gaping hole, soon to be replaced with a new, privately managed mixed-income development, one man asks the other what happened to the housing project. The second answers cryptically: "Slow train coming." The line is a nod to Bob Dylan's 1979 studio album of the same name, the first he recorded after converting to Christianity. For Dylan, the train is both a religious symbol and a commentary on the ambiguity of progress. The train may bring salvation or it may bring damnation; all that we can know is that it is slowly coming down the tracks.

The history of the Fairmount Corridor—beginning with a train, appropriately enough—is a story of slow, steadily unfolding, and often ambiguous progress. The forces pushing community development forward were not always direct, and the outcomes of policy decisions were not always immediately clear. In this chapter, I bring clarity to what may seem like a disjointed or unrelated series of policies and events—to identify, in other words, where the train came from and what structures allowed it to move slowly down the tracks.

Residents mobilized and now have a stronger voice in urban policy and community development politics. Community development projects are, accordingly, less destructive for poor neighborhoods. Yet this progress has also placed more political power and decision-making authority in the hands of *private* organizations. Unintentionally, the successful push for democratic inclusion in the 1960s undermined key structures of democratic governance in poor neighborhoods today.[8]

The Fairmount Line and Urban Growth in Boston

First called the "Midland Route" and later "the Dorchester Branch," the Fairmount Line has operated under a variety of owners since 1855. Originally, it ran from Boston's city center to the suburb of Dedham, where it connected to other rail lines continuing west to Providence and New York City. At its peak, the Fairmount Line included as many as eleven stations in the neighborhoods of Dorchester, Mattapan, and Hyde Park.

When the Fairmount Line came into existence, those neighborhoods were in fact independent, rural towns. That changed beginning in the late nineteenth century, when the development of electric streetcars and improved sanitation services led to significant population dispersion throughout the region. These technological innovations allowed middle-class Bostonians to live further from the city center, and by 1912, all of the neighborhoods in what is now the Fairmount Corridor had been annexed as Boston's new "streetcar suburbs."[9]

Passenger service on the Fairmount Line continued until 1944. I was unable to find a record of the rationale for the decision to end service—there were no meeting minutes or memoirs or letters about the decision in the transportation authority's historical archives. I was, however, able to find some evidence in my own family history. In the 1940s and 1950s, my great-Aunt Ethel commuted from my great-Grandmother Rose's apartment in Mattapan to her job in downtown Boston. She traveled down Blue Hill Avenue on a streetcar similar to the one shown in figure 1.1.

Ethel had no recollection of the Fairmount Line, even though Rose's apartment was located directly in between a trolley stop on Blue Hill Avenue and a Fairmount Line Station on Morton Street. My great-Aunt Shirley, who also lived in the apartment, remembered the train but never considered taking it. Due to higher fares, insufficient advertisement, or simple inconvenience—neither Shirley nor Ethel could remember which—they never saw the rail line as a viable mode of transportation.

Shirley and Ethel were not alone. Beginning in the 1940s, public transit ridership declined as people throughout the country shifted toward private automobiles. The precise reasons are hotly contested. In testimony during a 1974 hearing before the US Senate Subcommittee on Antitrust and Monopoly, a lawyer named Bradford C. Snell placed the blame on General Motors. GM, he claimed, conspired with associates in the auto and oil industries to

FIGURE 1.1. Blue Hill Avenue in Mattapan, 1955
Source: Boston Streetcars, "Dorchester's Blue Hill Avenue"
(https://web.archive.org/web/20191024074623/
http://www.bostonstreetcars.com/dorchesters-blue-hill-avenue.html).

undermine rail, electric streetcars, and other forms of public transportation. By destroying public transportation, the argument goes, GM executives effectively destroyed the private automobile's key competition.

Though plausible, Snell's theory lacks strong empirical evidence; a number of larger political and economic factors were at play, and it is likely that GM and others simply took advantage of processes already in motion.[10] The end result, however, is undisputed: Buses and cars soon overtook rail and trolleys as the dominant modes of transportation in cities. Indeed, a few months after the photo in figure 1.1 was taken, the Blue Hill Avenue trolley tracks were removed and replaced with two additional traffic lanes. With little investment in public transportation and growing consumer demand for private automobiles, it is perhaps no surprise that the state discontinued passenger service on the Fairmount Line.

Postwar Suburbanization and Residential Segregation in the Fairmount Corridor

The decision to stop passenger service preceded significant demographic change in the postwar period. In stark contrast with today's racial and ethnic composition, the Fairmount Corridor population was predominantly white and Jewish in the mid-1940s. At the northern end of the Corridor, Roxbury and

Dorchester each became predominantly Black in the 1960s.[11] Mattapan shifted to majority Black a bit later, in the 1970s. And Hyde Park, at the southern end of the Corridor, became majority nonwhite for the first time in the 1990s.

The story of postwar racial change is not unique to Boston. Between the 1940s and 1970s, four million Black Americans moved to Northeastern and Midwestern cities, hoping to take advantage of jobs in the industrial economy.[12] There were more jobs in the North than the South, but the move entailed significant costs—in particular, rampant racial discrimination and the constant threat of violence. Housing was a particularly fraught arena. As Black migration increased, white homeowners fled cities in overwhelming numbers. Historians refer to the process as "white flight": an interrelated "push" from the city and "pull" to the suburbs. On the "push" side, interpersonal racism combined with political and fiscal fears that Black migrants would decrease whites' political power, lower property values, and increase public spending.[13] On the "pull" side, federal housing policy drew white Americans to the suburbs at unprecedented rates.

An important Depression-era policy facilitated suburbanization across the country. In 1933, the federal government created the Home Owners Loan Corporation (HOLC) that would provide low-interest loans to keep small farms at risk of foreclosure afloat. The organization's method for assessing risk codified neighborhood value largely as a function of racial composition. Racially homogenous neighborhoods containing affluent white families received the highest rating: an "A," color-coded "green." Predominantly Black, low-income, and dense neighborhoods received the lowest rating, a "D," and were color-coded "red."

In the postwar period, the Federal Housing Authority (FHA) and private sector lenders adopted the HOLC's rating system. Through a process called "red-lining," these lenders provided low-interest loans to prospective homeowners in white, homogenous suburbs, and they denied loans for homeownership in predominantly Black neighborhoods.[14] Predatory real estate agents capitalized on discriminatory loan practices through a tactic known as "blockbusting." Real estate agents warned white homeowners of declining property values in integrating neighborhoods, and then, block by block, panicked homeowners sold their homes at below-market rates. Suburbanization caused population decline in cities, and with it, the loss of cities' tax base. Property taxes make up a significant share of cities' revenues, and so white and middle-class flight from cities meant fewer public resources for neighborhoods like those in the Fairmount Corridor.

Boston's story fit many of these national trends, but with one important twist: At the request of city officials, a consortium of bankers, called the Boston Banks Urban Renewal Group (BBURG), began to offer attractive federal loans to prospective Black homeowners in 1968—but only if they chose to live in certain non-white neighborhoods, including the vast majority of the present-day Fairmount Corridor. The bankers viewed their loan program as a way to "help rebuild an area of the city that was festering with decay" and "provide homes for the rootless in the ghetto area and thus help or avert disorders."[15] Limiting loans to Black neighborhoods, the bankers indirectly hoped to "stabilize" the predominantly white neighborhoods in which they had substantial investments. Integration destabilized neighborhoods, the bankers reasoned; residential segregation was taken for granted.[16]

Together, the intersection of federal housing policy, local real estate practices, and the racism of policymakers, lenders, real estate agents, and homeowners led to increasingly segregated cities and suburbs. Neighborhoods in the Fairmount Corridor became and remained poor, racially segregated, and starved of resources.

Urban Renewal and Government-Led Redevelopment

As postwar suburbanization transformed the racial and class composition of metropolitan areas, urban renewal transformed the physical layout of the urban core. Two pieces of federal housing legislation—the Federal Housing Act of 1949 and the United States Housing Act of 1954—provided billions of dollars for city governments to demolish "slum" neighborhoods adjacent to downtown business districts. In places like Boston's West End, new housing and commercial development replaced dilapidated buildings in desperate need of repair. A critical flaw of urban renewal—a flaw that would be repeated again and again in subsequent housing policies—was its lack of a right-of-return guarantee; residents displaced during construction remained displaced even after new buildings went up. A second flaw was architectural: Housing developments of this era adopted high-modernist, aggressively rational styles. Inspired by European architects like Le Corbusier, urban planners designed high-rise, high-density cubes of steel and concrete that towered over adjacent neighborhoods. Clusters of buildings formed grids, often separated by empty space. The brooding, impersonal structures became associated with poor living conditions in the developments.[17]

Another urban renewal–era policy, the Federal Aid Highway Act of 1956, created the nation's first interstate roadway system. Advocates portrayed interstate highways as a national defense policy: If an atomic bomb were on its way to a heavily populated city, the highway would allow residents to quickly and efficiently flee the bomb's blast. In practice, however, interstate highways facilitated the growth of segregated suburbs, as it became easier to commute to and from the city.[18] Just like "slum" clearance, new roadways did more to destroy than to improve urban neighborhoods. In Detroit, for instance, the Black neighborhoods of Paradise Valley and Black Bottom were razed in the 1950s in order to make way for Interstate 375.

Black activism proliferated in the wake of urban renewal. From Bedford-Stuyvesant in Brooklyn to the Seventh Ward in Philadelphia, residents in segregated Black neighborhoods organized in opposition to government plans.[19] The South End and Lower Roxbury—two predominantly Black neighborhoods located just north of the Fairmount Corridor[20]—became hotbeds of activism. In 1954, city officials (in consultation with business elites in the city) demolished a section of the South End known as the "New York Streets." Hundreds of families were permanently displaced. In response, South End residents formed more than a dozen organizations and voiced opposition to large-scale neighborhood demolition. As South End activist Mel King chronicled:

> A major purpose of [urban renewal] was to revitalize the residents right out of Boston's inner city neighborhoods to make way for higher income white residents that [renewal's] proponents hoped to entice back into the city. The West End and the New York Streets section of the South End were demolished without a trace to accommodate [urban renewal]. Other neighborhoods were severely altered before residents banded together to demand a role in the decision-making that affected their lives and homes.[21]

One of the organizations that would notch important victories was the Emergency Tenants Council (ETC). ETC was a small group of mostly Puerto Ricans who lived in an area of the South End known as "Parcel 19." Housing in the neighborhood was substandard, and in 1967, city officials slated Parcel 19 for demolition and redevelopment. ETC members, working alongside other activists, successfully halted officials' plans. In "an unprecedented act," the Redevelopment Authority designated ETC as the developer of a new housing development in Parcel 19. Residents named the resulting project "Villa Victoria," or "Victory Village."[22] "As a result of the efforts of ETC," sociologist Mario Small describes, "the Puerto Rican residents of Parcel 19 were among the few groups of the South End who were able to remain in the South End after urban renewal."[23] Residents created another organization, Inquilinos Boricuas en Acción (IBA), to provide social services in the neighborhood. IBA merged with ETC in 2013 and remains the key representative of Villa Victoria residents today.

Urban renewal also affected the development of the Fairmount Corridor—though the history here is fairly complex and, at times, involved seemingly unrelated policy decisions that would only affect Corridor development decades later. A clear example is the failed proposal for a new highway in Jamaica Plain, a neighborhood on the opposite side of the city. In 1968, the state prepared for the highway by demolishing hundreds of homes and businesses in the neighborhood. Officials hoped to build an eight-lane highway, dubbed the Southwest Expressway, which would connect Interstate 95 (to the south) with another future highway (to the north).[24]

The highway never came to fruition. A group of local activists, radicalized by urban renewal policies, mobilized against new highway construction. In 1973, Massachusetts Governor Francis W. Sargent formally canceled the

Southwest Expressway. "I have decided to reverse the transportation policy of the Commonwealth of Massachusetts," Governor Sargent explained. "We were wrong. Today we know more clearly what our real needs are—what our environment means to us—what a community means to us—what is valuable to us as a people."[25]

In place of the highway, Sargent proposed a realignment of the city's public transit lines to spur "restoration" and "rehabilitation" on the land that had been cleared in Jamaica Plain. The Orange Line, an elevated public transit line that connected downtown Boston with the predominantly Black neighborhoods of Roxbury and the South End, moved West to the now-vacant land in Jamaica Plain. Governor Sargent promised to replace the elevated rail line with a cleaner, safer alternative, then extend it through Dorchester and Mattapan—a promise that was never fulfilled.[26] He made no mention of the Fairmount Line even though the proposed extension ran directly adjacent to the Fairmount Line tracks (see figure 1.2).

How do these historical developments relate to community development in the Fairmount Corridor? As the Orange Line realignment construction began in 1979, commuter rail lines that used the Orange Line tracks required re-routing. The state shifted the displaced commuter rail service to the underutilized Fairmount Line tracks and re-opened two previously shuttered stations in Upham's Corner and Mattapan.

In 1981, budget pressures caused the state to briefly suspend passenger service on the line, but it was restored indefinitely in 1987 with the opening of the new Orange Line. There was no press conference, announcement, or ribbon cutting. Indeed, the editorial board of the *Boston Globe* called it the state's "hush-hush line": "The only people who seem to know these stations exist are the activists who complained that transit riders along the Roxbury-Dorchester-Mattapan border have been ill-served by the relocation of the Orange Line."[27]

The War on Poverty and Emergence of the Community Development Field

In the 1960s, as poverty and progressive social movements spread across US cities, the federal government radically altered its approach to urban policy. Urban renewal proved to be a social and political failure, drawing the ire of influential thinkers like Jane Jacobs and activists like the anti-highway group in Boston. Government's new approach was decidedly community-driven, based on an assumption that funding for local communities (and local community *organizations*) was the most effective way to combat urban poverty and its associated social problems. Nonprofits became eligible to receive federal grants, and public participation was codified in federal legislation. Importantly, new ideas about community development emerged from both the public and philanthropic sectors. The Ford Foundation, in particular,

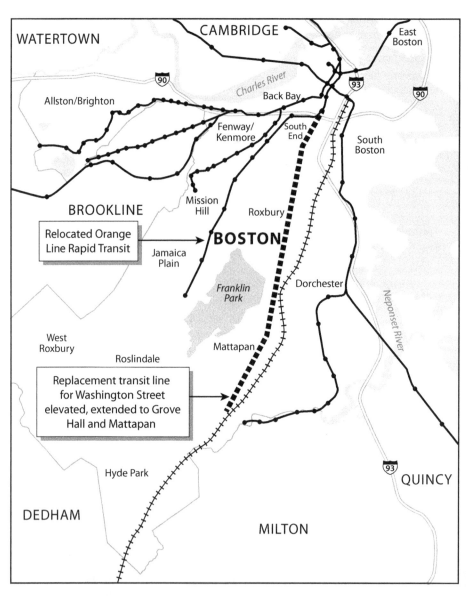

FIGURE 1.2. Proposed Orange Line Replacement in Present-Day Fairmount Corridor
Notes: The Fairmount Line tracks are shown—but not labeled or otherwise referenced—directly to the east of the proposed replacement of the Washington Street elevated transit line.
Source: Adapted from *Boston Transportation Planning Review Final Study Summary Report* (1973).

took an active role in promoting particular programs and practices, part of a broader shift toward foundations acting as strategic political actors.[28] By the mid-1960s, the two sectors were more interdependent than ever.

In 1961, President Kennedy signed the Juvenile Delinquency and Youth Offense Control Act, elevating the issue of youth crime and poverty to the national stage. Congress dedicated $30 million to the cause. The Act's true innovation was its model of allocation: Instead of providing grants to public agencies, like urban renewal policies, the Act allowed funds to go directly to a "nonprofit agency, organization, or institution." As historian Claire Dunning notes, "No funding precedent existed at the federal level to target social issues through private organizations."[29]

That same year, the Ford Foundation announced an antipoverty initiative called the "Gray Areas" program. It built on a burgeoning "community action" approach to social reform, encouraging citizen participation and relying on community-based organizations to manage local service provision. The initiative created new nonprofits to manage social service delivery and youth programs in five pilot cities: Boston, New Haven, Oakland, Philadelphia, and Washington, DC.[30] Rarely had foundations experimented with social programs on such a large scale.

President Johnson's Economic Opportunity Act of 1964—the signature legislation of the "War on Poverty"—combined Kennedy's funding model with Ford's commitment to community development. Title II of the Act was especially consequential. It established funding for Community Action Programs (CAPs), antipoverty initiatives "conducted, administered, or coordinated by a public or private nonprofit agency." The organizations tasked with managing federal CAP funds were called Community Action Agencies (CAAs), and they were typically nonprofits in the human services subsector.[31] Title II also stipulated that programs be "developed, conducted, and administered with the maximum feasible participation of residents of the areas and members of the groups served."[32] As such, the Act institutionalized two policy innovations: community-based nonprofits were eligible for direct federal funding, and public participation was a *mandated* step in the process of urban community development.

In 1966, Senator Robert F. Kennedy visited Brooklyn's Bedford-Stuyvesant neighborhood in his capacity as chairman of the President's Committee on Juvenile Delinquency. After meeting with neighborhood leaders, Kennedy offered support for an emerging kind of community development organization, modeled after the Gray Areas program: community development corporations (CDCs). CDCs planned and implemented brick-and-mortar redevelopment, complementing CAA social service providers. With Senator Jacob Javits, Kennedy co-sponsored an amendment to the Economic Opportunity Act called the Special Impact Program. The amendment diverted some of the War on Poverty funding into this new form of nonprofit organization. The Ford Foundation provided seed grants for new CDCs across the country, deepening connections between federal policymakers and organized philanthropy.

Recipients of War on Poverty funds were sometimes radical organizations critical of top-down government oversight. City politicians did not appreciate the rising power of federally subsidized opponents, and so they pushed Congress to limit the power of CAAs. The Green Amendment of 1967 did just that, stipulating that *only CAAs approved by city government* could receive War on Poverty funding. The measure was the beginning of the end for the ambitious policy experiment; budget cuts gutted the program in 1970. But the nonprofits it created and the public-private models of community development it promoted remained in place.[33] Community development organizations in the Fairmount Corridor likely would never have existed without the War on Poverty legislation and its subsequent amendments.

Congress grew weary of the Ford Foundation and its policy influence by the late 1960s. The foundation's "travel grants" to some former members of Senator Robert Kennedy's staff, as well as voter registration drives in predominantly Black neighborhoods, were particularly controversial. In an attempt to curtail foundation influence, Congress passed the Tax Reform Act of 1969.[34] The Joint Committee on Internal Revenue Taxation noted:

> In recent years, private foundations had become increasingly active in political and legislative activities. In several instances called to the Congress' attention, funds were spent in ways clearly designed to favor certain candidates. In some cases, this was done by financing registration campaigns in limited geographical areas. In other cases contributions were made to organizations that then used the money to publicize the views, personalities, and activities of certain candidates.

Previously, foundations were subject to the same "substantiality" test as other nonprofits; they could not spend "a substantial amount" of organizational resources on lobbying. The Act restricted all foundation lobbying with respect to legislation and limited foundations' ability to fund other organizations' political activity. The key language blocked foundations from "direct attempts" to influence legislation:

> One of the provisions of the Act specifically prohibits the incurring of expenses in connection with "grass roots" campaigns or other attempts to influence any legislation through an attempt to affect the opinion of the general public or any segment thereof . . . Another provision in the Act precludes direct attempts to persuade members of legislative bodies or government employees to take particular positions on specific legislative issues.

Congress left open an important loophole: Foundations could share nonpartisan analysis or research, as well as "technical advice or assistance." The Act continues:

Under the Act, it is clear that the expertise of a private foundation is not denied to lawmakers when the lawmakers or other appropriate persons have made written requests for such technical advice or assistance.

Foundations subsequently avoided overtly political activities and scaled back funding to radical, grassroots organizations. But the Act did little to curb foundations' influence in the public realm. The loophole that allowed foundations to offer "technical advice" to legislators, combined with the vague language restricting "direct attempts" to influence legislation, emboldened many in the field. Until 2018, no foundation was ever censured for its policy-related activities.[35] Foundations developed the ability to influence policy in the face of—and in accordance with—official regulations. That skill would prove critical for development in the Fairmount Corridor.

Federal Retrenchment and the Privatization of Community Development

To paraphrase political scientist Demetrios Caraley, Washington abandoned the cities in the 1980s and early 1990s.[36] Federal support for community development declined sharply, just as work and other resources "disappeared."[37] Take the Community Development Block Grant (CDBG), enacted by Congress in 1974. The CDBG program consolidated eight related but disconnected streams of urban development funding. Seventy percent of funds go directly to cities like Boston, whereas state governments control and distribute the remaining 30 percent. As urban planning scholars William M. Rohe and George Galster noted in 2014, "After 40 years, the CDBG program remains the primary federal source of funds for urban-improvement initiatives." Yet despite its symbolic importance, CDBG funding declined sharply in the 1980s. CDBG funding peaked at $13.3 billion in 1978. It was just $3.4 billion in 2018.[38]

In addition to declines in absolute funding dollars, funding allocation methods also changed. In the 1960s and 1970s, the federal government distributed urban development grants through formula-based apportionments. That changed in the 1980s, when Reagan-era reforms adopted market logics of competition. New allocation procedures forced local government agencies and nonprofit organizations to submit extensive applications detailing core competency, the ability to leverage private capital, and quantitative metrics of success. Similar reforms transformed foundations' funding practices. Not surprisingly, competitive application processes benefited already resource-rich applicants with the capacity to manage grants.

Privatization was especially acute in the housing arena. Over the course of seventy years, the federal government moved from a policy of public housing to "affordable" housing: publicly subsidized income- and rent-restricted apartments constructed by private developers and managed by private landlords.[39]

Starting in the 1930s, the federal government supported public housing managed by local housing authorities. In the 1960s and '70s, Congress shifted more of the nation's low-income housing burden to the private sector. Federal legislation provided below-market construction loans to nonprofit developers, and public housing authorities leased buildings from private landlords.[40] In the 1980s, tax credits further incentivized private developers to build and manage low-income housing. Privatization hit a high-water mark in the 1990s, when the HOPE VI program funded the conversion of existing public housing into privately managed mixed-income developments. HOPE VI ended in 2010. Public housing demolition did not. Between 1993 and the mid-2010s, local governments demolished approximately 250,000 public housing units.[41]

The Tax Reform Act of 1986, particularly its establishment of the Low Income Housing Tax Credit (LIHTC, pronounced *lie-tech*), was instrumental in the privatization shift. Each year, Congress determines the total number of tax credits available and apportions those credits to states based on population. Developers in cities like Boston then compete with other developers for the limited credits available at the state level. The credits are transferable, which means *nonprofit* developers are eligible to receive them because they can be sold to banks, corporations, or syndicators. The nonprofit developers receive cash for construction, and for-profit corporations reduce their tax liability. While for-profit developers receive the majority of LIHTC, the tax credit is also a critical source of funding for nonprofit developers. Community development corporations in the Corridor—and similar organizations across the nation—would simply not exist in their current form without LIHTC.[42]

As the federal government turned to the private sector for community development funding, the field of private funding organizations grew. Community development projects, once the sole responsibility of government, now draw on an extensive network of intermediaries and private foundations. Support from national intermediaries like Enterprise Community Partners and Local Initiatives Support Corporation (LISC) exploded during the 1990s, doubling in absolute dollars. These organizations' annual contributions are now in the billions; LISC awarded $1.1 billion in 2010 alone.[43] With partial funding from The Boston Foundation, LISC opened a Boston office in 1982 and remains a key funder of community development projects in the city.

Governments came to rely on this industry to help fund and implement community development projects. In fact, the Department of Housing and Urban Development (HUD) annual budget includes a line item to support LISC and Enterprise.[44] Public financing and tax incentives such as LIHTC still cover the bulk of up-front construction costs for certain projects like affordable housing development. But private organizations increasingly fund community development *planning*—the critical period before development, when project ideas become actual proposals.

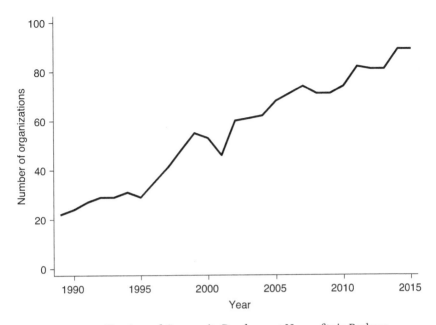

FIGURE 1.3. Housing and Community Development Nonprofits in Roxbury, Dorchester, Mattapan, and Hyde Park: 1989–2015
Notes: Analysis includes all public charities classified as housing or community building organizations in the Roxbury, Dorchester, Mattapan, and Hyde Park neighborhood districts, measured at the zip code level (02119, 02120, 02121, 02122, 02124, 02125, 02126, and 02136).
Source: Author's tabulations based on data from the National Center for Charitable Statistics Core Files (https://web.archive.org/web/20200409084628/https://nccs-data.urban.org/index.php).

The contraction of government resources led, in part, to the concentration of poverty and crime in poor urban neighborhoods. Hundreds of community-based organizations formed in response, created with the goal of improving safety, providing political voice, and acquiring resources for upward mobility. Between 1990 and the early 2010s, the number of community nonprofits in large US cities quadrupled.[45]

A similar growth occurred in Boston (see figure 1.3). In 1989, the first year for which data are available, twenty-two housing and community development nonprofits operated in the Roxbury, Dorchester, Mattapan, and Hyde Park neighborhood districts. That figure jumped to eighty-nine by 2015.

Growth in absolute numbers included *both* new organizational incorporation *and* organizational death—that is, organizations filing for bankruptcy protection, closing their doors, or otherwise disappearing. Figure 1.4 depicts the life and death of housing and community development nonprofits in Roxbury, Dorchester, Mattapan, and Hyde Park. Each line represents the length of operation for one of the 145 unique organizations that existed at some point

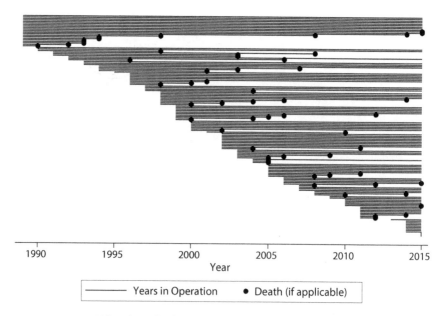

FIGURE 1.4. Life and Death of Housing and Community Development Nonprofits in Roxbury, Dorchester, Mattapan, and Hyde Park: 1989–2015
Notes: Analysis includes all public charities classified as housing or community building organizations in the Roxbury, Dorchester, Mattapan, and Hyde Park neighborhood districts, measured at the zip code level (02119, 02120, 02121, 02122, 02124, 02125, 02126, and 02136).
Source: Author's tabulations based on data from the National Center for Charitable Statistics Core Files (https://web.archive.org/web/20200409084628/https://nccs-data.urban.org/index.php).

between 1989 and 2015. A black circle indicates the organization's "death" date. Fifty-six (38.6%) organizations died between 1989 and 2015. Of the twenty-two housing and community development nonprofits in operation in 1989, only nine (40.9%) survived through 2015.

The nonprofits operating in the 1990s generally bore little resemblance to the radical, grassroots groups of the 1960s. Beginning in the 1980s, competition for funding led to sector-wide professionalization. Community-based nonprofits now rely more on paid staff than volunteers, develop systematic program evaluation tools with quantitative metrics, incorporate expert consultants and strategic planning into operations, and adopt managerial practices like annual audits. More and more nonprofit leaders have graduate degrees or certificates in management. Fewer and fewer live in the neighborhoods where they work. Figure 1.4 therefore reflects not just nonprofit *growth* over time, but nonprofit *change* over time.[46]

One of those newly formed organizations was the Greater Four Corners Action Coalition (GFCAC), located in the Four Corners section of

Dorchester.[47] GFCAC formed in 1991 following a neighborhood shooting, but quickly expanded its focus to other issue areas, including unequal access to public transportation. In 1999, Marvin Martin, the organization's Black director, attended a transportation forum with Noah Berger, a white policy analyst and member of the state transportation authority Advisory Board. Marvin mentioned a train—the Fairmount Line—that ran through but did not stop in Four Corners. He saw it as an injustice for a neighborhood lacking access to alternative rapid rail options. Noah agreed.

The two began meeting on a regular basis. By 2000, Marvin had formed a coalition of transit advocates including Noah and representatives from local neighborhood groups in Dorchester. Together, they sent a letter to the state transportation authority requesting new stations and improved service on the Fairmount Line. Half a dozen elected officials wrote letters of support, and state transportation officials responded by hosting public meetings and conducting a feasibility study in 2002. To the officials' surprise, the report concurred with the advocates' assessment and recommended the construction of four new stations. "Up until I received the (report) the other day, I was pessimistic. I didn't really believe there was big potential (there)," the general manager of the state transportation authority explained to a *Boston Herald* reporter. "But it just makes too much sense. This is a case where many of the advocates were right on target."[48]

Transit-Oriented Development and Mobilization for New Fairmount Line Stations

The state's recommendation for new stations on the Fairmount Line coincided with the growing popularity of transit-oriented development (TOD) in the early 2000s. TOD is a practice of urban planning that concentrates housing and employment opportunities in close proximity to public transportation nodes—typically, within a quarter- or half-mile radius. TOD often includes "beautifying" efforts as well, such as community gardens, bike paths, and small parks.

TOD is the bread-and-butter of nonprofit community development corporations (CDCs). These organizations grew exponentially across the country after receiving initial support from the 1966 amendment to the Economic Opportunity Act. Publicly subsidized cash flow vis-à-vis LIHTC, combined with consistent funding from private philanthropy and other intermediaries, helped many of these organizations secure sound financial footing. The directors of four CDCs in the Corridor—Dorchester Bay Economic Development Corporation (DBEDC), Codman Square Neighborhood Development Corporation (CSNDC), Mattapan Community Development Corporation (MCDC), and Southwest Boston Community Development Corporation (SWBCDC)—recognized the potential for TOD at the proposed Fairmount Line stations.

Public transportation advocacy was not necessarily part of their repertoires; they worked primarily in affordable housing development and, to a lesser extent, community organizing. But re-classifying their ongoing work as "TOD" introduced new funding opportunities.

In 2004, the four directors created a formal partnership they called the Fairmount CDC Collaborative. They then joined Marvin Martin's coalition, positioning themselves as the housing and commercial development complement to the ongoing advocacy for transit improvements. These coalitions each met roughly once a month. In 2005, the coalition of CDCs hired a consultant firm and produced a manifesto of sorts, titled "Boston's Newest Smart Growth Corridor"—"smart growth" referring to transit-oriented development with an eye toward equity. The document rebranded community development projects along the Fairmount Line as part of a cohesive *Corridor*, more impactful than projects in individual neighborhoods and thus worthy of special attention and resources.

City officials also recognized the possibilities for new TOD projects adjacent to the Fairmount Line's proposed stations. By March 2004, about 400 housing units were planned for the Corridor; 250 were scheduled for construction in 2004, and another 150 slated for 2005. "We have a housing problem, and we need to develop more affordable housing, so we started with that," a city official told a reporter from the *Boston Globe* at the time. "But the upgrading of the [Fairmount] line and new stops would be very important for the new developments, because we need to do more transit-oriented housing."[49]

The 2004 transportation bond bill passed by the Massachusetts state legislature included $43.5 million designated for the construction of four new Fairmount Line stations. But the bill was overly ambitious, listing more projects than the state could actually fund. Governor Mitt Romney's administration had to make critical decisions about which projects would receive immediate appropriations and which would be delayed.

It was the following year, in 2005, when a seemingly unrelated story of transportation policy from the 1990s converged with nonprofit coalition-building from the early 2000s. In 1990, the Conservation Law Foundation (CLF)—a Boston-based nonprofit environmental policy organization—sued Massachusetts Governor Michael Dukakis and State Secretary of Transportation Fred P. Salvucci for failure to comply with the federal Clean Air Act Amendments. The lawsuit centered on the environmental effects of the Central Artery/Tunnel Project, colloquially known as the "Big Dig," which rerouted Interstate 93 into a tunnel through downtown Boston. CLF's lawsuit argued that the project negatively affected regional air quality due to increased traffic, and the suit demanded a set of public transportation investments to mitigate increased carbon dioxide emissions. The state agreed to a number of public transit projects, though neither party suggested improvements to the Fairmount Line; again, as the *Boston Globe* editorial board noted in 1987, only resident activists seemed to know about the line at this time. The state never carried out those projects, and in March 2005, CLF threatened to sue again.[50]

In April, with CLF's legal action hanging over their heads, state officials hosted a groundbreaking for upgrades to two existing stations on the Fairmount Line. As the press gathered to cover the event, the coalition of community-based organizations, nonprofit developers, and neighborhood associations held a rally at the site of the proposed—but still unfunded—station in Four Corners. The idea was to pressure state officials to formally commit to the four new stations.

The pressure paid off. In May, the Romney administration announced $770 million in transit commitments. Central to the announcement was a reshuffling of the projects included in the state's 1990 air pollution mitigation agreement with CLF. At the time of the original lawsuit, the Fairmount Line was not in consideration; it was the transit authority's "hush-hush line," after all. But the nonprofits' advocacy prompted officials to remodel ridership projections. According to those new projections, the proposed stations would dramatically reduce carbon emissions by pushing car users toward public transit. CLF and the state settled the lawsuit in 2006 and included the new Fairmount Line stations in the final agreement.[51]

Public-Private Partnerships and Urban Policy in the Obama Era

Decades-long trends in urban policy were fully realized with the election of President Barack Obama in 2008. For policymakers, the key debate was no longer between destroying poor neighborhoods or ignoring them; it was about the relative weight placed on "people-based" policies—that is, direct cash transfers and other resources for poor people—or "place-based" policies—that is, income-restricted housing developments and other infrastructure improvements in poor neighborhoods.[52] On the place-based side, governments increasingly relied on community development organizations to implement a number of activities in poor neighborhoods, including housing development, social programs, job training, and public art.

Amidst notable changes, the technocratic logic of public-private partnerships still predominated. The Obama administration's cross-agency, cross-sector approach privileged private organizations, like CDCs and foundations, and structurally incentivized private capital investment through tax credits and other grants requiring "matching" funds from nongovernmental sources. The community development industry had matured in a way that mirrored the War on Poverty, combining the social service work of CAAs with the brick-and-mortar development of CDCs.

Consequently, foundations across the country became even more involved in urban governance decisions. One of those funders was Geeta Pradhan, associate vice president of programs at The Boston Foundation (TBF). To Geeta, the Corridor presented a once-in-a-lifetime opportunity: By combining affordable housing, economic development, and transit improvements all within Boston's historically disinvested neighborhoods, community development in the Corridor had the potential to make a real difference in the lives of poor Bostonians.

In 2009, Geeta took on a proactive leadership role in the Corridor.[53] Her first order of business was awarding a $1 million grant for operational support to the coalition of CDCs, paid out in $200,000 annual increments between 2009 and 2014. Geeta's second move was to tactfully insert the Fairmount Corridor into TBF's internal strategy areas. This set the stage for what would later become a stand-alone "Fairmount strategy" or "Fairmount frame" alongside the organization's larger mission of improving health and education in greater Boston. The foundation organized its entire 2014 Annual Report—titled "Corridor of Promise: This Is How We Build Vibrant Places"—around its grants to Corridor nonprofits. That same year, TBF committed an additional $10 million in funding for community development efforts in the Corridor.

This influx of private funding in community development reflects a broader shift in the nonprofit sector: Between 2002 and 2015, total foundation funding grew enormously, from $39 billion to nearly $63 billion in inflation-adjusted dollars.[54] More than ever before, private philanthropy sets public agendas with minimal public oversight, sometimes in competition rather than collaboration with government. This form of philanthropy has always existed to some degree; recall, for example, the Ford Foundation's Gray Areas program and the organization's influence in the 1960s. What has changed, however, is the broader institutional context in which foundations operate: Americans have grown less trusting of government and more willing to accept private solutions to public problems. Today, philanthropic institutions are, at a minimum, seen as government partners. They are also sometimes seen as a *superior alternative* to government, using grants to nonprofit service providers as a more efficient or effective way to "solve" public problems.[55]

Private funding organizations flourished in this context, including funders in Boston. Geeta saw the crowded funder landscape as a good thing—more money for community development—but she also worried about duplicating efforts. After all, two grants to the same Corridor organization for the same work does more to ensure organizational survival than improve the lives of Corridor residents. To avoid potential redundancy, she initiated regular meetings with Bob Van Meter, executive director of Local Initiatives Support Corporation's (LISC) Boston office, and Angela Brown, director of programs at Hyams Foundation. The three agreed to collaborate and complement their groups' grants in the Corridor. Together with the directors of the Corridor nonprofits, they also strategized ways to raise the Corridor's profile in policy circles and helped fill public funding gaps as they arose.

Policy influence was one of Geeta's strengths. After meeting with representatives from the EPA in early 2009, Geeta arranged a tour of the Fairmount Corridor with officials from three federal agencies: the EPA, the Department of Housing and Urban Development (HUD), and the Department of Transportation (DOT). Her timing was serendipitous. At that very moment, EPA, HUD, and DOT were in discussions to create a new interagency partnership, called the Partnership for Sustainable Communities. The partnership was built on the growing acknowledgment that greater public transit access improves regional air quality by reducing car use and that affordable housing is more affordable when it is energy-efficient and in close proximity to public transportation options. Like the private funders in Boston, the directors of these agencies wanted to better align their efforts. Officials told stories about looking at maps and realizing the spatial overlap of each agency's grants. They believed that a coordinated system would be more impactful.

The federal officials were impressed with the tour Geeta organized—so much so that in February 2010, the Partnership included the Fairmount Corridor as one of five pilot projects. The initial designation represented the beginning of increased federal recognition and support. The Dudley Street Neighborhood Initiative (DSNI), a nonprofit involved in other community development projects in the Corridor, received a $500,000 Promise Neighborhoods planning grant from the Department of Education in 2010. The organization leveraged that initial planning grant into a $6 million, five-year implementation grant in 2012. And in 2011, HUD committed a $1.8 million grant for private property acquisition and community outreach throughout the Corridor.

The most crucial federal resource for the Corridor, however, was a $20 million grant through HUD's Choice Neighborhoods program. Choice Neighborhoods was a response to the devastating effects of urban renewal, discussed earlier, and HOPE VI, a Clinton-era housing program. Inspired by sociologist William Julius Wilson's theory of concentrated poverty, HOPE VI replaced "distressed" public housing with mixed-income developments. Unfortunately, HOPE VI did not require a one-to-one replacement of subsidized units, so few public housing residents returned after redevelopment. Gentrification and residential displacement were more common consequences than revitalization.[56]

Responding to the shortcomings of HOPE VI, HUD proposed Choice Neighborhoods: "a comprehensive approach to community development centered on housing transformation." Ideal projects focused on the renovation of existing housing developments and proposed benefits for both people and broader neighborhoods. The allocation process was competitive, and applications were open to local governments, public housing authorities, nonprofit organizations, and for-profit developers applying jointly with public agencies. This meant proposed projects could be either public housing or privately managed subsidized housing, but they had to include a one-to-one replacement of subsidized units. Applicants were additionally required to "create partnerships with other local organizations including assisted housing owners, service agencies and resident organizations" and "undertake comprehensive local planning with input from residents and the community." The selection process weighted capacity heavily, at 49 percent of the total possible points (compared to need, which only accounted for 24%).[57]

In Boston, a city agency co-applied for the grant with Dorchester Bay Economic Development Corporation (DBEDC), a CDC located in the Fairmount Corridor. Their winning proposal requested funds to purchase and renovate 129 apartments spread out across eleven separate buildings on Quincy Street—just steps from the Fairmount Line. DBEDC created a new Limited Liability Corporation with another Corridor CDC and purchased the properties from a for-profit affordable housing management company. Two other Corridor nonprofits were included as sub-grantees, responsible for community organizing and other outreach tasks.

All 129 apartments in the new development retained federal subsidies; in housing policy terms, it was a one-to-one replacement, and current tenants were guaranteed right-of-return after redevelopment.[58] In addition to housing renovations, the project also included the construction of a new multipurpose community room as well as the redevelopment of a vacant factory into a shared kitchen space for small food production businesses. The Boston Public School Department received $3 million from the grant, theoretically tying the project to the nearby Promise Neighborhoods site. And millions more went to community-based public safety initiatives and public infrastructure improvements.

The Choice Neighborhoods project only affected one part of one neighborhood in the Corridor. But the policy structurally induced partnerships between government agencies and four local nonprofits, paving the way for a broader planning effort that would include the entire Corridor. Initially, city officials were intrigued but reluctant to coordinate with nonprofit developers. The issue was money and control: Corridor planning would be expensive, and city officials wanted to control the process with their own consultants. Kairos Shen, the chief planner for the Boston Redevelopment Authority (BRA), would only agree to get involved if the nonprofit developers ceded some control over the planning process—a testament to the power local nonprofits had amassed. Geeta worked behind the scenes during the spring of 2011 to assuage Kairos's concerns. She offered funding for consultants, and he agreed to share a draft of the work plan with the nonprofit leaders before moving forward with the initiative.

The Boston Foundation ultimately contributed $100,000, and Geeta persuaded the Garfield Foundation to pitch in another $60,000. City officials drew on internal sources and grants to fund the remaining difference. Formally launched in February 2012, the $350,000 project was the city's largest planning initiative in recent memory. Two officials from the BRA managed the process and hired their own consultants. But Kairos was unable to maintain *full* control; the initiative also included four advisory groups dominated by nonprofit directors, board members, and consultants.

Readers may notice the relative absence of district-based elected politicians in the preceding discussion. Indeed, in recent years, politicians like city councilors and state representatives have seen their power over community development plans ebb and flow. Elected officials undercut the growing power of local nonprofits in the 1960s when they successfully lobbied Congress to give them greater control over War on Poverty funding allocations. Yet by allowing federal grants to go *directly* to nonprofits, War on Poverty legislation nevertheless created the conditions to circumvent elected politicians in funding decisions. Title II, institutionalizing public participation, further elevated the role of community-based nonprofits, regarded as the natural facilitators of community outreach. The Green Amendment of 1967 limited community action grants to organizations approved by local government, but the floodgates had been opened. A small tweak to a single section of a single piece of legislation could not stem the tide of public-private partnerships.

By the time of my fieldwork, elected politicians were mostly bit players in Boston's community development field. City councilors and state legislators could get in the way of a particular project or delay its implementation, so nonprofits and other developers were certainly interested in gaining their support. But solicitations of support came *after* plans were created and drafted. Without formal control over private foundation money, and with diminished control over public money as a result of CDBG cuts, elected politicians had less leverage to influence community development plans.

Community development efforts in the Fairmount Corridor accelerated throughout the 2010s. A coalition including many of the aforementioned nonprofits planned a "greenway" of interconnected parks, gardens, and bike paths running along the train line. The Boston Foundation applied for and received a $480,000 grant from ArtPlace America (funded by the Kresge Foundation) to implement arts and cultural projects. Those efforts led to the creation of the Fairmount Innovation Lab, a small business development program. And in July 2013, the MBTA officially opened three new stations on the Fairmount Line, with the fourth following in 2019.

The preceding story of the Fairmount Corridor places it within the context of national, state, and local urban policy changes. The stories of urban planning projects across the United States are not interchangeable—not all neighborhoods in all cities followed the exact same path—but they are nevertheless inextricably linked. The social and political failure of urban renewal in the postwar period gave way to new, community-based approaches to urban policy in the

1960s. These institutional reforms empowered local nonprofit organizations and carved out new political roles for private foundations. Community-based organizations grew substantially following federal retrenchment, solidifying their place in the community development field. Over time, the focus of these organizations expanded. GFCAC, for instance, was founded in response to neighborhood violence in Four Corners, but eventually shifted to other issue areas, such as access to the Fairmount Line. The Obama administration's emphasis on public-private partnerships was the capstone to a trend that was decades in the making, providing grants to nonprofits and working hand in hand with private foundations. The historical evolution of the Fairmount Corridor cannot be understood without accounting for the larger policy context, even when those policies had only indirect effects on Corridor development.

A key takeaway is that since the 1960s, nonprofit organizations in general, and community development organizations in particular, grew in number, assets, and influence. In Boston, the shift from the demolition of the West End to the construction of the Fairmount Line Station in Four Corners was remarkable. Nonprofit leaders pushed for greater influence over community development decisions, and federal, state, and local policies helped enlarge and embolden the sector. By President Obama's first term, private nonprofits were taken-for-granted players in urban governance.

While some things changed over time, others stayed the same. Most notably, multiple levels of government coordinated urban development policy through the Obama era. War on Poverty legislation and the Low-Income Housing Tax Credit at the federal level, transportation policy at the state level, and the emphasis on transit-oriented development at the city level were all important pieces of the puzzle. The cumulative effect of different policies reflects a major theme of this book: To understand urban governance, we must look beyond the meeting rooms of City Hall to the ways different levels of government intersect with different organizational fields. The community development field today is an exceedingly complex network of public and private actors, all negotiating for seats at the figurative decision-making table.

CHAPTER TWO

A Seat at the Table

ROBERT, THE VICE PRESIDENT of programs at The Boston Foundation (TBF), stepped up to a podium and adjusted the built-in microphone. It was November 2011, and sixty "stakeholders" gathered at the Foundation's downtown offices to discuss development in the Fairmount Corridor. Pictures of construction projects broadcast onto a screen behind Robert as he spoke to a room full of nonprofit leaders, consultants, and government officials.

With a booming, energizing voice that seemed to reverberate against the walls, Robert welcomed everyone to the Foundation. He told a story about a recent trip to Los Angeles at which he and other foundation leaders from across the country discussed strategies for supporting low-income housing in disadvantaged neighborhoods. He recalled that he spoke highly of Boston's neighborhood advocates, especially their willingness to meet directly with residents and incorporate community input. "This is what Boston brings to the table," he said. That commitment to equity is what excited him about development in the Fairmount Corridor. "We're excited to be part of this with you," he concluded.

Geeta, TBF's associate vice president of programs, took Robert's place at the front of the room and outlined the day's objectives. The first was building greater communication between an increasing number of organizations involved in planning, funding, and implementing community development projects. "All of us are doing this work, but we haven't met each other," she explained. The second objective was more practical: to update everyone on the various initiatives underway in the Corridor.

A series of PowerPoint-assisted presentations followed. Inés, a Latina planner with the Boston Redevelopment Authority (BRA), described a new, Corridor-wide urban planning process. In the coming weeks, she and her colleagues would select multiple working groups to manage both an economic development plan for the entire Corridor as well as smaller plans for select neighborhoods near the Fairmount Line stations. The process would also include a Corridor "branding" initiative to stimulate economic activity in commercial areas. And, of course, there would be extensive resident participation at every stage of the process. "Geeta and I discussed over lunch the benefits of sharing information together," Inés told the crowd. The lines of communication would be open.

Five more government officials presented. One city official discussed housing development in the Corridor made possible by a federal grant, another presented on city government resources for small businesses, and a third described an education policy initiative for struggling schools in the Corridor. A state transportation official shared the Fairmount Line station construction timelines, and a federal housing official reiterated the importance of "breaking down silos." "Sometimes in Boston it seems like there are so many pieces," the official lamented before thanking Geeta and The Boston Foundation for bringing everyone together.

Notably, an equal number of nonprofit leaders spoke. Chris, the white executive director of the Metropolitan Boston Housing Partnership (MBHP), shared his organization's program to provide financial planning resources to Corridor residents. Bob, the white executive director of Local Initiatives Support Corporation (LISC), presented on an initiative to support resident-directed neighborhood planning in the Corridor. A coalition of community-based organizations described wide-ranging work, from housing development to policy advocacy, violence prevention to arts and cultural projects, environmental sustainability to community organizing. The organizations' directors managed affordable housing developments, advocated for more stations on the Fairmount Line, and planned to repurpose vacant land into a series of interconnected public gardens and parks. They had been the "face" of Corridor community development since the early 2000s and had amassed an extensive portfolio of projects. Their joint presentation was, by far, the longest of any that day.

It was a grueling afternoon full of acronyms and abbreviations, a dizzying rundown of different programs controlled by different people within different organizations. Everything related to community development and the Fairmount Corridor, but the issue areas and types of organizations were impressively diverse.

I had been sitting next to a nonprofit director all afternoon. For the last seven years, there was rarely a conversation about the Corridor that didn't involve or reference the director and the coalition of community-based organizations. But in the wake of that two-hour meeting, it was clear that the cast of characters had expanded. New faces now had seats at the table. In that moment, the director seemed to recognize the implications. As we gathered our things to leave, the director turned to me, leaned in close, and remarked with a tinge of sarcasm, "It seems like there's a lot of 'we' all of a sudden."

Urban governance did not always include "a lot of 'we.'" In the postwar period, when cities benefited from large sums of discretionary federal funding, local politicians and government officials held significant power and dominated community development planning—sometimes with devastating consequences. Government reforms in the 1970s and 1980s fundamentally changed the urban policy environment. Competitive grants replaced formula-based apportionments, incentivizing entrepreneurial collaboration. Nonprofit developers and philanthropic foundation leaders multiplied across the country, developing new, interdependent relationships with government agencies. The community development field became more crowded—and more institutionally diverse—than ever before.[1]

Who, then, planned community development projects in the Fairmount Corridor? How did these different players make sense of their respective roles? And what made claims for seats at the table more or less persuasive?

We could make a list of the various organizations and agencies that seemed to have a say and label it a powerful coalition that collectively made governance decisions. We could also rely on conventional wisdom and assume that access to the decision-making table depended on some combination of formal political authority, access to material resources, or elite social network ties. To the extent that community-based organizations were included, we might assume processes of cooptation were at play; perhaps more powerful players offered ceremonial seats that lacked any real authority.

Research by sociologist Josh Pacewicz suggests a different pattern.[2] In a study of two Iowa cities, Pacewicz shows how adversarial, partisan politics declined in city governance. Federal policies, discussed in chapter 1, unintentionally created an urban development game that favored entrepreneurial collaboration. The people who took on roles as creative partners played the biggest role in urban governance decisions.

My ethnographic observations revealed a similar structure of relationships. Against expectations and contrasting with much of the literature on urban governance, resource-holding funders or politically powerful public officials in Boston sometimes found themselves sidelined from community development efforts. And supposedly powerless neighborhood organizations sometimes controlled projects from initial planning to final implementation. This was because, much like Pacewicz observed in Iowa, seats at the table depended on one's ability to negotiate legitimacy and authenticity as a good partner with the community—convincing others in the field that their contribution to community development was necessary and complementary. That contribution could be money, but just as often it was something else, like community organizing skills or issue area expertise. Most important, *that role had to be negotiated and performed.* Partnership and collaboration were taken for granted. One's status as a partner was not.[3]

Historical changes paved the way for private nonprofits to become important decision-makers in urban governance. But inclusion was not automatic. This chapter shows *how* the various players in urban governance pursued seats at the table within a particular political system that favored consensus, collaboration, and partnership over dissent, conflict, and partisanship. There were diverse pathways to a seat at the table, seemingly democratizing influence. Yet those pathways were only open to certain organizations at certain times. The net effect was to introduce a new layer of nonprofit leaders, consultants, and other development professionals—an "asteroid belt of organizations," to borrow a phrase from organizational scholar Stephen Barley[4]—that separated urban residents from formal government institutions.

Structural Change and Urban Development Policy Networks

In December 2012, the Massachusetts Association of Community Development Corporations (MACDC) reserved a large conference room inside the Federal Reserve Bank of Boston. The registration-required event was the formal announcement of a tax credit that would help fund nonprofit community development organizations across the state. A variety of developers, state government officials, and other professionals lined up outside the room, presented their government-issued IDs to a security guard, and crossed their names off a sign-in sheet. They were then guided into the Connolly Center, the largest ballroom at the Fed, and took their seats at one of eighteen round tables.

I sat alone at an empty table until Jay, a white architect, joined me. "How are you connected with all of this?" he asked as he settled in to his seat. I explained that I was a graduate student studying community development in the Fairmount Corridor. He pressed for more specificity, and I responded that I was interested in "politics with a small 'p'—the negotiations to get stuff done." He smirked. Political negotiations interested him as well. But they were also the source of professional frustration. Jay worked for a firm that designed affordable housing developments, often for nonprofit developers. "For us, we kind of—we're at the periphery of the stuff you're [studying]," he said. He continued, articulating what he saw as the hierarchy of influence in Boston's community development field:

> As architects we like to think we're so important. But the fact of the matter is that we're really not. *It's the guys with the money. It's the guys*

with the political connections. The guys who put deals together. And that's what's happening. And for us, it's just a matter of whether they like us or not. It really, really has less to do with the quality of our architecture than, you know, *how we get along with people*, and whether they, you know—it's interesting. (emphasis added)

Jay's comments summarize the conventional wisdom: The people who influence community development are those with the most *capital*. That capital could be in the form of financial resources used to purchase land or cover development costs. It could be political connections and formal authority. Or it could be social network ties that facilitate trust and cohesion. It could also be the cultural knowledge, skills, and education that allow certain people to "talk the talk" and get along with other elite players in the field.

There was a time in Boston's history when the conventional wisdom rang true. In 1959, a group of bankers and other successful businessmen formed what they called the Coordinating Committee. Colloquially, they would be known as "the Vault," a reference to their meeting spot in the basement of the old Boston Safe Deposit & Trust Co. The Vault aligned with local government officials and dominated city politics for three decades. As journalist Yvonne Abraham noted in 1999:

> Since the late 1950s, these businessmen had played almost as important a role as the mayor in the life of the city, functioning as a kind of behind-the-scenes Cabinet. They were the ones who had helped bring [Mayor] White's predecessor, John Collins, to power, and in return, Collins had attended their Thursday afternoon meetings and listened to their ideas, transforming the way City Hall was run, partly on their recommendations.[5]

Through the 1960s and 1970s, the Vault helped finance major city initiatives and steered federal resources toward downtown redevelopment.

The Vault's rise to power occurred within a particularly favorable federal policy context. With massive amounts of discretionary urban renewal funding pouring into cities, different interest groups fought to control spending priorities. Throughout the country, urban policy generally reflected the will of politically connected groups like the Vault. Indeed, similar business-led coalitions dominated urban politics in Atlanta, Baltimore, Chicago, Cleveland, Detroit, Milwaukee, Philadelphia, Pittsburgh, and San Francisco.[6]

Over time, however, economic and political changes weakened the Vault's influence in Boston. Bank mergers and acquisitions eliminated many key members. Most of the remaining corporations moved their headquarters to the suburbs. New companies, especially those in the technology sector, were less attached to the city. To the extent that corporations still played a part in local politics, it was through corporate *foundations* that, sociologist

Edward Walker argues, "root companies in the nonprofit sector of their host communities."[7]

A new flavor of urban politics emerged as changes to federal funding formulas resulted in fewer discretionary grants for business organizations to capture. During the period of postwar urban renewal, different interests in cities could fight for large pots of federal money. Organizations like the Vault leveraged their economic power into political influence. Now, in a period of declining public funding and competitive federal grants, entrepreneurial "stakeholders" form technocratic partnerships and compete for smaller, piecemeal grants.[8] The titans of industry no longer dominate urban policymaking. "Whereas 30 years ago a bunch of leading business types might meet in the Vault and call the mayor up and ask him to attend, now it's the other way around," John Cullinane, founder of Cullinet software company, told Abraham in 1999.[9]

The move toward partnership in local politics opened up opportunities for the expanding nonprofit sector. Local community development organizations gained status and became key partners in urban governance. Greater local organizational involvement shifted policymaking: *Residential* redevelopment replaced an overwhelming focus on *downtown* redevelopment in urban policy priorities.[10]

The Vault disbanded in 1997. A new version formed in 2010, calling itself the Massachusetts Competitive Partnership. It was a far cry from its predecessor. "They can get people to pay attention, but it's not clear they can dictate the outcomes," David Luberoff, deputy director of the Joint Center for Housing Studies at Harvard, told a *Boston Globe* reporter in 2016.[11] The group was notably split on major proposals, like Boston's bid for the 2024 Olympics. And it was almost entirely disinterested in the city's poor neighborhoods, like those in the Fairmount Corridor.

If business coalitions like the Vault declined in influence, and if urban politics is focused more on residential neighborhoods than downtown redevelopment, then who made important decisions about community development in the Fairmount Corridor? Figure 2.1 begins to provide an answer. It depicts the network of private planning and strategy meeting co-attendance between 2010 and 2014.[12] Each node represents a community-based organization, government department or agency, intermediary, private funder, or group of consultants. Each line represents co-attendance during at least one private meeting where projects in the Fairmount Corridor were discussed. The size of each node is weighted based on the number of connections to other nodes. Nodes without ties provided funding for community development but did not engage in strategy discussions beyond the scope of specific grants.

The network is dense, a tangled web of public agencies and private organizations. There are nevertheless distinct clusters. Government fills the right side of the network whereas nonprofits fill the center and left side. Business is represented vis-à-vis corporate philanthropy, though these organizations are,

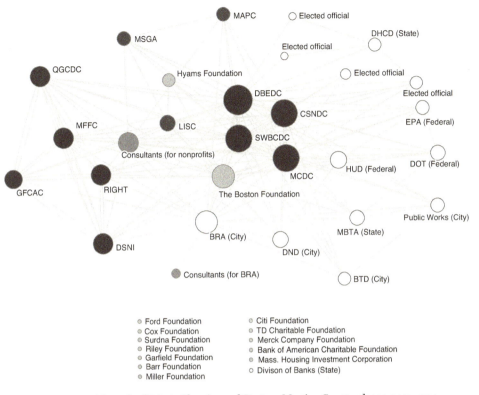

FIGURE 2.1. Network of Private Planning and Strategy Meeting Co-attendance, 2010–2014
Notes: Figure created using Pajek version 5.06 and modified for aesthetic presentation. In order from darkest to lightest, community organizations are color-coded black; intermediaries are color-coded dark grey; consultants are color-coded grey; private funders are color-coded light grey; and government departments are color-coded white.
Source: Author's fieldnotes and observations.

from a planning and policy perspective, marginal. The direct center of the network includes the Boston Redevelopment Authority (BRA), The Boston Foundation, and a coalition of four nonprofit community development corporations. Reflecting a core argument of this book, the diagram reveals nonprofit organizations as vital decision-makers in urban governance alongside formal government agencies.[13]

The network does not account for differences in resources; government agencies, for instance, have significantly larger budgets than community-based organizations. Nor does it account for differences in nonprofit leaders' cultural capital or consultants' social capital. A single network diagram is also static; it implies stable decision-making structures across projects where none may exist.

Here is where ethnographic evidence can provide a more complete picture. On the whole, I observed quite a bit of *instability*: Individuals or groups could have a seat at the table for one project, but face resistance on another. And rather than leverage money, political authority, or social network ties into seats at the table, I observed players in the field negotiate and perform their qualifications as partners in service of community. Certainly, some individuals (like the architect mentioned above) believed "the guys with the money . . . [and] political connections . . . who put deals together . . . [and] get along with people" dominated decision-making. What I observed, however, was a different story.[14]

"This Will Go Down as a Lesson Learned"

To someone living in the Fairmount Corridor, it was hard to keep track of the various government agencies involved in community development. No fewer than a dozen agencies or divisions played at least some role planning or implementing projects. By 2011, state and federal agencies were deeply involved. The Partnership for Sustainable Communities named the Corridor a pilot site for a new HUD-DOT-EPA interagency initiative, and the state transportation authority was designing new stations for the Fairmount Line. City government's absence was notable, particularly to nonprofit recipients of state and federal grants. Meeting with students from a Tufts University urban planning course, one nonprofit director in the Corridor joked, "We're waiting to be as famous locally as we are nationally."

That changed in March 2011, when city officials began thinking about a Corridor planning initiative. Things moved quickly: In May, a BRA official met with a senior TBF staffer to discuss funding options. In July, officials shared a draft work plan with the coalition of nonprofit developers in the Corridor. And in August, they invited the coalition and representatives from two funding organizations to meet and discuss the plans.

The meeting was held in a small conference room inside Boston City Hall. Approaching the building, it is hard not to feel a touch of vertigo. It is a case study in 1960s-era Brutalist architecture: an overbearing mass of concrete sitting on top of a large, almost completely barren brick plaza. The top of the building is wider than its base, giving the impression that it is looking down at its visitors. Protruding concrete frames surround three rows of recessed rectangular windows, all of which appear to rest atop tall concrete stilts. Inside, sterile hallways, wide corridors, and concrete continue the industrial theme. The building practically exudes raw power.

Still, the August meeting felt more collegial than intimidating. The BRA's Chief Planner, Kairos Shen, an Asian American man, explained that the purpose of the meeting was to share the scope of work before his organization hired a consultant team to manage the planning process. He said the planning process would continue and expand upon the nonprofit leaders' work. "We will follow your cues," he told them. "Everyone was concerned about repeating work, which we don't want to do, we assure you." He added, "We will jointly own what comes out of this." Kairos wanted to make sure the nonprofit directors' voices were heard, and he pledged cooperation, noting that federal grant applications favored partnerships between public agencies and community nonprofits.

Two other BRA officials presented more detailed plans. "Our job is about strengthening connections between [Fairmount Line] stations and communities," one said. He claimed that the city has "a lot to bring to the table for such an initiative," such as resources for capital improvements and zoning expertise. Everyone was onboard and interested in working together.

As the planning process was underway in 2012, city officials continued to situate their role as additive and complementary. At a November public forum, Kairos praised the Corridor nonprofits and explained:

> The [nonprofits] have done excellent work, and we're just piggybacking on what you've done . . . and the role [City Hall] can play in addition to bringing funding and support is kind of clarity in the vision and regulations, like zoning and land use controls.

In March 2013, during a tour of the Corridor for local reporters, another city official reiterated the idea of city officials "piggybacking" on past work in the community:

> We're sort of the cleanup hitter, if you will . . . [City Hall] was hearing all these great things from these organizations, and really, the organizations had the original vision. But now, the BRA, with the help of The Boston Foundation and other funders, have really sent their professional planners down to work on all the stations and the surrounding neighborhoods. So we're building on what has already been done in the community—done skillfully—and now hiring some independent consultants to look at traffic, to look at greenscape, to look at parks, to look at city land.

Government officials' deference to community-based organizations and other nonprofit institutions initially struck me as confusing. There is overwhelming evidence that government officials dominate urban governance. So why did city officials think nonprofit leaders and private funders deserved a private briefing before starting the planning process? Why make all of the assurances that they would build "on what has already been done in the community"? Why did they feel the need to justify their planning process to *anyone*? It seemed that government officials were asking permission to do their jobs. Instead of leveraging their formal political authority and simply initiating their own planning process, Kairos and the other city officials went to great lengths to justify their seat at the table, and most important, persuade other players in the field that city government would be a good partner with the community.

I later realized the city officials had good reason to feel pressured to make a substantive case for involvement. The BRA's special zoning authority was not necessarily critical for Corridor projects; not all development requires zoning changes, and project-specific variances, if necessary, were common.[15] Kairos also admitted that city funds alone were insufficient to plan and implement community development projects. He understood that strong applications for federal grants like Choice Neighborhoods (described in chapter 1) required joint applications with nonprofits from the Corridor. No matter what came of the planning process, city officials needed local nonprofits, developers, and other government agencies to help implement their plans.

Government officials' deference also made sense when I observed other players in the field explicitly *deny* them a seat at the table. Consider, for example, planning for the Fairmount Corridor Greenway. In 2008, a coalition of eight nonprofits received $750,000 from the Barr Foundation. With that funding, the coalition hired a consultant team to plan parks, community gardens, and bike paths along the Fairmount Line. The coalition received additional in-kind resources from the federal EPA to identify city-owned land parcels suitable for the Greenway. (City-owned parcels, the coalition correctly reasoned, would be easier to acquire than privately owned land.)

In March 2011, the consultants completed a forty-eight-page concept plan for the Fairmount Greenway. The nonprofit leaders shared the plan with city officials in August, five months after it had been completed.

The nonprofit coalition members also paid community organizers to host public meetings to solicit resident input. They did not invite city officials to these meetings; attendance was limited to organizers and local residents. At an October 2010 meeting of nonprofit directors, staff, and consultants, the group explicitly discussed the decision to deny city officials a seat at the table. Jeanne, a white director, explained to the group:

> They're catching up with us . . . and now they want to get involved. It seems like it's duplicative of what all the neighborhood meetings have been. So, I think we need to make sure that processes that happened already—don't let the BRA come in there and just shove all of that aside. We all need to make sure they work for us. We pay the taxes. They work for us. And I think they'll back away.

Others in the room agreed. They did not think city officials would be useful partners at this stage of the planning process. Even the fact that their plans targeted publicly owned land was insufficient to justify city officials' involvement. Instead, the nonprofit leaders believed they should be able to present city officials with a plan—a *community-driven* plan—and expect city officials to follow their lead.

City officials did not appreciate being excluded, as I learned during a car ride in December 2011. I was working in City Hall at the time and accompanied three officials—Richard, Jeremy, and Lara—to an unrelated event. I sat in the back seat, and the four of us discussed Richard and Jeremy's frustration with the Fairmount Greenway planning process.

Raising his eyebrows as he glanced at me through the rearview mirror, Richard complained that it was a big mistake for them not to invite city officials to the public meetings, and instead to only wait until the final presentation. No city department was involved at all, he complained.

I observed that he seemed upset, to which he replied, "That would be an understatement." He believed that "this would go down as a lesson learned: You have to consider the stakeholders."

Jeremy shared his view that this was a huge investment from the city, and so city departments couldn't be ignored. Richard agreed that the city should have been involved from the beginning.

Pushback from Richard did not stop the nonprofit leaders from continuing their planning process. Nor did it hinder their ability to get buy-in from other city departments or acquire more grant money to begin to implement their plans. By 2015, the nonprofit organizations had developed an urban farm in Codman Square and a community garden in Mattapan. Both were on city-owned land.

Cooperation with city government was ultimately necessary for full implementation. Yet if anything was to be noted "as a lesson learned," it was that initial support from city officials was unnecessary to push a project forward. Put differently, city officials' formal political authority was not enough to secure a seat at the table during initial stages of planning. The coalition of nonprofits had support from a federal agency and financial resources from a private foundation. Nonprofit leaders did not see government officials as useful partners in planning, and the officials were thus unable to exert the kind of control they would have liked.

"It's Just a Little Bit of Community Theater"

Part of the nonprofit leaders' confidence stemmed from their authority as de facto representatives of Corridor neighborhoods. Notably, a wide array of nonprofits could play the part of neighborhood representatives. All were ostensibly "community-based," meaning they managed programs intended to benefit the people living in particular neighborhoods. Some had staff in the single digits and small budgets. Others had multiple departments and millions of dollars in annual revenue. Some were run by neighborhood residents, others by middle-class professionals with little personal connection to the neighborhoods in which they worked. For some, it was just a job. But for most, their work reflected a moral drive to improve life for people living in poor neighborhoods.

Over the course of my fieldwork, nine different community-based organizations (CBOs) were the key members of three overlapping coalitions, each focused on a different substantive area.[16] It was a fairly complex, opaque

Table 2.1. Key Nonprofit Community-Based Organizations in Fairmount Corridor, 2010–2014[a]

Name	Location	Organizational Focus	Revenue	Staff
Dorchester Bay Economic Development Corporation	Upham's Corner	Community Development Corporation	$3,553,814	25
Codman Square Neighborhood Development Corporation	Codman Square	Community Development Corporation	$5,210,506	23
Mattapan Community Development Corporation	Mattapan	Community Development Corporation	$666,476	5
Southwest Boston Community Development Corporation	Hyde Park	Community Development Corporation	$283,536	5
Greater Four Corners Action Coalition	Four Corners	Community organizing	$369,842	9
Dudley Street Neighborhood Initiative	Upham's Corner	Community organizing	$1,140,943	66
Quincy-Geneva Housing Corporation	Grove Hall	Community Development Corporation	$371,390	6
Project RIGHT	Grove Hall	Community organizing	$1,115,529	32
Mattapan Food and Fitness Coalition	Mattapan	Community organizing and health promotion	$55,000	6

[a] Revenue and staff data come from 2012 IRS tax returns, except for Mattapan CDC and Mattapan Food and Fitness Coalition. The latest data for Mattapan CDC are from 2009. Data for Mattapan Food and Fitness Coalition come from the organization's chairperson. Mattapan Food and Fitness Coalition staff are all part-time. Dudley Street Neighborhood Initiative is located in the Dudley Triangle, technically adjacent to the Fairmount Corridor. However, their service area includes Upham's Corner. Mattapan CDC filed for bankruptcy protection and was voted out of the coalitions in 2012. Mattapan Food and Fitness Coalition joined the effort in 2012.

structure—even to most of the coalitions' members. One coalition was made up of four community development corporations (CDCs), a specific form of CBO that primarily develops housing and commercial space but also engages in local community organizing and related programming. A second coalition, including the four CDCs plus another CDC, two other CBOs, a social service agency, and a Boston-based environmental nonprofit, advocated for more stations, better public service, and lower fares on the Fairmount Line. And the third included the five CDCs and two CBOs from the public transit advocacy coalition, plus three additional CBOs and a different environmental nonprofit. This group planned recreational development projects along the rail line.[17] The coalitions met in-person monthly.[18]

When I began my fieldwork, Gail, Jeanne, Mike, and Spencer were the only members of all three coalitions. Each ran a nonprofit CDC. Gail, a middle-aged Black woman described in the book's introduction, lived in Codman Square before moving to Hyde Park. She was executive director of the Codman Square Neighborhood Development Corporation (CSNDC). Jeanne, executive

Table 2.2. Fairmount Corridor Nonprofit Coalitions and Member Organizations, 2010–2014[a]

Fairmount Transit Coalition (formed 2000)	Fairmount CDC Collaborative (formed 2004)	Fairmount Greenway Task Force (formed 2008)
Dorchester Bay Economic Development Corporation	Dorchester Bay Economic Development Corporation	Dorchester Bay Economic Development Corporation
Codman Square Neighborhood Development Corporation	Codman Square Neighborhood Development Corporation	Codman Square Neighborhood Development Corporation
Southwest Boston Community Development Corporation	Southwest Boston Community Development Corporation	Southwest Boston Community Development Corporation
Mattapan Community Development Corporation	Mattapan Community Development Corporation	Mattapan Community Development Corporation
Dudley Street Neighborhood Initiative		Dudley Street Neighborhood Initiative
Greater Four Corners Action Coalition		Greater Four Corners Action Coalition
Quincy-Geneva Housing Corporation		Quincy-Geneva Housing Corporation
Conservation Law Foundation		Boston Natural Areas Network
Mattapan Family Services Center		02136 "All Things Hyde Park"
		Mattapan Food and Fitness Coalition
		Project RIGHT

[a] Membership in each coalition fluctuated depending on staffing, funding, and interest level; the lists presented here represent membership *at some point* during my fieldwork. Other organizations, like Alternative for Community and Environment (ACE), were involved in the coalition before I began my fieldwork in 2010. Neither the Greater Four Corners Action Coalition nor Mattapan Food and Fitness Coalition are "coalitions" per se, but rather stand-alone organizations. "02136 'All Things Hyde Park'" is not really an organization, but rather a single Hyde Park resident, Bob Vance. It was nevertheless listed as an organization on both internal and external coalition documents. Mattapan Family Services Center was technically never a formal member of the Fairmount Transit Coalition. Rather, Karleen Porcena, a Mattapan Family Services Center employee and lead organizer for Mattapan United—a LISC-funded comprehensive community initiative managed primarily by the Mattapan Family Services Center—was an informal member starting in 2013.

director of Dorchester Bay Economic Development Corporation (DBEDC), was a white, middle-class woman in her sixties. Jeanne identified as "an old organizer" and claimed to "live in Upham's Corner, but sleep in Roslindale"—meaning she actually lived in the middle-class neighborhood of Roslindale, but identified strongly with the poorer neighborhood where she worked. Mike was a white man in his forties who grew up in Cambridge, Massachusetts. Like Jeanne, he lived just outside the Corridor in Roslindale. He served as executive director of Southwest Boston Community Development Corporation (SWBCDC), located in Hyde Park, until July 2013. Spencer was the executive director of Mattapan Community Development Corporation (MCDC) until he left the organization in 2011. He was a Black Vietnam War veteran who worked as a business development consultant for Texas Instruments in Dallas before moving to Milton, an affluent Boston suburb, in 2006.

In addition to individual organizational budgets, the coalition of CDCs collectively fundraised between $700,000 and $1 million annually for work in the Corridor each year. They developed housing and commercial projects, offered small business loans, and created a conceptual plan for a "greenway," a strip of land preserved for recreational uses along the train line. They also advocated for new stations and reduced fares for the transit service.

When BRA staff began a Corridor planning process in early 2012, the CDC coalition orchestrated a February conference call with senior BRA officials and advisors to the mayor. During the call, they claimed a necessary, interdependent role as partners in Fairmount Corridor planning.

"We know you are increasing the number of stakeholders, which we think is great . . . but we don't want to be pushed aside, marginalized, or not at the table," Jeanne told the officials. The directors stressed the organizations' track records of successes in the Corridor, from advocacy for more public transportation access to affordable housing development—actions that made them useful partners.

Howard, a white, middle-aged advisor to the mayor, listened quietly. Then he joked, "So we can't say, 'Thanks very much, we'll take it from here!'"

He paused.

"Just kidding! No, we do want to acknowledge the work—all the great work that's been done."

"What I don't think we want, Howard, is [for you to think] we're just community people and you have to throw us a bone," Jeanne said. "We're critical partners, and we want to continue to be."

"Got it," Howard responded.

Jeanne emphasized the organizations' goals of equitable development for residents and noted their willingness to plan joint ventures with for-profit developers, should opportunities arise. She also offered to help engage local residents with the new planning initiative. Community organizing capacity was a unique asset she and her colleagues could bring to the table.

The officials were convinced. Since the 1960s, urban planning processes in Boston and elsewhere mandated community participation, and local community-based organizations were uniquely suited to the task of mobilization. When city officials selected an advisory group for the initiative in June, each organization in the CDC coalition was invited to appoint a board member to sit at the table, meeting monthly.

Nonprofit leaders not only claimed to be uniquely suited to facilitate community engagement but also *performed* that role as they worked to win over private funders and public officials. Consider the plans for a plot of land on Ballou Avenue in Codman Square. In 2011, the BRA proposed using the 23,000-square-foot vacant lot for small-scale farming as part of a citywide urban agriculture initiative. But Gail wanted to develop the land into a garden and small park. She requested a series of private meetings in City Hall. At each, Gail insisted that "the community" did not want agriculture on the lot.

City officials agreed to remove the plot from their urban agriculture plans but tasked Gail's organization with submitting an alternative development proposal. The official in charge of city-owned property hosted a private meeting and asked if city officials could "meet with some of the neighbors, and Codman [CSNDC] being kind of the conduit or host."

The following month, staff from CSNDC strategized the best way to make their case to city officials during the upcoming visit. Their understanding of "the community" came from a small group of six nearby residents they called "The Friends of Ballou Avenue." When a consultant asked Isaiah, a Black community organizer with CSNDC, if he planned to include more residents than just the small group at the presentation, he replied:

> Yeah. Our [Friends of Ballou Avenue] group will do the presentation and the pitch, but kind of, for a little bit of community theater. It's nice when we go around and say, "I'm Miss Jones and I live at 40 Ballou Ave." and "I'm Mr. Johnson, and I live at 80 Ballou Ave." It strengthens it so that—it's a little bit of community theater. It's people we've engaged with, but also sends a stronger message that . . . it's not just these six "Friends Group" folks.

Isaiah knew that a small group would not be enough to convince city officials that the organization truly understood the overall community sentiment. Because city officials and funders relied on nonprofits to be the "voice" or "conduit" for local residents—that is, to be community-organizing partners—nonprofit organizers strategically displayed this special skill. In this instance, successfully performing local representation afforded the organization influence over future development of the vacant lot. In the spring of 2014, the organization was formally designated developer of the site.

The episode aligned with Jeanne's assumptions about the roots of power. To know Jeanne is to know that she thinks power comes from "organized people and organized money." The statement stemmed from her training as an Alinsky-style community organizer in Buffalo and a previous job as a fundraiser for an interfaith organization in Boston. According to Jeanne, powerful nonprofits organized constituents and had robust fundraising operations. Her definition captures a core insight: Nonprofit leaders' ability to get a seat at the table depended on visible displays of local support (organized people) and tangible evidence of their competence (organized money).

The flip side was that nonprofit leaders could be denied a seat when displays of community support or evidence of competence fell short. Perhaps ironically, Jeanne would become an illustrative example in my fieldwork. In June 2012, the BRA selected an advisory group for the Fairmount Corridor Planning Initiative. Jeanne applied, emphasizing her organization's community organizing reputation in Upham's Corner. The BRA denied Jeanne's application, citing a conflict of interest: Jeanne's organization might have an unfair advantage on development contracts if she sat on the board making development recommendations. While Jeanne and others viewed that as a reasonable concern on its face, other developers—including other nonprofit developers—*were* granted seats on the board.

Why did city officials deny Jeanne a seat? A conversation four months earlier suggests Jeanne's rejection stemmed not from a conflict of interest but from skepticism about her organizing acumen. In February 2012, I had coffee with a city government official. We discussed the BRA's planning process and the advisory group selection process. During our conversation, the official questioned the ability of nonprofit developers like Jeanne to be effective community organizers, despite their vocal bluster. Organizations tended to limit their outreach to their own developments rather than the community at large, the official said. She even reported that some other officials "rolled their eyes" when Jeanne attended meetings at City Hall and claimed expertise as a community organizer.

While I did not observe Jeanne fail to fulfill her organizing responsibilities before the selection of the advisory group, I did note several instances after its creation. In February 2013, for example, Jeanne offered to organize Upham's Corner residents for a forum (coincidentally, a forum planned by the advisory group from which she'd been excluded). Attendance was abysmal. Those who did attend were disproportionately community development professionals, not neighborhood residents. Jeanne was furious with her community organizing staff. She knew that the failed performance would diminish her standing in the field. It was, in her words, "a political mistake." As she explained to the other CDC coalition members on a conference call:

> I'll tell you what I also think is going on: Power is a funny thing . . . It's a process. It's relationships. And it's something you can gain and lose in a snap of a finger. And it's information. Power is relationships, a process,

information. And you can gain it or lose it *in a second*. And it's like they totally disempowered us, and we let them because we didn't have our troops out [at the forum]. We didn't prepare ourselves. (her emphasis)

Jeanne later apologized to the advisory group during a public meeting. She took responsibility for the low attendance and blamed it on a conflicting event. "Shame on us, because we didn't have appropriate communication," she said.

Jeanne's organizing failures continued the following month. A city official told me that she had relied on Jeanne and organizers from two other CBOs to bring residents to a meeting addressing street, sidewalk, and lighting improvements. There, too, turnout was sparse. "I mean, Jeanne has 129 families there [in a nearby affordable housing complex]," the official told me. Her voice got lower, and she leaned in closer. "If we had twelve people in that fucking meeting—that was all. I was pissed."

Unlike the "community theater" performed in Codman Square, Jeanne did not bring a sizable constituency to those neighborhood meetings. The failures validated claims that her organizing skills and connection to the community may have been overstated—thus rendering her unworthy of a seat at the table.[19]

"How Do We Know It's Not Full of Consultants?"

In May 2012, three consultants met in a small conference room at the offices of Dorchester Bay Economic Development Corporation (DBEDC). Joan, Mat, and Sherry held contracts with the coalition of nonprofit developers, who paid them by the hour using grant money. Joan, a white woman "of Medicare age" (as she joked with her colleagues), was the coordinator consultant, scheduling meetings for the nonprofit leaders, negotiating contracts with funders, and creating budgets. Mat, a white man in his sixties, was the senior economic development consultant, advising the nonprofits on real estate projects and other development financing. And Sherry, a white woman in her sixties, was the fundraising consultant. She sought out and applied for grants from private foundations and government agencies.

"Oh, I forgot to show you my favorite *New Yorker* cartoon that I recently came across," Mat told me before the meeting started. The cartoon depicted the ancient story of the Greek army sneaking into Troy while hidden inside a large, wooden horse disguised as a gift. The caption read, "How do we know it's not full of consultants?" The joke was that consultants infiltrate organizations and take over operations under false pretenses. "Should I give it to the executive directors, or would it [be] best not to?" Mat asked with a chuckle. "Don't fan the flames!" Sherry laughed.

Consultants like Joan, Mat, and Sherry offered strategic or technical assistance to nonprofits, government, or philanthropic foundations. Some formed long-term relationships with particular organizations and others cobbled together short-term contracts for individual projects or tasks, from creating websites to public relations strategies to market analyses for new commercial development.

It is hard to overstate their importance, though few in the field commented on it. Consultants made sure grant applications were submitted and plans were produced. Nonprofit leaders and government officials claimed the resulting reports as their own, but it was *consultants* who often completed the actual work and interfaced with different stakeholders. They filled a critical interstitial role—not quite insiders, but not quite outsiders, either. Their very existence glued disparate organizations together, bringing intelligibility to the network.

Because consultants, by definition, joined community development efforts only when they had issue area expertise, their voices could be rejected in certain domains. Joan, Mat, and Sherry often negotiated respective roles with the nonprofit leaders who contracted their services—the basis for Mat's Trojan horse joke. For example, Jeanne told Mat that he shouldn't be involved in discussions of transit development because he is "more of an economic development person," and she reprimanded Sherry for "mission creep" when Sherry asked to help coordinate a neighborhood planning process. Sherry could influence fundraising discussions (her official position) but had no seat at the table when other issues areas came under discussion.

These negotiations mattered even when individual consultants had extensive network ties in the community development field. Mat, for instance, worked in the Newark offices of HUD immediately following urban planning graduate school in the 1970s, then spent sixteen years as senior program director for a funding intermediary in Boston. He ran a nonprofit organization in the city and served as interim director for three others. He sits, or has sat, on numerous boards of housing organizations. Given this experience, Mat is often asked to speak about the Fairmount Corridor at events or sit on planning committees with funders and development professionals. He relished the opportunity to influence community development strategy and policy.

But in 2012, Mat faced strong resistance from Jeanne. Jeanne worried that Mat was becoming the go-to speaker at events about the CDC coalition's work in the Corridor, especially events hosted by private funders.[20] She saw it as a "boundary issue." "I *really* don't see your role as our primary spokesperson with funders," she told Mat, "and I don't want to let that keep happening too much. You can be a senior development strategist," but cannot speak on the developers' behalf. The directors of the organizations in the coalition could perform those duties on their own, she said. Mat agreed to accept future invitations only when approved by Jeanne.

Jeanne's attitude abruptly changed when Mat took over as interim director of Southwest Boston CDC. Mat replaced Mike, who resigned from his position during an organizational restructuring. At a meeting of the CDC coalition in October 2013, Mat offered to update the coalition on a park development in

Hyde Park. "What if we say no, Mat? What would you do then?" Jeanne needled. "Well, I'm in a different role now," Mat responded with a smirk. "You're now a peer! You have a real vote now," Jeanne lightly teased, giggling as she spoke. Nothing had changed with respect to Mat's individual educational background, expertise, or social capital. What *had* changed was his structural position in the field, now representing the Hyde Park community.

For other consultants, neither political connections nor financial resources were enough to get a seat at the table. Consider Peter Harnik, the white director of the Center for City Park Excellence, a division of the Trust for Public Land (TPL), a national environmental organization based in Washington, DC. In 2010, Peter received funding from the Barr Foundation to advise parks development in Boston. An official from the EPA put him in contact with the coalition of nonprofit leaders planning a "greenway" along the Fairmount rail line.

At an October 2010 meeting of the coalition, Javier, a Latino community organizer with CSNDC, made the case for enlisting Peter's services. He saw it as an "opportunity to have somebody with a national perspective and national connections to help us sort of bring attention to this 'greenway.'" Peter had emailed Javier with a number of ways he could be helpful. "We could certainly benefit from this additional sort of layer of analysis," Javier told the group, "and again, potential connections to sort of the [funding] contacts that TPL has at a national level." Javier reasoned that the national attention would result in more resources from national funders. The other coalition members agreed.

In February 2011, Peter met with the coalition for the first time. "I don't want to come in here with 'answers,' because this is really complex," he said. Instead, he explained, he wanted to be part of the conversation. For Peter, this project could "rejuvenate" his organization's work in the Boston area. In exchange, he could provide a national perspective on how to make this type of development a reality. "We give input on how other people do things," he told the group, "and put you into contact with experts and funders." As a way to get started, he said he could create maps and design a brochure to help market the coalition's vision.

Peter drafted the brochure in late 2011. It revealed an underlying tension between Peter's perception of a "greenway" and the nonprofit leaders' understanding. Peter recommended calling the proposed development something other than "greenway" because the project did not satisfy the technical specifications of a greenway. He first suggested calling it a "Healthway," then later, a "Fitway." Peter did not advocate for an alternative development plan; he merely produced a brochure rebranding the project. But the coalition members preferred their framing, even if it was technically inaccurate. "Greenway," they reasoned, resonated with residents in the Corridor. More important, they didn't appreciate being told that their vision, which they saw as the vision of "the community," was wrong.

Peter had remaining funding from Barr, so he continued to work on the concept and marketing brochure. The conflict reached a crescendo in

July 2012. Seven members of the coalition and a consultant met in the community room of a housing project in Upham's Corner. Peter and his work for the coalition was the last item on their agenda.

"He doesn't like calling it a 'greenway,'" Joan told the group, summarizing Peter's objections.

"Well who made him God in the first place?" Jeanne asked rhetorically. "Jesus, Mary, and Joseph."

Tracey, another coalition member, recounted a recent conversation with Peter. "He called me ... and he described this as *his* project—well, the brochure. *He* got money. *He* decided to use part of *his* money. And therefore—"

"He feels like he has something to deliver Barr, and if we don't pick what he likes, then it's embarrassing for him. So what? Too badskis," Jeanne interrupted.

Jeanne proposed the idea of firing him. Marvin, the Black coalition member introduced earlier in the book, started to argue, "If he's a consultant, he's supposed to—"

"He's not a consultant," Joan, a consultant herself, clarified, cutting Marvin off. "He's an employee of TPL."

"Well, ok. If he was a consultant, and maybe he is, it's our job to say—"

"You're working for us," Jeanne interjected, finishing Marvin's sentence.

Marvin agreed: The group should consider ending its relationship with Peter. He summarized the roadblock pointedly: "He keeps saying we don't have a greenway. We don't agree." The room erupted in laughter.

The nonprofit leaders did not hire Peter and did not hold the contract for his services. Yet he was *acting* like their consultant—one who had not fulfilled his duty to listen to his clients and reflect the community's vision in his work product. "Given your inability to fully share our vision, we concluded that is best for us to bring our association with you on the brochure to a close," Joan emailed Peter two days later.

Peter wanted to "rejuvenate" his organization's work in Boston by planning recreational development in the Fairmount Corridor. He came to the table with his own funding, ties to other national funders, and personal connections to EPA officials. None of that was enough to get him a seat at the table. The ultimate irony is that the coalition later adopted his reframing: By 2013, the nonprofit leaders began calling the "greenway" a "neighborway" because, as Peter had correctly noted, the development technically wasn't a "greenway." "Peter Harnik will be thrilled," Joan quipped when the nonprofits formally adopted the new terminology.

"We're an Influencer, and a Funder"

It might seem obvious that philanthropic foundations and other private funders would have a seat at the table. But private funders involved in Corridor planning tended to downplay their control over resources when attempting to influence community development plans. Instead, they highlighted their role as brokers connecting disparate organizations in the field.[21] It was a useful role, and it set them apart from other organizations. Geeta, at TBF, made this clear during a conversation in 2013. She told me:

> We are not the front face. We are not the ones who work directly with the communities. We don't do the organizing. We don't do the services. We don't build the infrastructure. We're an influencer, and a funder. We're a change agent, but we are not the direct change maker.

[margin note: private funders as "brokers", connectors, not creators]

Geeta distinguished what TBF could do, what was unique about her organization, juxtaposed against the skills and responsibilities of other organizations involved in the redevelopment process. Nonprofits work directly with communities. Government builds infrastructure. TBF staff carved out an interdependent and complementary niche.

Private funders publicly performed this role. They hosted formal conferences, like the one described at the beginning of this chapter. They also organized informal, ad hoc workshops that addressed specific issue areas, such as the use of data in community development planning or community-based research partnerships with local colleges and universities.

One of these events occurred in October 2012. At the request of HUD officials, TBF hosted a tour of the Fairmount Corridor for federal grantees from Connecticut. After the tour, the group of twenty-four professionals (and an ethnographer) sat for a catered lunch in one of TBF's conference rooms. The casual discussion was designed for the Boston group—TBF staff, city officials, and nonprofit CDC grantees from the Corridor—to share "what works" with the new grantees from Connecticut.

Barbara Fields, the regional administrator for HUD, explained to the group that the successes described during the tour did not emerge out of thin air. They required regular communication between a diverse cast of characters:

> What you saw today seems like seamless alignment between HUD, EPA, DOT, the state, city, and CDCs . . . Obviously underneath that you are smart enough to know that there's a lot of moving parts, a lot of disagreements, there's a lot of screaming and yelling, and talking to each other, and listening, and not listening . . . But again, I think this process that you saw today, um, as messy as it can be at times, has also been very, very productive and really astonishing . . . I'm hoping that the Sustainable Communities grant . . . is bringing people together that never met before, so that's a starting point. And we can kind of roll our eyes like that's not enough, but it is a starting point; it is important. So, getting people in the room, trying to have the resources, and you know doing some short-term things while you're doing some long-term thinking.

None of that was possible, Barbara emphasized, without a partner like TBF. Government is easily distracted and priorities can change from one administration to the next. Admitting that, "as someone in federal government" she "shouldn't be saying this," Barbara credited long-term conveners like TBF for helping achieve wins in community development implementation:

> One of the key things here, too, [is that] The Boston Foundation has been a key partner, and quite honestly, as someone in federal government maybe I shouldn't be saying this, but sometimes we don't stick with things long enough. And I do think outside partners sort of pushing at some of the government entities to stay the course and not shift and then refocus somewhere else [is important] . . . I was thinking of all the neighborhood tours that I've done over the years and it looks easy, almost, in a sense. But it's taken years and years and years and years and years, and that can outstrip anyone. . . . [so you need] the outside influences like The Boston Foundation staying the course.

Geeta agreed with Barbara's comments and cited the days' events as examples of TBF's important role. Private funders could convene community development partnerships in ways government agencies could not:

> I have to say that sometimes—I think partnering with foundations is always an imperative. It allows you to do these little things that people in government have a very hard time doing. Pulling people together for a lunch. I mean, it's such a silly simple thing, but it's like you said: It enables conversation, it enables relationship building, and ideas grow, you know, and you foster ideas, you know, little, little things, like paying for small things that's so much easier for foundations to do that, and I think it's really important to have a foundation partner . . . I think some of the biggest things we've done in the foundation . . . all we did was provide free lunches and people came together and talked, and ideas grew, and ideas grew.

TBF's value stemmed not only from the funding it could provide, but also from assuming a role as an "outside partner" that could "stay the course" when government agencies shifted priorities. Convenings were one way to publicly perform that role.

Yet neither the promise of funding nor the responsibility of convening stopped other players in the field from challenging TBF's policy influence. Grantees sometimes referred to program officers as "dilettantes" and "interventionists" when they took on policy objectives beyond providing grants. Boston's late Mayor Thomas Menino famously distrusted the organization, reluctant to share credit for mutual accomplishments and fearful that TBF's CEO secretly planned to unseat him as mayor. During my fieldwork, a city official called the organization "presumptuous." "They are a foundation," he said dismissively. "But they act like a public agency."

The comment reveals the occasionally blurry line between foundations and government. The very fact that the official felt the need to draw the boundary implies that others *did* sometimes treat TBF as closer to a public agency than a private foundation.

Even when the foundation financed a particular effort, such challenges to the organization's status as a helpful partner could limit its power. In 2011, for instance, the foundation committed $100,000 to the BRA for a Corridor-wide urban planning initiative. Some of TBF's grantees feared it was a blatant play for influence. "People are buying a seat at the table, literally," one grantee complained at the time.

The following year, as the BRA planning initiative was underway, the foundation unexpectedly found itself in city government's crosshairs. TBF staff applied for and received a nationally competitive $480,000 grant for arts- and culture-based programs in the Fairmount Corridor. They planned to manage the grant, though most of the money would be redistributed to local nonprofits for implementation. Geeta recalled that Mayor Menino was "furious" when she told him about the grant. He chastised her for not consulting with city officials before applying. In the mayor's eyes, this grant should have been controlled by city government, not an outside foundation. Rather than see it as something TBF brought to the table, Mayor Menino saw the grant as a resource TBF had stolen from the community.

The dressing-down made an impression on Geeta. She told the story to multiple people over the last two years of my fieldwork; I heard it directly from her, but I also heard it second-hand from other players in the field. The incident caused Geeta to "keep a low profile" during the BRA-led Corridor planning process. She did not attempt to influence the final product, even though the initiative would not have come to fruition without her organization's funding. In this instance, the $100,000 grant did not, in fact, buy a seat at the table.

"Just Act Like Partners"

The growing complexity of community development funding created the space for a variety of intermediaries to emerge. These predominantly nonprofit organizations pooled funding from multiple sources and repackaged grants to nonprofit grantees. Staff members saw their role as closer to the ground than large foundations, yet also more strategic and big-picture than local neighborhood organizations.

Intermediaries working in the Fairmount Corridor mostly managed multi-neighborhood community development planning processes. One was Local Initiatives Support Corporation (LISC), a national organization with thirty satellite offices. Bob was the executive director of the Boston office. During my fieldwork, Bob helped manage comprehensive community initiatives (CCIs) in two Corridor neighborhoods. The CCI program essentially entailed LISC staff co-managing neighborhood planning efforts with neighborhood organizations, primarily CDCs. The stated goal was to empower local communities and provide the structure for residents to determine what kinds of projects would most benefit their neighborhoods. To run the program, Bob received funding from local foundations and the LISC national office. A portion paid LISC staff to serve as program managers, and the rest went to neighborhood organizations to pay for community organizers.[22]

In 2013, I spoke with Bob about the program and its early implementation. He noted that he was laying the groundwork to get more support from city and state government. When I asked how elected officials fit into his strategy, Bob explained that getting them involved—by, for example, inviting them to announcements and other events—was a way to legitimate LISC as a useful partner in community development:

> I see the value in getting public [elected] officials [at the event] because essentially what you're doing is, is—it's kind of a mutual validation or legitimation thing, where they're seeing this as representing—in some measure—a legitimate expression of the neighborhoods' priorities, and they are also legitimating and validating that by saying "Yes, we think these are good ideas and we want to support them. We want to make them happen." . . . And it also—an event like that tends to focus peoples' thinking and get other people who might have resources, you know, thinking about how they might join up with you.

This "mutual validation or legitimation thing" operated on two levels: First, inviting elected officials to events legitimated the planning process as important for Corridor residents. Second, the visible display of official support signaled to other organizations—like government agencies—that Bob's *organization* was a useful partner. Bob leveraged the event into greater visibility and future meetings with city and state officials.

Intermediaries sometimes met challenges from other policy players. Take The Metropolitan Area Planning Council (MAPC), a quasi-public regional planning agency. In 2010, the organization applied for and received a $4 million grant from the federal government to support regional planning efforts in greater Boston. MAPC redistributed a portion of the grant to the coalition of nonprofit developers, and another portion supported urban planners on MAPC's staff to serve as a "go-between," or intermediary, between nonprofit sub-grantees and their city governments. MAPC staff hoped to leverage the grant into a seat at the table with city officials.

But MAPC staff and their grantees in the Corridor differed on the expectations of MAPC's role. The grantees preferred MAPC to be a direct cash funder, whereas MAPC staff proposed using a majority of the grant to pay themselves to mediate relationships between the nonprofits and city agencies.

In January 2012, an all-white group of MAPC staff met with a diverse group of nonprofit leaders inside an Upham's Corner housing project to resolve the grant allocation issue. Following a round of introductions, Joan, the coalition consultant introduced earlier, said the purpose of the meeting was to try to find common ground around a scope of work for the grant. Javier, a community organizer with CSNDC, stated the nonprofits' case. They "are in a unique position . . . at the community level," he said, and as such would be best supported with direct cash funding:

> We are in a unique position as community-based organizations to respond and bring value to the work of our residents . . . We're at a position at the community level to start implementing some of the things that are important for our communities, so we are looking for allies and resources to help us do that.

Joan added that MAPC's proposal to mediate relationships "struck us, frankly, as a bit over-reaching on your part."

Edward, an MAPC staffer, calmly but assertively explained that MAPC provides planning expertise for small towns, city agencies, and nonprofits throughout the Boston region. With respect to the Fairmount Corridor, Edward identified political challenges to community development. In particular, city officials resisted the recreational development. Managing those challenges was MAPC's bailiwick: "Figuring out how to get the project done through technical work and political jockeying." Another MAPC staff member told the nonprofit leaders she saw the group's role "more as a bridge between you—who bridge to the community—to [City Hall]."

Jeanne, DBEDC's director, responded that the nonprofit leaders didn't like "the feeling of being spoken for." She welcomed the technical expertise, "but *our* job is to bring residents to speak directly to City Hall." She also critiqued the educational background of MAPC staff. What others might interpret as a cultural signifier of expertise, Jeanne saw as "talk[ing] funny":

> I was telling [another MAPC staffer] the other day, you guys need to learn how to talk regular. You guys are all really smart; you've all been to MIT and Harvard, and sometimes you just talk funny . . . Sometimes you do sound funny to us. And it's not like I came out of an urban gang or anything, but you get down with the regular people. So some of it is a cultural issue. I think simplifying your thinking and your talking is helpful to us. And even the writing . . . You've got a lot of smart people, but we're not at Harvard anymore.

Jeanne did not mention that she held a Master's degree in history from the University of Wisconsin, or that Mike, another white nonprofit coalition member at the meeting, had a Bachelor's from Harvard and a Master's in city planning from MIT. Indeed, her critique did not necessarily appear substantive; it was a way to convey a message that cultural capital would not afford MAPC staff a seat at the table.

The meeting ended with an agreement to reformulate a new scope and meet at a later date. The following month, Angela, a white MAPC staff member, met with the nonprofit coalition members and their consultants. The conversation quickly shifted to MAPC's brokerage role.

"Frankly, I don't really think you need to convene us," Jeanne told Angela.

"Ok," Angela responded, scribbling notes.

"I think what we're trying to avoid is this patronizing thing. Just act like partners. You know things we don't know. You have connections that can add to our connections."

"Sure."

"But, I think that's a more realistic way of functioning . . . What we don't need is a facilitator slash convener slash hand-holder . . . What I would rather do, as we think about the scope and your role, is do things that you're really good at, that we're not so good at."

Joan interjected, suggesting that MAPC might have access to additional data, or research abilities. "I think that's an advantage here," she said.

"Ok. Alright," Jeanne agreed.

"You know, that's why we're having this conversation," Angela chuckled nervously.

The negotiation ended after follow-up conversations and meetings throughout 2012. Ultimately, MAPC provided technical assistance on the development of vacant lots, researched ownership options for recreational spaces, and partially funded a consultant to coordinate recreational development for the nonprofits. Staff from the organization abruptly stopped trying to mediate between the nonprofit leaders and City Hall—losing power and access in the process.

The crux of the debate centered on the legitimacy of each organization's role as a partner in community development planning. The nonprofit directors and organizers clearly stated their unique contribution: representing the voices and vision of the community. Edward and Angela listed their perception of MAPC's special skills: technical expertise and brokerage between the nonprofits, "who bridge to the community," and City Hall. But the nonprofit leaders challenged MAPC's claims and argued that the attempts to mediate between the nonprofits and city officials was not the behavior of a useful partner. In their "unique position . . . at the community level," the nonprofit leaders had a legitimate reason to be at the table with city officials, while MAPC staff—legitimate technical experts—did not.

In July 2013, the state transportation authority hosted three ribbon cuttings for new rail stations on the Fairmount Line. At the event in Four Corners, State Representative Marty Walsh, a Dorchester Democrat, walked to the podium as the Fairmount train sped down the tracks behind him. After thanking the governor, mayor, and state senators for their contribution to community development projects in the Corridor, Walsh reflected on the last few years of planning. "We came to many, many meetings about this station," he said. City officials, state departments, developers, nonprofits, and neighborhood groups were all present. In his words, they were all "at the table."[23]

In the Fairmount Corridor, those particular agencies and organizations all had seats at the table at different points in time, for different projects. Project by project, they negotiated for those seats by emphasizing and performing their qualifications as partners with or on behalf of the community. They all desired to plan and implement community development projects. Getting a seat at the table ensured organizational survival and allowed them to take credit for the projects they cared about. They also had an incentive to work *together*: Piecemeal grants required an all-hands-on-deck approach. This system of mutual dependence made complementarity necessary; no one group or agency could go about a project in isolation. At the same time, an organization's status as an effective, legitimate community partner was not taken for granted. It had to be performed, and only successful performances resulted in seats at the table.

I found less evidence that unequal access to capital—economic, political, social, or cultural—allowed certain groups to dominate others. If formal political authority afforded a seat at the table, then city government wouldn't have been rejected from the initial planning of the Fairmount Greenway. If money afforded a seat at the table, then the mayor wouldn't have berated Geeta after TBF secured a large grant, and she wouldn't have avoided the BRA planning process as a result. If social capital afforded a seat at the table, then Jeanne wouldn't have restricted Mat from sitting on certain panels when he worked as a consultant. And if cultural capital afforded a seat at the table, then nonprofit professionals wouldn't have rejected technical assistance from the MIT- and Harvard-trained MAPC staff. Performances of community partnership carried more currency than claims of capital, allowing nonprofit leaders to take on prominent roles in community development politics.

These findings may stem from the fact that I focused on community development plans in poor neighborhoods. Some actors, like for-profit developers, have a vested interest in more general pro-growth development policies, and other actors, like construction companies and labor unions, might gain access to the table once plans are put into action. Their absence in my analysis should not be interpreted as powerlessness per se, but rather suggests that they may be more influential at higher levels of government, "hotter" housing markets, or different stages of development.[24]

The interactions described in this chapter were also notably mundane. Peter Harnik was fired for his work on a *brochure*, after all. These were not the high-stakes debates about whether a public housing development would be demolished, or if new housing would be accessible to poor renters.[25] For a number of important reasons, controversial projects receive most of the attention in the scholarly literature and fill the pages of local newspapers. This chapter adds to our understanding by focusing on the ordinary projects that do not give rise to similar levels of controversy. The outcomes still matter: Losing a seat at the table, even when the stakes seemed comparatively low, meant losing power, influence, and access to resources.

This raises an important methodological point. Existing research in sociology, political science, and urban studies typically describes city governance in terms of ideal types: Scholars take a top-down view, identify the central players in urban governance, and then label cities accordingly. I hesitate to create a label for this particular structure of governance insofar as it could obscure the mechanisms of influence. My bottom-up, ethnographic fieldwork revealed shifting constellations of decision-makers in which the same people could be included as legitimate community partners today but be treated as unnecessary tomorrow. These important interactional mechanisms of power and influence may have remained hidden had I relied on alternative analytical approaches.

Even though involvement in project planning fluctuated, everyone in the field agreed that the Fairmount Corridor was an important place. In the next chapter, I show how people constructed the Corridor's geography—what, where, and who it included—in different ways in order to further their respective political interests. A seemingly banal practice, making the Corridor legible as a place nevertheless had important implications for neighborhood inequality.

CHAPTER THREE

In Search of Spatial Legibility

GEETA AND I STOOD side by side in a room full of maps. We were both attending an event to celebrate the formal end of the Upham's Corner Working Advisory Group. Managed by the Boston Redevelopment Authority (BRA), the thirteen-member Working Advisory Group had met monthly with a team of consultants and created a community development plan for the neighborhood. It was the first of three planning processes for neighborhoods in the Fairmount Corridor, part of a larger Corridor-wide planning effort. At the event that evening, about fifty people milled around, looking at poster boards depicting the geography of housing, parks, transit, and other forms of land use in Upham's Corner—shown specifically as the area within a half-mile radius of the Upham's Corner Station on the Fairmount Line.

Seeing all of the maps prompted Geeta to reflect on how far the idea of the Fairmount Corridor had come. "When I look back over three, four, five years—five years back, there was no idea of a [Fairmount] Corridor," she told me. "And, slowly, I think it was just talking about it and bringing people together that created this idea of a 'Corridor.' So, someone the other day asked me, 'What is the geography?' And there actually is no geography for the Corridor, right? It's a constructed geography." I was struck by her astute observation: The Corridor did not have a self-evident geography. It had a *constructed* geography.

Nowhere was the constructed geography more apparent than during one of the first meetings of the Upham's Corner Working Advisory Group. A few months earlier, BRA officials had announced four advisory groups: One would guide community development planning for the entire Fairmount Corridor, and the other three would focus on specific neighborhoods. BRA officials selected Upham's Corner because they had previously promised a neighborhood planning process there. The Upham's Corner Working Advisory Group, embedded within the larger Fairmount Corridor initiative, was their way of fulfilling the promise by proxy.

At 6:30 in the evening, about thirty-five people gathered in a conference room inside the newly constructed Salvation Army Kroc Center, just steps from the Upham's Corner Station. The first meeting, held the previous month, was limited to introductions. "Now we really get into the work," a BRA official told the assembled nonprofit leaders, developers, landowners, and scattered residents. The advisory group sat at rectangular tables arranged to form three sides of a square, with a drop-down projection screen at the fourth side. Members of the public—about ten of us—sat in chairs around the room's perimeter. At the back of the room, there were three trays of food provided by a local Caribbean restaurant.

From the beginning, the advisory group had to adjust to some new ideas about geography. Josh, a white consultant hired by the BRA, led the evening's presentation. After talking through the background and history of the neighborhood, he displayed a map labeled "Upham's Corner Existing Conditions—Station Area Boundary." Josh acknowledged that the study area boundaries did not exactly align with this or any other Corridor neighborhood. Most Bostonians would place the center of Upham's Corner at the intersection of Columbia Avenue and Dudley Street, the main commercial area and bus route thoroughfare, with the Fairmount Line framing the western border. By contrast, Josh's station area map placed its center at the Upham's Corner Station, about a quarter mile west of the Columbia Avenue/Dudley Street intersection. Josh acknowledged the discrepancy, but argued that this map fit better with the practice of urban planning and transit-oriented development:

> This is the boundary that we've struck, and we can talk later if we have some time for discussion about what the boundary of Upham's Corner is, and what people recognize it as. But for the case of this study, this is what we started with. And it's focused on the station itself. And typically in transit-oriented development communities, what is recognized as the "catchment area" of the station is a half-mile walking distance—that's what people can comfortably walk 10 or 12 minutes, and that's what our expectation is for the population that would make the journey to this station, as opposed to a station further down the line.

The map showed Census tracts and blocks inside a circle drawn around the station. "We didn't include any of the tracts or blocks that are more than 50 percent outside of this imaginary circle," he said—again acknowledging the somewhat arbitrary construction of the geographic boundary. "So that's the methodology that we use to construct. But we will show you right before we get into discussion that Upham's Corner as an area or neighborhood might be typically associated with this quadrant of the circle [to the east], but we are expanding that a little bit to the west, I guess, so that it's more of a concentric circle around the station."

WORKING ADVISORY GROUP DISCUSSION
What is Upham's Corner to you?

FIGURE 3.1. PowerPoint Slide from Upham's Corner Working Advisory Group Presentation, September 2012
Source: Boston Redevelopment Authority, "Fairmount Indigo Planning Initiative, Upham's Corner Working Advisory Group (WAG) Meeting #2."

For forty minutes, Josh described neighborhood conditions, from housing affordability to zoning to transportation. Each slide included a colorful map of the Census tracts and blocks within a half-mile of the station. He showed forty-one maps in total.

When he finished, Josh asked the advisory group members if they'd like to have "a discussion about what is Upham's Corner to all of you, and how can that inform the work that we're set off on now." He then showed two maps side by side, reproduced in figure 3.1. The one on the left showed the half-mile circle around the station, the basis of the preceding analysis. The one on the right showed a street map with two slightly different boundaries of the neighborhood—both more in line with local definitions. The consultants cropped both maps tightly so that they appeared to cover the same amount of land area even though they were projected at different scales. Few streets were labeled. The tight cropping, different projections, and scant labels made the two maps difficult to compare.

Josh paused and stared at the pull-down screen. He puzzled over the two maps, his eyes darting back and forth between them. After a moment, he said to no one in particular, "Yeah, it's pretty similar to the circle. It's not too far off."

There would be only one comment from the advisory group about the neighborhood's geographic boundary. Drew, a white nonprofit leader, said he understood why the consultants placed the station at the center of their map. The urban planning exercise required capturing information about people who might use the station, even if those people weren't necessarily residents of Upham's Corner. He wasn't sure, however, how that would translate into people's actual understanding of the space. It was "really easy to see" how someone who got off the train and walked down Dudley Street toward Columbia Avenue would feel as if they were in Upham's Corner—it was well-established as the western half of the neighborhood, after all. But "if we are talking about expanding to the west, you know, to think about Dudley in *this* direction," here he pointed to the left side of the map, "I'm interested to hear from *residents* what they think about 'Upham's Corner' extending down to" areas not typically associated with the neighborhood.

Jeremy, a white BRA official, interjected dismissively: "I wouldn't consider it 'Upham's Corner, continuing down.' Let's consider [it] 'the study area.'" The planners and consultants wanted to study community development around the station. It didn't matter to them that their definition of the neighborhood conflicted with traditional boundaries.

Nor did it matter that, as a result of this newly imposed geography of Upham's Corner, the southeastern corner of the neighborhood had been cut out. That particular area was home to one of the city's most violent gangs and would be the site of a major drug raid four months later.[1] The people who lived there were excluded from participating in the planning process. Had these residents been included, issues of crime and violence may have factored more prominently in the discussions and recommendations. Their absence was especially notable considering this planning process took the place of one promised for the neighborhood.

The Upham's Corner Working Advisory Group's final report, released in 2014, included fifty-three maps. The study authors admitted that "some of the areas included within this study area may not be traditionally considered Upham's Corner," yet referred to the area as "Upham's Corner" throughout the text.

Maps represent geographic relationships. They situate points on the earth's surface and illustrate the relative distance between particular locations. They display terrain and delineate sovereign territories. They are snapshots in time, vulnerable to both ecological and political shifts. As sea levels rise or states splinter into independent nations, maps evolve in order to convey the most accurate, up-to-date information.

Maps also communicate where *communities* are in relation to other communities. This was a central concern among early Chicago School sociologists.

The now-famous "concentric zone" map created by Robert Park and Ernest Burgess in 1925 depicted communities as functionally interdependent "natural areas." According to the theoretical map, community areas emanate radially from the city's central business district and spatially segment groups based on race, class, and family structure. The demographic composition of communities may change when some groups "invade" and others "secede." But community boundaries are geographically stable, demarcated by particular streets, transit lines, or bodies of water, and systematically catalogued by external authorities—Park and Burgess among them.

Later Chicago School sociologists rejected the "naturalness" of community areas, pointing instead to the "social construction" of "symbolic communities."[2] Local communities do not exist outside of social interaction; individuals and organizations actively create neighborhood identity and boundaries. As Albert Hunter argues:

> [L]ocal urban communities should not be viewed as immutable, static social units whose names, boundaries, and other defining characteristics may be permanently and authoritatively fixed. The "mapping" of local areas will inevitably be "wrong," because of historical change and because of the different criteria that observers or participants may use in "their" definitions of community.[3]

No map can accurately reflect the local understanding of communities because there is no one, single understanding of any given community. For some places, reputations are sticky, and local traditions sustain differences between places over time.[4] For others, demographic change leads to different groups relying on distinct definitions of community boundaries depending on race, class, or length of residence.[5] Communities are neither wholly objective nor definitively defined by external authorities. They are, in short, constructed.

A large body of literature in geography and critical cartography has analyzed maps as *political projects*. Mapmakers decide what is included, how it is represented, and what is left out. As historian William Rankin observes, "Maps are thus laden with the specific political or cultural goals of those who produce them: they are descriptions of how the world is, but they are simultaneously arguments about how the world should be."[6] Sometimes those goals and aspirations are relatively banal. The map of "Upham's Corner" presented by Josh and Jeremy was a particular vision of the neighborhood that centered on the Fairmount Line. Other times, maps serve more nefarious purposes. Maps created by the Home Owners' Loan Corporation (HOLC) and the Boston Banks Urban Renewal Group (BBURG), described in chapter 1, allowed lenders to justify systematic discrimination against prospective Black homeowners. The ostensible neutrality of mapping helped do the dirty work of segregation.

Like any territory, the Fairmount Corridor's boundaries were fluid and open to interpretation. Different people and organizations defined its boundaries in different ways. Importantly, *private* actors—consultants and nonprofit leaders, in particular—played a prominent role in making the Corridor legible as a place. And they did so for *political* reasons, shaping and reshaping geographical boundaries to gain access to resources.[7] Private political interests came first. Community geography was constructed second.

Some definitions of the Corridor's boundaries excluded areas included in other definitions; the Working Advisory Group, for instance, excluded certain parts of Upham's Corner in its definition of the neighborhood. On the surface, decisions like these might seem inconsequential. But for those on the other side of the boundary, it meant less resources and fewer opportunities to shape community development policy. The difference between inclusion and exclusion was the difference between investment and disinvestment, between policy attention and political indifference.

The discussion that follows underscores three broader themes of this book. First, private nonprofit leaders played important roles in urban governance by determining how geographical boundaries were drawn. Second, transit policy—and transit-oriented development (TOD), in particular—carried unintended consequences. While TOD has many benefits for poor neighborhoods, it skews decision-making in other policy areas, anchoring neighborhood planning to *transit* rather than the *neighborhood* at large. Finally, community development was as much about the construction of communities as the construction of "community" as an idea. The Fairmount Corridor and its neighborhoods were treated as malleable communities, subject to shifting boundaries. Shifting boundaries empowered certain organizations and benefited certain neighborhoods but could ignore other people and places in the process.

How Many People Live in the Fairmount Corridor?

No one seemed to know exactly how many people lived in the Fairmount Corridor. Government officials and their consultants cited no fewer than eight population figures over the course of my fieldwork. Sometimes officials directly contradicted one another in public. During a panel at the 2011 National Smart Growth Conference in Charlotte, North Carolina, Carl Dierker from the EPA listed the Corridor's population as "about 90,000 people." In the same session, Mary Beth Melo from the Federal Transit Administration (FTA) said 160,000 people lived in the Corridor. No one acknowledged the discrepancy.[8]

Local government officials were just as inconsistent. In early 2012, the Boston Redevelopment Authority (BRA) began a Corridor-wide urban planning process. At the February "kick-off" event announcing the initiative, Mayor Thomas Menino referenced "130,000 people living along the Fairmount Line." Press coverage of the event listed the population as "over 160,000."[9] The next day, at a "bidders conference" for consultants applying to manage the process, a BRA official said "roughly 190,000 people," but four months later he would say "upwards of 180,000 people." Two months later, a consultant hired by the BRA offered somewhat more precise numbers: The Corridor included either 131,946 people or 121,624 people, depending on "how you cut the data." And in the final report of the planning process, published in 2013, the Corridor population was put at a relatively modest 93,104.

There was a technical, sometimes unspoken reason for the varying population numbers. The Fairmount Commuter Rail Line runs approximately 9 miles between South Station (the northern terminus) and Readville Station (the southern terminus). The Corridor is generally understood as the area within a half-mile of the stations, as this is the standard definition of "walking distance" to public transit. If it extended any farther, community development projects would have no formal relation to new or existing stations on the line.

Given these parameters, data analysts had to make three decisions when describing the Corridor. The first was whether to include the area within a half-mile of the rail *line* or a half-mile of the rail *stations*. A large oval around the train line would seem to better signify a "Corridor" than a series of circles around existing stations. But that would mean including areas that did not fall within a half-mile of any existing or to-be-constructed station. On the other hand, defining the Corridor as only the area around existing or to-be-constructed stations precluded planning in areas that might gain access to the line at a later date, if the state were to decide to build more stations—something that was under consideration.

The second decision stemmed from the fact that economic and demographic statistics are only available at aggregate levels, like US Census tracts, block groups, or blocks, and these units do not fall cleanly within a half-mile of the stations or the line. Analysts could include all tracts that *at least partially* intersected with the half-mile boundary, though this would mean including geographic areas beyond the boundary. Or they could include only tracts that fell *completely* within the boundary, though this would mean excluding geographic areas within the boundary. Or, they could apply some other arbitrary criteria, like including only tracts that were more than 50 percent within the boundary. Once, I observed a consultant apportion population as a function of the percentage of a tract's land mass included within the boundary. This decision, however, relied on a questionable assumption: that population is spread evenly within tracts.

The third and final issue was whether to include the area around South Station. South Station is located in downtown Boston, near the booming (and, at the time, gentrifying) Seaport District. It is nearly two miles north of the next nearest station on the Fairmount Line, separated from the rest of the Corridor by an interstate highway. It is the northern terminus of the line, but it is also quantitatively and qualitatively distinct from any other area along the Corridor.

Each of these decisions produced a unique set of results. Some analysts included South Station in their definition of the Corridor, while others did not.

Some included all tracts at least partially within a half-mile of the rail *line*, while others included all tracts at least partially within a half-mile of the rail *stations*—a difference of eight tracts. Some ignored tracts altogether in favor of smaller geographic units that fit more closely within a half-mile of the stations—like block groups or blocks—but doing that meant sacrificing accuracy as well as any demographic information available only at the tract level. No decision was more "correct" than any other. The Fairmount rail line bisected established neighborhoods and passed over major thoroughfares. A shape on a map, no matter how well thought out, would not correspond with any standardized administrative units or local understandings of community boundaries.

The confusion over the Corridor's population nevertheless bothered Mat, a consultant for the coalition of community development corporations (CDCs). In particular, he was troubled by the fact that BRA officials generally cited population numbers (between 130,000 and 190,000) nearly twice as high as the coalition's estimates (between 88,000 and 120,000). The coalition needed accurate demographic statistics for grant applications, and so in late 2012, Mat set out to understand the true population number.

His quest ended nearly as soon as it began. Mat realized that the coalition benefited from a larger number, regardless of the "true" population figure. A larger population meant the coalition could claim a bigger impact, incentivizing public and private funders to financially support its plans.[10] "Frankly," he told members of the coalition during a conference call in September, "if anything the BRA . . . number possibly over-counts the population, and I don't think that hurts us."

Mat's realization reflected two important aspects of the Corridor. First, its geography was malleable, open to different interpretations. Different boundaries—not different data sources—contributed to the varying population estimates. Second, geographic considerations did not exist in a vacuum. There were technical reasons for the varying population numbers, but there were political reasons as well.

Puzzling over the Corridor's Boundaries

For the most part, people like Mat could pick and choose population statistics that suited their interests. Yet there were key moments when a boundary had to be collectively defined, when community development plans could not proceed without a shared understanding of the Corridor's geography. One of those instances was the BRA-managed Fairmount Corridor planning process. Recall that the Menino administration created four advisory groups in early 2012. In addition to the three neighborhood-based groups, there was an overarching twenty-six-person advisory group made up of nonprofit leaders, development professionals, and a few residents who met monthly with a team of outside consultants.

"We have such an unusual opportunity to start to think about a whole segment—this whole corridor of the city that has been in some ways invisible," noted Steve, the white consultant leading the planning process, at one of the first meetings of the Corridor-wide advisory group. Yet making the Corridor visible—that is, making it legible as a community—proved difficult. It was clear from the start that the Corridor did not align with any local understanding of community boundaries. The group of government officials, urban planning consultants, and advisory group members puzzled over the Corridor's boundaries, debating what to include and what to exclude. The constructed geography had little connection to traditional community boundaries. It did, however, satisfy their respective political interests.

BRA officials had two interests in conducting the planning process. First, they wanted to connect the Corridor to the Innovation District, an area near South Station designed for the growing technology sector and a major priority of Mayor Menino's late career. They also wanted to give the Corridor a legible identity as a place. Officials were not ignorant of the fact that the Corridor included neighborhoods with few common elements. Yet they also knew the Corridor needed a cohesive identity if they were to be competitive for federal urban development grants. Like Mat, the officials realized they could make a better case for resources if they could claim a greater impact—and a "corridor" of interdependent development projects was perfectly suited to make that case.

The first working meeting of the advisory group occurred in August 2012, inside a Mattapan social service agency. Pam, a white consultant, presented data on economic activity in the Corridor. She offered two sets of analysis, one including and the other excluding South Station. The difference was enormous. South Station is in the heart of downtown Boston, and its inclusion meant one analysis indicated considerably more job growth, commercial establishments, and higher income residents in the Corridor than the other.

As a consultant hired by the BRA, Steve had an interest in connecting the Corridor to the Innovation District near South Station. He therefore pushed for South Station's inclusion, arguing that one purpose of the planning process was to help bring Corridor residents to downtown jobs:

> This is really looking at the citywide context, and where the Fairmount Corridor *is* in the city . . . The point about the South Station area, looking at a half mile—of course, that's the center of Boston. That's the center of the region, the center of New England . . . And we have an extraordinary ability to increase the access to the jobs and economic opportunity. (his emphasis)

Members of the advisory group resisted Steve's framing of the planning process. They had an interest in securing resources for the neighborhoods they represented, not just opening up access to downtown jobs. The inclusion of the South Station area distorted statistics about the Corridor—making it appear more advantaged—and thus undercut the case for more jobs and economic opportunities in the neighborhoods. Mat, the CDC consultant who was also an advisory group member, understood the desire to connect Corridor residents to currently existing jobs downtown. But he hoped the planning process would spend serious time on the areas lacking economic opportunity:

> And I think one of the things that has to be decided is, is the focus going to be how to get people who live in the Corridor to South Station, to the Innovation District, to [the suburbs along] Route 128—and that certainly has some value. Or is the emphasis going to be how to create more economic activity within the Corridor. And both things have to be looked at. I certainly hope there's going to be more emphasis on the latter.

Mat's argument did not focus on whether South Station was part of the Corridor's geography. Instead, it was about who should benefit from the planning process. The geography was a second-order corollary.

Glen, a white nonprofit leader, Upham's Corner resident, and advisory group member, put forward another reason to exclude South Station from the analysis: Downtown Boston was socially and culturally distinct from each of the residential areas within the Corridor. While neighborhoods in the Fairmount Corridor were quite distinct, and most residents would not feel any special connection to those living on the other side of traditional neighborhood boundaries, absolutely no resident would consider their neighborhood in the same breath as downtown Boston. He explained:

> Just to comment on what's been presented thus far, and the whole South Station including, excluding [issue] . . . It doesn't strike me as very apples-to-apples. As a *resident*—I mean, I live a few hundred feet off of the line—it *never* would have occurred to me to think of somebody living in a loft [downtown] as a *Corridor* resident. So when you're talking about, you know, these folks versus these folks, including/excluding—it seems like it skews [the analysis]. (his emphasis)

Steve responded by offering to remove South Station from the consultants' economic analysis because it "blows the data up in ways that aren't really helpful."

"Personally, I would rather be focused on excluding South Station, and not even talking about it [at all]," Glen pushed.

The consultants agreed to think it over. "Part of it is just getting our head wrapped around it too," Pam said sympathetically. As the meeting wound down, Steve added, "Believe us, we're puzzling this through. Looking at all the data, how it is cut."

At the next advisory group meeting, held in an Upham's Corner community center, the consultants proposed a compromise: They excluded South Station from all data analysis, but continued to frame the planning process in terms of getting Corridor residents to downtown jobs—furthering the interests of city officials while also conceding the advisory group's concerns. Steve showed the group a map of the consultants' new definition of the Corridor. It excluded South Station and displayed Census tracts and blocks that at least partially fell within a half-mile of the stations. Steve stared at the map projected on to a pull-down screen. The ill-fitting Census tracts were "a *pretty close* match" to the half-mile boundary, he said—"close enough for the purposes of planning."

In public, city officials agreed that South Station—and by extension, the Innovation District—was not part of the Corridor. But in official documents, they continued to include South Station in their definition of the Corridor's boundaries. They did so by distinguishing the geography of "the Fairmount Corridor" from the geography of "the Fairmount Focus Area." In a January 2013 report, a caption of a map explained the distinction:

> For the purpose of this profile we have defined the geographic area of the corridor to be a 0.5-mile radius from the rail line. We have included data for the Fairmount Corridor (Corridor) from Readville to South Station recognizing that South Station is a key employment hub for both the city and the region. In addition, this profile provides data for the Fairmount Focus Area (Focus Area) from Readville to Newmarket that allows data to be compared to the Corridor and the City of Boston (Boston) overall.

Mat, Glen, and the rest of the advisory group had their preferred geography represented. So did the city officials. The final report of the Fairmount Corridor Planning Initiative, published in September 2014, retained the distinction between the "Corridor" and the "Focus Area."[11] Two geographies of the Corridor's boundaries coexisted in the same report, reflecting each side's respective interests.

To understand the importance of the compromise, it is worth considering the counterfactual: If the boundary had not included South Station, then city officials would not have been able to tap downtown resources, include downtown business representatives, or connect their plans to major downtown initiatives. The resolution—negotiated by their consultants—gave them the power to satisfy their interests.

Branding the Corridor

"And that's the way we're cutting the data generally," Steve said during an advisory group meeting, "to figure out what's true about the Corridor compared to other sorts of places." Steve's reference to "what's true about the Corridor" segued into the next problem: The Corridor did not have a single, cohesive identity. Excluding the South Station area was a start. But Newmarket, Upham's Corner, Grove Hall, Four Corners, Codman Square, Mattapan, Logan Square, and Readville are all distinct neighborhoods, in some cases separated by miles and united only loosely by their relative disadvantage compared to more affluent neighborhoods in the city. There was nothing necessarily "true" about the Corridor beyond an oval on a map. Nevertheless, if BRA officials wanted to complete their planning process and compete for federal urban development grants, they needed to define the Corridor as something more than a collection of individual neighborhoods.

Steve told the advisory group that this would be the next task, to make visible a geography that had previously been invisible:

> We should say to ourselves, "Our job is to think about a corridor of Boston that is *less visible* in a way, than other places, but has been made visible simply because of how the line was drawn and connected in the Fairmount Line." And start talking about the communities, and how communities can be made better ... The question that comes up ... is: What is common about the Corridor? In other words, what is it that really makes this Corridor? (his emphasis)

To define the Corridor's identity, two additional consultants joined the team: Terry Shook, a white, Charlotte-based brand management consultant specializing in urban design, and L'Merchie Frazier, a Black Codman Square resident and activist. Terry and L'Merchie developed a branding strategy, what the consultant team called "a big idea—a vision for the Fairmount Corridor."

That "big idea" inadvertently reaffirmed the incoherence of the Corridor's geography. At the April 2013 advisory group meeting, held in a Codman Square community room, Terry shared the findings from their analysis. Each neighborhood had its own "cultural anchors," "genuine, local experiences," and "genuine, authentic, local food"—distinct features that made the neighborhoods "real places," according to Terry. Rather than see the incongruence as a challenge, Terry and L'Merchie reframed it as an asset and defined the overall Corridor identity as "Diversity." L'Merchie explained to the advisory group:

> I think one of the jumping off points about the [Fairmount Line] is that there are diverse neighborhoods. And with that diversity, it becomes the identity. The identity that there are so many different representations ... that there are interesting cultural pockets. That becomes part of the identity of the *entire* line, and not that the entire line—that each place has to be branded the same as another. That is the real opportunity we have here, to keep these—not necessarily *differences*, but these aspects of culture highlighted. (her emphasis)

Terry suggested a tagline, "The entire world is at home here."

Broadly stated, the idea was that residents from each station area could create and control their own identity, and that these identities cumulatively reflected nearly every culture in the world. Put more critically, the consultants concluded that the only "common element" across the Corridor was that it had no single common element.

The idea that each neighborhood in the Corridor was special and unique, and that diversity was its central asset, certainly resonated with the advisory group members.[12] And it suited the BRA officials' desire for a single Corridor identity that would make projects more attractive to federal officials and other funders. Branding it as "diverse" helped make the space legible and marketable in the face of incoherence. As a result, it empowered the people and organizations invested in the idea of "the Fairmount Corridor."

"One Community Is Benefiting from All of This, and That's Just Not Right"

The BRA's planning process involved more than just one Corridor-wide study. It also included sub-area studies for three of the eight Fairmount Line station areas. As mentioned earlier, city officials had previously committed to a neighborhood plan for Upham's Corner, and so the advisory group had two more areas to choose.

At a March 2013 meeting in a Hyde Park community center, the advisory group made its selection. Nearly seventy people attended. Jeremy, the BRA official managing the process, stood at the front of the room facing a three-sided table where the advisory group members sat. The rest of the meeting's attendees sat behind the advisory group in four rows divided by a center aisle, with additional seating around the room's perimeter.

Jeremy began with a slideshow presentation and revealed the BRA's preliminary selection. He hedged as he described the agency's quantitative selection criteria: "It's not scientific"; "This was just to start the conversation"; "If we were to put numbers to rank these station areas, this is how it *might* fall"; "This is give or take; these numbers aren't perfect. You can go either way, but this is an *estimate*." The criteria included categories such as "Ability to engage diverse corridor communities" and "Availability of potential development parcels." Station areas were scored from 1 to 4 in each category, with a "4" indicating highest priority. Jeremy did not explain how the officials assigned each rating.

After more hedging, Jeremy finally announced the BRA's recommendation: One station area planning process in Mattapan and the other in Four Corners. "Our hope is that we're going to get some kind of consensus tonight," Jeremy told the group, "and we're going to strive for that."

For the next two hours, advisory group members discussed the merits of a planning process at each station area. A resident from each area presented facts and information about ongoing initiatives, making a case for the additional resources. After the presentations, the advisory group conducted a hand vote. Fifteen votes went to the station area in Codman Square, ten to Four Corners, three to Mattapan, and two to Hyde Park.[13]

Christian, the Black co-chair of the advisory group and Codman Square resident, noted that a decision had been made: Judging from the advisory group's votes, the residents from Codman Square and Four Corners had made the most compelling case for resources. But murmurs spread throughout the room. One advisory group member, Milly, an immigrant from the Dominican Republic, director of a social service agency in Mattapan, and resident of Hyde Park, observed that the Codman Square and Four Corners stations were directly adjacent to one another. Residents saw them as distinct, but Codman Square and Four Corners were nevertheless within the same larger neighborhood district: Dorchester.

"I'm not saying one or the other, but in terms of the city of Boston, and the Fairmount [Corridor] benefiting from this, that is way too close for other communities that are being left out," Milly complained. "Way too close." She asked about the sub-area planning resources already earmarked for Upham's Corner. "And isn't Upham's Corner also in Dorchester? So that's three for one neighborhood."

A consultant countered that, technically, the Upham's Corner Station area is just as much in Roxbury as it is in Dorchester. "The Roxbury-Dorchester line is actually . . . in the Upham's Corner half-mile circle," he said.

"Right," Milly retorted, "but [the Fairmount Corridor] includes Hyde Park, Mattapan, *and* Dorchester." To her, it didn't matter that the Upham's Corner Station area included Roxbury if it also included Dorchester. "So now we got everything concentrated in just Dorchester, so what happens to Mattapan and what happens to Hyde Park? One community is benefiting from all of this, and that's just not right." A dozen mostly white residents from Hyde Park, sitting directly behind Milly, applauded in agreement.

The scope of the debate shifted immediately. At the beginning of the discussion, each station area was a distinct subcommunity within the larger Corridor. Milly effectively redrew internal neighborhood boundaries. Now, multiple station areas within the same large neighborhood district—Upham's Corner, Codman Square, and Four Corners—were part of Dorchester, a *single* subcommunity within the Corridor. By this logic, eight neighborhoods intersecting with the Fairmount Line stations collapsed into three larger neighborhood districts.

Audience members from Hyde Park picked up on Milly's reframing of the Corridor geography. A white resident argued that "everyone's gonna be upset" if planning resources only went to Dorchester, and advocated for a planning process in "each community":

> Why don't you just do one from each community? Because when you just do Dorchester—because all of your hard work is gonna be for nothing, because everyone's gonna be upset. Do one from Mattapan, do one from Hyde Park, and do one from Dorchester. And then everyone will

be—it won't be upsetting. If you do all of Dorchester—then all of your hard work—and I know all of the work this committee has put into it, is going to be for nothing.

When the Hyde Park resident referred to "one from each community," she meant "one from Mattapan, ... one from Hyde Park, and ... one from Dorchester." Because resources were already earmarked for Upham's Corner, her proposal effectively called for resources to be distributed to Mattapan and Hyde Park. A few advisory group members nodded their approval.

Christian's neighborhood, Codman Square, would be excluded under the Hyde Park resident's proposal. That is, if the Corridor were limited to distribution across three larger neighborhood districts, and "each community" deserved resources, then Christian's neighborhood would be ineligible because resources were already earmarked for Upham's Corner. But if the Corridor were eight distinct neighborhoods around the stations, and "each community" deserved resources, then Christian's neighborhood would be eligible. And so, Christian offered a new proposal, implicitly reframing the station areas as separate communities: Split the planning resources *across all of the station areas*. The rhetorical sleight of hand seemed to slip under the radar; both Christian and the Hyde Park resident agreed that there should be "one [planning process] from each community," yet each had a very different community geography in mind.

The BRA officials resisted the call for geographic equity—no matter how the geography was defined. Inés, a Latina urban planner, justified the BRA's recommendation to allocate the resources to Mattapan and Four Corners, and *not* Codman Square and Four Corners (the advisory group's original recommendation), Mattapan and Hyde Park (Milly and the Hyde Park resident's demand), or all of the station areas (Christian's compromise). In doing so, she implicitly rejected Milly's attempt to classify Four Corners and Upham's Corner as part of the same community:

> In talking to people in the community, and what I'm hearing tonight, is Four Corners definitely has good momentum, and [Mattapan] ... [the BRA thought] it would be a great way to sort of bring the community together around an issue ... Bringing resources to the community through this process and sort of galvanizing folks around the Fairmount Line—that was a thought that we very much talked about with folks in the community.

Inés wanted to devote resources to Four Corners and Mattapan, so it served her interests to treat each station area as a distinct community and allocate resources where there was "good momentum." As the three-hour meeting wound down, Inés promised to consider the proposals for broader geographic equity.

In an email to the advisory group on April 3, a BRA official used the passive voice, writing that "the decision was made to move forward" with Mattapan and Four Corners—the agency's original selection.[14]

The episode revealed the geographically fluid definitions of the Corridor. It also illustrated how different community boundaries created power imbalances and competing claims for resources. When Milly and the Hyde Park residents defined large neighborhood districts as single communities—rather than collections of subcommunities surrounding each station area—they undercut the advisory group's vote in favor of their own interests in seeing the resources allocated to Mattapan and Hyde Park. And when Christian and Inés ignored those claims and framed the area around each station as a distinct community, they pursued *their* own interests in seeing resources devoted to Codman Square (in Christian's case) or Four Corners and Mattapan (in Inés's case). Each side constructed community boundaries in a way that supported their access to resources.

The existence of nested neighborhoods, and the fact that individuals can pick and choose different geographic referents, fits with sociologist Robert Sampson's assertion that "[t]here is no one neighborhood, but many neighborhoods that vary in size and complexity."[15] Neighborhoods are best understood as "a mosaic of overlapping boundaries."[16] It was this social fact of urban life that allowed Milly, Christian, and Inés to puzzle over the geography of the Corridor's sub-neighborhoods. If communities had fixed boundaries, there would be far less room for debate.

More notable, however, was how people defined geographic boundaries *as a political strategy to secure resources and empower some people at the expense of others*. A straight vote from the advisory group would have resulted in resources for Codman Square and Four Corners, but Milly's reframing of community boundaries effectively changed the scope of debate. Milly did not debate the appropriate geography of the Corridor, as such; she was interested in affecting resource allocation. With a planning process in Mattapan, Inés satisfied Milly and rendered her initial geographic critique ("one community is benefiting from all of this") moot. Mattapan and Four Corners received urban planning resources. Codman Square and Hyde Park did not.

A Greenway with Grapes

The Fairmount Greenway Task Force had a problem. The coalition of nine nonprofit organizations wanted to develop a linear greenway along the Fairmount Rail Line. The problem was fairly significant: It was impossible to do so under current conditions. Greenways require a significant amount of land, and the Fairmount Line tracks ran right up against busy public streets and private backyards.

Boston already had two well-known greenways. The Southwest Corridor Park includes 4.7 uninterrupted miles of parks, gardens, and bike paths running from the South End to Jamaica Plain. It opened in 1990 on land cleared by the state in preparation for an expressway that never came to fruition. The 1.5-mile Rose Fitzgerald Kennedy Greenway opened in downtown Boston in 2008. Built on land cleared during the "Big Dig" (the project that moved a segment of Interstate 93 underground), it features gardens, fountains, and rotating public art installations. Both greenways indirectly contributed to the existence of the Fairmount Corridor: The Southwest Corridor project shifted commuter rail service to the Fairmount Line, and the Big Dig's negative impact on the environment prompted the state to build new stations on the line to comply with the Clean Air Act of 1990. Both are also well funded and incredibly popular, so nonprofit leaders in the Corridor wanted one, too.

With a $750,000 grant from the Barr Foundation, they hired a consultant firm to create a concept plan. The consultants, tasked with drawing a continuous path on a map, were forced to call it a "nontraditional" greenway: a bike path, winding up and down city streets, that linked to "destinations" or "loops"—that is, existing parks and other open space not necessarily falling along the zigzagging path. It was a greenway with "grapes," "twigs," or "polka dots," as one nonprofit director variously explained.

There was another problem. Each nonprofit leader in the coalition had an interest in securing resources for their respective neighborhood. During an October 2010 coalition meeting, Javier, a Latino community organizer with Codman Square Neighborhood Development Corporation (CSNDC), explained that residents "want to see results." "For neighbors," he said, "the transformation of a vacant lot in their neighborhood, sort of may seem, sort of—or may represent a bigger victory than a bike path from Hyde Park to South Station." The group decided to select "priority parcels," evenly spread throughout the Corridor, so that each organization—and by extension, residents of each neighborhood in the Corridor—could benefit from the development.

Of course, the very idea of "priority parcels" conflicted with the premise of a continuous greenway. Funders and government officials were interested in the potential of an unobstructed pathway, not strung-together individual projects. "Whether I like it or not," Javier continued, "it's the path" that was the bigger selling point to outside funders.

Javier's comments frustrated another coalition member, Marvin, the Black executive director of the Greater Four Corners Action Coalition (GFCAC). Marvin did not think the coalition had to pursue the path at the expense of neighborhood-specific projects. That was a "traditional" way of thinking. The Fairmount Greenway—lacking a true "way"—would be more "innovative":

> You know, I'm sorry, I just have a problem with that response. You know, they're coming out [of] a traditional [way of thinking,] that we said we want to change. When we first had this conversation about putting this urban greenway through our neighborhoods, and we had this conversation about the term "greenway." And remember, we said . . . we're going

to define greenway the way we want to define greenway! And so—and [we] knew that the purists was going to say, "Oh that's not a greenway!" Right? But, so, you know, do we have to break this apart because of funding? Or do we say to them, "Look, this is a new way of thinking about it, maybe *y'all* need to catch up!" Because it's not only happening here in our neighborhoods; you're starting to see it in other cities. Because people are looking at ways to connect green to their neighborhoods, in neighborhoods that don't have a lot of green. So you got to be innovative about how you do that. You know, there's no way that the people in our neighborhoods are going to be more excited about the [path] than they would the parcels they've identified, just because it's "right." And so, you know— . . . [We need to] start thinking outside the box, and it just sounds like they're trying to put us back in the box. (his emphasis)

Other coalition members agreed with Marvin's attempt to reimagine the Corridor's geography as an asset, not an impediment to development.

The coalition faced other resistance. During a February 2011 meeting, a white consultant for a parks organization told the coalition members that a greenway in the Corridor was impossible. A "greenway," he insisted, has two elements: It is green, and it has an unobstructed path. The Fairmount Greenway had no path, and the idea of "priority parcels" in individual neighborhoods only made the absence of a path more apparent. "One of the issues you have is that there are [nonprofits] with their own political boundaries and you're trying to put a greenway on top of it. A greenway needs continuous development—a way," the consultant said.

Gail, CSNDC's executive director, wondered if it was still possible to market the idea as a greenway. Did it matter from a *marketing* standpoint if their greenway didn't fit the urban planning definition of a greenway? The consultant responded affirmatively; the group would have trouble funding the development of a greenway that was quite clearly not a greenway.

"I disagree," Gail countered, dismissing the consultant as she answered her own question. "We should call it what we want to call it. It's a way for us to talk about our neighborhoods as a cohesive plan. We want people to start *seeing* us this way—as a unit—and I'm less interested with the nomenclature." That the "priority parcels" were not on a continuous path was irrelevant to Gail; the nonprofit leaders could make the ad-hoc parcels legible as smaller parts of a larger geographic whole.

The coalition, undeterred by the consultant, contracted a regional urban planning agency to create maps of its Greenway concept. Created in 2014, the maps depicted the zigzagging route on city streets, spin-offs or alternative paths called "spurs," "loops" to existing parks, and the "priority parcels." Figure 3.2 displays one of those maps, showing the segment of the greenway between the Talbot Avenue Station and the Blue Hill Avenue Station on the

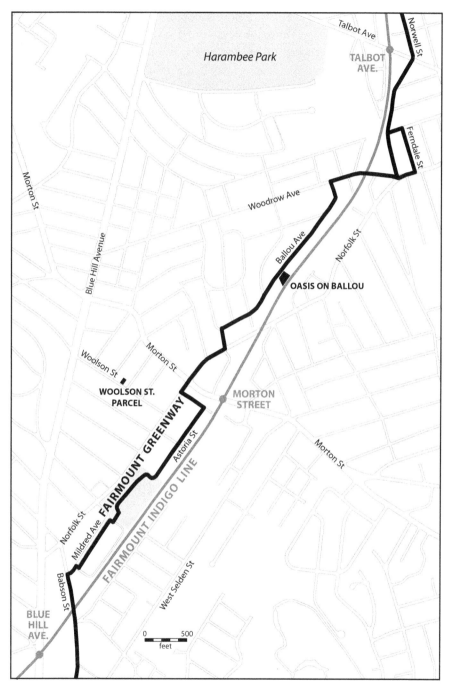

FIGURE 3.2. Map of Fairmount Greenway Segment, Talbot Avenue to Blue Hill Avenue
Source: Adapted from a map created by MAPC for the Fairmount Greenway Task Force.

Fairmount Line. It labels two "priority parcels": a small urban farm on Ballou Avenue in Codman Square, and a community garden on Woolson Street in Mattapan. The Woolson Street parcel was selected as a priority because it was the site of the murder of four people, including a two-year-old boy, in 2010. The location, however, is a significant distance from the proposed path.

The maps proved beneficial for the nonprofit coalition. By 2018, the nonprofit leaders had acquired resources for three projects on "priority parcels": the aforementioned urban farm in Codman Square and community garden in Mattapan, as well as a playground in Hyde Park. There was no connection among the projects other than a color-coded shape on a map. By the time I completed my fieldwork, little progress had been made on constructing the continuous path.

The nonprofit leaders each had an interest in acquiring resources for their respective neighborhoods. The "greenway" was a way to satisfy those interests, but making it a useful, legible concept required reimagining the Corridor and reframing disjointed projects as strategically tied to a particular geography. Barring mass resident displacement, the Fairmount Corridor will never have a continuous "way" similar to the Southwest Corridor Park or Rose Fitzgerald Kennedy Greenway. That did not stop the coalition members and their consultants from drawing a path on a map and leveraging the idea into additional resources. Manipulating the Corridor's geography allowed them to satisfy neighborhood-specific resource needs.

Distinguishing Fairmount Neighborhoods from the Fairmount Corridor

Geeta wanted The Boston Foundation (TBF) to do more to address poverty in the city. She controlled the foundation's housing and community development strategy, and through her leadership, TBF provided community development grants to organizations in the city's poorest neighborhoods, including Roxbury, Dorchester, and Mattapan. TBF also funded organizations located in poor sections of gentrified neighborhoods, like Inquilinos Boricuas en Acción (IBA) in the South End and the Hyde Square Task Force in Jamaica Plain.

The problem, according to Geeta, was that these "investments" were not "coordinated"; the grants were ad hoc and did not follow an intentional antipoverty strategy. The Corridor, however, provided Geeta with a potential solution: It cut through Roxbury, Dorchester, and Mattapan—the core of Boston's urban poverty. Reframing grants to the Corridor as TBF's antipoverty strategy imposed thematic consistency on disparate grants. "So I just called it the Fairmount initiative!" Geeta told me with a laugh in 2011. Problem solved.

Solving one problem unintentionally created another: No reasonable definition of the Corridor included Roxbury, and *all* definitions of the Corridor included Hyde Park, a neighborhood that was 85 percent nonwhite, but more middle-class than the rest of the Corridor. The Fairmount Corridor included some—but not all—of the city's poor neighborhoods, and it included more advantaged areas as well.

Geeta's solution was to distinguish the Fairmount *Corridor*—the area around the rail line—from what she called the Fairmount *neighborhoods*—the poor neighborhoods in or near the Corridor. As she explained to me in 2013:

> The stations are also not centrally located strategically; they're not in the business districts. They are always a little bit "off," you know? . . . What we are calling the Fairmount neighborhoods, is that we took a look at—we said, "This corridor impacts the neighborhoods of Roxbury, Dorchester, Mattapan, and Hyde Park." Our principle investments have been in Roxbury, Dorchester, and Matta—very few in Mattapan [because of the small number of nonprofits in the neighborhood] . . . So we actually—because the nonprofits are there, because poverty is concentrated there, because all of the disparities are concentrated there, we found that most of our investments were falling in these neighborhoods. And so, we are calling the neighborhoods of Roxbury, Dorchester, [and] Mattapan as "the Fairmount neighborhoods."

Geeta drew a diagram on a piece of scrap paper to show me the distinction. She first drew a long oval signifying the half-mile border around the rail line. "This is the Corridor," she said. She then drew smaller circles inside the oval signifying the areas within a half-mile of the stations. Two half circles—one at the top left of the oval and the other at the bottom right—signified the neighborhood of Roxbury and the portion of Dorchester that was beyond a half-mile from the rail line. The Fairmount neighborhoods are "a much bigger geography" than the rail corridor, she explained. To Geeta, "the Fairmount Corridor" was shorthand for the neighborhoods of Roxbury, Dorchester, and Mattapan—including parts of those neighborhoods inaccessible by, and thus unconnected to, the Fairmount Line.

Not everyone at TBF agreed with Geeta that the Fairmount Corridor represented a unique opportunity to coordinate the foundation's antipoverty work. Another program director at TBF was largely dismissive as she talked with me about the so-called Fairmount frame in 2013. This program director indicated that TBF would have awarded the same grants to the same organizations, regardless of the train line running through them. TBF "ended up there because we all can read. And we all can see the data driving us there":

> We are in that space because it's low-income, often disproportionately minority, or people of color. Often disproportionately immigrant.

> Absolutely, as a result, the worst health slash economic slash educational outcomes. Highest incidents of violence. I mean, our grants around [a violence prevention program], our education [grants] . . . our career advancement work, our health work—it's all there because you go to where the problem is.

Much to her frustration, however, the Fairmount Corridor's geography did not include *all* poor neighborhoods in the city. In particular, no reasonable definition included East Boston, a neighborhood near Logan International Airport on the northeast side of the city. On every indicator of disadvantage, East Boston is on par with "the Fairmount neighborhoods":

> We have a concentration of investments [grants] in these neighborhoods because, well, they're high need . . . People wound up there not because of the train line, but because, well, if you're working in Boston, [then] Roxbury, Dorchester, Mattapan, and . . . East Boston are the places that tend to have the worst outcomes in "fill in the blank." Every single measure we could come up with, the outcomes are going to be poorer in those four communities.

Whereas TBF had recently incorporated a "Fairmount frame" into operations, "[n]obody really talks about 'the East Boston frame.'" The issue with TBF's "Fairmount frame," she suggested, was that it ignored other places in need.

The emphasis on the Fairmount Corridor also ignored other poor, primarily Latino inner-ring suburbs like Lynn, Revere, and Chelsea. The program director explained that the same rationale justifying special attention for the Corridor also applied to these low-income Latino areas:

> Do I think that we could as easily step back and have a cohort of investments that look like this in Lynn, Revere, Chelsea, and East Boston, and call it our "Latino" frame? Absolutely. I mean of course we could. Anybody's paying attention to those communities knows that those communities—I mean East Boston is probably, what, 70 percent non-English-as-a-first-language speakers. They're probably a *majority* . . . Spanish-speaking Latino immigrant. If you tack on Chelsea, you tack on Revere, you tack on Lynn? The low-income [suburbs]—you know, you could do this exact same work. (her emphasis)

When Geeta treated the Fairmount Corridor as a stand-in for TBF's grants to poor neighborhoods, that meant other disadvantaged neighborhoods weren't being considered. Coordinating grants in a particular geography made the Corridor legible in a way that suited her interests, but it also inadvertently narrowed TBF's vision and provided an incomplete picture of poverty in the city.[17]

"The Corridor is a constructed concept," Geeta told me over coffee in 2016. "It's funny. Like, it's in the newspapers, [city government's] talking about it, and there really was no—there really is no 'Corridor'!" The Corridor's geography was a product of "myth creation," she said, and the myth had become a reality.

Geeta was right: There was no such thing as *the* Fairmount Corridor. There were many Fairmount Corridors, each with a slightly different geography. Various players in urban governance made the Corridor legible in distinct ways that corresponded with their individual interests and pursuit of resources. Sometimes that meant reimagining the Corridor as Roxbury, Dorchester, and Mattapan—and not Hyde Park. Other times that meant depicting a continuous greenway adjacent to the railroad tracks—a form of land use that was incompatible with the reality on the ground. And other times it meant creating a single, top-down identity for distinct neighborhoods that intersected with a rail line. The Corridor became a *politically* salient place even if it lacked any unifying *social* or *geographical* identity.

The shifting boundaries suggest two findings about power in urban governance. First, certain people, including nonprofit leaders, foundation staff, and consultants, had the power to reshape geographical boundaries. Second, there is an important brand of power inherent in community boundaries. If consultants had excluded South Station from the Fairmount Corridor Planning Initiative, then BRA officials would have had a harder time connecting their plans to other city government priorities. If Milly had depicted the Corridor as eight independent neighborhoods rather than three large neighborhood districts, then it would have been more difficult to claim planning resources for Mattapan. If the Fairmount Greenway did not include "grapes" along its zigzagging path, then nonprofit leaders in the Corridor may not have been able to secure resources for community gardens and parks. If Geeta did not propose a "Fairmount frame," then TBF would have appeared less intentional in its grant-making, and organizations in the Corridor may not have been able to acquire the same level of philanthropic support. Defining community boundaries was not merely an academic exercise; it was a materially consequential process that affected both resource allocation and policy attention.

These findings also reveal unintended consequences of urban policy's emphasis on transit-oriented development (TOD). The logic of TOD is sound: Dense development near public transit reduces residents' reliance on cars and is good for the environment. The problem was that people working in other policy areas—housing, open space, philanthropy, and so on—twisted themselves into pretzels trying to tie their work into the rail line. Geeta reoriented TBF's grants knowing full well that Boston's poorest neighborhoods extended beyond walking distance to the Fairmount Line. City officials spent a nontrivial amount of money on consultants to "brand" the transit corridor for economic development planning, but, as one city official later admitted to me, "In all honesty, it's not like we at the City are going to be implementing it." "Would

I do it again for a corridor in a planning study?" he continued. "Probably not." The branding exercise may have benefited nonprofits hoping to market the *transit line*, but it did not include enough economic analysis for much beyond that. Tying neighborhood planning to transit inadvertently limited policymaking in other domains.

Given this emphasis on transit, how generalizable are the scenes described in this chapter? Some, like branding the Corridor and redrawing neighborhood boundaries in relation to transit, may only apply to transit corridors and transit-oriented development projects. Others are more broadly applicable. It should not surprise us that Milly reframed the eight Corridor neighborhoods as three neighborhood districts; Chicago School sociologists and the many critical urban theorists who followed persuasively depict *all* urban communities as more symbolic constructions than "natural" areas. Nor should we interpret the Fairmount Greenway Task Force's squiggly line on a map or TBF's antipoverty strategy as unusual. Community development organizations and their funders work on a variety of projects, many of which are not spatially connected. To be seen as competent, strategic, and mission-oriented, these organizations have an incentive to portray projects as geographically aligned. There is an additional parallel here with gerrymandering, a common practice in which politicians redraw voting districts in order to maintain political power.[18]

Private funders and other nonprofit leaders proposed variations on the Corridor's boundaries to pursue their political interests. In the next section, I turn my attention to these organizations. Focusing on their roles in urban governance, I reveal the important, sometimes unintended, ways nonprofit leaders affected democratic representation and neighborhood inequality.

Part II

CHAPTER FOUR

Representing the Community

THE ERIE-ELLINGTON HOMES, an affordable housing project in Four Corners, is named for its cross streets. In addition to nineteen duplex and triplex townhomes, the project includes a stand-alone community center. It's the kind of place with well-worn linoleum floors, where a few folding tables line the walls and stackable plastic chairs are arranged in rows. The space is part public, part private; it mainly hosts events for people who live in the privately managed Erie-Ellington Homes, but it can also be rented out for public meetings pertaining to broader neighborhood issues.

On a rainy night in September 2011, about thirty people shuffled in to the community center to hear a proposal by City Growers, a Black-owned, for-profit agriculture business, to convert a vacant, city-owned lot on nearby Glenway Street into a small, half-acre urban farm. The company co-sponsored the meeting with city officials and the Greater Four Corners Action Coalition (GFCAC), a local community-based organization. Two city officials—one white, one Black—sat in the front left corner of the room. Marvin Martin, GFCAC's Black executive director, moderated.

The meeting began at 6pm, but Four Corners' Black city councilor, Charles Yancey, wouldn't arrive until 6:45.

Councilor Yancey was the first to speak after City Growers' presentation. He rose from his seat in the audience and moved to the front of the room, facing the crowd. He called the plans "seductive," but he worried about environmental hazards associated with construction. And he had an even bigger concern: "The project is not from the community," he declared. "It was imposed on the community, top-down." He asked neighborhood residents to stand next to their seats. Just three of the thirty people in attendance stood up. Councilor Yancey asked each of them, one by one, how they had heard about the meeting and whether they agreed with his objections to the urban farm.

Behind Councilor Yancey, the city officials appeared frustrated. One sighed deeply and threw his hands up in the air as the councilor questioned participants. Another called out, "Oh, Lord!" and rolled his eyes as Councilor Yancey speculated—without any evidence—that dangerous gas tanks might be buried beneath the proposed farm.

Marvin sensed the meeting was getting out of control. As Councilor Yancey spoke, he walked quietly around the perimeter of the room and approached the councilor from behind. He tapped Councilor Yancey's shoulder and whispered into his ear. When he finished, Councilor Yancey abruptly sat down.

"I've been informed that I've overstayed my welcome," Councilor Yancey announced from his seat, "in my own district."

Marvin resumed his position at the front of the room. "We need to have a process, and you can't just ask ten questions," he told the group. Turning to Councilor Yancey, he added, "You will never overstay your welcome, Councilor Yancey. But at the beginning of the meeting, we set rules for a process."

Out of earshot, the Black city official muttered, "Thank you!"

Saving face, Councilor Yancey let out an embarrassed chuckle. "I was just trying to forward it along!" he yelled out from his seat.

The meeting continued with routine questions about limiting pollution from idling trucks and the process for hiring local residents to work on the proposed farm. Earnest, Councilor Yancey's Black manager of constituent services, asked the final question of the evening:

> At what point has the community told you that they want this? From my understanding—and I've been at just about every single meeting—we've had members of the community tell you that they *don't* want it. So at what point has a majority of the community, from each of these parcels that you're proposing this for, stated to you, "Yes, this is something I want"? Because we just continuously hear otherwise. (his emphasis)

The white city official asked Marvin to respond, but Earnest interrupted. "I'm asking the city. I'm not asking Mr. Martin, with all due respect."

"Mr. Martin is part of the conversation, though," the Black city official quickly responded, "because he runs the community group—the local community group in the area."

"Excuse me," Councilor Yancey interjected, standing back up. "But I represent the community. And am elected. And *I* think that question should be answered." He said that he supported urban agriculture in principle but remained concerned about this project's negative environmental impacts and what he believed was insufficient "community support." He asked rhetorically, "How can I be a responsible elected representative from this area if that's not [addressed]?"

"I have to be forthcoming, and say that we also spoke to people," Marvin responded, "and the majority of people we talked to were in favor of this project." Nevertheless, he agreed to conduct more outreach and organize a second meeting. "It's not unusual for us to have more than one community meeting to resolve an issue."

Ralph, a Latino community organizer with GFCAC, spoke from his spot in the back of the room. He told the group that the organization would submit a letter to city officials regarding soil testing and other issues discussed at the meeting. "Let us do our jobs," he insisted. Councilor Yancey sat back down, and the meeting ended shortly thereafter.

City Growers began farming on the Four Corners lot the following summer.

Social scientists have long been interested in questions of organizations and politics, representation and democracy, and urban neighborhoods and poverty. Only recently have we begun to consider the intersection of these topics: how organizations' place in politics impacts local democracy and the availability of resources in poor neighborhoods.

Nonprofit community-based organizations (CBOs) deserve special attention. Like other tax-exempt nonprofits, CBOs cannot endorse candidates for office or otherwise participate in partisan electoral politics. Lobbying is allowed, though it can only account for an "insubstantial" amount of an organization's resources. The ambiguity causes some nonprofits to avoid lobbying altogether.[1]

Yet nonprofits *do* engage in politics, particularly at the local level. Some scholars depict CBOs as third-party arms of government. Because government often funds CBOs to implement community development plans, this perspective depicts CBOs as an extension of government, distributing public resources to urban residents.[2] Others see CBOs as interest groups, persuading government agencies and politicians to allocate resources to certain populations.[3] For still others, CBOs replaced urban political machines: Nonprofit leaders encourage clients or other organizational participants to vote for particular district-based elected politicians, and in exchange, winning politicians steer government-controlled grants and contracts to the mobilized CBOs.[4]

The scene from Four Corners points to an alternative understanding of CBOs' place in urban governance. When the meeting took place, Charles Yancey was an elected representative—a fifteen-term incumbent, in fact. And yet, in that room of nonprofit leaders, government bureaucrats, and neighborhood residents, he was hardly treated as the representative of his own district. Instead, staff from GFCAC took control and acted as if *they* were the neighborhood's true representatives. Councilor Yancey attempted to assert his legitimacy as an elected official—a person elected to represent his constituents in this neighborhood—but was unable to overrule Marvin and other GFCAC staff.

This was not an unusual occurrence. In the Fairmount Corridor, nonelected government officials, private funders, and other redevelopment players viewed nonprofits like GFCAC as more authentic neighborhood representatives than were elected politicians. Nonprofit leaders acted as "gatekeepers" over local neighborhood development, and similar to a state senator or city councilor, tried to steer the allocation of public and private resources to their districts. Elected representatives never missed a ribbon cutting or ceremonial groundbreaking, what political scientist David Mayhew identifies as the important act of credit-claiming.[5] But they were largely absent from private discussions of community development planning—the moments when actual decisions were made. Nonprofit leaders were, in effect, nonelected neighborhood representatives.[6]

The results were a mixed bag for Corridor residents. On the one hand, community organizations were empowered and neighborhoods with strong CBOs gained notable access to resources. It was, in many ways, an improvement on the past and exactly what progressive social activists in the 1960s had hoped for. Yet on the other hand, resource access came at the expense of democratic representation. CBOs lack formal accountability mechanisms, and moreover, professionalization in the sector removed any expectation that directors live in the neighborhoods they claimed to represent.

CBOs' ascent also unintentionally created a new mechanism of inequality: Neighborhoods lacking effective CBO representation had limited access to resources. An elected politician alone could do very little without a CBO to accept grants, manage funds, and implement community development plans. The emergence of CBOs as nonelected neighborhood representatives therefore affected urban inequality in complex ways, offsetting some mechanisms of disadvantage while introducing others. It presented a central tension in community development politics today: a tradeoff between democratic representation and access to much-needed community development resources.

"This Is Like the Senate"

One of the first things I noticed while observing nonprofit leaders in the Fairmount Corridor was that they referred to neighborhoods in the possessive—as in, "*my* neighborhood" or "*our* neighborhood"—even when they weren't residents themselves. Jeanne, executive director of Dorchester Bay Economic Development Corporation (DBEDC) in Upham's Corner, was a prime example. She consistently referred to predominantly Black, low-income Upham's Corner as "my neighborhood" in conversations with government officials, funders, and other nonprofit leaders. Yet Jeanne, a white woman in her sixties, lived in the white, middle-class neighborhood of Roslindale.

The grammar of community ownership extended beyond CBO directors. Neighborhood names served as shorthand for organizations; Codman Square Neighborhood Development Corporation (CSNDC) became simply "Codman Square." Individual staff embodied both the organization and the neighborhood. If, for example, someone asked if "Codman" attended a meeting, they meant a particular person working for a specific CBO located in the Codman Square neighborhood.

Nonprofit leaders also adopted a language that mirrored electoral politics. They referred to their coalitions as "caucuses," organizational goals as "campaigns," and local residents as "constituents." Goals were not *always* referred to as "campaigns" and residents were not *always* viewed as "constituents," but it happened frequently enough to stand out as I conducted my fieldwork.

Assertions of neighborhood representation were especially salient when CBO leaders negotiated their positions vis-à-vis other players in the community development field. Consider the Boston Redevelopment Authority's (BRA) Fairmount Corridor Planning Initiative, announced in February 2012. As outlined in chapter 3, the mayor selected a twenty-six-member advisory group to help guide the initiative. The advisory group included board members from each of the nonprofit developers in the Corridor, as well as a seat for Mat, the white consultant who represented the coalition of nonprofit developers. Other members included landowners, for-profit developers, architects, bike advocates, and historic preservationists. The group met monthly to vet ideas prepared by a BRA-hired consultant team.

Mat recognized an opportunity to influence the allocation of planning resources—but it would require some politicking. He suggested forming a "caucus" of the nonprofit developers and their board members on the advisory group. These seven members—Mat plus the three directors and their three board members—would "strategize about upcoming [advisory group] meetings and agendas," he proposed, and "see if we can . . . have a clear unified position."

The caucus met monthly, at 8am, at a Dorchester diner known for hosting campaign fundraisers and other political meetings. Fittingly, the diner abutted the Fairmount Line, so passing trains could be seen through large windows as the group ate breakfast and strategized.

The December 2012 meeting focused on BRA resources for local economic development plans. The Corridor planning initiative, you'll recall, included a plan for the entire Corridor, as well as additional plans for three Corridor subneighborhoods. By this time, BRA officials had selected Upham's Corner as one of those three neighborhoods. They would consult with the advisory group and begin planning processes in another two of the remaining seven Corridor neighborhoods. The caucus members represented Upham's Corner, Codman Square, and Hyde Park, and so they hoped to steer the remaining resources to Codman Square and Hyde Park. But how?

In between bites of her omelet, Jeanne suggested recruiting "allies" on the advisory group and "building relationships" with them. "This is like the Senate," she said:

> Think about the Senate, how they make all these deals. I just saw [the 2012 film] *Lincoln* the other night, and the way they had to get

the [Thirteenth Amendment] ok'd, they had to deal one, by one, by one. And this is like being on the Senate, where you got people in the room who may not be your friends, but if you build relationships with them... you end up with allies.

Jeanne's metaphor reveals the extent to which CBO directors considered themselves legitimate district representatives. She did not see CBO leaders as one advocate among many, but political actors fundamentally responsible for the development of urban policy and the allocation of resources to "their" neighborhoods. The rest of the caucus members agreed.

At Jeanne's recommendation, the group conducted a "power analysis," following one of Saul Alinsky's well-known community organizing techniques. Jeanne wrote the names of each advisory group member on large sheets of paper and listed relationships of work, family, religion, and politics. The nonprofit leaders believed these relationships revealed each person's "self-interests." Self-interests, in turn, could be exploited to form alliances with advisory group members and influence their decisions. Each director used this knowledge in one-on-ones with BRA officials, members of the advisory group, and other supporters.

Gail dove head-first into the approach. Over the next three months, she met with five advisory group members and asked both a neighborhood association and a funder to send letters of support to city officials. Gail's efforts impressed the other members of the nonprofit caucus. "Great organizing Gail," Mat told her during a conference call in February 2013. "Fabulous. I think that's wonderful."

In March, the chief planner for the BRA called Gail to say that resources would be earmarked for Codman Square under the following fiscal year's budget. As Gail revealed to her fellow caucus members, another BRA official told her in no uncertain terms that the letters of support "made a difference for the way the BRA is looking at it."

Gail lived in Hyde Park during this episode. Yet, by taking charge as Codman Square's representative and gathering supporters who treated her accordingly, Gail secured a commitment for new resources. It is particularly notable that the money under discussion was for outside consultant-led neighborhood planning. These were resources for the *neighborhood*, not the organization; none of the funding supported CSNDC programming or operations—meaning that Gail was acting on behalf of the neighborhood, not just her organization.[7]

Neighborhood Gatekeepers

In February 2013, nonprofit leaders from the Fairmount Corridor gathered at City Hall to meet with city officials about plans for a "greenway"—the integrated, if sometimes disjointed, system of proposed parks, gardens, and bike paths along the Fairmount Line train tracks (discussed in more detail in chapter 3). They prepared a list of priority development sites on city-owned land and hoped to push city officials for a firm commitment of support.

Latoya, a Black community organizer, described a steep hill in Four Corners that GFCAC hoped to convert into an "urban wild" with new trees, a winding path, and signs describing local wildlife. "No arguments here," Karen, the white city official in charge of property disposition, responded. The incline made the site unappealing to city officials, so they were happy to transfer ownership to a local organization.

Jay, a Black architect with the city, spoke up from the back of the room. "We have a meeting with a neighborhood organization that's interested in a license to turn it into some kind of farm, or orchard farm," he said. The nonprofit leaders and organizers flashed each other quizzical looks.

"Those same parcels?" one asked.

"Yeah," Jay responded. "I thought they had talked to you [all]."

"That's interesting," Latoya said, speaking fast. "Because I know Greater Four Corners Action Coalition made that a priority parcel."

"Yeah, it's some sort of local organization, I guess," Jay said sheepishly. He didn't remember the organization's name.

"Well maybe you can give her that information of who it is," Karen directed Jay.

"Yeah," Latoya retorted. "Because I would love to know."

Jay agreed to dig through his email and find the contact information, and Latoya said she would pass the information on to GFCAC's executive director, Marvin, who was unable to attend the meeting.

In March, the coalition of nonprofits met in CSNDC's conference room to debrief from the meeting. As people trickled through the front door and passed out agendas, Latoya asked Marvin whether he had learned any more about the mysterious organization with plans for a development project in Four Corners. As it turned out, the organization wasn't an organization at all; the unknown developer was a landscape architect from Four Corners.

"I know about it, yeah. They're going to be working with us," Marvin replied confidently.

"When I heard it at the meeting [in City Hall], I was like, 'Wait, what? I don't think so!' . . . Because I know not much goes underneath Marvin's nose. He's pretty much on top of everything," Latoya observed with a knowing smile.

Everyone in the room chuckled.

"Yeah," Marvin responded, slowly dragging out the word. "It's gonna be hard for anyone to get anything there without coming to us and getting our blessing."

Over the next few months, Marvin met with the architect and took over the planning process. The architect could participate in the design of the development—providing his architectural expertise, free of charge—but Marvin, the neighborhood's representative, retained ultimate authority over the project. It was a project for Four Corners, and no project proceeded in Four Corners without approval or direction from the local community-based organization.

Conduits for the Community

It is not easy to enter the CSNDC offices. The floor-to-ceiling glass windows and bright green storefront certainly look inviting. But the building is always locked. Visitors must press a small button to the right of the front door, alerting a receptionist. The receptionist pushes another button, the door buzzes, and visitors gain temporary access to the building. CNSDC is the kind of place you only visit if you have an appointment.

In August 2012, Gail hosted an 8am meeting in the organization's conference room. Attendees included Gail, her colleagues from the coalition of nonprofit developers, and representatives from three private funding organizations. Over bagels and coffee, the nonprofit grantees shared their accomplishments from the past year and, when appropriate, asked for additional resources to overcome specific gaps in their upcoming budgets.

The meeting was also a chance for the funders to explain why they offered financial or political support—reasons above and beyond typical benchmarks of "impact," like housing units built or jobs created. Geeta, associate vice president for programs at The Boston Foundation (TBF), succinctly explained why TBF had previously awarded the coalition a $1 million grant: "You're the holders of community," she told them. "You're the community presence."

The statement was neither unusual nor remarkable. From the perspective of private funders like Geeta, nonprofits are grassroots organizations, working on the ground to help local residents. They exist, by definition, to advocate on behalf of the communities in which they are located—even if their offices are not easily accessible.

That assumption is rooted in a structural relationship between resource holders and nonprofit grantees. If a funder wanted to provide a grant to a neighborhood, the funder needed a CBO to accept the money and manage the funds. This grant-giving relationship directly incentivized funders to defer to nonprofit leaders as de facto community representatives. In 2010, for example, Local Initiatives Support Corporation (LISC), a community development intermediary, announced a $400,000 neighborhood development planning initiative in two Corridor neighborhoods. They selected a CBO "partner" in each neighborhood to act as their local liaison. LISC staff referred to these CBOs as "communities," using each CBO's name and "the community" interchangeably, as if one was a stand-in for the other. Funders wanted to give money to *communities*. The only way to do that was to fund *CBOs*.

City officials behaved similarly. Consider, again, the Fairmount Corridor Planning Initiative. The BRA relied on a mayor-appointed committee of

CBO = community

Corridor stakeholders to relay information from local residents. The group, dominated by CBO leaders, was officially called the Corridor Advisory Group. But during a September 2013 meeting, a white urban planner referred to it as the "Community Advisory Group"—a Freudian slip implying that the CBO leaders were, in fact, stand-ins for "community" oversight. He called them "a much better conduit to the people and neighborhoods than I can [be]." At a meeting later that month, the same planner noted, "While you are the advisory group and the focal point, it's really . . . the community. But you guys are my point folks to these stakeholder groups . . . I look to you first, as conduits."

This is an *expectation* of representation—an expectation that foundation officers and public officials conveyed explicitly when meeting with CBO leaders. Take Tom Tinlin, the head of the Boston Transportation Department. In November 2012, he told representatives from three Corridor CBOs, "You know the neighborhoods better than we will," and asked for *their* guidance when redeveloping city streets.

Officials also communicated this expectation to residents. In January 2012, for instance, city officials hosted a public meeting to discuss the development of parks and other types of recreational spaces in Codman Square. The meeting began at 6pm. Within an hour, there were approximately fifty people in attendance. Officials stood at the front of the room, near aerial photographs of empty lots. During a question-and-answer period, an elderly white woman asked, "So if the community wants open space, would they need a nonprofit to buy [the land parcel]?" Yes, a white city official replied; if a nonprofit were interested, they could buy it for as little as $100. A middle-aged Black woman asked a follow-up question. She wanted to be sure that the plot would remain recreational space "if the community wants to keep it that way." "It's ok for it to stay in the community," another city official, a Black man in his early thirties, responded, "but the community needs to be an organization like a nonprofit that has the capacity to manage the plots." The officials were clear: As far as city government was concerned, a *CBO* moving forward with a project—specifically, one "that has the capacity to manage the plots"—was functionally equivalent to *the community* moving forward with a project.

In favoring CBOs as representatives, government bureaucrats sometimes intentionally bypassed local elected politicians. In July 2011, Theresa McMillan, deputy administrator for the Federal Transportation Administration (FTA), requested a tour of the Corridor and a meeting with CBOs to discuss transportation development in the Corridor. An FTA official emailed the CBO directors and deferred to them as neighborhood "stakeholders" in charge of representing "your community/communities" at the meeting. The official also noted that elected representatives were barred from participating:

> As indicated, this is a meeting between FTA and you, Fairmount/Indigo Line stakeholders—*there will be nobody from the [state transportation*

authority], the State, the City; no elected officials & no press. The intent is a frank discussion of what went well and is going well with respect to meeting the needs of your community/communities (e.g., the capital investments), as well as what might not be living up to your expectations (e.g., a commitment to provide rapid transit-type service levels or fares), and what is still a work in progress. (emphasis in original)

The tour and meeting occurred on July 11. No elected officials attended.

Other organizations, like government agencies and private funders, validated CBO leaders' claims and legitimated their roles as representatives. With few direct links to poor neighborhoods in the Corridor, these outside groups and agencies were incentivized to defer to CBOs. Treating CBOs as "conduits for community" allowed other players to feel as though they were attuned to the community without having to put much effort into determining whether that was actually true.

A Political Strategy without Politicians

While nonprofit leaders in the Corridor spoke about "politics" in terms of elected officials, they rarely developed political strategies targeting state legislators or city councilors. Instead, they focused their energy on appointed bureaucrats and foundation program officers—those with direct access to community development resources.

CBO leaders consistently brought up these political targets during their meetings. One especially acute instance occurred during a December 2012 meeting of the CDC coalition. Six months earlier, the BRA had begun the Corridor planning initiative. It was a sign that city government would commit more resources to the Corridor, and the members of the coalition (at the time, Jeanne, Gail, and Mike) strategized ways to access those resources and attention. Gail suggested targeting the person who "really is in charge": the redevelopment authority's chief planner, Kairos Shen. As she explained:

> If our goal is to see if we can get them to ... work with us and actually think about getting some things off the ground and writing some joint proposals and not passing up opportunities, then it feels like to me it's a meeting that needs to happen with someone like Kairos, or someone who really is in charge of this whole planning process. Not the mayor, but Kairos.

A month later, Jeanne reiterated Gail's suggestion. She recommended the coalition adopt a strategy aimed at "who really has the power at the [redevelopment authority], besides the mayor": the agency's director, Peter Meade, and its chief planner, Kairos Shen. Both men were appointed city executives.

Private funders were targets of CBO political action, too. This was especially apparent when funders balked at nonprofits' funding requests. In November 2010, for instance, the CDC coalition received a $7,500 grant from a national bank for foreclosure assistance. Jeanne was upset about the size of the grant and suggested "a political power meeting" to make bank officials understand how little can be accomplished with the paltry sum. The strategy worked: ongoing conference calls and emails with bank officials led to two $100,000 grants in August 2012 and November 2013, respectively.

Throughout my fieldwork, Jeanne repeatedly encouraged Sherry, the CDC coalition's fundraising consultant, to "be more political" as she did her job. Jeanne referred to her own fundraising strategy, which involved targeted calls with trustees and board members of national banks and foundations, as "relational politics." She was particularly interested in making connections with major national foundations like the Surdna Foundation, Annie E. Casey Foundation, Ford Foundation, and Barr Foundation—sources of huge sums of money that were, at that point, largely uninterested in the Fairmount Corridor. During a meeting of CDC directors and consultants in December 2012, Jeanne compared the fundraising strategy to warfare, declaring, "We need a political organizing strategy—not just Sherry looking for grants on the Internet. We need a war room strategy."

After that meeting, Sherry gave Mat, who was also a consultant at the time, a ride to the nearby train station. I sat in the back seat, listening as they discussed Jeanne's instructions to initiate a "political" fundraising strategy.

"When she says be more political, does she mean with the funders? Or the politicians?" Mat asked Sherry.

"She means with the funders," Sherry replied. "But by going and sitting down. Going to New York and talking to [the large foundation]."

"Well that is a big part of fundraising," Mat agreed, "the schmoozing." He recommended Sherry speak with the director of Communications at the Massachusetts Association of Community Development Corporations (MACDC), a statewide association of nonprofit developers. "He's someone you should get to know . . . [He] really knows the funding world well." Sherry heeded his advice, committing to a more proactive, relationship-driven fundraising strategy.

Lists of political targets offered another window into nonprofits' political priorities. On seven occasions between 2011 and 2013, I observed nonprofit leaders from the Corridor develop these strategic documents. In each instance, private funders and bureaucrats were the key targets, and elected representatives were either the last noted, or completely ignored. On one advocacy strategy document, the coalition of nonprofit leaders listed elected officials under the head "Potential Supporters" rather than "Decision Makers" or even "Key Players."

In today's political context, appointed bureaucrats and foundation program officers, not elected representatives, controlled many community development grants. And so, when CBO leaders wanted to influence the allocation of these resources, they negotiated with bureaucrats and funders directly, speaking on behalf of poor neighborhoods.

Avoiding and Outsourcing Electoral Politics

In late March 2013, Mayor Thomas M. Menino announced that he would not seek reelection. To put it mildly, the announcement was a big deal in Boston politics. With a twenty-year tenure, Menino was the city's longest-serving mayor, and he'd been a district city councilor for ten years before that. More than a dozen candidates pulled papers to run in the September primary. And that wasn't the only hotly contested position up for grabs: Nineteen candidates ran for four citywide City Council seats, and there were twenty-eight candidates for nine district City Council seats. The city was poised for a major political shakeup.

With such high stakes, I expected to see nonprofit leaders in the Corridor coalesce around preferred candidates—particularly in the mayoral race, a presumably important position with respect to community development policy. But, beyond speculating about possible entrants into the race or casually chatting about candidates' strengths and weaknesses, there seemed to be no strategy to support any particular candidate's election bid.

Like me, consultants for the nonprofits were surprised. During the lead-up to the election, Michael and Mat discussed their employers' political strategy as the three of us waited for a bus after a meeting. Michael was recently hired, and he asked Mat about the history of Corridor CDCs working with elected representatives. "There is *no* history!" Mat exclaimed, his eyes wide. Michael was incredulous.

Mat had plenty of experience working with elected officials, he explained. In 1983, when Mat was the director of another CDC in Boston, "we basically ran one of our former directors to be on the City Council." When a development project faced resistance from City Hall, Mat called this councilor who, in turn, called the appropriate agency directors. The project was reconsidered. "That's how it works!" Mat exclaimed. "That's how it works! And these guys [the Fairmount Corridor CDC directors] don't get it!"

Mat's experience in the 1980s fits with research by sociologist Nicole Marwell—the basis of my expectations. Marwell argues that CBOs mobilize local constituencies to vote for particular candidates, and winning candidates reward CBOs with special privileges, such as grants and contracts. The theory draws on the case of State Assemblyman Vito Lopez, a Brooklyn Democrat and founding director of the Ridgewood Bushwick Senior Citizens Council (RBSCC), a social service nonprofit. In the 1990s, RBSCC staff helped mobilize the organization's client base to vote for Lopez. Once in office, Lopez steered state social service contracts to the organization.[8] Yet, even though the Corridor CBO directors seemed politically astute, they did not engage in a similar strategy.

It is possible that these activities did in fact occur and I did not observe them because of incomplete access. One particular case gives me pause. In 2013, John Barros resigned as director of the Dudley Street Neighborhood Initiative (DSNI), a Corridor CBO, and declared his candidacy for mayor. Barros resembles Vito Lopez, but with one important difference: Barros lost the election. It was a crowded primary field, including twelve candidates, and Barros tied for sixth place, receiving just 8 percent of the vote. In the general election, Barros endorsed eventual winner Marty Walsh and accepted a job as chief of economic development when Walsh took office. In the primary, most of the Corridor coalition *directors* expressed support for candidates other than Barros. However, I do not know whether DSNI *staff* mobilized voters for their former director, nor can I say whether DSNI staff mobilized voters for his eventual preferred candidate, Marty Walsh, in the general election. Undoubtedly, many DSNI staff personally supported Barros, but it was unclear whether they collaborated in any organizational effort around the election.

Aware of potential holes in my fieldwork and motivated by the existing literature, I decided to dig deeper. While catching a ride to another meeting, I asked Joan, a consultant and former DBEDC board president, why the nonprofit directors did not select preferred candidates and advocate—even informally—for their election She ignored my insinuation and responded by telling me *her* preferred mayoral candidate.

I tried to rephrase and clarified that I meant a broader organizational effort, not just support as individuals. By way of response, Joan referenced legislative advocacy by associations and intermediary organizations, such as the Massachusetts Association of Community Development Corporations (MACDC). The statewide organization's staff hosted an annual "lobby day" at the statehouse and encouraged community development nonprofits to meet regularly with state representatives.[9]

A number of times during my fieldwork, I observed the kind of outsourcing of legislative advocacy Joan described. In one instance, Corridor CBOs relied on Transportation for Massachusetts (T4MA), a regional coalition, to pressure state legislators on transportation issues. When Governor Deval Patrick proposed a transportation bond bill in 2013, T4MA lobbied members of the House to vote the bill down in favor of a larger budget. The coalition of Corridor CBOs symbolically "signed on" to that effort, but they did not send representatives to a T4MA-sponsored public demonstration in April. When the Corridor CBOs engaged with transportation issues, they met privately with executives. Legislative politics was left to the regional association.

"But, I love this [electoral politics] stuff," Joan admitted in the car. She described door knocking and phone banking for candidates, and she happily claimed to have persuaded one of her neighbors to vote for her preferred candidate in a recent special election.

That particular candidate supported the work of Corridor nonprofits. I used the example to prod: "So, she gets elected, everyone will support her *personally*, but *organizationally—*," I started to say.

Joan cut me off. "Well, nonprofits really can't make endorsements," she said with indifference.

"Right, sure," I responded. There was a pause. As I opened my mouth to discuss the point further, Joan started speaking at the same time, and our conversation moved to another topic.

I also asked Mike, executive director of Southwest Boston Community Development Corporation (SWBCDC), about the two candidates for the District 5 City Councilor race. One candidate was a former SWBCDC board member, and another was the director of a nonprofit business development organization in the neighborhood. Had Mike been approached to support either candidate?

"I haven't been," Mike told me in May as we waited in the lobby for a meeting at the state transportation authority. "You know, maybe because they're keeping in mind that I'm in kind of a public position, or whatever. I don't know." I pressed further, explaining that I understood the legal restrictions on political endorsements, but organizations in other cities *informally* rallied behind particular candidates. "I just try to keep it as bright, a hard line as I can, you know. Because I just don't want to mess with that," he responded. He then told me how a local resident had asked if he would host a fundraiser at SWBCDC for a mayoral candidate from the district. "If we want to lose our nonprofit status!" Mike responded in a mocking tone. "You know, that's the implication."

A Haphazard Attempt at Electoral Politicking

In their official capacity, nonprofit leaders in the Corridor saw their work as political, but generally steered clear of elected politicians. There was one exception. In April 2013, organizers and other staff from the coalition of Corridor CBOs met to discuss high fares and infrequent service on the Fairmount Line. At the time, each trip on the line cost $5.50 (compared to $2 on the rapid rail system), and there was no weekend or evening service. To many, the pricing—determined by concentric "zones" around the city center—seemed arbitrary. The state transportation authority classified the Fairmount Line as "Zone 1," so a trip on the line was priced the same as a trip to the suburbs, even though it ran completely within the city of Boston.[10] The coalition members agreed that a mayoral forum of some sort could help achieve a fare reduction. They began calling the prospective event "Get on Board"—a play on words signaling support for reduced fares and increased service.

In May, the nonprofit leaders began planning the forum in earnest. The meeting included a mix of mostly white directors and consultants and mostly Black and Latino organizers. From the start, there was confusion about the purpose of the forum. Mela, a Black community organizer, called it "a community forum with the mayoral candidates and elected officials." "We haven't had this type of meeting with the public, as of yet," Mela reminded everyone. "And so we need the public to get on board. And we need the candidates to get on board. And we need our elected officials to get on board." The focus would be on the community, she said, and mayoral candidates would be "special guests."

Mike responded with concern about the logistics of a forum that included both candidates *and* other elected officials. To him, that wasn't a mayoral forum. Typically, candidates sit on a stage and field questions from a moderator. Similar forums were occurring throughout the city, and he worried that this alternative model would confuse both the candidates and audience members.

For approximately fifty minutes, the group debated the framing and target for the event. Should it be "a candidates' forum," where nonprofit leaders pressed the mayoral candidates about their support for improvements on the Fairmount Line? Or should it be "a community forum," in which the central purpose was to gin up community support and candidates were invited to observe? And why should the event be limited to mayoral candidates? Shouldn't current elected officials, in both city and state government, be invited? The conversation moved in circles, and the group tossed out contrasting proposals: Structure the event as "a candidates' forum," "a community forum," "a community forum, with invited guests," or "a candidates forum for the community."

Finally, Jeanne proposed a structure that everyone seemed to agree with: First, get the mayoral candidates to agree to support improved service and lower fares; then, reeducate the broader public about the benefits of the transit line. They would invite incumbent officials but would not offer them a special platform to speak. "An odd tradition about Boston, for me," Jeanne wryly observed, "is that they always recognize the elected officials like they're gods. And I guess you have to do that here, huh? Or you're rude."

The conversation was confusing. At times, even the attendees seemed to have trouble following. Part of the problem was structural: The framing kept drifting away from a focus on mayoral candidates because mayors do not control statewide transportation budgets and scheduling. Though no one at the meeting said it in these terms, a mayor cannot change state policy directly. The best-case scenario was that a new mayor would be willing to help the Corridor nonprofits lobby the state for more favorable transportation policy. The nonprofit leaders saw mayoral forums springing up around the city and believed a similar forum might help them achieve their transportation policy goals. The back and forth about the format of the event suggests an unstated acknowledgment that electoral politicking may have been insufficient to achieve those goals—and electoral politicking with mayoral candidates may have been *particularly* insufficient.[11]

Nevertheless, after two more meetings to hash out the precise language, the final flyer for the event read:

A Community Discussion with
MAYORAL CANDIDATES
and other elected officials

"MAYORAL CANDIDATES"—bolded, underlined, all caps, and printed in green—stood out from the rest of the flyer's text. Below, the phrase "and other elected officials" dangled like an afterthought.

The event occurred in mid-June. It drew about seventy-five people, including six mayoral candidates and representatives for two more. A columnist for the *Boston Globe* wrote, "[T]hey all agreed: Taking the Fairmount Line is too expensive."[12]

"This Has Nothing to Do with What the Candidates Were Out There Doing"

Nonprofit leaders in the Corridor considered the mayoral forum a major success. Did it affect transportation policy? At first blush, it seemed so. Six days after the event, Dr. Beverley Scott, the Black general manager for the state transportation authority, invited the coalition to her office, where she announced an eighteen-month to two-year fare reduction pilot program. It would coincide with the opening of three new stations in July and bring the cost of a ride on the Fairmount Line to $2—just like the other rapid rail lines.[13]

Digging deeper, the causal link between the forum and the transportation authority's decision is murkier. The fare issue was nothing new; it had been part of the nonprofits' advocacy for more than a decade. And the idea of a fare reduction pilot program was proposed during a meeting between the nonprofit leaders and state officials in *February*—before the forum, and before Mayor Menino even announced his retirement. A detailed sequence of events suggests it was state transportation officials' desire to avoid negative press, not support from mayoral candidates, that spurred the price drop.

On May 17, an article in the *Boston Globe* described the Fairmount Line as "fraught . . . with controversy," noting poor service, low ridership, and high fares.[14] Around the same time, Mela, the community organizer, said she received a call from a state representative relaying a message from Governor Patrick. The governor wanted to host ribbon cuttings for the new stations some time that summer, but worried there might be protests related to the Fairmount Line fares. Mela said that her organization's director was in active talks with the governor's office to ease any tension and plan a successful event.

The following week, Mela and other nonprofit staffers met with Dr. Scott at the transportation authority's downtown offices. Mela pressed for—but did not get—a commitment on a fare reduction, insinuating that even a proposed timeline would help avoid any "drama" at the new station openings. In response to this implicit reference to the governor's concerns, Dr. Scott replied decisively: "I'm just gonna tell ya: To wind up going to a Thrilla in Manila where everybody's out there with protest signs about fares, is not something that's gonna be productive." She would consider a fare reduction but could not fully commit. Seniors and youth were also "knocking down my door," Dr. Scott said, and she was unsure how much wiggle room she would have in the budget. The group agreed to reconvene in June.

The mayoral forum occurred on June 12; a reporter from the *Boston Globe* referred to it as a candidate forum focused on "the . . . controversial Fairmount commuter rail line."[15]

A week later, the group of nonprofit leaders and organizers from the Corridor met, again, with Dr. Scott and state transportation officials. Dr. Scott announced the fare reduction pilot program and everyone was elated. Jeanne wondered aloud whether, after what she saw as a successful forum, her nonprofit coalition could take credit for the fare reduction. Instantly, the tone of the meeting shifted. "Well, no, let me just tell you I don't—let me tell you what I don't do," Dr. Scott said. "This has nothing to do with what the candidates were out there doing. We had this already pre-determined, and so, I'm not trying to play to—whatever. Ok? You know what I'm saying?"

"Yeah, yeah," Jeanne acquiesced.

The meeting pivoted to publicity. It was at this point that the state officials presented an alternative motivation for the fare reduction. "There's been a series of articles in the *Globe* recently," a white official at the transportation authority said, referring to the articles from May and June. "The Fairmount Line has been—the adjective that the news reporters have used has been, 'The Controversial Fairmount Line.' But we're trying to change that."

In July, the ribbon cuttings for the new stations went off without a hitch. The press lauded the fare reduction.[16]

The mayoral forum and its aftermath reveals a somewhat confused foray into electoral politicking. The nonprofit leaders had a difficult time planning the forum, in part because it was focused on an issue beyond mayoral control. The format may have been easier to decide if they had focused on housing, zoning, or street repairs along the Corridor—in other words, something a mayor had the power to change. In fact, a second key takeaway is that the forum's ultimate targets—regardless of how the organizers described it—were clearly state bureaucrats and private funders. The nonprofit leaders did not follow up with the candidates on transportation issues after the forum. They did, however, describe the forum alongside other examples of accomplishments in their annual reports to funders, and used it as a talking point in meetings with Dr. Scott and other state transportation officials. The ultimate purpose of the group's intervention in municipal electoral politics was to get more money from funders and persuade state bureaucrats, not necessarily push city politicians toward any particular policy decision.[17]

In this regard, we can see a third takeaway: The forum was likely unnecessary. What no one mentioned, but is also worth noting, is that the state had reduced fares on the Fairmount Line before. In 1987, when the Upham's Corner and Morton Street Stations re-opened, the state used a fare reduction to raise awareness and increase ridership. It may have happened again in 2013, regardless of whether the nonprofits were involved with a mayoral forum.

Jeanne's ambivalence toward elected officials reveals a more general point. It is only an "odd tradition" to treat politicians "like gods" if they do not have much power. If they were key decision-makers in urban community development policy, it would have been a given that they would need to participate in a public forum. There is no doubt that the nonprofit leaders in the Fairmount Corridor were politically savvy; political savvy in the community development field just didn't necessarily require *electoral* savvy.

Nonprofit leaders in the Corridor expressed reverence for their elected representatives as "allies" and "supporters." But they did not refer to elected officials as neighborhood representatives. When meeting with other nonprofit directors from the Corridor, Gail once referred to two state representatives as "our political Geeta's," comparing them implicitly to funders who consistently praised the Corridor CBOs to appointed bureaucrats. The implication was that politicians and funders played roughly equivalent roles as outside advocates. In this particular place, in this particular historical moment, politicians supported CBOs, not the other way around.

The Marginal Role of Elected Representatives

Nonprofit leaders' ambivalence toward electoral politics makes sense when we consider elected representatives' diminished role in community development policymaking. During my fieldwork, elected officials rarely attended working meetings to plan projects. When they were present at public meetings, it was more often as passive spectators than active participants.

Even their spatial positions at these meetings were revealing. At a September 2013 meeting about the redevelopment of an abandoned factory in Dorchester, State Representative Carlos Henriquez entered an hour late and stood alone at the back of the room, unacknowledged. At a January 2011 meeting on transportation improvements in Roxbury, Dorchester, and Mattapan, State Senator Sonia Chang-Diaz stood against a wall in the back left corner of the room. At a May 2012 meeting about parks development in Mattapan, State Representative Russell Holmes sat at the *front* right corner of the room—but spent the majority of the meeting reading his mail. At a February 2013 meeting about street improvements in Dorchester, then-State Representative Linda Dorcena Forry sat in the back left corner for fifteen minutes, then left for another event. City Councilor Charles Yancey joined Dorcena Forry, Holmes, and Chang-Diaz at a November 2012 meeting about transportation access in Mattapan, and all four elected officials leaned against a wall on the right side of the room. They offered generic, clichéd remarks at the end of the meeting, after the substantive conversations had ended.

Elected officials' roles as neighborhood representatives were undermined—sometimes publicly, as when Marvin and GFCAC staff overrode Councilor Yancey's objections to urban agriculture in Four Corners. But at least officials there had recognized Charles Yancey as an elected representative. Surprisingly, many government bureaucrats were not personally familiar with the politicians elected to represent the Fairmount Corridor neighborhoods.

In December 2011, Lieutenant Governor Timothy Murray toured one of the Fairmount Corridor's new transit stations. City and state bureaucrats joined nonprofit leaders and local elected representatives on a cold, rainy morning to discuss redevelopment efforts. After the event, I rode in a car with three city officials—two white men and a Latina woman—on their way back to City Hall. An official with the redevelopment authority hadn't recognized one of the state representatives. "Who was that young Black man that spoke?" he asked as we exited the car. We explained that he was Carlos Henriquez, a state representative elected the previous year. "Huh," he shrugged.[18]

By the same token, some of the Fairmount Corridor's elected officials were unfamiliar with resource-controlling government bureaucrats. In February 2013, the BRA hosted a large public forum to plan community development projects in Upham's Corner. The forum followed six months of planning meetings, but it was the first time two elected officials attended anything related to the planning process. Neither State Representative Henriquez nor at-large City Councilor Ayanna Pressley knew the city official managing the process, who introduced himself and gave each a business card. The official recognized the politicians, but the politicians—who had been serving as constituent representatives for two and four years, respectively—were unfamiliar with the officials responsible for allocating community development resources.

Local politicians can still exert influence over bread-and-butter neighborhood issues like trash collection schedules or the placement of stop signs. They may also spend their time working on issues other than community development, like education, basic city services, or public safety.[19] Some of course do take on issues broadly related to urban development. In October 2019, for instance, at-large City Councilor Michelle Wu proposed a plan to abolish the Boston Development and Planning Agency, the umbrella agency created in 2016 that includes the BRA.[20] And while government bureaucrats design *policy*, new *legislation* requires bills that only elected officials can sponsor and vote on.

Consider for example the Community Investment Tax Credit (CITC). Signed into law by then-Governor Patrick in August 2012, the legislation provided a government incentive for private donations to community development nonprofits. Donors received a $1 tax credit from the state for every $2 donated to a community development organization—and this state tax credit could be taken on top of the federal tax deduction for charitable donations. Community development organizations registered with the state, and tax credits were allocated on a competitive basis, limited to $150,000 per organization per year for up to three years, and capped at $6 million annually.[21] State Representative Linda Dorcena Forry of Dorchester and State Senator Sal DiDemenico of Cambridge were the bill's lead sponsors—though it had forty-four additional co-sponsors as it made its way through the statehouse. It passed unanimously. The Fairmount Corridor nonprofits benefited tremendously from the new legislation, receiving more than $1.1 million in grants and tax credits as of 2017.

The CITC partially indicates the importance of elected representatives, who pass legislation to benefit their districts. But notably, the idea for the CITC began with Joe Kriesberg, MACDC's white executive director, and discussions at the Community Development Innovation Forum, a regular meeting of nonprofit development professionals Joe helped establish. In 2011, Joe wrote language for what he originally called the Community Development Partnership Act. He recruited Forry and DiDemenico to sponsor the bill and hounded the governor to work out the details. As a reporter for the *Boston Globe* put it, Joe "proposed the program and received legislative support" from the two elected officials.[22]

I do not want to suggest that this is an unusual arrangement; an important body of literature in political science shows how powerful interest groups craft legislative language and recruit elected officials to sponsor the resulting bills.[23] The scenario is common at all levels of American politics. Instead, my purpose is to show the implications of these relationships for local nonprofits, which were treated as neighborhood representatives in the process.

On this point, Joe's framing of legislators as "supporters" (rather than representatives) stood out. It was especially evident during the December 2012 meeting to introduce the new legislation. About seventy-five people attended the registration-required event, held in the Federal Reserve Bank of Boston. At the beginning of the meeting, Gail took the stage and thanked Representative Dorcena Forry and Senator DiDemenico, who she called "our legislative champions." Dorcena Forry and DiDemenico, the nonprofit director said, "really understood community development and the critical role it plays in our communities." The legislators, she added, were "two people who know how the legislative process works, who know how to rally their colleagues, and who know how to move legislation forward. When they agreed to serve as our lead sponsors, we know we had a chance to win."

Throughout the meeting, other nonprofit leaders used that same term—"legislative champions"—and, like Gail, used possessives as they described "their" neighborhoods.

The lawmakers seemed to acknowledge their relatively small role in the whole process. After accepting a modest plaque from Gail, Senator DiDemenico took the microphone and admitted, "The people in this room have worked very, very hard for this legislation. And Representative [Dorcena] Forry and myself, we're just the people that helped bring it along. But you folks did all the work. You folks put the language together."

That language—the text of the law itself—defined local nonprofits as neighborhood representatives. To be eligible for the tax credit allocation, organizations had to identify a geographic area of focus and "any particular constituencies the organization is dedicated to serving"—a direct overlap with elected politicians who represent particular constituencies within designated geographic areas. After community development organizations articulated neighborhood representation, the state allocated tax credits to organizations with "strong track records" and the "highest quality" plans for community development.

Three years later, there was a new governor, Republican Charlie Baker. He continued to support the CITC. At a meeting hosted by MACDC in November 2015, Governor Baker pledged to nearly double its funding. He, too, referred to the community development nonprofits as neighborhood representatives, noting, "[T]hey are absolutely the core of their communities."[24]

Elected politicians were necessary for passing the Community Investment Tax Credit. They had a formal function as lawmakers and played a ceremonial role during public announcements. They were notably not referred to as neighborhood representatives—at least not to the same extent as local nonprofits. The taken-for-granted logic of the law—from its original genesis to its final implementation—was that *CBOs* were the ultimate representatives of "their" neighborhoods.[25]

Neighborhood Representation and the Distribution of Resources

How did neighborhood representation affect the distribution of resources? One way to answer this question is to compare two neighborhoods, one containing a CBO and the other lacking a CBO representative. Midway through my fieldwork, the Mattapan Community Development Corporation filed for bankruptcy protection. By comparing community development efforts in Mattapan after that point with those in neighboring Codman Square, I show how important CBOs were for neighborhood political representation, and by extension, neighborhood inequality.

AN OASIS IN CODMAN SQUARE

Twenty thousand square feet of vacant land sits between 94 and 116 Ballou Avenue in Codman Square. It is in the middle of a residential neighborhood and directly abuts the Fairmount Line. During the summer of 2010, two separate plans for the site emerged. The first was a city government plan for an urban farm, similar to the one developed by City Growers in Four Corners (discussed earlier in this chapter) and part of a larger urban agriculture initiative. The second was a Codman Square Neighborhood Development Corporation (CSNDC) plan for small-scale food production, gardens, and a playground.

Between 2010 and 2011, city officials hosted public meetings to introduce the urban agriculture initiative. Gail attended an April 2011 meeting on behalf of CSNDC. During the public comment period, she presented her organization's alternative plan for the Ballou Avenue site. She called it "the community's" plan. "The community already looked at it [the site]," she said, "and found a use other than urban agriculture." The response was tepid. One official assured Gail, "We won't put an urban farm where the community doesn't want it," but no one would commit to abandoning the city's plan for an urban farm.

After the meeting, Gail spoke privately with Evelyn Friedman, the city's white chief of housing, at the back of the room. At the time, Evelyn led the city's property disposition department. Gail explained that her organization had completed its own planning process in the neighborhood, and she requested greater involvement with the site's redevelopment. In early May, Gail followed up with a formal letter requesting a meeting with Evelyn as well as the BRA's white director, Peter Meade.[26]

As Gail negotiated behind closed doors, City Councilor Charles Yancey led a public crusade against the entire urban agriculture initiative. After the episode in Four Corners, Councilor Yancey hosted a public hearing in Codman Square to discuss soil testing and other concerns related to urban farms. For two and a half hours, residents and other meeting participants testified about possible soil contamination and their general confusion regarding the selection of sites for the pilot program.[27] Councilor Yancey berated BRA officials for a "rushed" process that occurred "without neighborhood input." He pointed at Cullen, a Black community organizer with CSNDC, who was seated in the audience. "Cullen has participated in a number of [meetings] on the parcels along the Fairmount Line," Yancey said. "And was he consulted? He was not."

Councilor Yancey admitted to the crowd that his role was limited. "My job is done," he declared as the meeting ended. "I provided . . . a forum for the community to speak." More work was necessary, to be sure, but "my only job here is to make your voice heard."

Gail met privately with city officials in July. They agreed to remove the Ballou Avenue site from their urban agriculture initiative and asked Gail to produce a feasible alternative development plan. In September, city officials began a second round of public meetings re-introducing the urban agriculture initiative—responding, in part, to Councilor Yancey's public criticisms. The Ballou Avenue site was no longer mentioned as part of the initiative.

For a full year, from June 2011 to June 2012, Gail fundraised and hired consultants to assist with development plans for the Ballou site. Two consultant groups drafted health impact reports and graduate students from a Boston University urban planning class drafted designs. In addition, community organizers from CSNDC established a "Friends Group of Ballou Avenue."

In October 2012, Gail met with representatives from a funding intermediary to provide an annual update on CSNDC's accomplishments. She described the momentum CSNDC built behind the Ballou Avenue project, though refused to take full credit. "It was the community, also," she told the funders. "The community—we had a lot of support from the neighbors." In Gail's narrative, CSNDC was simply working on behalf of the community:

> It was a groundswell that was, you know, led by the community, with our strong support, against that. So the City agreed to take out... Ballou Ave., at our request, out of the lots [for the urban agriculture initiative].

The funders were impressed, and they offered to support the project in any way they could.

In February 2013, representatives from CSNDC met with the new head of the city's Department of Neighborhood Development, Karen. By this time, CSNDC was calling the project "The Oasis on Ballou Avenue." They described holding regular meetings with the "Friends" group, the conceptual plans, and the findings from their consultants' environmental impact reports. Karen said she supported the project—as long as it was feasible, just as her predecessor had stipulated in 2011. She asked for a meeting with residents, with CSNDC acting as "the conduit" in charge of scheduling and hosting.

The meeting took place in June 2013. City officials were impressed with CSNDC's work and placed the Ballou site on a list of protected land parcels. Monthly meetings of the "Friends" group continued throughout the summer, and consultants created another design concept plan. In October 2013—after CSNDC had developed initial plans for the site—city officials hosted another public meeting in Codman Square. The officials advertised the meeting as an open conversation with residents, but it functioned more as an unveiling. Representatives from CSNDC shared their plans for gardens, a shared kitchen space, and a playground. The few residents in attendance supported the plan.

City officials trusted CSNDC to represent the interests of Codman Square residents, going so far as to equate the *organization* with the *community*. "The neighborhood in the past asked us to slow down the process and continue to work with the community," an official told a reporter after the meeting, repeating the narrative Gail had presented to local funders.[28] In fact, it was *Gail* who wrote a formal letter and met with city officials three times in 2011. It was *Gail* who claimed the community wanted the Ballou site pulled from the urban agriculture initiative. And it was *Gail* who obtained resources to develop alternative site plans. Codman Square residents were not necessarily opposed, but city officials never actually asked them. The officials accepted CSNDC as the legitimate, authentic mouthpiece for the neighborhood.

In December 2013, city officials issued a Request for Proposals (RFP) to develop the Ballou Avenue site. The guidelines were tailored specifically for an organization like CSNDC, and for a plan like the one they had developed over the previous three years:

> The development concept for this is site is to have a non-profit entity acquire the property and improve it such that the land is suitable for the production of food crops. These improvements must be designed in a manner that is complementary to the neighboring urban fabric.

CSNDC was the only bidder when proposals were due in February 2014. The organization was named developer in March, and Gail met with city officials in April to discuss the disposition process.

Through four years of debate, discussion, and backroom negotiations, Gail leveraged plans for the Ballou Avenue site into even more resources for the Codman Square neighborhood. She linked the site to a larger "Eco-Innovation District" plan, which focused on reducing energy costs for neighborhood residents. In July 2014, CSNDC was one of just nine organizations in the United States to receive funding from a national organization to update existing buildings with environmentally efficient improvements.

The case of the vacant lot on Ballou Avenue illustrates how a nonprofit leader can claim to represent a neighborhood, gain legitimation from other players in the community development field, and then leverage representation into resources for "their" neighborhood. Publicly and privately, city officials referred to CSNDC as a "conduit" for Codman Square residents. Councilor Yancey, the neighborhood's elected City Councilor, admitted that his influence was limited to airing grievances at public forums. Indeed, Gail did not need Councilor Yancey's influence to obtain resources; she used private funding to hire her own consultants and met directly with local government bureaucrats no less than five times before securing use of the Ballou Avenue site. CSNDC developed site plans with minimal input from a handful of residents, but Gail was still able to frame the effort as "community-driven" and to procure even more funding to benefit the Codman Square neighborhood.

A NONPROFIT GOES BANKRUPT IN MATTAPAN

What happens when a neighborhood lacks a representative like Gail or CSNDC? The Mattapan Community Development Corporation (MCDC) provides a case in comparison. MCDC was the only nonprofit CBO dedicated to real estate development and community organizing in the predominantly Black neighborhood of Mattapan. Halfway through my fieldwork, the organization filed for Chapter 11 bankruptcy protection. In the absence of a community development organization, other people in the field turned to local elected officials to represent the neighborhood's interests. But because elected officials needed nonprofit organizations to implement community development plans, projects slated for the neighborhood stalled when the organization closed its doors.

In 2010, MCDC employed just five staff members and faced considerable financial difficulties; the organization's 2009 tax return indicated a $221,000 budget shortfall and a negative net worth of $781,445. MCDC's executive director, a former director of strategic business development for Texas Instruments, left the organization abruptly in April 2011. A year later, MCDC owed nearly $30,000 in taxes on six properties. City officials were deflated when the nonprofit filed for bankruptcy protection. "In Mattapan, the big problem we have is that they are the only game in town. It's a big loss," the city's chief of housing told a reporter at the time.[29]

City officials weren't the only ones concerned about the loss of MCDC. Private funders partially funded the organization's work, and the directors of the Corridor CBO coalition depended on the organization to fulfill the requirements of their collective grants. These groups searched for alternative representatives to advance the neighborhood's interests and quickly settled on two elected politicians: State Representatives Linda Dorcena Forry and Russell Holmes.

Their ascent was swift. City officials called Representative Holmes in the first week of November 2011, seeking his advice and leadership in the neighborhood when MCDC's financial struggles became apparent. A month later, Representatives Holmes and Dorcena Forry brokered a meeting in City Hall between housing officials and outside developers in an effort to continue unfinished real estate projects. With this information, the Fairmount Corridor coalition members assumed Representative Holmes was City Hall's new "point person" for Mattapan.[30]

The nonprofit coalition members began taking their cues from the two elected politicians. In December, Representative Holmes asked the coalition members to cancel all meetings regarding ongoing development projects in Mattapan and to consult with him and Representative Dorcena Forry before holding any additional meetings in the neighborhood. The nonprofit leaders complied. Although they had brainstormed a potential replacement organization to fulfill their grant obligations in Mattapan, all efforts remained on hold until the elected officials could vet the candidate. It was not until October 2013—two full years later—that the Mattapan branch of a citywide social service organization joined their coalition, after getting the officials' approval.

Private funders also consulted the two representatives before moving forward with community development projects in Mattapan. In April 2012, representatives from LISC met with the legislators about the future of development in Mattapan. LISC had recently committed more than $200,000 for community development planning in the neighborhood, and the organization was a longtime funder of MCDC. LISC's executive director met with Representatives Holmes and Dorcena Forry throughout the summer of 2012. As he later explained, it was to "make sure they understand where the funders are coming from in relation to the demise of [MCDC] and the future . . . of this work in Mattapan."[31] The pair of state legislators filled the political vacuum left after MCDC's demise.

Although the neighborhood's informal political representation stabilized, MCDC's bankruptcy caused a number of development projects to stall or falter. In 2011, the organization received funding from the EPA for a mixed-use project that included thirty-three units of affordable housing and 7,000 square feet of commercial space. The project never materialized. In 2010, MCDC initiated a joint venture with another CDC to develop twenty-four units of affordable housing across three buildings; that project also stalled. Other CDCs in Boston initially avoided pursuing development projects in Mattapan for fear of being labeled, in their words, "interlopers" or "carpetbaggers." In 2013, the state fulfilled a previously negotiated commitment and opened new transit stations in Newmarket, Four Corners, and Codman Square—where CBOs actively advocated for the stations. But in Mattapan, $25 million for a new station was left on the table for years.[32] While CBOs in the other Corridor neighborhoods continued to seek out and apply for new resources, Mattapan residents lacked the required organization not only to pursue and accept grants, but to make use of the ones already secured.[33]

Another challenge emerged after my fieldwork ended. In 2018, a suburban-based real estate investment company, pursuing a "strategy of purchasing underutilized properties at transit-oriented locations," bought a 347-unit apartment complex in Mattapan. The company renamed the complex "SoMa Apartments at the T"—a reference to the nearby stop on the Fairmount Line—and immediately raised rents.[34] Similarly, as I was finishing writing this book in 2020, a 207-unit apartment complex went up for sale, further validating fears of impending gentrification and displacement.[35] Without a long-standing, high-capacity CBO to develop subsidized housing and advocate for current residents, the future of affordability in the neighborhood remains uncertain.

Community-based organizations have always claimed to represent urban neighborhoods. What is new is the broader context in which those claims are made today. Public funding reductions, combined with the growth in private funding, eroded elected politicians' control over many community development resources. At the same time, government became ever more reliant on CBOs to implement community development projects in poor urban neighborhoods. Private funders, for their part, want to fund *communities*, and the only way they understand to do that is to fund *CBOs*, thereby creating an additional incentive to assume CBOs are conduits for communities. Under these conditions, CBOs assumed expanded roles as nonelected neighborhood representatives.

Importantly, the rise of public-private partnerships in urban policy made CBOs necessary for poor neighborhoods to access resources. Neighborhoods lacking these organizations couldn't even *compete* for scarce resources, let alone acquire them. Unlike Codman Square, where CSNDC successfully secured funding for energy-efficient development, in Mattapan, the flow of resources to the neighborhood stalled when MCDC closed its doors. The comparison returns to a central argument of this book: that CBOs' structural position in larger systems of urban governance affects neighborhood inequality.

For neighborhoods with strong CBOs, greater access to resources came with a significant cost. Unlike elected politicians, CBO leaders are not subject to formal structures of democratic accountability. Nonprofit leaders may claim to represent neighborhoods, but they are still motivated, in part, by organizational survival. If and when organizational and neighborhood interests conflict, residents have no petition authority, veto power, or voting rights to remove CBO leaders from their positions. Adherence to government mandates or foundation funding requirements can also curb nonprofits' appetite for political advocacy—thus limiting what CBO leaders may be willing to do for residents.[36]

Nonelected representatives are not *necessarily* undemocratic; as political theorist Laura Montanaro argues, democratic legitimacy is still achievable if the nonelected representative "functions to give political presence to those whose interests are affected"—in this case, neighborhood residents—"and empowers them to exercise authorization and demand accountability."[37] In the Fairmount Corridor, neither the authorization nor the accountability standard was met. To paraphrase Montanaro, this form of representation may be preferable to the absence of representation, but it is not democratic.[38] Or, to borrow from political scientists Benjamin Page and Martin Gilens, we can think of the best-case scenario as "democracy by coincidence":[39] CBOs appear democratic because their interests generally align with residents', but residents have only modest influence over CBO decision-making.

We might worry that nonelected representatives are less likely to accurately reflect the views of the public they claim to represent. Democratic accountability should force representatives to be more attuned to the policy views of their constituents. Yet recent research challenges this assumption. Political scientists David Brookman and Christopher Skovron show how state legislators systematically overestimate constituents' support for conservative policies.⁴⁰ Experimental research points to a more generalized phenomenon of "nonrepresentative representatives" in which elected politicians prefer the status quo (regardless of policy substance), escalate commitment when faced with sunk costs, and are influenced by framing effects.⁴¹ When it comes to accurately representing the interests of constituents, more ideal forms of democratic representation are rife with shortcomings, too.

A second concern is that CBO leaders are not necessarily neighborhood residents. Professionalization in the nonprofit sector means that community-based organizations do not need to be led by community-based directors. Jeanne, for example, lived in Roslindale but represented Upham's Corner, and Gail lived in Hyde Park but represented Codman Square. Some Corridor CBOs were in fact residents, and all employed at least a few on staff, but it was clear that community representation was largely decoupled from community residence. Logically, the practice seems to undermine the "community" base of community-based organizations. For some scholars and many activists, professionalization is an indictment of the entire sector.⁴²

Still, given the evidence presented in this chapter, it is difficult to evaluate the political role of nonprofit community organizations in purely positive or negative terms. Whether urban residents are better off in this particular system—or, more specifically, whether residents of Codman Square are better off than their neighbors in Mattapan—depends on our criteria of evaluation. CSNDC brought resources to Codman Square while arguably undermining certain forms of residents' political advocacy. MCDC's bankruptcy limited resources for Mattapan residents but may have also relieved them of an undemocratic, nonelected representative. It underscores another central theme of this book: Inequality does not get any clearer the closer you get to the ground. It would be a mistake to make a blanket statement—or to even assume that one is possible—when the reality is so untidy. Urban politics belies sharp distinctions and clean categories. In this murky context, it is important to understand the structure of governance in terms of tensions and tradeoffs rather than dichotomies of good and bad.

This chapter focused on the role of CBOs in urban governance. Another group of organizations, private funders, were an important part of the story, legitimating CBOs' claims of representation. Like CBOs, private funders were neither elected nor subject to formal democratic oversight. I turn to these organizations—their role in urban governance, limits placed on their influence, and the impact of funding practices on neighborhood inequality—in the next chapter.

CHAPTER FIVE

Following the Money

IN EARLY 2012, I had coffee with Inés Palmarin, an official with the Boston Redevelopment Authority (BRA). The BRA had recently embarked on a Fairmount Corridor Planning Initiative, partially funded by two philanthropic foundations. I had reached out to Inés to learn more about the relationship between private funding and community development policy. Sitting inside a small deli on the eighth floor of Boston City Hall, we were only a few sips into our coffee when Inés mentioned Geeta Pradhan. Geeta, she told me, was "the godmother of Fairmount."

Geeta immigrated to Boston in the 1980s. She earned a graduate degree from the Harvard Graduate School of Design and worked in city government before eventually joining The Boston Foundation (TBF). In the late 2000s and early 2010s, she steered TBF resources toward nonprofits in the Corridor and was instrumental in capturing the attention of federal policymakers. Though she herself lived in Jamaica Plain—a more affluent, gentrified neighborhood—she nevertheless felt a deep personal and moral obligation to support the city's most disadvantaged residents.

People gravitated toward Geeta. Her personality is somehow both effervescent and understated; her short stature does not give her an imposing physical presence, but her full-body laugh is magnetic and her warm embrace makes it impossible not to smile in her company. That she is a master of behind-the-scenes politicking is no surprise; she is the kind of person who can walk down a hallway completely unnoticed by everyone except those with the power to move the gears of city policy.

When Geeta attended a public event or community meeting, people practically lined up to greet her—a movement of bodies resembling a receiving line at a wedding reception. In many respects the Fairmount Corridor is her child, and like the mother of the bride, she would happily hold court before or after meetings as a sea of officials, developers, and other players in community development politics extended their well wishes.

This was the scene in Upham's Corner on a blustery winter day in 2013. Seventy "stakeholders"—nonprofit leaders, business owners, funders, and some residents—filled a large room inside a community center to discuss development opportunities with consultants hired by the BRA. After a formal presentation, the attendees split into smaller discussion groups of nine or ten. A lunch of sandwiches and chips separated morning and afternoon discussion sessions. It was the culmination of months of work, an extensive urban planning process that Geeta, through TBF, had helped fund.

Geeta arrived as the morning session drew to a close. She stood by the windows of the large, open room, and as was custom, men and women approached her, one by one. Steve, the lead consultant for the meeting, sauntered over with a smile and engaged her in small talk. At 11:50, Karen, a city government official, entered and didn't even remove her coat before first greeting Geeta with a hug.

I joined the chorus of greeters at lunch. As I stood chatting with Geeta, Mat, a consultant, walked up to us. With a big smile, he hugged Geeta and asked, "How are you?" before disappearing back into the crowd. A BRA official was the next to interrupt. "Oh, excuse me, just a quick make-out session," he announced, his arms already opened wide as he came into sight. Geeta laughed, they hugged, and he too disappeared out of sight.

"This is like coming for a family wedding!" Geeta joked. "Hugs and kisses everywhere!"

We continued talking until Jeanne, the director of Dorchester Bay Economic Development Corporation (DBEDC), walked up to us with a mouthful of food and a half-eaten sandwich in her hand. Geeta stopped our conversation mid-sentence. "Hello!" she exclaimed. "Hi! How are you?" Jeanne asked. They exchanged small talk about the meeting and strategized about a grant for arts and cultural development in the Corridor.

Like the sun at the center of the solar system, "the godmother of Fairmount" greeted friends and colleagues as they flowed around the room in orbit.

Private funders are central actors in densely connected networks of organizations. They use financial contributions to influence others' behavior. They develop alliances to reduce uncertainty. They try to focus on distinct programmatic areas to avoid overlap and ensure complementarity with colleagues and competitors alike. They are also seen as fair and trusted—neutral parties to turn to for help when problems arise.

A growing body of research explores the role of philanthropic foundations in American politics and public policy. We know, for example, about the history of organized philanthropy and its changing relationship to the federal government over time.[1] We know about the influence of large, national foundations in specific areas of policymaking, like education.[2] We know about foundations and other funders supporting but sometimes moderating social movements.[3] And we know about foundations claiming to promote social change, but more often than not failing to upend unequal power relations.[4] This literature is largely limited to the activities of major national foundations, and it is typically framed as either critique or celebration. We know comparatively less about the full range of private funders affecting city development policy, their impact on the day-to-day gears of urban governance, and structural limits to their influence.[5]

Funders played important roles in the Fairmount Corridor. Most directly, they supported community development financially through grants for project planning and low-interest loans for up-front construction costs. They also played two absolutely essential, albeit more hidden functions: convening the various community development players who would not otherwise interact and brokering disputes between organizations in conflict. These roles should not be taken lightly. Urban policymaking in the United States is increasingly diffuse and complex. Some sort of coordination is needed, and in the Fairmount Corridor, that responsibility largely fell on private funders. With this responsibility came tremendous power, including the ability to determine invitee lists, set agendas, and define the rules of the game.

Still, the evidence presented in this chapter suggests it would be a mistake to assume a dominating class of funders. In fact, grantees had significant leverage to push back against funder directives. The reason, I argue, was structural: Many funders of Corridor projects received funding from *other funders*; they pooled and repackaged multiple lines of funding before providing a grant to a government agency or nonprofit organization. The ultimate grantee completed progress reports for the direct funder. That funder then submitted similar paperwork to their own funders, meaning *they* were being held accountable for the success of *their grantees*. As mid-level actors, these funders' organizational reputation depended almost entirely on the grantees' successes. The complexity of funding relationships and incentives inverted power imbalances and reduced funders' leverage over their own grantees. It allowed grantees to, at times, resist funder control.

This multilayered funding structure had another effect: It incentivized funders to support well-resourced, high-capacity organizations—"safe bets" that were most likely to produce successful projects. This makes perfect business sense, particularly for funders who called their grants "investments." But it also pushed funders to cut their losses in order to maintain their own organizational reputation and viability. In the Fairmount Corridor, this sometimes meant ignoring the people and places in greatest need of funding. Funders may not be as all-powerful as is typically assumed, but the structure of governance nevertheless incentivized certain behaviors that, in effect if not intent, compounded neighborhood inequality.

Policymakers have, to a large degree, uncritically embraced philanthropy as a solution to a variety of social problems. At a minimum, foundations are considered potentially useful partners. My analysis of the funder field in the Fairmount Corridor shows how funder incentives were not always aligned with neighborhood need. Given this evidence, policymakers have good reason to view the influence of private foundations with considerably more caution and skepticism.

Funders, Funders Everywhere

The scholarly literature on private funding and public policy generally focuses on large philanthropic foundations with deep pockets and complete discretion over grant-making. With respect to community development projects in the Fairmount Corridor, funders did indeed include well-known national foundations, like the Ford Foundation. Yet these funders only indirectly supported projects, mostly by funding *other* funders or intermediaries. Large foundations were less involved in day-to-day urban governance and played second fiddle to a number of smaller, local foundations.

Directors and program officers from three family foundations—The Herman and Frieda L. Miller Foundation, The Hyams Foundation, and Garfield Foundation—played a far more active role in the Corridor, and to a varying extent, regularly funded community development organizations and projects. The Barr Foundation fell somewhere in between local and national funders, a self-described "regional" foundation that "selectively" distributed grants nationally.

Notably, Boston is also home to one of the nation's premiere community foundations, The Boston Foundation (TBF). As of 2017, TBF had more than $1 billion in assets, making it the sixteenth largest community foundation in the United States. Community foundations differ from family foundations in a number of key respects. First, they dedicate resources to local communities (cities or regions) rather than national or international projects. Second, they are technically public charities, receiving funding from multiple sources rather than a single wealthy benefactor. This means that the organization must actively fundraise and solicit donations from wealthy individuals and other private funders. It also means that program officers, staff, and board members do not have full discretion over the distribution of resources. Certain funds, like "donor-advised funds" and "designated funds," are earmarked for particular recipients and projects. In the case of donor-advised funds, the community foundation is simply a pass-through for individual donors to transfer money to the donor's cause or organization of choice. Unrestricted or discretionary funds are what foundation staffers use to fulfill the organization's larger mission. There is not always an even balance between restricted and unrestricted assets; at TBF, for instance, only 14 percent of grant dollars distributed in 2016, or about $16 million, were unrestricted.[6]

Another layer of funders included what are best described as intermediaries. These groups seek out and receive grants from larger foundations or government agencies, generally keep a portion for overhead and staff time, and then redistribute the remaining money to local nonprofits. There were two such organizations funding projects in the Corridor: The Massachusetts Smart Growth Alliance (MSGA) and Local Initiatives Support Corporation (LISC).[7] Three other Boston-based funders primarily funded MSGA: The Barr Foundation, The Herman and Frieda L. Miller Foundation, and TBF. MSGA oversaw community development initiatives and also lobbied for sustainable development policies at the state and local levels. LISC focused more on brick-and-mortar affordable housing development, awarding grants and loans to community development corporations (CDCs). Its national headquarters is in Chicago, though its thirty-one branch offices—including the one in Boston—have notable discretion over day-to-day operations and politicking.

Major corporations make up a final category of private funders. It is now commonplace for corporations to funnel a portion of profits into charity.[8] During my fieldwork, the charitable wings of TD Bank, Citi, Bank of America, and Merck, a pharmaceutical company, allocated grants to organizations in the Corridor. These funders were peripheral, following a more passive model of grant-making.

Ensuring Complementarity

Funders of Corridor organizations exhibited notable differences in organizational form and function. Yet distinctions blurred as organizations on the ground engaged in dense networks of collaboration. It began informally in the late 2000s with three individuals representing a community foundation, a family foundation, and an intermediary, respectively: Geeta Pradhan, the Indian American associate vice president of programs at TBF; Angela Brown, the Black director of programs at Hyams; and Bob Van Meter, the white executive director of LISC's Boston office. In many respects, Boston is a small community. The major funders all knew each other. They shared grantees and saw each other at various ribbon cuttings, groundbreakings, and professional conferences. Through these informal channels, Geeta, Angela, and Bob realized that the coalition of nonprofit CDCs in the Fairmount Corridor had requested similar support from each of their funding organizations. So they had an idea: Why not coordinate grants to reduce redundancy and ensure greater impact? As Geeta told me in 2013, "We started to meet together about ways in which we could find synergies in our support . . . to make sure our funding to the CDCs was aligned. That there was a way that we could support them, that was not duplicative."

Table 5.1. Structure of RC/RF and GNI Initiatives[a]

	RC/RF	GNI
Managed by:	LISC	MSGA
Steering committee included (in part):	MSGA MAPC	LISC MAPC
Funded by (in part):	TBF Barr Hyams	TBF Barr Ford Miller Garfield
Included grants to (in part):	CSNDC MCDC	CSNDC MCDC DBEDC SWBCDC

[a] Both initiatives included additional funders, steering committee members, and grantees. MCDC was an initial lead applicant for LISC's RC/RF initiative but filed for bankruptcy protection in 2012.

In 2007, these funders met as a group and began communicating on a regular basis.[9] They also met collectively with their nonprofit grantees to review progress and discuss political strategy.[10] The funders' coordination was so significant that one grantee called them "the local Magi," a reference to the Three Wise Men who presented gifts to Jesus in the Gospel of Matthew.

There were more formal networks of collaboration, as well. Consider two programs, LISC's Resilient Communities/Resilient Families and MSGA's Great Neighborhoods Initiative. The overlap of managing and funding organizations was extensive, and the seemingly never-ending acronyms can be overwhelming to an outside observer. A table (table 5.1) can barely do it justice. But the confusing word salad of program names and organizational labels is instructive in its own right, revealing the dense structure of relationships between private funders and their programs.

In 2010, MSGA created a program to support sustainable development and equitable urban planning. The multiyear program was called the Great Neighborhoods Initiative, or GNI for short. Before selecting grantees, MSGA first hosted a Great Neighborhoods Summit, bringing together different organizational leaders to inform the design of the program. TBF funded the event.

At the same time, LISC began fundraising for its multiyear program, named Resilient Communities/Resilient Families, or RC/RF. RC/RF was a "comprehensive community initiative," a program that funded nonprofits to organize local communities and plan community development projects. RC/RF had its roots in the New Communities Program, a "comprehensive community initiative" developed by LISC's national headquarters in Chicago. By the early 2010s, LISC-Boston was one of twenty-three LISC branches that had replicated the New Communities Program.

For the GNI program, MSGA received funding from five foundations, including the aforementioned Barr, Ford, Miller, and Garfield foundations. It was enough money to support grants to local nonprofits in five Massachusetts areas. The organization selected the Fairmount Corridor as one site, offering a grant to the coalition of nonprofit CDCs.

For the RC/RF program, LISC received initial funding from Barr, Hyams, and TBF—enough resources to implement the program in two neighborhoods.[11] But the grants from Barr and TBF each had a catch: Barr required one of the two sites to be a neighborhood funded through MSGA's GNI program, and TBF required one of the two sites to be a neighborhood in the Fairmount Corridor, where TBF had previously committed $1 million in grants to local nonprofits. In other words, funding of RC/RF from both foundations was contingent on earmarking a portion for organizations that each foundation already funded through other, separate initiatives.[12]

The overlap didn't end there. Melissa Jones, a LISC program officer, managed RC/RF and was on the steering committee for GNI. Ina Anderson, partnerships director at MSGA, managed GNI and was on the steering committee for RC/RF. Staff from MSGA coordinated with staff from TBF to make sure the respective funders' grant requirements did not overlap. TBF funded and managed an evaluation of RC/RF, even though LISC staff ran the program independently.

Making matters *even more* complicated, all of these funders additionally coordinated with the Metropolitan Area Planning Council (MAPC), a quasi-public regional planning agency. As the GNI and RC/RF programs got up and running in 2010, MAPC received a grant from the federal Department of Housing and Urban Development (HUD)'s Sustainable Communities program. A portion of the grant funded nonprofits in the Fairmount Corridor— the same organizations funded through the GNI and RC/RF programs. Angela Insinger, senior regional planner at MAPC, managed the grant and sat on both the GNI and RC/RF steering committees.

Melissa, Ina, and Angela met frequently and coordinated their grant requirements with representatives from the Corridor nonprofits. As Ina later explained in an interview, "[W]e sat down, we made a column in that work plan [with the Corridor nonprofits] that said, like, here's what Sustainable Communities money is gonna cover, here's what Great Neighborhoods money is gonna cover, here's what Resilient Communities/Resilient Families covers, and does this make sense to use this funding for X." Similar to the informal coordination between Geeta (TBF), Angela (Hyams), and Bob (LISC), Ina (MSGA), Melissa (LISC), and Angela (MAPC) formally coordinated their respective organizations' funding streams as a way to avoid redundancy.

The previous paragraphs are difficult to follow. That, in part, is precisely the point I want to get across: Private funders were *densely connected* through grants to each other, programmatic coordination, and overlapping grantees.[13]

In the eyes of funders, coordination was a form of strategic behavior. It made perfect sense to leverage grants into more resources for their grantees, increasing the likelihood of project implementation or programmatic success. But there is another implication of coordination, one that had an important impact on inequality. By concentrating resources in particular areas, funders instituted high costs of entry for new organizations and alternative community development ideas. This benefited organizations that already had access to funding or proposed ideas that already appealed to funders. For everyone else, it was an impediment to organizational survival.

"But I Will Take Her Out to Lunch and Get Her Drunk So She Commits!"

Funders wanted to fund successful projects. They also wanted to influence community development policies, programs, and ideas. The most obvious way to do both was through grants. In the late 2000s, for example, Geeta used TBF's grants to draw more attention to the Fairmount Corridor. Part of her strategy entailed increasing the size and number of grants awarded to Corridor nonprofits. More money meant a greater likelihood of successful projects, which in turn meant more attention for the Corridor.

Another part of Geeta's strategy involved persuading other grantees in the city to expand their programs into the Corridor. In 2010, for instance, TBF offered Metropolitan Boston Housing Partnership (MBHP) a $500,000 grant to expand its Family Self Sufficiency (FSS) program. Primarily funded by HUD, the program provided job training and other financial planning resources to low-income families living in federally subsidized housing.[14] The goal was to increase family incomes. Under normal conditions, that increased income would go toward rent, since HUD sets rent in subsidized housing as a percentage of family income. For participants in the program, however, earnings increases were instead deposited into an escrow account. Participants received that escrowed money after they completed the Family Self Sufficiency program.

MBHP staff had no special interest in the Fairmount Corridor, but did have a broader goal of program expansion. HUD wouldn't fund an expansion, so MBHP needed to find a private funder willing to take the risk. As Chris Norris, the organization's white executive director, explained during an interview:

> We had 200 families that were participating in our region. With The Boston Foundation, we wanted to take that to 500 families in our region, which [extends] beyond Fairmount, but a significant portion

is in Fairmount. But in order to do that, we were sort of in a catch-22. We couldn't increase the numbers until we had staff. We wouldn't get [funding for] staff from HUD until we increased the numbers. So The Boston Foundation funding really served as that link or that bridge, almost a bridge subsidy to cover bringing staff on, doing the outreach, expanding awareness of the program so that we could increase our numbers that we had participating in the program.

In 2010, when TBF awarded the grant, approximately one-third of the participants in MBHP's Family Self Sufficiency program lived in the Fairmount Corridor. That number climbed to two-thirds in 2012. MBHP expanded their program, and residents of the Fairmount Corridor benefited.

Funding also *indirectly* influenced community development plans when grantees developed programs in response to available grants. Take the Barr Foundation and its strategic focus on the environment. In 2012, program officers informed their current grantees that future grant applications would require the inclusion of specific plans to offset climate change. As Gail, director of CSNDC, interpreted the message at the time, "[They said,] 'Everything we fund we want to see clear connections to reductions of carbon emissions.'" Barr made it clear that some of the foundation's previous grants to Corridor organizations were only marginally related to climate change. The projects were not necessarily bad, nor were they necessarily unworthy of funding. They just didn't fit Barr's strategic objectives.

Grantees in the Corridor took note and adjusted their work accordingly. For Gail, this meant promoting a new idea for energy-efficient, sustainable development in Codman Square. "We got this whole concept of a local energy district," Gail told her colleagues in the CDC coalition. "Really deep level [planning], in response to Barr, which we're trying to get money from."[15]

There was another way private funders affected community development, and it had little to do with money: They co-developed policy ideas and built relationships with government bureaucrats. The strategy was not new; recall the Ford Foundation and the Gray Areas program, described in chapter 1. In short, in the 1960s, Ford officials worked together with policymakers to incorporate "community action" into federal urban policy. Funders in Boston similarly attempted to influence policy ideas, albeit at a smaller scale. In 2010, for instance, Angela (Hyams) collaborated with Bob (LISC) and Geeta (TBF) to write a "white paper" for state housing officials. The document proposed a land acquisition fund, integrating philanthropic and state support, for Corridor housing and commercial development. That same year, when LISC began planning the Resilient Communities/Resilient Families program, Bob met with city and state officials to share his idea and plant the seed for future material and political support. In late 2011, Geeta told me about a Boston Housing Authority official who was reluctant to help MBHP staff enroll participants in the FSS program. "But I will take her out to lunch and get her drunk so she commits!" Geeta said with a hearty laugh.

Geeta's joke illustrates how funders valued informal relationships with government bureaucrats. Grants certainly mattered and were a central way for funders to influence the behavior of other players in the field. Ongoing relationships with bureaucrats, however, were part of a larger strategy to influence policy *ideas*.

The Partner Who Brings the Donuts and Coffee

Funders knew that relationships did not emerge out of thin air and ideas did not spread on their own. To develop deeper connections across the field, funders in the Corridor intentionally brought various players together in structured settings. For Geeta and TBF, this form of strategic coordination was a core aspect of the foundation's work. Connecting otherwise disconnected players in the field was just as important as obtaining grants. "We were in a unique place, at The Boston Foundation, where we could bring other things to the table," Geeta told me in 2013, reflecting on the previous four years. Namely: "We had a *set* of relationships."

Geeta leveraged those relationships from the beginning of her involvement in the Corridor. In the 1990s, she had worked with officials from the EPA on a cleanup and redevelopment project in the neighborhood of East Boston. In 2008, Geeta reached out to some of those officials and invited them to tour the Fairmount Corridor. As it turned out, an interagency Partnership for Sustainable Communities—including staff from the EPA, HUD, and the Department of Transportation (DOT)—was in the works, as described in greater detail in chapter 1. Geeta saw the Partnership as an opportunity to connect federal officials with TBF's grantees in the Corridor. She arranged an in-person convening as well as a bus tour so that the officials could see projects in progress.

The event was a major success. Federal officials developed new ties to Corridor nonprofits, thanks to Geeta's intervention. As she explained to me:

> And again, fortunately this was the time when the federal agencies were starting to develop the Sustainable Communities partnership, and they hit on this idea that, wow, [the Fairmount Corridor] would be a great opportunity for the federal agencies to illustrate how they work together. And, um, we convened them. Um, we did a tour. And then, it just took off! . . . The federal agencies are [now] bringing in more resources. The communities [now] have their own relationships with them. You know, and I feel like that was our role, to be the connector.

Invite-only get-togethers were key sites of idea diffusion. I observed a half dozen during my fieldwork. These events initially focused on nonprofit-led projects, but eventually expanded as more players became involved in

Corridor development. In 2010, TBF staff organized a tour of the Corridor for other funders and public officials. In 2011, they hosted one meeting of just grantees—hoping to create more collaboration between them—as well as a larger event, informally co-hosted with city government officials, in which TBF's key grantees described their recent accomplishments. At a separate event, they invited nonprofit grantees and faculty from Boston University to discuss possible community-based research projects. In 2012, they hosted program officers from Pittsburgh-based Heinz Endowments to learn more about TBF's strategic funding of Corridor nonprofits. That same year, at the request of federal officials, they hosted federal grantees from Connecticut to learn community development lessons from Corridor nonprofit leaders and city government officials. Later, in the fall, they convened a large group of local organizations and officials—the largest and most comprehensive of any meeting—that was formally co-hosted by city government. And in 2013, TBF expanded their work to include the press, organizing a bus tour for reporters from WBUR, Boston's National Public Radio affiliate.

Other players in the field valued TBF's role as convener, especially when compared to the alternatives. A state transportation official explained in an interview why TBF was a better candidate to host these events than government agencies like his own:

> There are somewhat landmines of who gets brought to the table and who doesn't . . . So, at least what I see as the role of The Boston Foundation as sort of the critical—as an important role in being what I would call a convener . . . [It] is not the state—who doesn't have the same baggage as the state. But in terms of the partner who not only brings money to the table, but can, you know, bring the donuts and the coffee.

Given that funders are hardly apolitical, it is perhaps ironic that the official saw TBF as a neutral party, unhampered by "landmines" and other "baggage." Perhaps it speaks to how fraught relationships were between other groups that TBF, by comparison, appeared impartial. Regardless, it illustrates the organization's reputation and position in the field: centrally located, highly respected, and valued for neutrality.

Each TBF convening had a specific objective, whether it was to facilitate connections between nonprofit leaders and academic researchers or to gain more publicity for projects in the Corridor. But there was a larger strategy that tied the events together: It was a way for TBF staff to create an epistemic community of organizations and agencies engaged in Corridor development. A political action in its own right, it effectively changed how different players in the field thought of themselves and their collective responsibility. That community-building created an opportunity for TBF staff—and Geeta, in particular—to institutionalize their vision of development in the Fairmount Corridor.

It is important to note that these events were not open to just anyone. The ability to convene afforded funders like TBF the power to determine who was and was not invited, what was and was not discussed. Convening power elevated the political status of private funders and cemented their place as key decision-makers in urban governance.

Brokering Behind the Scenes

Funders influenced organizations with their grants, built relationships with government bureaucrats, and convened the various players in the community development field. They also brokered fractured relationships between grantees and policymakers. At no point was this more apparent than during Geeta's years-long effort to convince city officials to embrace the Corridor CDC coalition.[16] City officials were initially skeptical of the coalition, part of a larger love-hate relationship with the nonprofit sector.[17] And the CDC directors in the coalition—the driving force behind community development since the mid-2000s—worried about city government taking over and excluding them from future development initiatives. Yet funders of the Corridor nonprofits knew public support would be necessary to fully implement their grantees' ambitious plans. If TBF's goals of community development in the Corridor were to be realized, then the two sides would need to resolve their conflict.

Geeta led efforts to develop stronger links between the CDC coalition and various public agencies. Her first move, discussed above, was to draw on preexisting relationships with officials at the EPA. She framed projects in the Corridor as a matter of civil rights and social justice, an opportunity for the federal government to make a difference in the everyday lives of people struggling with poverty. After piquing initial interest, Geeta orchestrated a series of large group gatherings, including the tour with EPA officials in 2008, which led to the Corridor being named a pilot site for the new Partnership for Sustainable Communities initiative.

Geeta worked with Bob (LISC) to leverage the federal attention into face time with city government officials. It was certainly beneficial to be in conversation with national policymakers, but local officials had access to more resources that could be immediately applied to community development efforts. With this understanding, Geeta and Bob orchestrated a presentation by the CDC coalition at the Mayor's Economic Development Sub-Cabinet meeting in early 2010.

City officials remained skeptical. In September, I met with an advisor to the mayor to try to figure out why. In her office, I noticed a large three-ring binder with the word "Fairmount" printed in bold letters. She called the Corridor a "sleeper," something that made sense on paper but, for some reason, lacked department buy-in and did not excite the mayor. As Geeta told me later, "The response to [the sub-cabinet meeting] was a very negative response. They had a lot of questions and concerns. Just the general attitude was not very embracing of this thing." The federal attention was a good start. But it was clearly not enough.

In 2011, Geeta and her staff tried to change "the general attitude." They contacted city bureaucrats with whom they had good working relationships. Geeta spoke with Richard, an urban planner with whom she'd previously worked. Another TBF staff member reached out to Karen, an advisor to the mayor. Those conversations led to Geeta and Karen meeting for lunch in early May. Geeta expressed her desire to arouse greater excitement among city officials about community development in the Corridor and even offered to help fund a Corridor-wide urban planning process. For her part, Karen shared insights as to why city officials weren't jumping at the chance to collaborate. City officials, she said, worried that local nonprofit developers were self-interested and parochial.[18] The mayor also hated "land-banking," a common CDC practice in which developers collect multiple adjacent parcels of vacant land until enough is "banked" for a large development project. The mayor preferred to see immediate development rather than let land sit idle for extended periods of time. Most important, city officials wanted control over the process. They were reluctant to cede authority or share credit because they wanted something to claim as their own.

Three weeks later, Karen arranged a follow-up meeting, pulling in Kairos Shen, the chief planner for the Boston Redevelopment Authority (BRA). Geeta offered Kairos a $100,000 grant for the initiative and helped persuade the Garfield Foundation to award another $60,000. In exchange, Kairos shared the BRA's idea for a Corridor planning process, partially drafted by Geeta's former colleague, Richard. Kairos agreed to share the proposal with Geeta's grantees in the Corridor. Four days later, the directors of the CDC coalition received an email with a four-page attachment titled, "Fairmount Corridor and Crossroads Planning Initiative, DRAFT as of May 31, 2011."

After another two weeks, the CDC directors sent comments to Kairos regarding the BRA's proposal. Geeta did as well. In July, Kairos responded in writing to the CDC directors, promising to "respect and build upon" the nonprofits' previous work. In August, Kairos hosted Geeta and the nonprofit directors in City Hall to review the proposal and discuss any disagreements with respect to the scope of work.[19] Geeta sat in the center of the table, a figurative broker between the two sides. The tone was collegial and productive; everyone appeared committed to working together. Geeta's work over the past year had paid off.

When the initiative officially began the following year, city officials created an advisory group that included a representative from the CDC coalition, as well as a board member from each organization.[20]

More than money, brokering between nonprofit grantees and government bureaucrats allowed funders like TBF to influence community development policy. In the case of the BRA planning process, Geeta wanted city officials and nonprofit leaders in the Corridor to work together. Both sides were skeptical, but through private meetings and informal, backstage communication, Geeta achieved her goal. "I feel like we've played this glue role, you know, connecting this one, connecting that one," Geeta told me in 2013, reflecting on her influence to date. "You know, just chit-chatting here and there . . . Behind the scenes. A lot of behind the scenes stuff."

Funders Funding Other Funders

In 2013, while waiting for a ribbon-cutting ceremony to begin, I struck up a conversation with Ina, partnerships director at MSGA. She made an offhand comment about funders in a way that implied she did not see herself as one. It surprised me, because during my fieldwork with Ina's grantees, they all referred to her as a funder. I had assumed she felt the same way.

"So, do you not think of yourself as a funder?" I asked.

"Not me, personally."

"How do you see yourself, then?"

"As funded by the funders," she responded quickly. "Passing it on to other people. I guess some people would call that an intermediary."

"Some people, but not you?"

"We like to say partners."

To nonprofit grantees in the Corridor, Ina was a funder: She provided grants that funded community development plans and projects. Where that money originated was largely immaterial. Considered from the perspective of funders, it was more complicated: The dense network of funding redistributions made some organizations simultaneously funders *and* grantees. Ina's self-identification as a "partner" was a way to rhetorically reconcile a somewhat contradictory position—a position that affected funders' incentives and behavior.[21]

The Great Neighborhoods Initiative provides an instructive case. MSGA received funding for the initiative from a number of foundations, including the Barr Foundation. MSGA redistributed a portion to the Corridor CDC coalition. MSGA was Barr's grantee and the CDC coalition's funder. In practice, this meant that the nonprofit grantees at the end of the money trail submitted annual reports to MSGA. MSGA staff, in turn, used those reports to submit their own reports to Barr. Barr effectively held MSGA accountable for the work of the CDC coalition.

In 2012, the nonprofit grantees proposed using a portion of MSGA's funding for a new coordinator position. The coordinator would manage the planning of the "greenway" along the rail line. But Barr staff had little interest in funding a coordinator position; they wanted to fund project *implementation*—ideally, for projects related to climate change—and did not want to fund project *planning*. MSGA staff also preferred to see a finished product, though they were sympathetic to the need for more planning. That put MSGA in a bind: Going against Barr's wishes could cost them future funding. But pushing their own grantees to meet Barr's expectations could *also* cost them funding, if the grantees failed to deliver.

Two consultants from the Corridor CDC coalition had prepared a draft work plan for the grant, and in July, they met with an MSGA staff member to iron out the details. The MSGA staff member honed in on the coordinator position and expressed concern that Barr might not approve:

> What I need to be able to—so, Barr is interested in implementation. They want to see something at the end of this. So that's why our focus has really been to try to be able to explain to them what the deliverable will be, you know, related to these investments, you know, that they're making.

One of the consultants, Joan, asked for a clarification. "Do you have to sell this to Barr, which has not approved anything yet? Or, do you have to sell it to [your] board?" The staff member responded, "I think—I think more, to Barr." She continued, making it clear that the biggest concern for this budget item was making sure MSGA's work plan aligned with Barr's expectations, rather than making sure the nonprofit grantees were held accountable to MSGA:

> And I don't think of it so much as "selling" it to Barr, as just giving them a very clear—"sell" isn't the right word. Well, ok, yeah, you sell. We have to be—we're accountable to Barr for implementation of these things. So it's really helpful for me to be able to lay out when I explain this to Barr . . . about, you know, what the outcome is—how that outcome is leading really to implementation, rather than, you know, coordination.

The consultants agreed to edit the wording in a way that would meet Barr's expectations. But they still wanted funding for the position.

Three months later, the group discussed revisions to the work plan. André, MSGA's director, joined the conversation alongside the directors from the CDC coalition. André explained that the coordinator position remained a problem. If the nonprofit leaders were to demand funding for it, they would have to frame the position in a way that aligned with Barr's goals. He offered to "serve as a buffer" and help his grantees make the case:

> One thing I want to put on the table is a bigger issue, which is that Barr is pretty, I think, ambivalent about funding the [position]. And so, we've done our best to . . . I think serve as a buffer for that. But I think it's going to be really important for us to have as clear outcomes as possible so that we can talk to them about why we're doing what we're doing. And I think in particular, you know, they're very focused

on implementation, so, you know, the more we can show them actual things that are moving into, you know, design or construction . . . activities, is going to really help us out a lot.

What André *didn't* say was just as important: He never directly told the nonprofit leaders that their proposed use of funds conflicted with the purpose of the funding. Instead, he *deferred* to his own grantees rather than holding them accountable to Barr's stipulations. Barr eventually approved the grant, and a portion of the funds paid for a new coordinator.

In funding relationships, we might expect power to flow from the top: Barr should exert control over its grantee, MSGA, and MSGA should exert control over *its* grantee, the CDC coalition. But for the Great Neighborhoods Initiative, it worked in the reverse: The CDC coalition told MSGA how the funding would be used, and MSGA "[served] as a buffer" to get Barr to approve it. In the end, MSGA staff aligned with its grantees to persuade their own funder to rethink the use of the funding.

Funders Evaluating Other Funders

In some cases, deference to grantees directly undermined funder power. The evaluation of LISC's Resilient Communities/Resilient Families (RC/RF) program was one such situation. In April 2013, LISC hosted an event announcing the initiative. Bob, LISC's director, opened the event by thanking two public agencies and seven private foundations for supporting the initiative. With a slight chuckle, he called them "the funders of funders."

One of those "funders of funders" was TBF. Three years earlier, Geeta had provided a grant for the RC/RF program, stipulating that a portion of the resources benefit organizations in the Fairmount Corridor. At the same time, she also hired a team of consultants to evaluate TBF's grants in the Corridor. Evaluating the grant to LISC effectively meant evaluating LISC's RC/RF program. It was an awkward arrangement borne of a complicated funding structure: TBF hired consultants to evaluate LISC-funded grantees. I became a consultant and joined the evaluation team in 2012.

As the initiative was underway, TBF and LISC staff spent months debating which outcomes were appropriate for inclusion in the evaluation. Geeta wanted it to be about whether grantees reduced poverty and violence in the Corridor. Melissa, the Black LISC program officer managing the program, wanted the nonprofit grantees to select their own evaluation metrics. Her approach followed a long line of thinking coming out of both the practice and academic literatures challenging the belief that experts know what's best for poor neighborhoods.[22] Top-down funders, this work argues, can disempower local neighborhoods by imposing goals that conflict with the goals of local residents. There is an important racial component as well: It is often predominantly *white* philanthropists imposing their values and worldviews on predominantly *nonwhite* neighborhoods. In practice, Melissa deferred to nonprofit organizations as representatives of local neighborhoods and successfully pushed for evaluation metrics that she knew her grantees had already achieved. Geeta was unable to fully realize her vision of an evaluation, even though she paid for it.

These diverging evaluation goals culminated during an August 2012 meeting at TBF's offices. Attendance included Geeta, two TBF staff members, Melissa, five staff from the nonprofit grantees, and five members from the evaluation team. Throughout the meeting, Melissa aligned herself with the nonprofit grantees, exchanging looks and smirks, encouraging them to critique the evaluation plan, and privately conversing with them outside the conference room. On thirteen separate instances during the two-hour meeting, Melissa translated the contents of the evaluation plan for her grantees or critiqued the plan for not capturing activities that were already underway.

At one point, I reviewed the key questions guiding the evaluation—questions that the team developed based on the stated program goals. Melissa turned to the grantees and told them, "This is really the opportunity to look and see if they seem like the right questions." One grantee mentioned partnerships she had developed. Others chimed in with similar stories. Melissa worried that those activities weren't included in the evaluation. She explained:

> I actually would love us to go back ... and take a look at these [questions] again, from *that* context. So you're right, there's a lot of richness in what you're each learning, both about your neighborhood, and what it means for people to come together, to work on things together. And all kinds of other things in terms of partnerships and things that are coming out of it. So can you look back at these questions, and see if *these* questions get us to *that* richness? You know, get us to that diversity of things that you're seeing? (her emphasis)

After a pause, she turned to her grantees and added, "I know they look like very general questions on a page, but what we're really trying to figure out is if we're spending all our time focused on this [evaluation], are we going to get to the things that really matter that are happening in your contexts?"

One grantee pointed to a question about increasing resident participation. He said he found it useful. "And those sub-questions look right, too?" Melissa asked with a slightly skeptical inflection. He looked down at his papers and didn't answer. Another grantee, Monica, described partnerships that had begun to emerge through the program, as well as noticeable increases in resident participation. Melissa asked, "So Monica, do you see questions in here that will get us there, to that stuff?" Monica briefly paused before responding,

"I think some questions are missing." She then asked for more time to think about what, exactly, was missing. Forty minutes later, as the meeting drew to a close, Melissa and the grantees offered to give the evaluation team feedback at a later date.

Melissa met separately with the grantees, and the following week, she sent a memo to the evaluation team in which she emphasized the need to capture the grantees' accomplishments. She said she was less interested in proving (or testing) her own organization's "theory of change," a phrase used in the nonprofit sector in reference to how and why programs produce expected outcomes. As she wrote:

> [T]here is a general concern that the evaluation does not seem to be of sufficient benefit to the neighborhoods' attempt to understand their impact. *The group's current sense is that the evaluation seems focused on developing lessons for people who might undertake this work in the future, and is not sufficiently focused on the outcomes that the groups have achieved or the progress they are making on these outcomes.* The group is interested in finding ways to ensure their needs to evaluate outcomes are met at the same time the document attempts to fill holes in the research world or proving LISC's theory of change. . . . The group also shared a general concern about a lack of sufficient focus on how people in the neighborhood are benefiting from this work. (emphasis added)

The evaluation team included the metrics in the final evaluation plan.

Everyone depicted in this scene—Geeta, Melissa, the evaluation team, and the nonprofit organization grantees—was in a difficult bind. If LISC were the sole funder, then Melissa would have had no need to justify her approach to the evaluation team; if the team did not conduct the kind of evaluation she wanted, she could simply terminate the contract or not hire them in the first place. The problem for Melissa was that *her* funder, TBF, funded the team.

Meanwhile, because TBF was only one of ten funders for the RC/RF program, Geeta was also unable to impose her will. Some of those funders were hands-off, others less so. Geeta was well aware of the position LISC's staff members found themselves in. At another meeting of the evaluation group, she asked Bob, LISC's director, "What are the expectations of your funders?" "Well, they vary," Bob responded. He continued:

> I would say, The Boston Foundation and The Hyams Foundation are at two different places. The Hyams Foundation is very much about the organizing and engagement and the process. I think you all have consistently been more about the poverty reduction and then the, kind of, broader social indicators . . . And the Barr Foundation was about greenhouse gas reductions [laughs].[23]

Varying expectations are a challenge for any organization. In this particular situation, it presented a challenge for the entire *network* of funders: With so many different interests and perspectives in play, it was difficult to draw clear lines of authority. It reduced the power of any one funder and shifted incentives toward defending grantees rather than holding them accountable to a funder's programmatic goals. This applied to both LISC *and* TBF: It was hard for Melissa and Bob to control the evaluation because it was being funded by TBF, and it was *also* hard for Geeta and TBF staff to control the evaluation because LISC received funding from a number of other funders.

The dynamics were complicated further by the racial politics of the evaluation. The members of the evaluation team who attended the meeting were all white, but four of the five grantees were nonwhite. I learned years later that Melissa had specifically recommended people of color to add to the evaluation team, but her suggestions were ignored by TBF, her funder—a fact that added to her skepticism about the team's recommendations.

The structure of "funders funding funders" pushed organizations like LISC and MSGA to align with and even cede power to their grantees. A network of funding has its advantages for funders: When multiple funders each contributed a relatively small amount of money to a large community development effort, each could claim full credit for that effort's outcomes.[24] The tradeoff for funders, though, was that complicated funding structures diffused authority and inverted the traditional power imbalance between funder and grantee. We might assume funding is a series of dyadic relationships between individual funders and individual grantees. But for LISC's RC/RF program and MSGA's Great Neighborhoods Initiative, it was far more complex. Yes, LISC and MSGA were funders. But they were also grantees. TBF and Barr were caught in a similar web: They were funders, but not the *only* funders. The tangle of distributions and redistributions meant that nonprofits were rarely fully reliant on a single funder—meaning, conversely, that funders rarely had full control over their grantees.[25]

Picking Winners and Losers

In 2004, Geeta, Angela, and Bob encouraged four community development corporations (CDCs) in the Fairmount Corridor to formalize a partnership and coordinate their work. The funders agreed that a "Corridor" of community development was more impactful than scattered projects across multiple neighborhoods. Geeta went so far as to pay a former family therapist-turned-consultant to meet with the nonprofit directors and help them work on their communication skills.[26]

Yet funders did not treat each CDC in the coalition equally. They saw great value in funding Dorchester Bay Economic Development Corporation (DBEDC), located in Upham's Corner, and the Codman Square Neighborhood

Development Corporation (CSNDC). Each was well capitalized and had a long track record of successful projects. Those successes made funders look good, even when each funder's individual grant only accounted for a small portion of total project costs. Funders rewarded DBEDC and CSNDC with relatively ample resources and sizable lines of credit—special privileges that gave these organizations breathing room to complete expensive projects and continue showing success.

Funders were more reluctant when it came to Mattapan Community Development Corporation (MCDC), located in Mattapan, and Southwest Boston Community Development Corporation (SWBCDC), located in Hyde Park. These two organizations were "low capacity" and "politically weak" according to funders, unlikely to translate funding into tangible program outcomes due to small staff sizes and limited development portfolios. Unlike DBEDC and CSNDC, which boasted $5.2 million and $3.5 million annual revenues in 2012, respectively, MCDC took in just $666,476 and SWBCDC made only $283,536. It was a catch-22: Funders treated them as poor candidates for funding because they were underfunded.

Both MCDC and SWBCDC experienced significant financial difficulties during my fieldwork, and private funders played a pivotal role in affecting organizational survival. MCDC's struggles resulted in its bankruptcy. SWBCDC survived, largely in spite of funders' indifference. In each case, when private funders denied initial funding requests, community development projects were delayed or abandoned altogether.

FUNDERS TURN THEIR BACKS ON MCDC

In spring 2011, Spencer, MCDC's director, went on vacation and never returned to work. Michelle, a Black staff member, became interim director. She inherited a history of financial mismanagement, including a budget shortfall and tens of thousands of dollars in taxes owed on six properties.

Michelle's colleagues in the CDC coalition grew concerned about MCDC's precarious financial state. Their worries peaked during a monthly meeting of CDC directors and their consultants in October 2011. The email invitation for the meeting noted a single agenda item: "[A] request to address both the financial stability of each member CDC and the status of the Mattapan CDC in the [coalition]." At the meeting, Gail, the Black director of CSNDC, revealed that the request was hers. She said she did not mean it as a personal attack, but she questioned the leadership of the organization. The coalition couldn't afford to look "weak," particularly to funders and government officials.[27] Mike, the white director of SWBCDC, brought up a lack of communication on Michelle's part, and Jeanne, the white director of DBEDC, raised specific concerns with respect to MCDC's financial obligations. A consultant revealed his perception that city officials considered MCDC "a dead organization" and would not fund it. "It's the wide nasty world of politics," Jeanne noted.

Gail had lost confidence in Michelle and MCDC, and she wanted to vote the organization out of the coalition. But Mike and Jeanne advised caution: MCDC deserved a chance to present a plan that would alleviate their concerns. More important, Mike and Jeanne stressed, they needed to hear what the coalition's key funders thought of the situation. Everyone agreed that a follow-up meeting with the funders was necessary. And it should be held somewhere other than MCDC—a neutral site, Gail proposed, like one of the funders' offices.[28]

The group convened at TBF a week later. Geeta and three other funders were present. In addition to the four CDC directors, MCDC's Black board president also attended. Gail chaired the meeting and reiterated her "serious concerns" about MCDC's finances and the organization's ability to satisfy the requirements of the coalition's grants.

Geeta spoke after Gail. She stated TBF's position plainly: "Our concern is the needs of the Mattapan community and what works best, not the viability of an organization." Geeta questioned MCDC's ability to plan and implement community development projects. Further, she charged, the organization lacked crucial political capital: She had heard city government officials express concerns about the organization's capacity. She revealed that she had decided to fund a consultant group to develop strategies for MCDC's future—strategies that included dissolution. "We've put too much into this for it to be weakened and not strengthened. This is considered by [city government] to be a weakness," she said, emphasizing the perception of MCDC in the broader community development field.

The meeting danced around the central issue of MCDC's future for an hour and a half. Finally, Geeta asked Michelle and the board president pointedly: What did they want to do next? The board president responded with a direct request for funding:

> I'd like a commitment from the funders. I wouldn't be surprised if you rejected it, but I'd like a commitment. We need to operate one to two months before we can be functioning right. We can give you a monthly operating budget that we would need. Short of that, we're just trying to find money to stay open.

"I just don't see a plan there," Geeta responded. "Operating support isn't a solution." The other funders agreed. The meeting ended with each refusing to make a funding commitment.

Without funding, MCDC was forced to cease operations. It filed for bankruptcy protection in May 2012. As described in the previous chapter, the neighborhood of Mattapan suffered greatly. There was no organization to accept resources earmarked for the neighborhood, implement community development projects, or compete for new grants. Some minor projects continued with for-profit developers or social service providers. Nothing, however, rose to a level comparable to the efforts occurring in other neighborhoods in the Corridor.

SWBCDC SURVIVES, IN SPITE OF FUNDERS' INDIFFERENCE

A month before MCDC's bankruptcy filing, Mike, SWBCDC's director, faced his own financial crisis. He, too, called a "neutral-site" meeting with the same three private funding organizations and his fellow coalition members. Mike brought along a pair of board members for support.

The situation, he explained, was dire: Staff raises had been postponed for the third year in a row, all staff hours had been cut to part-time, and if no assistance was forthcoming, he would have to resign as director. By calling this meeting, Mike said, he was "turning to family, so to speak, during challenging times."

The funders offered no reprieve. "Frankly, our resources for the rest of the year are spoken for. There's nothing we can do," Geeta told Mike. "So it feels frustrating, you know. Maybe three months ago, you know, I could have eked out something. But I have nothing for you." The funders encouraged Mike to consider alternative organizational models that may not result in many development projects but would allow SWBCDC to continue to operate with a leaner budget. One funder suggested he turn to a "virtual" real estate portfolio of joint ventures and consultant-led work.

Mike was visibly frustrated after the meeting. But he vowed to keep the organization afloat. He took loans from some board members, other organizations in the coalition, and family members. Because MCDC had folded, some of the coalition's funding that had been proposed for MCDC transferred to SWBCDC. And while TBF and Hyams refused to offer anything beyond what had already been committed, LISC was more receptive. Its funding came with an important catch, however: LISC would *not* support general operating expenses. The available funding could pay for some of Mike's salary, but only if he used it to design a long-term plan for the organization. That funding, plus the money that came in at the beginning of the new fiscal year, helped Mike keep the organization's doors open for another year.

SWBCDC's financial stability was only temporary. During a meeting of the CDC coalition in June 2013, Mike announced that he was stepping down as director. SWBCDC was in the red again, and his salary was the last expense they could cut. If the organization were to survive, it would need a part-time interim director at a lower pay grade.

After the meeting, I spoke with Mike. He told me that earlier in the year, TBF had funded a consultant group to complete an organizational plan for

SWBCDC. "They [the consultant group] basically said, 'You know, it sounds like what this will boil down to, to a larger degree, is how much do funders care? Because you're not in a position . . . to not need substantial assistance for still the . . . short- to perhaps mid-term.'" The firm interviewed fourteen different "stakeholders" to see how much funders did, indeed, care. The very last interview was with Geeta. Though the specifics of the interview were confidential, the consultants gave Mike the gist of it: As far as TBF was concerned, community development in Hyde Park was not a priority, particularly in comparison to the other Corridor neighborhoods. They had no interest in additional support beyond funding the consultant group. At that point, the scope of the consultants' work shifted from strategic planning to transitional planning.

It wasn't exactly a shock. As Mike reminded me, "We went through this last year. And the funders did not respond." Private funders saw smaller organizations as liabilities, unlikely to produce successful projects. Mike and SWBCDC faced an additional challenge related to the geography of race and class. Recall chapter 3, and the discussion of TBF's strategic framing of "the Fairmount Corridor" as Roxbury, Dorchester, and Mattapan—segregated neighborhoods of concentrated poverty. Hyde Park lacked the same history of disadvantage, and few funders even realized how racially segregated it had become by 2010.[29] Mike understood the situation. He had raised the issue with TBF staff before, when Hyde Park was ignored during one of TBF's tours. As he recalled, "The less senior staff basically tried to explain that away, when we raised it, as 'Oh, I think that's just a way to kind of not have to, you know, utter such a mouthful.' And I can remember thinking, 'That's a crock of fucking shit.'"

While SWBCDC did not file for bankruptcy protection like MCDC, community development in the neighborhood still suffered. Mike had been working on a new housing development since 2010, but with the organization's financial struggles, he lacked the time and energy to make it a reality.[30] Staff cuts made it difficult to apply for new grants, and as a result, Hyde Park did not receive the same attention as other neighborhoods in the Corridor.

"It's not the money you bring in," Geeta told me in 2013, "It's your power." As we talked in 2013, Geeta was describing a $20 million HUD grant for Corridor development. She said it was "no accident," but a product of TBF's efforts to cultivate the federal government's interest in the Fairmount Corridor. TBF's influence, she concluded, extended far beyond the organization's grants.

Money is of course a form of power. But as this chapter showed—and as Geeta implied—it would be a mistake to assume funders *only* used grants to affect community development plans. Funders like Geeta developed informal relationships with government bureaucrats, convened large groups of players from across the field, connected grantees to other resource-holding organizations and government agencies, and brokered disputes between organizations in conflict. These activities bear a striking resemblance to the case of the Ford Foundation and its Gray Areas program. In the 1960s, Ford concentrated resources in a few select cities and then used lessons from its pilot demonstrations to influence national urban policy. As historian Alice O'Connor argues, Ford "played the role of intermediary, providing the seed grants, technical assistance, and intellectual brokering that would put the 'Gray Area' cities into the pipeline for more substantial federal dollars."[31] Notably, the US Congress attempted to curb Ford's and other foundations' growing influence through the Tax Reform Act of 1969, restricting foundations from directly influencing legislation. Yet formal rules did little to stop subtler, behind-the-scenes forms of politicking.

From the perspective of funders, these behaviors were hardly controversial. Influencing policy and persuading other funders to support their grantees made their grantees' work easier. Yet these taken-for-granted practices inadvertently contributed to neighborhood inequality. Geographic agglomeration benefited resource-rich neighborhoods and disadvantaged all others. And because funders wanted to support successful projects, they were incentivized to ignore the people and places in greatest need. Mattapan and Hyde Park residents would certainly have benefited from community development projects, but funders felt little responsibility or obligation to fund MCDC and SWBCDC, two organizations that struggled to plan and implement projects. Funders saw grants to these organizations—which were regarded as neighborhood proxies—as a poor investment.

The underlying issue is not specific to these particular organizations or this particular place. It is worth noting that the federal government also approached funding with a similar bias toward "capacity." Recall the Choice Neighborhoods program, detailed in chapter 1. The official application rubric weighed capacity (49%) twice as high as need (24%). By privileging strong leadership and previous experience, government officials hoped to make the most efficient use of public resources. We would expect private funders to be more flexible than government, more willing to take risks with respect to social programs that might fail. Risk-taking and innovation are two widely proclaimed benefits of institutional philanthropy. As detailed in this chapter, however, private funders could be just as risk-averse as public agencies, valuing capacity above all other factors when making allocation decisions.

One way to make sense of the bias toward capacity is to understand the incentive to fund successful projects. Drawing on a case study of international humanitarian aid, sociologist Monika Krause shows how philanthropy functions less like charity and more like a market for projects. Managers at humanitarian nonprofits seek "good projects" with measurable outcomes, clearly delineated time horizons, and defined budgets. The "good project" becomes a commodity that nonprofits sell to both institutional and individual donors. But only certain projects fit the technical parameters of a "good project." Problems like urban poverty will never fit in this framework; they are too complex, too costly, and have no obvious end date. And because nonprofits *sell* projects in the donor marketplace, value and efficiency can supersede mission and need. As one respondent in Krause's study said, "If you were doing it solely according to need, would you be giving everything to Somalias and Central African Republics? Surely the needs are greatest there. But then would nothing be going to the Kenyas?"[32] Each site may need resources, but relative need was not the ultimate deciding factor. For policymakers who rely on foundations' funding and policy expertise, this is a significant limitation to consider.

Still, funder power was not infallible. Yes, their central position in the field helped them build relationships with other agencies and organizations. It also placed structural limits on their influence. Large, national foundations tied to wealthy families are less likely to solicit funding from other funders. For small and mid-size funders—those who had the biggest effect on the day-to-day functioning of urban governance—money flowed through more complex arrangements. The resulting web of grant distributions and redistributions made some funders simultaneously funders and grantees, dispersing authority and reducing individual funders' leverage over their direct grantees.

On this point, the scenes described above may be unique to this particular policy area. Community development metrics are notably ambiguous. Even short-term outcomes, like developing new housing or improving public transit, can take many years beyond the scope of a single grant—and that is to say nothing of longer-term goals, like poverty reduction or environmental sustainability. By contrast, other policy areas operate with a clearer set of socially accepted metrics of success. In education, for instance, metrics rarely go beyond grades, graduation rates, or test scores. Broadly accepted outcomes leave little room for grantees to push back against funders; the test scores go up, or they don't. Community development projects operate on a much longer time horizon than education interventions. And the causal links between individual grants, short-term project outcomes, and long-term social goals are less well established. The lack of institutionalized metrics may explain why funders exhibited less power and control than we might expect.

How, then, should we evaluate the role of private funders in urban governance and community development? If we are concerned about a dominating class of funders, then we may be comforted by the fact that there are limits to funder control. If we are concerned about funders' ability to hold their grantees accountable, then we may be discouraged to see the effect of dense funding networks on organizational incentives. If we are concerned about neighborhood inequality, then we may view funders' ability to pick winners and losers in a negative light, structurally disadvantaging neighborhoods represented by under-resourced organizations. That funders turned their backs on Corridor organizations in need seems to go against the very idea of charity. If we are concerned about nonprofit organizations' survival in spite of poor performance, then we may view funders' role as crucial for making sure resources are put to good use. It is not unheard of for community-based nonprofits to become institutionalized and persist even when they do not produce benefits for local residents.³³

Still, the contrasting concerns listed above are somewhat second order compared to a more fundamental issue: These are *private* organizations influencing *public* policy. It is worth remembering that private funders operate with little public oversight and almost no public accountability. It can be a good thing when philanthropic resources help reduce poverty or contribute to worthwhile community development projects. Yet as a growing list of scholars including Sarah Reckhow, Rob Reich, and Megan Tompkins-Stange show, the fact that private funders have influence is, in and of itself, a threat to democratic governance.³⁴ In the Fairmount Corridor, private funders influenced policy behind the scenes and allocated resources as they pleased. To the extent that residents even knew about funders' political negotiations, they lacked democratic mechanisms to determine how resources were spent.

In Mattapan and Hyde Park, neighborhood residents suffered as a result of funder ambivalence. Because the system of urban governance required a community-based organization to represent a neighborhood's interests, private funders' rejection of an *organization's* needs effectively cut off the *neighborhood's* access to resources. Allowing community-based organizations to die or weaken also affected neighborhoods' voice in community development politics—the topic of the next chapter.

CHAPTER SIX

Community Power

THE CODMAN SQUARE TECHNOLOGY CENTER was bustling. It was late March 2010, and inside the building's entryway, twenty people waited to sign a visitor's log. After signing in, some entered a room where free tax preparation services were being offered. A few others made their way to a room filled with desktop computers. But most entered a third room, the largest in the building, where sixty or so people were already settling in for a public community meeting.

Paper plates and plastic forks in hand, several attendees hovered around a buffet of red beans and rice, cabbage, marinated oxtail, and fried plantains. The rest sat, eight across, in neatly arranged rows of chairs. The meeting was an opportunity for residents of Four Corners to meet with Steve Early, the president of S&R Construction Company. S&R, a New Hampshire–based firm, had recently won a bid to construct a new Fairmount Line station in Four Corners, just up the street from the Technology Center. The Greater Four Corners Action Coalition (GFCAC), a local community-based organization, co-sponsored the meeting with the state transportation authority.

Steve, a middle-aged white man dressed in a light brown button-down shirt, jeans, tan work boots, and thin-framed glasses, was at the front of the room near a lectern. Three officials from the transportation authority stood next to him, including Wanda, a Black woman in her forties from the State Transportation Authority's Office of Diversity and Civil Rights, and Pablo, a Latino community relations manager in his fifties. Marvin, GFCAC's Black executive director, chatted with residents at the back of the room, while Mela, a Black community organizer with GFCAC, moved up and down the aisle, handing out copies of the meeting agenda.

Of the seventy people in the room, only ten were white. The rest were people of color.

At 6:30, the dull roar of conversation quieted as an older Black man approached the lectern. He did not introduce himself, but his assumed authority suggested he was somehow affiliated with the meeting's sponsors, and his casual, untucked shirt hinted that he was likely linked to the nonprofit co-sponsor, GFCAC. "Good evening, ladies and gentlemen," the man said, speaking with a West Indian accent.

> For more than twenty years the Four Corners community have lobbied for stops on the Fairmount Line . . . We have fought hard, and it was agreed after our struggles that we'll have four stops along the Fairmount Line. We have been involved from the selection of the sites, to the designs. Everything, we've been involved in . . . This is a community-based—what do you call it?—a community-based project in that we, the community, were the force behind this . . . And, as we go forward, this is our first community meeting that involves the principal of S&R Construction, Mr. Steve Early.

In the crowd, a cell phone's muffled ring was silenced. After a brief pause, the man continued. "There's jobs involved," he said, referring to construction jobs, "and what we're fighting for is jobs for the neighborhood people. Too often, again, people from the outside benefit from what we have fought for. Away with that." He clarified that GFCAC itself was not hiring, but the organization could help steer people in the right direction. "We don't control the construction site. We're not contactors. We're just neighborhood persons trying to make sure that justice prevails for neighborhood people—people of color."

The man finished his portion of the talk and introduced Pablo. In turn, Pablo invited Wanda to talk about workforce diversity.

"Good evening," Wanda began. "We're happy to be in the community and getting this project started." She detailed the demographic goals for the project workforce: 30 percent minority workers and 6.9 percent female workers across all subcontractors. S&R Construction, she said, had "made every effort to reach out to the community and get everyone involved."

Steve, S&R's president, echoed Wanda's overtures. "We want to hire more from the community," he said, noting that half a dozen women and people of color were currently working on the project. "We *are* taking an interest in this community, to making it right for everybody."

Pablo told the audience that state officials would distribute monthly reports to keep track of the quotas. Everyone who signed in to the meeting would receive updates via email. "Again I'd like to thank all of you for inviting us to this meeting, and we will continue working very closely with the community throughout this process. Any questions, please pick up the phone and call me." Pablo provided a phone number where he could be reached.

The next item on the agenda was a question-and-answer period, moderated by Mela. Residents lodged questions about pest control and other matters, but the conversation quickly zeroed in on the Fairmount Line workforce goals. How would they be enforced? Who would be responsible for connecting workers from the neighborhood to S&R? And could the community see workforce statistics weekly rather than monthly?

On the issue of a weekly report, Mela moved from moderator to participant. "When we pre-met with all of the [transportation authority officials], and the contractor, Mr. Early and his crew, and the Office of Diversity, we were told that we would get a weekly or biweekly report," she said, directing her comments at the state officials. "So, the monthly report is not really what we had agreed to . . . We had a few meetings before we got here so that we could make sure that all of our bases were covered, so that we would be able to come and bring you the real information and all the issues that were brought to us so that we could have those things addressed, so that we could come here with some agreements that the community would accept. And so I just want to know why the change happened since the last meeting."

An official from the state explained: The state's contract with S&R stipulated a monthly pay schedule. In order to get paid, S&R would submit payroll information that would contain the demographic statistics used to verify workforce quotas. The data on workforce demographics would, as a result, only be available monthly.

"That's fine," Marvin called out from the back of the room. "But I don't like surprises at a community meeting. So when we agreed to something, and you found out later that you couldn't live up to that, it would have been nice if you called our office and said 'Look this is what we found out' since then."

"That's fair," Wanda responded meekly.

The remaining questions centered on the logistics of monitoring the workforce quotas, potential coordination with local organizations, and the design of signage around the new station. As 8pm approached, Marvin moved to the front of the room to summarize what had been discussed and give assurances about future opportunities for residents to hold the contractor accountable. It would be a long process moving forward, but he reminded everyone that GFCAC had already negotiated a number of concessions. "This is a working process," Marvin explained. "I think what we got from S&R to this point, before we even came here, was a major accomplishment . . . I think you need to know, as Mela has mentioned about our pre-work that brought us to this, to get us to this point, where we did come in here with some agreements already."

After the meeting, about a dozen people mingled. They chatted and exchanged information. By 8:30, the room had emptied and the building closed for the night.

When residents of the Fairmount Corridor wanted to influence projects in their neighborhoods, they attended meetings like this one. As a technology of governance, public participation is by no means limited to poor neighborhoods—or even urban politics, for that matter. Indeed, participation has been a centerpiece of American political institutions since the colonial era, often romanticized in the nostalgic image of a New England town meeting. Participation is fundamental to Americans' notions of democratic citizenship. Today, sociologist Caroline Lee notes, "Americans face proliferating invitations to 'have your say!' and 'join the conversation!'"[1]

Participation is increasing everywhere, though it has become *particularly* common in poor neighborhoods. Demands for community control and self-determination among low-income communities of color were fueled, in part, by the Black Power Movement in the 1960s. In response, government policies like the Community Action Program, with its requirement for "maximum feasible participation" in local antipoverty efforts, helped institutionalize the practice. And emerging organizational forms, like community development corporations, continued the tradition long after specific government reforms ended. This combination of ideas, policies, and organizational structures transformed radical demands for resident participation into a mundane, taken-for-granted step in community development planning.

In theory, participatory governance expands decision-making power beyond elites and experts to everyday residents equipped with experiential knowledge. Participation enables democracy by incorporating that unique knowledge into public decision-making. Advocates of participatory democracy expect that neighborhood conditions will necessarily improve when the voices of local residents are considered.[2]

Recent research, however, critiques the ways participation unfolds in practice. An entire industry of participation experts has emerged, professionalizing participation in ways that can decouple deliberation from authentic grassroots mobilization. In fact, elite actors often use lay participation to *counter* social movements and protests. "Rather than serve as a challenge to elite and expert authority," sociologist Michael McQuarrie argues, "participation is now deployed as a tool of that authority."[3]

These tensions were evident during the meeting in Four Corners. At first blush, the residents at that meeting certainly seemed empowered. Public officials like Wanda and Pablo deferred to "the community" as a valued stakeholder and structured the meeting accordingly: Hosting the meeting in public implied transparency. Using a sign-in sheet to distribute updates signaled open lines of communication. And matching the food to the ethnic composition of the neighborhood suggested respect for local residents.

Yet initial impressions can be deceiving. Under the guise of a free-flowing conversation, the event actually followed a fairly rigid structure. Public officials may have intimated deference, but they offered no real *concessions*. Promises to hire more people "from the community" are not, after all, enforceable commitments. And who, exactly, qualified as "the community"? Residents of Boston? *People of color* from Boston? People of color from *Four Corners*?

It was never clarified. The commitment to ongoing communication similarly lacked adequate follow-through. Even though I had signed in at the meeting and provided my email address, I never received any updates on the station, nor did Pablo return my calls when I dialed the number he had provided to the crowd.

References to "pre-meetings" and private agreements between nonprofit leaders and government officials were also curious, potentially undermining the democratic promise of participation. No one voiced concern when Marvin said he "[didn't] like surprises at a community meeting" or when Mela said GFCAC "had a few meetings before we got here . . . so that we could come here with some agreements that the community would accept." At the time, even I thought their comments were ordinary. Only after conducting fieldwork in similar "pre-meetings" and returning to my field notes did I find it noteworthy. But these hidden conversations happening outside of public meetings are significant. They suggested that much of what appeared to unfold organically in public were in fact privately predetermined. And they hinted at the powerful role community-based organizations played in translating the act of participation into the realization of political voice.

A Promising Community Process—On the Surface

In the Fairmount Corridor, community meetings followed a particular script. There was an official sponsor, such as a government agency or a local nonprofit. Meetings were announced by distributing flyers—often including the text "Community Meeting" in large font—via email, social media (Twitter and Facebook), and, less frequently, hard copies left at community centers or other public places. The central targets for outreach were immediate residents near a particular development project ("abutters") or other knowledgeable residents and nonprofit leaders ("stakeholders").

Meetings were held in the late evenings or weekends, most often beginning at 6 or 6:30pm, Monday through Thursday. Rain or shine, participants shuffled into church basements, public gymnasiums, or nonprofit conference rooms. A center aisle would divide rows of metal or plastic folding chairs. The room could be new, like the Mattapan Library's multipurpose room, with modern light fixtures dangling six feet from the ceiling. Or the room could be old, like the Great Hall in Dorchester, with creaking wood floors and the kind of civic sediment that can never be fully cleaned from nooks and crannies.

A small table was usually placed somewhere near the main entrance. It held a meeting agenda and materials, as well as a sign-in sheet with spaces for participants' names, affiliations, phone numbers, and (sometimes) email addresses. The sign-in sheet gave the impression that officials systematically collected contact information and would notify participants of future meetings or decisions. Depending on the meeting sponsor's budget, there might be a spread toward the back of the room—sometimes the food aligned ethnically with the neighborhood, like oxtail or tamales, but other times it was more generic, like chicken casserole or turkey sandwiches.

Participants filtered in, as early as fifteen minutes before the meeting started and as late as one hour after the meeting began. The rows of chairs incrementally filled as people first sat with one or two seats separating themselves, gradually occupying the vacancies. Long-time neighborhood leaders congregated in the back of the room. They informally welcomed new faces as self-appointed stewards of the neighborhood.

The meeting's moderator—a government official or nonprofit community organizer—opened the meeting with an introduction, a welcome, and a description of the meeting's purpose. They would ask elected officials and members of the press to identify themselves, giving the meeting a sense of official importance. A formal presentation from the moderator followed introductions. Sometimes, it was a slick slideshow with before-and-after schematics of a proposed streetscape. Other times, it was simply a moderator standing in front of the room reading from prepared remarks.

After 15–30 minutes of formal presentation, moderators "opened it up" for feedback. The vast majority of meetings included fewer than fifty participants, and so these feedback periods resembled a classroom lecture. Anyone present could raise their hand at any point, and when called on by a moderator, could raise any point they felt like raising. The practice conveyed equality and openness; it gave the impression that no topic was off-limits and that no attendee received unfair preference. At government-sponsored meetings, an official or consultant recorded notes ("meeting minutes"), which they sometimes distributed via email or uploaded on a website after the meeting ended. An official note-taker signaled a transparent process, but more important, it encoded the ceremony with a sense that participants' remarks were acknowledged and taken seriously.

After approximately two hours, the moderator would close the meeting by addressing "next steps": the schedule of the development project, the process for incorporating feedback, and a promise to notify attendees about future meetings. Officials would note, "This is just the beginning of the process," even if there had already been many meetings on the same development project—a statement implying indefinite future opportunities to influence community development plans.

Claiming Community Credentials

In these participatory processes, residents and nonprofit leaders claimed authority based on their representation of "the community." These references, what I call *community credentials*, preceded specific points or suggestions, imbuing individuals' comments with an added sense of value. One example occurred during the Four Corners Station meeting, when, during the question-and-answer period, Mela called on a Black man in his forties.

The man, wearing a black baseball hat, black sweatshirt, and paint-stained jeans, stood up and announced, "My name is Frank Hart, and I'm representing the community." Heads turned to face him. Bodies shifted. Frank spoke in a lyrical cadence that captivated the room. "For this particular project to be substantial, and for it to move forward, *we* as the community must make sure that we hold everybody that's supposed to be held accountable, accountable to make sure that these quotas are met. That's the first piece."

Frank went on to equate racial quotas with the moral significance of Barack Obama's recent election, raising his voice incrementally with each sentence:

> My solution, and my suggestion, is very clear, and it's very simple . . . It is not saying *could* you [subcontract to minority businesses]—no, you *have* to [subcontract]. We have an African American president—first time. We got a healthcare reform—first time. We got a commuter rail—first time. I'll be *darned* if I'm gonna . . . sit here for the millionth time to see business ran as usual. Not today. Not now. (his emphasis)

A dozen people in the audience nodded their heads in support. "Now, I also want to say that, you have the—just bear with me because this is important."

"Go 'head brother, you got the floor," an older Black man exhorted from his seat.

Frank looked directly at Steve, S&R's president. He referenced the goal, established by the state Office of Diversity and Civil Rights, for 30 percent of subcontractors to be minority-owned businesses. "I am holding you accountable, my man, because there's a 30 percent manpower goal that must be *met* by each contractor." Then Frank turned his attention to his fellow audience members. "Now let's not get it twisted: At the end of the day, if they don't fulfill their obligations, then this man here—it will be held on the general contractor to make sure that 30 percent is *acquired*. So that's my piece."

He briefly paused before nearly shouting, "Because I'm not here to play games!"

"Ok now!" a woman in the audience called out in support.

"I'm here to make sure folk work and make sure we do what we gotta do. That's it. Thank you."

Frank took his seat to the sound of loud applause.

For Frank, his representation of "the community" was couched in racial symbolism. He tied racial quotas for construction jobs in his neighborhood to the election of a Black president. The broader symbolism associated with "the community" bolstered his call for minority employment opportunities.

At the end of the meeting, the Black proprietor of a dirt-hauling company introduced herself to Steve Early. Her firm would later receive a subcontract and join the construction team. She and the rest of the subcontractors completed construction in 2013.

Residents can also evoke the boundary of "community" membership in attempts to delegitimize the positions of opponents—a practice I call *policing the boundaries of community membership*. As conflicts arise, the discursive tactic of policing community representation is used instead of countering competing claims directly; to be classified as an outgroup member is enough to have one's substantive comments invalidated for not representing the common good.

In 2010, for instance, residents of the Fairmount Corridor appeared to persuade government officials to award a contract for a transit needs study to a consultant team with greater community representation, subjectively defined. The state Department of Transportation had received five bids for a contract to conduct a Roxbury-Dorchester-Mattapan Transit Needs Study. Before the contract was awarded, officials required the two finalists—Arch Professional Group and McMahon Associates—to present study plans to local residents at a meeting in a Roxbury public library.

The consultant team assembled by Arch included mostly people of color who identified as residents of Roxbury, Dorchester, or Mattapan. A Black man led their presentation. One of the first questions from the audience was, in fact, a statement: "It's nice to see so many folks from the community on this team," a middle-aged Black man said. "I don't know how many planning processes I am a part of, and the consultants are never from our communities, and not familiar with our communities." One of the consultants took the opportunity to equate her own interests with the interests of the common good, noting, "With our being part of the community . . . I can continually stay in touch, as a member of the team. But also as a resident, I have a vested interest in this being successful because this means that *my* neighborhood can [benefit]."

McMahon's team, comprised of five firms, presented next. Their group was predominantly white. They emphasized their technical expertise and past experience working in low-income neighborhoods. With a South Asian accent, one of the consultants emphasized the McMahon team's desire to "really meet the needs of you, the community: the businesses, the residents, the people who live and work here."

After this presentation, Marcus, a Black independent laborer and Mattapan resident, questioned how policy recommendations would emerge from the study. In particular, he challenged the ability of the McMahon consultants ("they") to represent the community ("we"):

> I hear you saying "we." I'm trying to understand clearly, who is "we"? Is that the [consultant] team? Does it involve community participation in that? And have you talked at all about the finances of "we," and who's getting paid, and how much, and how does the community fit into that

structure? Because I see us constantly having this battle of "we" versus "they"—you're doing something supposedly for our benefit, but *we're* not included financially, in the planning . . . Can you talk a little bit about that, and how you set that in motion so that people who are part of these communities—people who live in those communities—actually participate in the planning, and get paid for doing it just like you're getting paid? (his emphasis)

An elderly Black man asked a more direct follow-up question, attempting to clarify Marcus's opening query: "How many people from the district represent your company? And your company? And your company?" He pointed to each consultant sitting at the front of the room.

Ralph, a white consultant from McMahon, replied, "How many people *live* in the study area? I don't know that we have an answer for that."

"Is it zero? Is it zero?" Marcus pressed, his deep voice booming across the room.

"I don't believe it's zero, no. But I don't know . . . What I do know is that the folks you see before you have been working in Roxbury, in Dorchester, in Mattapan, throughout the city of Boston, on transit projects—"

"C'mon, let's keep it real!" Marcus shouted dismissively.

The elderly man kept pressing the consultants. "But how many live in the district?"

"In the study area? I don't know."

"Not one," Marcus asserted, sitting back in his chair.

The lone Black consultant with McMahon's team, Arthur, said that he lived in Dorchester, a few blocks from the specific study area. Then he asked why the question was important in the first place.

Marcus scrunched his brow. "We're not included, man! That's the answer!" he said. "We're not included. I see five groups up here and they're all from outside making money—huge amounts of money—at our expense, and we're not included! What are you—it's a no brainer! You brought five groups up there. How many of them include people from our neighborhoods? . . . How many of them? One? *Your* group?" Marcus pointed at Arthur, the lone Black man on the team, scoffing, "That's one person? C'mon!"

The moderator, a white state official, attempted to deflect. "Marcus, if I may, it sounds like they don't have an answer."

"Exactly! There's no answer. It's obvious we're being taken advantage of, and we have continuously for years," Marcus replied.

"We have a limited amount of time, Marcus."

"I got you. It's very limited when we start asking hard questions."

The interrogation lasted until a security guard politely asked everyone to leave so that he could close the building for the night.

Arch Professional Group won the contract and completed their study in September 2012. On the surface, this was a clear victory for local residents of the Corridor. At the same time, it is important to recognize the stakes at hand. Awarding the state contract to Arch Professional Group did not go against officials' stated interests. Nor did it involve a substantive claim or request for resources. Money for consultants had already been allocated, and officials did not express a preference for one consultant team over another. Marcus's query about paying residents, however, was ignored; a state official steered the conversation away from the racial politics of redevelopment consulting and limited the interaction to clarifying questions and matter-of-fact answers.

The meeting about construction jobs in Four Corners also appeared to produce a win for residents. Frank's emphatic comments directly resulted in the subcontract going to the Black woman's dirt-hauling company. Yet it is also important to consider the counterfactual: The dirt-hauling company counted as *both* a woman-owned and minority-owned business, making it especially valuable for S&R's workforce diversity numbers. It is possible that she would have received the subcontract even without the participatory process.

A Community Process, But Without Community Influence

When residents like Frank and Marcus made claims of authority during public meetings, they invoked their representation of the community. I heard that word—"community"—spoken thousands of times throughout the course of my fieldwork in Boston.[4] Sometimes it referred to feelings of solidarity and cohesion, like a "sense of community." Other times it referred to a racial group, like "the Black community," or a spatial territory, like a neighborhood. And other times it referred to a narrow group, like the specific people in attendance at a specific public meeting.

When government officials used the word, it was frequently a tactic for placating meeting participants. Objections to government plans were met with assurances that "the community" would be properly consulted—and once vetted, "the community" would benefit. Of course, officials never explicitly articulated who, precisely, they meant when they invoked "the community." The rhetoric was a nod to the *cultural value* of "the community," without any commitments or concessions to specific people or groups.

If "the community" is merely a vague ideal, then officials cannot be held accountable to a specific group or population. Officials can publicly praise the community, go through the motions of a community process, and claim due diligence toward satisfying residents' needs. But that means community empowerment is effectively reduced to a bureaucratic procedure, and officials can circumvent participating community members without appearing to do so.

Consider, for example, a "community visioning forum" held in Upham's Corner in February 2013. Residents and other stakeholders were asked to describe the sort of development they'd like to see in the neighborhood.

Demographically, the crowd was hardly representative of the neighborhood: Only one-third of the seventy participants lived in the neighborhood, 40 percent reported incomes greater than $100,000 (compared to a median family income in the neighborhood of $34,659), and more than 40 percent identified as "white" (compared to only 10.5% of the neighborhood).[5] After a formal presentation, officials from the Boston Redevelopment Authority (BRA) separated participants into small groups. City planners and employees served as moderators and note-takers for the small group discussions. Officials explained that the note-takers would aggregate comments from the groups in order to channel residents' interests into development plans.

In one group, Lara, a Latina BRA employee, was the official note-taker. She diligently recorded comments ranging from complaints about local transit service to recommendations for business district improvements. The tone of the conversation shifted, however, when a specific housing development came under discussion. Nancy, a white Upham's Corner resident, was upset about what she saw as City Hall's failure to adequately represent local interests in the development plans. "The community already came up with a plan," Nancy claimed. These plans included a community center, subsidized housing, and a shared parking garage. She continued, forcefully declaring that City Hall had "completely ignored what we as a community want."

Lara did not record Nancy's comments.

Still, Nancy continued. She identified a local nonprofit developer—"a stakeholder in the community"—that had not been mentioned by the officials in their presentation. This nonprofit had been in conversation with the owner of the infamous Leon building, an abandoned 60,000- square-foot storage facility. She demanded that the local nonprofit be included and considered in community development discussions.

At this, Lara wrote: "Identify vacant parcels/abandoned buildings." The resident, of course, did not realize Lara had misrepresented her comments. Yet Lara's misleading notes would go on to serve as the basis for a summary of development recommendations.

The BRA hosted a public meeting the following month to present the plans. Speaking in front of a dozen residents, a consultant hired by the BRA introduced the results as "information coming from the community and the forum." However, the recommendations—calls to "integrate training and job incubator clusters" and "concentrate clustered uses and convert to housing," for example—were far more technical than the actual recommendations residents raised during the forum. The official made no mention of Nancy's concerns about the housing development or her request to include a local organization in future planning. The few residents who attended the plan meeting sat in silence as the consultant detailed complex plans full of urban planning jargon.

Empty gestures to "the community" continued when the final report was published. It included a section, "Community Process," that contained eighteen uses of the word "community" and a picture labeled "Community participation and break-out sessions." In the picture, ten people are seated around a table as an eleventh person writes on a large poster board. I am at the center of the picture, even though I was not, and have never been, a community member according to any definition of the word. Adding to the absurdity, the picture was taken at an entirely different planning process meeting, held in November 2012.

At the forum, Lara's overtures—being the note-taker at a public "community vision" meeting—implied a level of transparency and respect for meeting participants. But the *content* of her note-taking revealed a deceptive disregard for residents' recommendations. Although Lara selectively omitted certain resident concerns, that didn't stop officials from calling the process "community-driven." More generally, the unrepresentative demographics of meeting participants went unchallenged, subsumed under the banner of "the community process." Further illustrating the hollowness of officials' deference to "the community," Lara was later promoted to deputy director of community planning—a position that entails engaging "community members" to execute a "community vision . . . informed by the community's input," according to the BRA's website.

Deference to "the community" silenced residents from disadvantaged neighborhoods in more explicit ways, as well. For example, in 2013 the BRA held a meeting in Dorchester to solicit input about bike lanes, traffic congestion, and other transportation issues. A white transportation consultant contracted by the BRA presented plans to consolidate a pair of Dudley Street bus stops. The state transportation authority had already committed to the consolidation; the consultant was just explaining the change as background context for her additional recommendations.

Residents at the meeting were both unaware of and upset with the bus stop consolidation. Stephon, a Black resident in his forties, argued that the bus stops were important for "this community." The consultant responded that a "robust public participation process" had already occurred, and during that process, "people were invited to submit comments." A young Black woman asked if it was too late to comment on the decision. The consultant paused as the room fell silent, then admitted, "it has pretty much been closed out." There were public meetings, she claimed, "and this was ultimately the decision that was made with the consensus of the community working with the City of Boston and working with the [state transportation authority]."

Residents at the meeting raised concerns about just how robust that public participation process could have been, given that this was the first they were hearing about the city taking away one of their bus stops. One claimed, "[W]ith all this community input, I was never invited. I didn't even know it was going on." Stephon expressed his concern that "the citizens that's being affected by this are not being made abreast of this until after the fact." He added, "That plan there, I see all the complications that's going to come with it. For the community. That's going to affect the community. You know, as residents."

Their objections were fruitless. Jeremy, a white BRA official, shrugged his shoulders and said that the consultants were simply relaying the information. The transportation authority, he said, "[already] went through a public process." As the consultant had articulated, the decision was made "with the consensus of the community." The discussion was closed.

Resident resistance was similarly shut down when parking came under discussion. The transportation consultant presented the benefits and disadvantages of resident-only on-street parking. "It's a tradeoff," she observed casually. Irritated, Stephon shouted, "I don't believe—see, you're saying it's a 'tradeoff.' I don't believe it's a 'tradeoff' when you're coming into someone's community and you're telling me I have to . . . take it or leave it." He argued that, "*as a resident*," he found the consultant's tradeoffs unacceptable.

Stephon's attempt to elevate the value of his argument—clarifying that he was a resident, objecting to the consultant "coming into someone's community"—was met with deference. Jeremy placated Stephon by claiming that these parking stipulations were not being imposed by the consultants but had emerged from "the community." With another shrug, Jeremy argued, "The context that got this all started here, came out of the community vision . . . We're not just throwing this out, pie in the sky. This started percolating at these community visions a lot of people had." He added dismissively, "If any of this is implemented, it's got a lot of community process to happen." Everyone agreed that "community process" was critical for any redevelopment project. Stephon slumped in his chair and did not respond.

In both discussions, resident dissent was met with discursive deference to "the community." In the case of the bus stop consolidation, a "community consensus" had already been reached. And in the parking case, the official assured, "[I]t's got a lot of community process to happen." For these officials, references to "the community" signified an abstract general public that attended, or would attend, community meetings. Dissenting residents were disempowered because they had not attended the previous community process, and by default, had not yet attended any future community process. The "community process" was a nod to the *value* of "the community" that nonetheless limited community participation to predefined times and ironically placed individuals outside "the community" if they had not attended. Further, a "community process" implies an unspecified future. Assurances of a future "community process"—regardless of whether there are actual plans for participation—can silence residents when they express dissent. Empty gestures to "the community" as a *concept* obscured the fact that these participatory processes undermined the power of community *members*.

The Community Contests a Transit Station in Mattapan

In 2005, the state responded to transit advocates in Boston by agreeing to build four new stations on the Fairmount Rail Line, including one on Blue Hill Avenue, in the predominantly Black neighborhood of Mattapan. State officials studied at least four different locations for the station, ultimately settling on a segment of tracks behind Woodhaven Street. A group of elderly Black middle-class homeowners, whose backyards abutted the proposed site, strongly contested the new station. They were a politically connected group; one member, Virginia Parks, was the widow of Paul Parks, a longtime civil rights activist and former education secretary under Governor Michael Dukakis.

Public meetings to discuss the design and location of the Blue Hill Avenue Station began in 2009. Residents from Woodhaven Street attended each meeting, stalwart in their resistance. They believed construction would damage their homes' foundations, negatively impact property values, and disrupt their quality of life. They cited one of the alternative segments, further south, as a more appropriate location for the new station.

In 2010, they sent a letter to Massachusetts Governor Deval Patrick and recruited two elected officials to advocate for them at the city and state levels: Rob Consalvo, a white city councilor, and Jack Hart, a white state senator. Senator Hart served on the Committee on Ways & Means, a powerful committee in charge of budget appropriations. In 2011, he hosted a series of private meetings in his office with state transportation officials and a handful of residents from Woodhaven Street. The residents expressed their concerns, and the officials promised to study alternative locations.[6]

State officials hosted a public meeting in June 2011 and reviewed the results of their analysis: Because of a variety of technical factors including the curvature of the tracks, the Blue Hill Avenue location was the only viable option. Buying in to the promise of participatory democracy, Woodhaven residents again voiced their opposition. One resident, Barbara Fields, a middle-aged Black woman and retired head of the Boston Public Schools Office of Equity, was especially adamant. "We're concerned about the damage to our homes," she said during the question-and-answer period, establishing her credentials as a community member. "We live there. We're invested in it. We're concerned about damage." She defended her statements as reflecting a broader sentiment in the neighborhood. "I think it is really *unfair* to paint this picture, you know, that 'This is good for this community, and it's a small group of people opposed.' It's not a small group. And our neighborhood association . . . covers *eight streets*." She concluded forcefully:

> The [transportation authority] is making decisions about this community without involving this community. And so I don't think it's fair.

We *are not* accepting of this ... It's not the same quality of life. And we opposed it [two years ago], we oppose it now, and we're going to fight you. If we have to lay down in front of those trucks, you're not putting that station behind our homes. (her emphasis)

Ten Black men and women sitting around her applauded as she sat back down.

Officially, the station remained "in design" for the next two years. But its progress was a hot topic during public meetings about community development in Mattapan. At an April 2013 meeting, Barbara addressed a crowd of mostly nonprofit leaders, city redevelopment officials, and state transportation officials. Speaking quickly and confidently, she again made the group's opposition clear and repeated their threat to physically block construction:

We've been dealing with this issue for the last three or four years, when we found out, after the fact, that it was going to be sited there. So I won't go into all of that, but I will say that we remain opposed to it, for reasons that we've stated over the years, and that we intend to continue our opposition to it, whether it's political, whether it's legal, whether it's— some of us have said that if the truck goes to develop the station, that we will lay down in front of it and we are serious as a heart attack. That's how opposed we are to it ... We're the abutters. And we stand *most* to either be harmed by this or impacted in some way. (her emphasis)

Barbara's intensity had only heightened a year later, when she spoke at a meeting specifically devoted to discussing concerns about the station. About one hundred people attended the forum, held in the auditorium of a Mattapan school. Participants lined up next to a microphone stand near the front of the room, and each in turn directed comments, questions, and concerns at state policymakers. Barbara's comments—repeating her and her neighbors' opposition to the station and emphasizing the support from local elected officials— garnered the most crowd reaction.

"One observation I'll make, is that in our community, it seems that we have things *imposed* on us," she began.

"Yup!" a Black woman seated in the audience called out in support.

"And we do not make decisions for ourselves ... And one of those decisions has to do with what happened in my *immediate* neighborhood in which I live in," Barbara continued. "And one truth of the matter is, is that when we were dealing with these issues, it was [State] Senator Jack Hart, and [City Councilor Rob] Consalvo, who supported our efforts around the rail stop."

"Uh-huh!" another audience member yelled out.

"It was Senator Hart, who in fact put some of this stuff on hold for a while, while we looked to try to work out something ... We felt very strongly that it's damaging the foundations of our homes. We are the immediate abutters. And your community process says that we're supposed to have some say... Well I ask you a question, have you ever heard of democracy?"

Barbara stopped speaking amidst yelling, clapping, and cheers of approval from the crowd.

"We live in a democracy, and we will continue to fight this, because it's not in our best interests... We are the abutters!"

"Amen!" a Black man in the audience called out.

"We don't support it, we won't support it, and we'll do whatever we have to do to not have that station there!" Satisfied, Barbara walked away from the microphone amidst raucous applause.

Other meeting participants supported Barbara. "I don't want this station here," one said. Another admitted that even though he personally supported the new station, "if the community doesn't want it—the community that's affected the most, on Woodhaven... then we shouldn't have it. If Woodhaven doesn't want it, then we shouldn't have it." Only two others spoke in support of the station. The overwhelming impression was that the new station was not welcome on the Woodhaven site.

As progress on the station ground to a halt, it seemed as though the opposition's efforts had paid off. However, plans for the new station were never formally abandoned. And by 2014, Woodhaven residents' elected allies were both out of office; Senator Hart became partner at a downtown law firm and Councilor Consalvo moved to the private sector after losing his mayoral bid.[7]

Woodhaven residents privately worried that they were not being perceived as "stakeholders." Following one public meeting in November 2012, two residents, Marcella and Marcus, pulled the director of a local social service agency aside and bent her ear. They expressed concerns that they might be viewed as overly radical and unnecessarily adversarial—characteristics that could undercut their authority as community members. "We have developed a negative profile, and we've become these pariahs," Marcella complained. "Instead of stakeholders," Marcus interjected. "Stakeholders. Community stakeholders."

Indeed, state policymakers did *not* see the group of residents as "stakeholders." Part of this stemmed from behind-the-scenes actions of nonprofit leaders advocating for the new station—"organizing for a 'yes' on the Mattapan Station," as one director referred to it.

Organizing the Community to Support the Transit Station in Mattapan

When I began my fieldwork in 2010, nonprofit leaders and community organizers in the Corridor were well aware of the opposition to the station emanating from Woodhaven Street. It directly threatened a Corridor-wide coalition of eight nonprofits, including seven community-based organizations and one citywide environmental association. Since the early 2000s, the coalition had been the main force behind the push for new stations on the Fairmount Line. The proposed Blue Hill Avenue Station was an integral piece of their broader housing and economic development efforts in the Corridor, as well as an important symbol of racial and environmental justice for poor Mattapan residents.

Their first reaction was to depict Woodhaven residents as unrepresentative of "the broader Mattapan community." At a coalition meeting in June 2011, Mela, the GFCAC community organizer, dismissed "the Woodhaven group" as "bullies" whose bluster "make it seem like the opposition is strong." "It's a tactic," she said. "And the press picks it up." The station didn't just affect residents of Woodhaven Street; "It's the whole community, not just Woodhaven, that will benefit," Mela reasoned—recognizing Woodhaven residents as community members but denying them full authority and status.

The group decided that Michelle, a Black community organizer with the Mattapan Community Development Corporation (MCDC), would lead the counter-organizing effort because MCDC was the only Mattapan-based organization in the coalition at the time. Jeanne, the white director of Dorchester Bay Economic Development Corporation (DBEDC), suggested a strategy to drown out Woodhaven residents at public meetings. "You need a group of big men and women to make sure the rabble rousers are silenced," she told Michelle. When the coalition met again six months later, the official meeting notes—distributed to all members via email—were similarly blunt: "We need to have residents who support the station at future meetings."

In 2012, MCDC filed for bankruptcy protection, causing the coalition to lose its community organizing presence in the neighborhood. The response was twofold. First, the group sought alternative allies who could reasonably claim to represent the Mattapan community. Churches seemed like a logical choice: Organizers could draw on church membership, and Boston's religious organizations have a long history of social justice advocacy.[8] Jeanne had a connection to Pastor Ronald Williams of Triumph Church, a Black mega-church located near the proposed station in Mattapan. The value of the church, according to the coalition, was its ability to manufacture public support. "All [Pastor Williams] needs to do is blink and the whole church jumps," Jeanne told the other coalition members at a May meeting.

Jeanne arranged a sit-down with Pastor Williams a few weeks later, and he agreed to write a letter to state transportation officials declaring his support for the station. "He'll put it on his stationery once his council approves, which he said they would," she wrote in an email to some of her colleagues in the coalition. Pastor Williams sent his draft to Jeanne for edits. "The Board of Elders of [Triumph Church] supports the construction of a rail line station on Blue Hill Avenue in Mattapan . . . Our Mattapan residents feel a [Blue Hill Avenue] Station would provide 'rapid' rail transit much needed for work, school, and shopping," he wrote, adding that building a new station "is the right thing to do."

Pastor Williams sent the letter to state officials later that month.[9]

Organizational allies in place, the coalition's second step was to shore up its community organizing infrastructure. That required financial resources. In June, directors and organizers from three Corridor nonprofits met with a program officer from a local family foundation. The nonprofit leaders requested funding to, in part, pay for a community organizer whose key responsibility would be ginning up support for the proposed station. They framed Pastor Williams's letter as evidence that residents of Woodhaven Street, however loud and persistent, did not represent the broader community sentiment.

During the meeting at the foundation, Jeanne shared the news of Williams's letter with Prentice, a white foundation program officer. "Well," she explained, "it took a visit, and some time and thought, and the right personal connections. So we had a good visit. He and I have been sending letters back and forth. He's *extremely* positive. He's *guaranteeing* the participation of his church with his 7,000 members."

"Yeah, I was gonna say, there's 7,000 people *that can show up*," Prentice added excitedly.

"The largest church in Boston."

"Exactly."

"So he's on board. He's sending letters. We asked him to send them to the head of the [state transportation authority]—"

"And, and that's the NIMBY site, right?" Prentice interrupted, referring to the residents of Woodhaven Street. NIMBY is an acronym for "Not In My Backyard," a phrase used to describe people who resist a particular form of development, not in principle, but only when it is planned for their own neighborhoods.

"That's where—right across the tracks from him is the NIMBY site," Jeanne answered. She continued, "Once you get these churches going, now you really got the numbers, and you've got people that are there for the long haul. And they meet every week. And so, he's fired up—I can send you his letter once we got it all on his stationery." She smirked, conveying a sense of pride that the letter would carry official church markings.

"And what's the policy action that we need to get—," Prentice started to ask.

"They're going to fight to get that station there," Jeanne answered before he could finish his question, "where the people, the neighbors are fighting against it."

"Okay."

"They [the church leadership] want it there. The [state transportation authority] wants it there. So I think it's very winnable. And now, if they have a 7,000-member church fighting for it—it's *abutting* the station—it just changes the whole dynamic."

A $50,000 grant from the foundation arrived in 2013. It primarily funded a new "lead organizer" to manage the organizing "campaigns" initiated by the nonprofit coalition.

But Gail, another coalition member and executive director of Codman Square Neighborhood Development Corporation (CSNDC), did not think an organizing *manager* was enough; the issue, she believed, required an additional on-the-ground organizer. Her concern grew as Barbara Fields spoke out at the public meetings in April 2013. Three weeks after Barbara threatened to lie on the tracks and block construction of the new station, Gail joined two other coalition members on a conference call and strategized ways to undermine the opposition. She proposed setting aside resources to hire a part-time community organizer whose *sole task* was elevating support for the proposed station—"to get the 'yes' on the station, to counter some of the things, like, that Barbara Fields said."

In August, the coalition's newly hired "lead organizer" drafted an advertisement for a part-time organizer around the station initiative. The document listed a set of "goals," including a bullet point to "Organize the broader Mattapan Community around a 'yes' vote in support of a new stop on the Fairmount line at Blue Hill [Avenue]." The first person they hired did not work out. A second advertisement was distributed in January 2015. Among other minor grammatical changes, the new document capitalized each letter of the word "YES" in the aforementioned bullet point.

Nonprofit leaders in the coalition also met privately with state transportation officials throughout 2013. The email invitations referred to each meeting as a "Fairmount Corridor Stakeholder Meeting." The guest lists, however, included only state officials and representatives from Corridor nonprofits. No residents from Woodhaven Street were invited; indeed, no Mattapan residents were at the table at all. Marcus's fear, that Woodhaven residents weren't seen as "community stakeholders," was even more accurate than he realized at the time.

On October 16, 2014, Governor Patrick held a press conference across the street from the proposed station, marking the beginning of construction. Woodhaven residents remained defiant. Quoted by a local reporter, Barbara argued, "The opposition has fallen on deaf ears because the powers-that-be have decided that this is what is best for this community."[10]

Barbara and her neighbors resisted the project. They articulated alternative locations. They made their wishes known in the press. But alliances with particular elected officials proved risky, given regular elections and political turnover. Subsequent threats of protest fell on deaf ears. Meanwhile, nonprofit leaders produced evidence of public support and managed to establish an identity as "community stakeholders," affording them unique access to state policymakers. Planning for the station continued, despite vocal resident opposition at public meetings.

The Community Blocks a Lighting Storage Facility in Upham's Corner

We can contrast the case of the Blue Hill Avenue Station in Mattapan with the redevelopment of the Maxwell Building in Upham's Corner. In 2009, the City of Boston foreclosed on an 84,000-square-foot warehouse that had been home to the Maxwell Box Company. It sat vacant for four years. In the spring of 2013, the city's property disposition department quietly transferred the property to the Department of Public Works in a backroom agreement—a favor from one department to another. The head of Public Works planned to demolish the abandoned factory and replace it with a street lighting storage facility.

As these plans unfolded, a parallel neighborhood planning process was underway. Beginning in 2012, the BRA had convened an advisory group of local nonprofit leaders and residents to discuss community development in Upham's Corner. The advisory group held monthly meetings, open to the public, where members planned and reviewed development scenarios for the neighborhood. Early discussions showed the potential for residential apartments on top of 54,000 square feet of light industrial or commercial development at the Maxwell site (emphatically *not* a storage facility).

In June 2013, the advisory group met at an Upham's Corner community center and discussed the rumors that the Maxwell Building was going to become a Public Works storage facility. Chris, a Black resident, Dudley Street Neighborhood Initiative (DSNI) board member, and advisory group co-chair, explained the situation: Public Works had plans for a storage facility, but this project directly contradicted the group's hopes of housing and job opportunities for residents. He suggested they send a direct but cautious letter to the mayor, asking for more information and a meeting about the property disposition process. "Because all of our understanding was that it's [the Maxwell Building] a part of the community process—part of *this* community process—and we want to make sure that actually is a part of the community process."

The advisory group agreed: They would send a letter emphasizing the important role of the community in any appropriate course of action.

That letter, sent on July 11 and addressed to the mayor and the head of the property disposition department, noted that the advisory group was considering alternative plans for the site. The group requested a meeting to discuss the following:

> As we move forward with the creation of an economic development plan for the area, the [advisory group] would like to understand the process and the timeline for the disposition of the Maxwell Building and the role the [advisory group] and community members will play in deciding the development that happens on the site. We would like to request the officials from the Department of Neighborhood Development and other relevant City departments attend the next meeting of the Upham's Corner [advisory group] to discuss the disposition process for the Maxwell Building and share our plans to date.

No one from the mayor's office responded.

In July, the advisory group met again. There were thirty-three people in the room, nearly double the normal attendance. Ten advisory group members and two city officials were seated around a U-shaped configuration of tables, all looking toward a pull-down screen. Twenty-one members of the public were seated in a circle around the advisory group. Many of the newcomers were Cape Verdean residents from the streets adjacent to the Maxwell Building who had heard about—and objected to—the proposed storage facility.

They weren't alone. Nearly everyone in the room voiced anger over the proposal. One white resident (an advisory group member) said, "This ranks among the top of the most outrageous and stupid ideas that I have heard in a long time." Another called it "a slap in the face to the neighborhood." She added that she was "unhappy" and "disturbed" that "they're [city officials] not including the community in this. This is horrible."

"The community process has been short-circuited," Chris said, "in a major, major way":

> We're at a point where [city officials] are now saying, "Yep, all that time you invested means nothing." On the largest, most significant, integral part of the footprint of what you're looking at. "We're going to do what we're going to do." So to me, I think it raises the question, in my mind, as to whether or not—you know, if in fact, all that happens is they come and meet with us, and they say, "Here's the way the process lays out," then I have to ask myself, one, is it worth finishing [this] process, and two, how loud do I need to yell on behalf of myself, and more importantly, on behalf of the community [to stop this] . . . We were convened by the mayor, but we were convened to represent our community.

Jeanne, the director of DBEDC, frowned from her place in a chair against the wall. After members of the advisory group vented and aired their concerns, she raised her hand and passionately called on everyone in attendance to fight the decision:

> I just think it's an outrage—and I don't think we're going to take this . . . Because we need to find out, where was the decision made, and then we need to fight it! And if we all stick together, I think we can win it! . . . We fought a lot of other battles. Let's do it!

No one responded to her call to arms. Max, a white nonprofit director and advisory group co-chair, ignored her and suggested writing a second letter that asked, again, for a meeting to discuss plans for the property with city officials. Jeanne interjected, her voice cracking as she suggested a more active display of collective action—a sit-in:

> Let's take a group of fifty people down, and have a meeting, and just *go* if they won't give us a date [for a meeting]. And we'll go into

[Department of Public Works]'s office and *sit* there 'til they throw us out! That *used* to work in the good ol' days! (her emphasis)

After Jeanne finished, there were some chuckles. A few people smirked. Most people sat and stared blankly at her.

Breaking the awkward moment, an advisory group member simply listed names of officials that should receive the letter, ignoring the call for a sit-in. Jeanne sat back in her seat and crossed her arms.

Max summarized the next steps: The advisory group would draft a letter and try to get a meeting next week. "It would be more pressure going in to City Hall," Jeanne grumbled—loud enough to be heard, but lacking the fervor of her earlier comments. No one in the room reacted.

Jeanne spoke with Joan, a white Upham's Corner resident, member of the advisory group, and consultant for nonprofits in the Corridor, after the meeting. "Why was everybody so tame? Why weren't they all yelling? What's the matter with them? C'mon! Let's go, let's go!" Jeanne urged. "We should just take forty or fifty people and just go. Say, 'We're coming down . . . we're going to go to the mayor's office, and we're going to have a *sit-in*,'" she pushed. "We haven't had any fun like that in decades! That was all fun stuff, back in the '60s. C'mon! Everybody's so damn anesthetized [now]. Send a letter?!?" Joan nodded passively but didn't respond directly to any of Jeanne's recommendations. As was the case in Mattapan, there may have been threats of protest, but by and large, collective action was not necessarily seen as the most effective path forward if the community wanted to be at the table.

The second letter, sent on July 25, asked "what the community's role will be," and requested a meeting:

> At our [advisory group] meeting last night, neighbors of the Maxwell Building and other residents expressed serious concerns about lack of communication about plans for the site, especially with reports that the building will be demolished in the fall. We would like to request a meeting with you and your key staff to discuss the disposition process for the Maxwell Building, including the role that the [advisory group] and community members will play in deciding the type of development that happens on the site.

On July 26, an editorial questioning the Maxwell Building disposition ran in the *Dorchester Reporter*, a neighborhood weekly. The article quoted Joan, who repeated the arguments from the previous week's meeting: Residents do not want a storage facility in their neighborhood, they prefer alternative housing and commercial development, and most important, redevelopment planning should not occur without consultation from the advisory group.[11]

Three days later, city officials reversed course. From the *Dorchester Reporter*:

> A spokesperson for Mayor Tom Menino today said that the mayor believes that a key city-owned parcel along the Fairmount Line in Uphams Corner should be redeveloped as a "transit oriented development"—a strong indication that the city will put the brakes on an emerging plan to turn the site into a warehouse for city street lights.[12]

City officials met with the advisory group and other residents in August. "The City was going to use the site for a [lighting] pole yard and desperately needs one," Sheila Dillon, the head of property disposition, told the group. "The mayor was on board with that, but after getting a number of calls he changed his mind and said, 'There's a better use for this site.'"[13] She announced a new community-driven process to guide the site's redevelopment. It was a clear victory for the residents and their nonprofit representatives.

"Community Consensus" in Practice

The case of the Maxwell Building was a grassroots triumph over government officials' harmful plans—a situation in which participation at public meetings helped transfer power to local residents. After blocking the city's plans for a storage facility, the question became: What type of development should take its place? Generating consensus about what *not* to do was easy. Getting any sort of meaningful agreement on what should replace the abandoned factory proved far more difficult.

City officials hosted a public meeting in September 2013 to set development guidelines for the Maxwell Building site. Fifty-five people attended the 6pm meeting, including Joan; Glenn Knowles, a white resident and former board president of the Dudley Street Neighborhood Initiative (DSNI); Harry Smith, a white community organizer with DSNI; and Carlos Henriquez, a Black state representative.

Patrick, a white city official, led the meeting from a podium at the front of the room. He described the site and explained the general disposition process. The purpose of the meeting was to develop guidelines for the Request for Proposals (RFP). Any recommendations would be nonbinding, but they gave residents the ability to signal what types of development—e.g., affordable housing, market rate condominiums, or commercial storefronts—they would like to see.

Patrick brought a handout of draft guidelines to the meeting. He said they were based on conversations with the Upham's Corner Advisory Group "and in cooperation with neighborhood residents." Those guidelines included a preference for light industrial development, though housing would also be acceptable. They would also include some sort of "community benefits," like a small park or "community room." And ideally, the project would be an energy-efficient development.

Patrick then opened the floor for discussion. After a few clarifying questions about the selection process and possible uses for the site, Joan raised her hand. She established her residence in the neighborhood and then asked Patrick to "respect the community" and slow down the disposition process:

> I'm Joan Tighe, and I'm a resident of Eastman Street, from Eastman-Elder Neighborhood Association. I'm also a member of the [advisory group]. And it seems—I'm feeling like we're being pushed to affirm what's in your proposed guidelines here. And I think if we do that tonight, then we'll miss a huge opportunity to really influence what the neighbors want—and I've heard several things already... And I think there needs to be time allotted for us to have that conversation before you go back to [City Hall], and you know, sign on the dotted line and issue the RFP. I mean, this whole thing—it started back in July with that outrageous proposal, but I feel like that was the tipping point to just rush this building into development... And, um, it just doesn't make any sense. So I'm asking you tonight to respect the community. And give us some time.

"We're not rushing anything," Patrick responded in defense, raising his hands in the air and shaking his head. "The goal would have been—if there was consensus—to move forward. We were under the impression that a lot of this stuff had been discussed [at the advisory group meetings]... And if that's not the case, that's fine. Believe me: We're not trying to rush anything. If people aren't ready, there's not consensus, then we'll wait."

A handful of residents in the room asked for more meetings so that residents could come up with their own ideas and then share them with city officials—a suggestion that left Patrick confused, since that was his plan for *this* meeting. Glenn, DSNI's former board president, offered DSNI's services to manage a community process that would lead to consensus. "We have a long, long history of working with [city officials] to put together community meetings to get community input," he said. "We would love to help in any way we can and partner with [city government], because that is what we do."

But another city official worried that it would be a conflict of interest if a nonprofit submitted a proposal after facilitating the creation of proposal guidelines. Perhaps it would be better if city officials managed the community process. "We're hyper, hyper critical of conflict of interest," Glenn responded. "I'm just saying, we are offering, because this is what we do, and we are offering to help in any way we can." The official agreed to share the offer with the head of property disposition and get back to Glenn.

At 7:20, State Representative Carlos Henriquez arrived. He stood alone at the back of the room. Harry approached and whispered in his ear, presumably filling him in on the previous eighty minutes of discussion. After a few more questions were asked, Representative Henriquez offered to lead the community process, thereby rendering the potential conflict of interest question moot:

> In terms of conflict [of interest], I want to offer myself. My name is Carlos Henriquez, the state representative for this neighborhood. These are the people I serve and work for. I'd be happy to lead the meeting in any way you want it to lead, so there's not a conflict of interest, because I do serve and work for them . . . And I will challenge my City Councilor counterpart, who is Councilor Jackson, to help co-sponsor that meeting and lead it, if that helps eliminate the conflict of interest with [community development corporations] and organizing groups. So whatever we can do to play that role, I'd be happy to help.

Patrick responded that he would also share this suggestion with the head of property disposition. As the meeting wound to a close, Patrick promised to coordinate with "the elected officials and the [advisory group]" to plan a follow-up meeting.

Some participants were happy with the outcome of the meeting, but others considered it a waste of time. After two hours, all that was accomplished was the promise of more meetings. "Well, that was pointless," one nonprofit director muttered as he packed up his things.

The next meeting occurred in October, at the same social service organization. Unlike the government-led meeting in September, this one was formally hosted by DSNI. Thirty-three people—including about a dozen white, Asian, Cape Verdean, and Black residents—grazed on the cheese and crackers set out at the back of the room. Patrick and another city official were present, but sat in the audience as observers. State Representative Henriquez attended, too, but again was more than an hour late. Similar to the scenes described in chapter 4, no one acknowledged him, and he did not announce himself, though he did quietly take a photo of the meeting and post it to his official Twitter account.

The meeting started at 6pm with a round of introductions. Community organizers from DSNI then divided everyone into three groups to continue discussing development priorities. Each group listed the kind of development they wanted at the Maxwell Building site, the kind of development they did *not* want, and any additional comments that could inform the RFP.

The participants moved their chairs into semicircles, and a DSNI staffer joined each group to take notes on a large notepad. The city officials joined a reporter to observe the conversations from the side of the room. After an hour, Harry, the community organizer with DSNI, asked each group to select a representative to share their recommendations. He wrote each comment on poster board.

Each recommendation contradicted another. One resident requested a park for neighborhood children; another said absolutely no parks. One wanted an industrial facility with on-site parking and absolutely no housing; another wanted only housing and no commercial uses. Some wanted strictly affordable housing, while others were open to market-rate condos. And still others suggested a mix of uses, such as a ground-floor commercial development below two floors of apartments.

"There was a lot of um—I won't say *consensus*," Harry told the group as the meeting drew to a close, attempting to reconcile the contradictory recommendations. "But there was a lot of agreement about some of the broader goals of the development." The city officials frowned when Harry asked if they had anything to add. In a tone that could best be described as checked out, one said drily, "Yeah, I think we're in a good place."

In March 2014, city officials unveiled the final RFP. Reflecting the lack of consensus at the October 2013 community meeting, the guidelines invited proposals for mixed-use, housing, and/or light industrial uses with some element of public recreational space—broad recommendations practically indistinguishable from Patrick's original draft guidelines.[14]

Three proposals were submitted in October, and another round of community meetings began. "The community in Upham's Corner has been a wonderful partner to help us envision what they'd like to see in this space," Sheila Dillon, the head of property disposition, told a local reporter. "We're expecting a lot of community involvement as they [potential developers] make presentations. Their opinion and input will be critical to our analysis."[15]

The potential development teams presented their proposed projects at a public meeting in January 2015. The first was a joint venture between Dorchester Bay Economic Development Corporation (DBEDC), a nonprofit community development corporation, and two for-profit developers. It included ninety-two housing units (with 50% designated "affordable"[16]), 20,000 square feet of commercial space for light industrial uses, public recreational space, and a community room. The second proposal came from Corcoran Jennison Associates, a for-profit development firm. It included 123 housing units, with sixteen designated "affordable,"[17] as well as 28,000 square feet of commercial space and 7,300 square feet for public recreational space. Weld Management Company submitted the third and final proposal: a 40,000-square-foot light industrial facility.

DBEDC was designated developer of the site in May.

After another round of public meetings, the BRA board formally approved DBEDC's project in June 2016. The final project plan included eighty apartments reserved for families earning at or below the area's median income. Due to Boston's extremely tight housing market, that stipulation meant all apartments would rent below market rate.[18] Nine additional townhomes were reserved for market-rate homeownership. The project also included space for four or five light industrial tenants, like wholesale distributors, small manufacturing, or food businesses. There was also a community room, and all of the apartments would be built to energy-efficient standards.[19]

Finally, after three years of public meetings and, according to the head of property disposition for the City of Boston, "a lot of community involvement," DBEDC's accepted proposal lined up almost exactly with the original recommendations from the Upham's Corner Advisory Group, as well as the draft RFP guidelines that followed. Participation effectively blocked the lighting storage facility, but it did not meaningfully determine what happened next. A cynical take is that, due to the lack of consensus, the community process simply delayed an outcome that may have happened regardless of community participation. Put in even starker terms, the pursuit of community consensus put development of new affordable housing at risk: As organizers searched for a singular community voice, the value of the Maxwell Building increased, making it even more attractive to for-profit developers who ultimately proposed fewer, if any, subsidized apartments.

Participatory democracy is an appealing form of governance for good reason. Theoretically, power is transferred from elites to everyday residents, democratizing public decision-making. Yet in practice, government officials can still circumvent citizens even under the guise of open participation. During public meetings, officials expressed deference to the community, but they were implicitly referring to *the abstract moral significance* of community, not actual community *members*. By going through the motions of a "community engagement process" and publicly praising the community in the abstract, officials reduced community input to a bureaucratic procedure. In these instances, residents appeared empowered as members of the community, but, by design, had little actual influence.

The work of formal organizations was an additional mechanism affecting the outcomes of resident participation. In Upham's Corner, a nonprofit-led advisory group helped residents resist government plans for a lighting storage facility. In Mattapan, residents of Woodhaven Street lacked similar connections to nonprofit allies. Instead, they formed alliances with elected politicians and threatened protest. Coming full circle with the arguments presented in previous chapters—that local nonprofits are now major players in urban governance and can supersede politicians as de facto representatives of poor neighborhoods—alliances with nonprofits were more successful than alliances with elected politicians, and protest was not necessarily seen as legitimate political action.

When thinking about the value of participation in neighborhood politics, both the Blue Hill Avenue Station and Maxwell Building cases should give us pause. One reaction to the Blue Hill Avenue Station case might be to critique the coalition of Corridor nonprofits for deliberately undermining neighborhood residents. Another interpretation is that the failure of relatively affluent

Woodhaven residents' complaints was a victory for poor Mattapan residents who depend on public transportation. A new station significantly reduces the commute time to downtown Boston—an unnecessary public resource for the middle-class car owners on Woodhaven Street, but critical for their neighbors living in poverty. Yet another interpretation is that Woodhaven residents' participation actually undermined *their own* stated interests: Some research suggests that geographic proximity to transit significantly increases residential property values.[20] Without a station, they suffer through all of the negative externalities associated with train tracks in their backyards—the diesel fumes, the sound pollution, and so on—and benefit from none of the positive externalities of public transit access in a major city. Ironically, by *not* getting their way in the political arena, these residents may have ultimately "won" in the economic arena.

The Maxwell Building case challenges our normative predispositions in a different way. We may assume that more community participation is always better than less, but what happens when the community lacks consensus? The scenario is not hard to imagine; in any neighborhood, opinions will vary. In a study of community life in Chicago, sociologist Mary Pattillo vividly belies the notion that urban neighborhoods are monoliths. When it came to support for a new magnet school or grilling food on a public median, Pattillo found no single "community" position. The complex intersection of race and class created cross-cutting, sometimes divergent interests.[21] Such was the case in Upham's Corner, where residents may have agreed about what they did *not* want but did not agree on an alternative. A notable challenge of bottom-up participatory governance as it is currently practiced—expecting consensus after asking residents, open-ended, what they'd like to see in their neighborhood—is that it requires a level of unanimity that is simply unlikely to exist in the real world.

There is a larger point I want to make about community, and what it means, in policy and practice, to "empower the community." In the Blue Hill Avenue Station case, does empowering the community mean improving public transportation access in the neighborhood, or does it mean helping the residents of Woodhaven Street succeed in their efforts to block a new train station? In the Maxwell Building case, does empowering the community mean building a new park, as one resident suggested, or building new housing, as another requested? Nonprofit community-based organizations seemed to support the community in one instance (Maxwell Building) and not the other (Blue Hill Avenue Station)—but supporting the community and supporting poor urban residents did not always mean the same thing. When advocating for greater community control, scholars and policymakers implicitly assume that participatory processes will eventually reveal a unified community voice. The entire exercise relies on this assumption. Yet no matter how segregated or disadvantaged, neighborhoods still contain some level of diversity, and a normative policy to "empower the community" ignores the complexities and contradictions inherent in local political life.

There is a second point that reflects a major theme of this book: Urban politics is fuzzier than national or even state politics. Allegiances and alliances are not always clear-cut. Winners and losers are sometimes ambiguous. And our moral inclinations and normative assumptions do not always hew to politics in practice. The polarization that increasingly characterizes national US politics becomes much murkier, marked more by grey than by black or white, when we look to urban politics. We can rightly criticize government officials for systematically suppressing citizen demands, but the counterfactual—more community control with fewer top-down constraints—does not necessarily bring about better outcomes for neighborhoods. We shouldn't forget, for instance, that racially restrictive housing covenants of the 1920s, '30s, and '40s were enforced by resident participation, or that anti-busing activism (virulent in Boston) was a form of resident participation, or more recently, that resident participation helps affluent Americans resist affordable housing development in their cities and neighborhoods. Participation may empower urban residents and lead to more equitable outcomes, or it may sustain segregation and support discrimination—it just depends on *which* residents participate, and *whose* voices are empowered as a result. We can analyze why urban residents are more powerful in some cases than others. It is much harder to conclude whether the pursuit of community control through participation, as a general practice, produces positive or negative outcomes for the urban poor.

[Handwritten note: participation doesn't automatically lead to more equitable outcomes → depends on who is participating]

Conclusion

MIDTOWN DETROIT, INC. (MDI), a nonprofit organization in Detroit, exemplifies today's community development industry. Led by a white director in an overwhelmingly nonwhite neighborhood, the organization's staff develops new housing and commercial storefronts. They landscape boulevard medians and planned a Midtown Greenway. They put lights on trees during the winter holidays. They encourage businesses to set up shop in the neighborhood. They have collaborated with nearby Wayne State University's police department to help initiate patrols when the Detroit Police Department was unable to. In short, MDI provides public services to the residents of Midtown—and in many respects does so more effectively than Detroit city government.

In a 2012 article titled, "Welcome to Your New Government: Can Non-Profits Run Cities?" journalist Anna Clark profiled MDI alongside three other nonprofits.[1] Like many of the organizations described in *Constructing Community*, MDI emerged out of 1960s-era radical activism but has since transformed into a highly professionalized neighborhood institution. As Clark notes, "tactical collaborations with major anchor institutions in Detroit—including City Hall—have elevated it from the antiestablishment fringe and into the establishment itself."

Clark writes that the growing influence of community-based nonprofits like MDI "speaks to larger trends of governments outsourcing what had once been their own jobs." And with those trends come important costs: While nonprofits may ensure regular trash collections and support affordable housing development, "communities cede a certain amount of accountability when private hands . . . take charge of public services." What's more, "the dominating influence of a handful of non-profits can create a sort of civic hierarchy," leaving the city's poorest neighborhoods behind. In other words: Nonprofits have been empowered to take on important governance responsibilities, undermining systems of democratic accountability and introducing new forms neighborhood inequality.²

Detroit and Boston are very different places. One city faced municipal bankruptcy and became a national symbol of urban decline. The other is the sixth largest metropolitan economy in the nation, known for its array of globally recognized education and medical institutions. One city is 79.7 percent Black. The other is 53 percent white. The median rent in one city is half that of the other. In one city, nonprofit leaders stepped up when local government struggled. In the other, a high-capacity local government experiments with innovative policy solutions to pressing social problems.

On the surface, the two cities appear as similar as apples and oranges (or Coney dogs and clam chowder, to use more local references). Yet digging deeper reveals a shared governance structure. Private nonprofits perform many functions that we would typically ascribe to government—sometimes alongside and sometimes in place of public officials. This is true not just of Boston and Detroit, but of cities across the country. Nonprofits' degree of influence no doubt varies from city to city and neighborhood to neighborhood. But, as Clark notes in her article, there has been a general trend over time toward incorporating community-based organizations and philanthropic foundations into informal governance structures.

Through a case study of the Fairmount Corridor in Boston, I analyzed the resulting tensions: What happens when community-based organizations take on roles of nonelected neighborhood representatives, foundations influence local policy and programs, and participation during public meetings does not always transfer power to poor urban residents? I now turn to the future and suggest three recommendations for urban policymakers and community development practitioners. For a more democratic and equitable urban governance, we should increase nonprofit diversity, push foundations toward capacity funding, and reimagine participation beyond the public meeting. These policy recommendations relate to a final lesson for social scientists: By appreciating the symbolism of community—that is, how people *use* the concept in local politics—we can develop a more refined understanding of democracy and inequality in American cities.

Who Governs?

One of this book's central contributions is to make sense of the particular roles nonprofit organizations now play in urban governance. Though my empirical focus is on community development politics, similar changes have occurred in other policy areas. As Americans have grown less trusting of formal government institutions and more supportive of private solutions to public problems,[3] we now see private nonprofits assuming leadership roles in fields as diverse as education, social services, public safety, and public health.

This is, in part, what many social movement activists in the 1960s fought for: community organizations capturing resources on behalf of the urban poor. Yet there are also significant risks for democracy when nonprofit leaders supersede or override elected officials—when they act, in other words, like nonelected neighborhood representatives. Nonprofit leaders are neither democratically elected nor subject to term limits. Although nonprofit leaders ostensibly work on behalf of the public, they are not required to be residents of the neighborhoods they represent, and the public has few, if any, formal mechanisms to hold them accountable. Nonprofit organizations carry a certain amount of moral authority based on their altruistic motivations, but altruism is assumed, not guaranteed. Seemingly selfless organizations are still motivated by organizational survival and not, necessarily, the broader public good. Philanthropic foundations embody many of the same problems, influencing public policy with little public oversight.

It is not as though government has disappeared, of course; public funding and subsidies still outweigh private funding in absolute dollars. But we currently find ourselves in a situation where private nonprofits can come up with policies first and then expect support from public officials second. It is an inversion of the way many Americans assume urban policy works. Government responded to the growing power of nonprofits in the 1960s with stricter regulation: The Green Amendment of 1967 stripped Community Action Agencies of control over War on Poverty funds, and the Tax Reform Act of 1969 restricted foundations' influence in electoral politics. That resistance—and other attempts at suppression—was successful in the short term but largely failed over the long run. With retrenchment and shrinking budgets, government officials have acceded a great deal of practical, on-the-ground power as they came to rely on the funds and follow-through of the nonprofit sector.

As a result, many poor urban residents today face a resource-representation tradeoff: Nonprofits can bring more resources to their neighborhoods, but at the expense of democratic representation. How should policymakers and practitioners respond? One option is to try to make nonprofit organizations more democratic. We could, for instance, mandate resident representation on elected boards of directors. Enforcement could be formal, like government regulations tied to tax exemption, or informal, like requirements tied to private foundation grants. Another option is to provide resources to poor neighborhoods without using nonprofits as pass-throughs. We could place more power in the hands of local politicians by increasing the amount of public resources under their control or by creating quasi-public organizations to implement community development policy.

Each of these potential solutions has significant downsides. Individual organizational reforms, like requiring elected boards of directors, will not change the basic contours of a field that has few formal mechanisms of democratic accountability. Nor do I think more stringent government oversight is an appropriate answer. A central premise of nonprofit organizing is to place a check on government power, not the other way around. To erase political gains made by nonprofits could mean going back to 1950s-style "urban renewal" in which local governments, assisted by the federal government, demolished whole neighborhoods like Boston's West End and Detroit's Paradise Valley. An important value of community-based nonprofits—part of their reason for existence—is to counteract these and other harmful urban policies.

And so we return to the central dilemma. It is a tension we can trace back to the eighteenth century: Nonprofit organizations both enhance and undermine democracy, simultaneously. They are central to democracy and civil society, providing a voice for "the people" that complements representative government. Yet nonprofit organizations are also detrimental to an egalitarian society, in that they give some people a more powerful voice than others. They are funded by private groups with private agendas, they serve some neighborhoods more ably than others, and they are just as capable as any politician of ignoring the truly disadvantaged.

Taking all of this into account, I would suggest an alternative solution that may seem ironic given my emphasis on the rapid growth of the sector over the last few decades. We should support *more* nonprofits. Rather than scale back nonprofit advocacy or enforce organizational reforms, we should instead incentivize *greater organizational diversity*. That we need organizations of more types, structures, and missions is not a new argument. In the community development literature, scholars have long advocated for separating technical project development from other activities, like community organizing.[4] The idea here is that complex development projects and community organizing require very different kinds of expertise, and the funding relationships required for development are incompatible with the contentious politics of organizing. To these, I add an additional motivating factor: When multiple issue areas and functions are collapsed within a *single* organization, it can become the *single* voice of neighborhood residents. As I have shown throughout this book, there is a big difference between being *a* nonelected neighborhood representative and *the* nonelected neighborhood representative.

Insofar as policymakers engage with local neighborhoods, they prefer to have one organization serve as the representative; it's easier for officials to manage. Consider policy proposals like the Massachusetts Smart Growth Alliance's (MSGA) Community Benefits Districts (CBDs). The CBD proposal involves a payment by local property owners, similar to a condo fee, that would be paid to a local nonprofit and be used for services like security, signage, or cultural activities.[5] According to MSGA's fact sheet, CBDs would be "run by a nonprofit organization with community governance."⁶ Like other policy proposals that encourage public-private partnerships, the implicit expectation is that a *single* nonprofit organization will be in control.

Let's imagine an alternative scenario, in which any given neighborhood contains development organizations, community organizing groups, transit advocates, and block clubs. Citywide and regional organizations would focus on interrelated issues, such as environmental sustainability or policing. Elected politicians would act as neighborhood political representatives, held in check by these varied, coordinating, and even contentious organizations and associations. The underlying principle is to "let a thousand flowers bloom": to support diverse organizations advocating for a wide range of interests (including underrepresented or niche interests) and empowered to hold democratically elected leaders accountable. I'm not coming up with something new in this hypothetical scenario—I'm describing what many nonprofit leaders in the field articulate as their ideal, too. But funder incentives and public policy narrow that vision, expecting single organizations to operate as the lone neighborhood representative. Recognizing and rejecting that impulse would alleviate many of these tensions and help democratize urban governance.

The Will to Fund Capacity

When staff from The Boston Foundation (TBF) denied Mattapan Community Development Corporation's (MCDC) last-ditch funding request, they did so without reservation. As they explained, TBF funds successful projects. It is not in their interests to throw money at a struggling organization. In fact, MCDC's weakness was seen as a *liability*: Funders like TBF have their own reputations and survival to consider, and it reflects poorly on them when they fund ineffective organizations. If private funders were disinclined to keep MCDC from bankruptcy, they were even less interested in funding a new organization to take its place. Such an effort would be even riskier and would require considerably more capital to build capacity. MCDC ultimately closed its doors, and Mattapan residents suffered as a result.

Social scientists generally think of urban inequality in structural and cultural terms. My analysis of the Fairmount Corridor builds on important work in urban sociology and shows how politics and organizations matter, too: The place of organizations in politics mediates poor neighborhoods' access to resources. Incorporating community organizations and foundations into urban governance unintentionally introduced new mechanisms of inequality. To be clear, it is not necessarily a problem that organizations like CSNDC leveraged initial grants into even more resources for Codman Square residents—in fact, it is a notable improvement from past decades. But it is a problem that Mattapan residents lacked those same opportunities.

One way to make sense of this issue is to consider public and private funders' bias toward capacity. Government officials ostensibly want to make the best use of public money, and private funders want to attract more donors and prestige. A straightforward way to ensure successful projects is to only fund community organizations with extensive experience and highly trained staff—in other words, to fund high-capacity organizations. From a more critical perspective, privileging capacity in grant applications can systematically disadvantage the people and places in greatest need. Organizations like MCDC are caught in a catch-22: They can't secure funding because they don't have the capacity to produce successful projects, and they don't have the capacity to produce successful projects because they can't secure funding.

To solve this problem, we need to rethink funder incentives. And a significant share of the burden should rest on the shoulders of *private* funders. As political theorist Rob Reich argues, foundations' lack of public accountability can be used as an asset: Shielded from public view, foundations can take greater risks. They can (though rarely do) fund new organizations or support struggling ones—efforts that may not result in immediate "success," narrowly defined.[7] One of the country's best-known community organizations, the Dudley Street Neighborhood Initiative (DSNI), discussed in chapters 4 and 6, would not exist without a risky bet and initial operating support from the Riley Foundation.[8] The same was true for the Fairmount Corridor CDC coalition, which received a $1 million general operations grant from The Boston Foundation in 2009.[9]

There are a number of ways to steer funders toward grants that support nonprofits' capacity and, as a result, increase organizational diversity. The first is through public policy. Current tax law requires foundations to spend only a small amount of assets each year: just 5 percent, which can include staff salaries and other related costs. Foundations are also allowed to exist in perpetuity. Changing the annual payout requirement and instituting lifespan restrictions would incentivize foundations to give more money to more nonprofit grantees.

Both ideas have historical precedent. When John D. Rockefeller sought a federal charter for his foundation in 1909, he proposed a cap on total assets ($100 million), a requirement to spend all investment returns annually, and a time limit on the lifespan of the foundation (50 years).[10] The bill to establish the charter ultimately failed when it reached the Senate in 1913. Rockefeller then sought and received a charter from the State of New York, abandoning many of the concessions he had previously offered federal lawmakers. The federal government should revisit nonprofit tax policy and consider an increase in the annual payout requirement as well as a lifespan limit. Adhering to such regulatory changes would be a small price to pay for the privilege of tax exemption.

Social norms can also make a difference. In particular, we know that denser network ties between philanthropic leaders and other local elites lead to more philanthropic giving.[11] To facilitate more ties, private funders can convene local elites on a regular basis, similar to the way TBF "[brought] the donuts and coffee" at semi-annual events and symposia.

In addition to increased funding, there also needs to be a change in *how the money is used.* As we have seen throughout this book, program grants are far more popular with funders than grants for general operating support. Programs produce measurable outcomes, and funders like to see exactly how their money will make a difference in people's lives. To the extent that private funders supported capacity in the Corridor, it was generally in the form of consultants. Recall that when MCDC and SWBCDC faced budget shortfalls, TBF and LISC, respectively, provided funding for strategic planning consultants, not direct operating support. It is a well-known problem in the field. Some practitioners like Dan Pallotta make the case for operating support, arguing that higher overhead can result in more absolute dollars for charitable causes even if the percentage devoted to operations increases.[12] And some funders have made strides in recognizing the value of operations. The Ford Foundation, for instance, committed $1 billion in operating support for social justice nonprofits in 2016.[13] More funders should take Ford's lead.

If private funders are to embrace capacity funding, they will need to rethink what a "successful" grant looks like. More specifically, they will need to reject the idea that success can be measured through quantifiable metrics.[14] Evaluating the effectiveness of operating support is very different from evaluating program outcomes. Organizational capacity allows nonprofit leaders to keep the lights on, raise additional revenue, and advocate for particular causes. These activities are ill-suited for a random control trial or any other technocratic method of evaluation. Funders will never meaningfully increase organizational diversity—and, I would argue, never meaningfully change patterns of urban inequality—if they continue to hold grantees accountable to quantifiable outcomes.[15]

Government can play a supporting role in these efforts. In particular, tax credits that incentivize private investment in the nonprofit sector have broad appeal and can be redesigned in ways that build organizational capacity and diversity. Take the Community Investment Tax Credit (CITC) in Massachusetts, described in chapter 4. The CITC only funds one kind of nonprofit—community development corporations (CDCs)—and only funds organizations "with a track record" of successful projects. By denying capacity funding for organizations that lack capacity, policies like CITC do little to change the unequal distribution of resources across poor neighborhoods.

Operating with little public oversight ironically puts private funders in a unique position to tackle urban inequality. Making good on that potential will require a fundamental reimagining of their purpose and role in urban governance. Current funding practices amplify government's bias toward capacity and systematically disadvantage those in greatest need. It will be politically difficult and financially costly, yet institutional philanthropy can make strides by performing the functions that government and markets are ill-equipped for: the risky, long-term capacity-building efforts in the places that need it most, where quantifiable outcomes may be hard to define.

Decoupling Participation from Community Control

Participation is a central pillar of democratic politics and civic life in the United States. Bolstered by federally mandated "maximum feasible participation" during the War on Poverty, participation has become a dominant approach to governance in cities. In poor neighborhoods, the idealized outcome of participation is community control: The community should have a say and determine neighborhood priorities. Conditions in poor neighborhoods are expected to improve when the community is in the driver's seat.

No mechanism of achieving community control has been more common than the public meeting. In the scholarly literature, critiques of participation and public meetings abound. Public meetings are disempowering, overly technical, or insufficiently advertised. Homeowners and middle-class residents tend to dominate discussions, undermining the voice of the poor.

Throughout *Constructing Community*, I have introduced a number of additional critiques. For one, community control requires *the* community to control development. The case of the Maxwell Building in Upham's Corner, described in chapter 6, shows how difficult this can be in practice. The community wanted a park, and the community also didn't want a park. The community wanted housing instead of commercial development, and the community also wanted commercial development instead of housing. The community wanted only affordable housing, and the community also didn't want any affordable housing. And on, and on. It is unclear what the appropriate outcome of community control should be when the community's demands are inconsistent and irreconcilable.

There is also a question of who, exactly, we are referring to when we say "the community" should control development. Some forms of community control can actively harm the urban poor. For instance, white homeowners who collectively resist integration and block affordable housing are in a very real sense exercising community control. Even if we clarified that the community in "community control" refers only to poor people of color who are longtime residents of poor neighborhoods, valuing some community members over others seems inconsistent with the democratic ideal of community control. Another normative inclination is to value proximity; the opinions of those who live closer to a project matter more than those who live farther away. But what are the cutoff points? How close must one live to claim authority as an "abutter" or a "stakeholder" in a given project? Places are not isolated islands. Residents of a poor neighborhood have good reason to worry about encroaching gentrification in surrounding neighborhoods, crime has spillover effects, and pollution from factories spreads across a region. Why, then, shouldn't residents of nearby neighborhoods have a say in projects that might affect them?

In the Fairmount Corridor, DSNI enacted a particular vision of community control by instituting quotas on its thirty-five-person board of directors. Sixteen seats were reserved for community residents, and according to the organization's website, "[e]qual representation is provided for the community's four major cultures—African American, Cape Verdean, Latino and white."[16] DSNI's approach creates a structure that avoids what sociologists Leslie Martin and Derek Hyra each call *political displacement*: instances when long-time, predominantly poor residents "become outvoted or outnumbered by new residents."[17]

Though well-intentioned, such practices introduce additional complications. In particular, this form of community control gets messy for precisely the reason it exists: When neighborhoods change, the composition of "the community" changes. At DSNI's annual meeting in 2010, there were a number of Asian immigrants in attendance. How many Asians must move into DSNI's service area before Asians could gain guaranteed seats on DSNI's community-controlled board? Conversely, to what percentage would the Latino population have to decline in order to no longer qualify for special recognition on the board? Consider a poor, predominantly Black neighborhood. If affluent white newcomers moved there in large numbers and assumed positions on the local community-based organization's board, we would rightfully identify it as an example of political displacement and worry about the implications for poor Black residents. The catch is that, because the community changed, the organization would nevertheless remain, by definition, "community-based." Simply put, *community control* does not necessarily mean *marginalized peoples' control*.

I want to suggest one possible path forward: We should decouple participation from the idea of community control. Rather than treat participation in local politics as a means for the community to control development projects in their own neighborhoods, urban policymakers should instead treat political voice as an end in and of itself. Poor people, people of color, and poor people of color face intersecting institutional barriers that can push their voices out of politics.[18] Some of those voices might propose innovative ideas to reduce inequality. Some might make unrealistic suggestions. Many will disagree. And still others might demand policies, programs, or projects that would ultimately make life *worse* for the urban poor. There is little reason to expect a single community voice, and so we should reframe public participation as a way to elevate the political voice of *specific people* rather than vague notions of "community control."

These theoretical problems with participation and community control are magnified by the design of public meetings. Limited in time and space, public meetings restrict broad participation. The optimal outcome is consensus—*a* position from *the* community to be juxtaposed against government officials or a potential developer. When community agreement is required to move a project forward, the people who say "no" will inherently have more power than the people who say "yes"; all it takes is a handful of opponents to demonstrate a lack of consensus. Transparency is also virtually nonexistent. Officials never say what they did with public comments, nor do they explain how participants influenced decisions beyond uncontestable claims that "the community" played a part.

What if, instead, policymakers and practitioners invested more in low-cost, ongoing exercises that produce a high volume of information, persist even after particular projects are completed, make priorities transparent, and neither seek nor assume a singular position from "the community"? What if, in other words, we invested in organizations and techniques that focus specifically on generating ideas from marginalized people less likely to participate in politics?

Consider Design Studio for Social Intervention (DS4SI), a nonprofit in Boston. In 2014, DS4SI staff solicited input about public improvements for the Four Corners Station on the Fairmount Line. They built a mock refreshment cart next to the station and called it "The Imaginary Tea Stop"—a play on words referring to Boston's public transit system, colloquially known as "the T." Next to it, there was a booth with rows of cups affixed to a wooden wall. Each cup represented a different category, like "Better Signage" or "Wifi," and people voted for their priorities by placing wooden popsicle sticks into the cups. They could write on the sticks, adding context to their votes or proposing different ideas beyond what was listed on the cups. The exercise was creative, low-cost, and attracted participation from people who may not attend public meetings. Most important, it was structured to collect many different ideas, not reach consensus.[19]

Pairwise wiki surveys are another, related technique.[20] These innovative survey instruments present a single question and collect multiple, crowdsourced answers. The information is housed online, but like any other survey, can also be collected in person through the use of handheld devices. The key difference, as articulated by sociologists Matthew Salganik and Karen Levy, is that pairwise wiki surveys solicit (and can account for) both heavy and light contributors, are inherently collaborative, and adapt to new information. In the basic setup, participants make pairwise comparisons between two answers. The instrument presents them with a new pair after every vote, and they can vote as little or as much as they want. They can also add their own answers to the instrument, and those answers are then presented to future participants. As such, the survey constantly evolves. Each response helps the instrument learn and use past information to inform future pair selections.

For an example, let's return to the question of the Maxwell Building, discussed in chapter 6. A pairwise wiki survey could ask: What should replace the Maxwell Building? The instrument would present participants with a pair of answers, like "Affordable housing" and "A playground." Participants would then vote for one answer or indicate that they could not choose between the two options. After voting, another pair of answers would appear, and so on. Along the way, people could add alternative answers for future participants to consider, such as "Light industrial development." The backend algorithm would then rank the various answers based on the totality of pairwise voting and give an overall sense of participants' priorities.

Pairwise wiki surveys do not overcome some of the challenges listed above, such as normative concerns about who should have the most say over community development plans. But, like DS4SI's "Imaginary Tea Stop," they generate a substantial amount of information at a relatively low cost, without assuming consensus is preferable or even possible. Here, *the entire point* is to reveal contradictory recommendations and force a public conversation about why some ideas are better or worse than others. Transparent ranking of priorities also forces government officials' hand, putting pressure on them to explain *why* they pursued a certain path without resorting to the kind of "community" talk I observed in Boston.

In practice, public participation and the pursuit of community control has not lived up to its promise. No additional meeting, alternative community organizing strategy, or clever urban planning activity will make a difference. Community control is elusive because there is no singular voice of *the* community. As such, we should not judge success by whether the community controlled development. Instead, we should work to ensure marginalized people had ample opportunities to express ideas or opinions about decisions affecting their neighborhoods. There is so much untapped, imaginative, innovative potential out there—ideas that approach problems in ways policymakers and activists never even considered. Poor neighborhoods would benefit from a policy orientation aimed at getting more ideas—even conflicting ideas—on the table, so that residents and organizations can mobilize around the proposals that they believe are best.

Constructing Community

Since the 1960s, urban policy has been predicated on the idea that the community should be incorporated into public decision-making. The challenge is to find the community's authentic voice: to facilitate an effective participatory process or to find the right community organization to represent the community's needs and concerns. Urban scholars make similar assumptions. We ask how the community is socially organized, the extent to which the community influences public decisions, or how new policies and development projects affect the community. The questions themselves imply that the community's social organization has positive effects, the community should influence policies and plans, and the community should benefit from new projects and programs. Even in public discourse, community has come to signify the common good: a valued, moral state to aspire, the preferable alternative to individual interests and elite domination.

Yet while the use of the concept invariably connotes something positive, it also eludes definition. "The community" can refer to a particular neighborhood, a group of people with a shared identity, the dozen people who attend a community meeting, or a vague collective existing only in the abstract. During my fieldwork, it was not unusual to hear sentences like: "After organizing the community, there was a meeting in the community and the community expressed support for a new project"—roughly translated to: *People who live in a place* were informed about a meeting, there was a meeting in that *place*, and *the people who attended the meeting* expressed a favorable opinion. The sentence is comprehensible, yes, but it uses a single concept to refer to three distinct objects of reference.

Scholars, policymakers, and even self-described community leaders nevertheless operate as if *the community* is a cohesive object and has a single, unified voice. The concept's vagueness—the fact that it is a floating signifier of the common good—allows people to invoke different definitions at different times in order to pursue particular political ends. Boundaries and membership are *inherently* fluid and *intentionally* open-ended. No organization can ever effectively mobilize the community, and no participatory process can ever fully empower the community, because, I would argue, <u>there is no such thing as "the" community</u>.

What does this mean for urban policy and social science scholarship? First, the sooner professional urban planners acknowledge that politics entails winners and losers, the sooner we can move past farcical claims of "community consensus" and have honest debates about whose ideas should win and why. Pretending there are win-wins and then claiming community consensus does little to increase participation *or* positive outcomes for the urban poor.

Community development practitioners should engage in similar self-reflection. As the nonprofit sector became increasingly professionalized, the field's mission drifted further and further away from its radical roots. There are strategic and rational reasons for this shift, including, as I have described throughout this book, the structure of urban governance and the dynamics of foundation funding. But the most high-profile, ongoing critique is that community development professionals, in pursuit of organizational survival, have lost sight of "the community" in their work. Organizational leaders should continuously ask, "Who, *specifically*, are we working for, and are we actually helping those people?" Any answer that reflexively references "the community" is wholly insufficient.

As scholars, we are also guilty of imprecise language. Even if we were to accept one denotation of "community" and discard all others, referring to any form of community as "*the* community" ignores the fact that people and places are diverse no matter how demographically similar. As sociologist Monica Bell argues, we shouldn't think "in a static way about what 'the community' wants or needs."[21] To say that "the community" is in support of anything is a misnomer. At best, the way we talk about community in our research lacks specificity. At worst, we reify the misleading notion that communities are self-contained, homogenous places or groups of people.

We don't need, and probably can't find, a precise definition of the word community. Trying to pin one down creates analytical blinders and obscures the different ways people actually *use* the concept. Instead, we need to identify when the concept's positive connotations are being invoked for political purposes, appreciate how people strategically deploy the *symbolism* of community in urban politics, and recognize that the concept is as constructed as the projects it so often bolsters. That is, community development is as much about the political construction of legitimacy and authenticity as it is about the physical construction of buildings. By coming to terms with this reality, we can better understand how urban governance works on the ground, and how it can be changed to produce more equitable outcomes.

METHODOLOGICAL APPENDIX

THIS STUDY DID NOT FOLLOW the conventional path of urban ethnography—though it was no doubt urban and certainly ethnographic. The prototypical urban ethnography is a study of life in poverty: The ethnographer typically lives in a poor neighborhood and writes about interactions with his or her poor neighbors. Unfortunately, it is difficult to "live in the field," so to speak, when your field is governance and political decision-making. So I did what I believed to be the next best thing: I tried to be present for as many discussions of Corridor development as was possible. I couldn't live in politics like an urban ethnographer lives in a poor neighborhood. But I could still be a part of the political process.

Between 2010 and 2014, I observed 367 meetings and events related to the Fairmount Corridor: 268 private strategy sessions, 23 semi-private professional conferences or symposia, and 76 public community meetings. Of the private meetings, 69 were conference calls and the remainder, in-person gatherings. The vast majority (218) included only community-based organization (CBO) leaders, government officials, or foundation staff. As table A.1 shows, meetings were held throughout Boston, and I observed a wide range of participants.

I did not strive for parity across meeting type or participant. Instead, I tried to follow the planning process as *it* traveled through multiple field sites— "follow[ing] the thing," as anthropologist George Marcus describes the technique.[1] Some people and organizations thought about community development in the Corridor more than others, leading to more or fewer opportunities for observation. Table A.1 does not include all meetings that occurred; there were some meetings I missed or did not have access to, discussed in more detail below. That said, I made sure to observe at least some meetings including each of the relevant organizations and agencies that contributed to community development plans.

Those meetings included 11 planning processes and discussions of 51 different projects, detailed in table A.2. Meetings ranged from 1-hour conference calls to 5-hour forums, for an average of approximately 2 hours.

I also received two research fellowships that allowed me to work inside Boston City Hall for a total of 10 months (3 months full-time in 2010 and 7 months part-time in 2011). My specific tasks were unrelated to the Fairmount Corridor.[2] But I leveraged those contacts and connections into additional information that helped contextualize my fieldwork. In particular, I happened to have a cubicle next to Sheila Dillon (then the mayor's advisor to housing, she would later be promoted to director of the Department of Neighborhood Development). Casual conversations with Sheila were especially helpful when

Table A.1. Number of Observations at Private and Public Meetings, by Participants and Location

	Private Meetings	Public Meetings
Participants		
CBO Leaders	212	62
Consultants	253	57
Private and Quasi-Public Funders	53	32
City Government	23	53
State Government	15	42
Federal Government	7	4
Location[a]		
Upham's Corner	70	25
Codman Square	51	8
Other parts of Roxbury and Dorchester	50	15
Mattapan	23	18
Hyde Park	32	6
Downtown	66	4

[a] Five private meetings were held outside the Corridor or were multi-neighborhood tours.

Table A.2. Community Development Activities in the Fairmount Corridor, 2009–2013

Category	Number	Illustrative Example
Housing	12	Housing development in Hyde Park (27 apartments)
Commercial	4	Pearl Food Production Small Business Center in Upham's Corner
Mixed-Use	14	Mixed-use project in Codman Square (24 apartments and commercial space leased to a nonprofit arts organization)
Transit	5	New public transit station in Codman Square
Public Realm	3	Street and sidewalk improvements in Grove Hall
Open Space	8	Community garden in Mattapan
Economic Development	5	NECAT job training center in Newmarket district
Planning Processes	11	Fairmount Corridor Planning Initiative
TOTAL	62	

the Boston Redevelopment Authority undertook the Fairmount Corridor Planning Initiative.

I also worked as a consultant. For 12 months (part-time) between 2011 and 2012, I joined a team of applied researchers from the UMass–Boston Center of Social Policy. They had been hired by The Boston Foundation (TBF) to evaluate the foundation's impact in the Fairmount Corridor.[3] I was involved during the initial data collection stage in which the team reviewed internal TBF documents and conducted 45 interviews with nonprofit grantees, government officials, and other funders.[4]

Finally, I supplemented observations with ongoing informal interactions—going out for coffee, a brief phone chat, and so on—and the analysis of an extensive database of newspaper articles and official reports mentioning community development projects in the Fairmount Corridor.

Together, those various pieces of information and fieldwork observations constitute the primary data used in this study. But that only tells part of the story—indeed, it only tells the *outcome* of the story. In this appendix, I describe how I balanced the professional expectations placed on urban ethnographers with the practical realities of studying a process that did not lend itself to residence in a poor neighborhood. My approach yielded unique insights as well as unique challenges.

Evolution of the Study

I stumbled upon the Fairmount Corridor in 2009. A friend in my graduate school cohort told me about a sign he saw announcing a new transit station in Codman Square, a disadvantaged neighborhood in Boston. The development piqued my interest. At the time, I was searching for a dissertation topic related to neighborhood poverty, and I had grown particularly interested in unequal access to public transportation. In my reading of the literature, I had noticed that sociologists generally wrote about urban inequality in terms of jobs, housing, crime, or education. Transportation access, fundamentally linked to these other policy areas, stood out as an underexplored issue.

The Codman Square transit station was part of a previously negotiated agreement to build four stations on a commuter rail line called the Fairmount Line. The Fairmount Line, I later learned, cut right through neighborhoods underserved by the traditional subway system. Not coincidentally, those neighborhoods had some of the highest concentrations of poverty, violence, and other forms of disadvantage in the city.

I didn't know it then, but federal officials were also thinking about the Fairmount Line. In the summer of 2009, the Obama administration announced a new interagency partnership including the Department of Housing and Urban Development (HUD), the Department of Transportation (DOT), and the Environmental Protection Agency (EPA). The idea behind the partnership was as novel as it was simple: Building affordable housing in close proximity to public transportation is good for the environment and makes daily life less costly for the urban poor. The departments' outcomes were related, but their strategies were not. The three agencies pledged to better coordinate their efforts and target specific underserved areas.

In February 2010, the three agency directors named the Fairmount Line a pilot project for their initiative. Significant national attention and millions of dollars for development projects around the stations soon followed. It was around this time that I decided to study development along the Fairmount Line for my doctoral dissertation, research that would eventually become the basis of this book.

Even though I had selected the Fairmount Line as a research site, I still had no idea *what* I wanted to study about these neighborhoods and the new transit stations. My first thought was to study the effect of increased transportation access on poverty. Given the timing of the proposed stations, I thought I had a unique opportunity to observe life in the neighborhood for two years before and two years after the new stations were built. When I presented this idea in a graduate seminar, the professor, a senior political scientist, gently urged me to come up with a plan B. The reason, she said, was that public infrastructure projects rarely finish on schedule. She was of course correct: The state initially announced a December 2011 deadline for new station construction. In reality, three new stations opened in July 2013, and the fourth did not open until 2019.

Turning to Google, I began to read any and every news article, blog post, and website discussing the Fairmount Line. A number of sources mentioned a coalition of nonprofit organizations located in neighborhoods that intersected the rail line. Beginning in the mid-2000s, the coalition strategically built housing and other commercial development near the sites of the proposed stations. Insofar as there was any action to observe, it was clear to me that these nonprofit leaders were a good place to start.

In 2010, I conducted eight exploratory interviews to get a better sense of the Fairmount Line's history and the ongoing work by the coalition of nonprofit developers. After one of those interviews, the director of a community development corporation (CDC) invited me to attend a private coalition meeting. I was then invited to another, and then another. Meanwhile, I was soon attending all public meetings about development projects in the area. And so my fieldwork began.

I quickly came to two realizations. First, transportation access was only one piece of a much larger puzzle of development in these neighborhoods. There was also affordable housing construction, arts and cultural events, community organizing, and a variety of other programs and initiatives. Moreover, the social effects of increased transportation access—or any other form of development, for that matter—occurred only after long debates about who gets what. I had to understand these *political decisions* if I wanted to understand any bigger story about poverty and neighborhood inequality.

At this point, my initial point of access—nonprofit leaders—started to look like a limitation.[5] The directors of nonprofits in the Corridor were incredibly important players, to be sure. But the community development field was vast and multifaceted. If I wanted to understand that wider ecosystem of decision-making and decision-makers, I had to gain access to other agencies and organizations. By 2012, I was observing a wide range of government officials, foundation program officers, consultants, nonprofit directors, community organizers, and residents of the Fairmount Corridor.

In true inductive fashion, I had expanded my fieldwork but had not yet decided how to situate my research in an existing body of scholarship. That changed two years into data collection. Alongside other graduate students, I had breakfast with a political sociologist invited to speak at our department colloquium. As is customary during these kinds of visits, we went around the table and discussed our respective research interests. When I described my growing interest in the political decisions surrounding urban redevelopment, the visiting sociologist made a connection to Robert Dahl's classic work, *Who Governs?* Something clicked. Up until that point, I thought my research was a study of urban poverty, not a study of urban governance.

Not everyone agreed with my change in direction. One urban ethnographer urged me to abandon my study of political decisions and instead follow a few families negatively impacted by new development projects. A gritty portrayal of hardship is what gives ethnography its emotional punch, the scholar explained. If I was determined to study urban development, then I should move to a neighborhood in the throes of change and conduct an ethnography of poor people struggling to get by. In terms of professional advice, these points were valid. With few exceptions, "urban ethnography" has come to signify "the lived experience of poverty." If I wanted to be seen as an urban ethnographer, and if I wanted my ethnographic study to be read by other sociologists, it would make sense to conform to these norms. But this is precisely the reason why an ethnographic study of urban governance is so necessary. Many studies document the hardships of urban poverty. Far fewer investigate the people and organizations proposing and implementing the policies that make a difference in poor residents' lives.

Getting In

Access is not a one-shot deal; it is an ongoing process of negotiation and renegotiation. I initiated this project by asking a few nonprofit leaders and government officials for formal interviews. The eight I asked agreed to be interviewed, but I found it difficult to get sufficiently detailed answers from them. These were people used to providing sound bites, either to news reporters or to Master's degree students completing theses in one of Boston's many urban planning or public policy schools. I was as skeptical about the veracity of their answers as I was concerned about what my interviewees *weren't* saying. I made the decision at that point to prioritize observations over interviews. In doing so, I followed the advice of sociologists Colin Jerolmack and Shamus Khan, who warn against the "the error of inferring situated behavior from verbal accounts."[6]

Gaining access to private meetings and conversations was, in some ways, easier than I had anticipated. By and large, people were proud of the work they were doing in the Fairmount Corridor and wanted their story told. In some instances, I obtained access before I asked for it. During my first fellowship in City Hall, I introduced myself during a meeting of the Education, Health, and Human Services sub-cabinet. I described my background, the work I was doing for the fellowship, and briefly mentioned my dissertation research on the Fairmount Corridor. An advisor to the mayor approached me after the meeting. She pulled me into her office, showed me a binder labeled "Fairmount Corridor," and proceeded to tell me, unprompted, how the mayor viewed the Corridor.

Similarly, in June 2011, I received an email out of the blue from Geeta's assistant at TBF. "Geeta asked me to reach out to you to find a time to meet to explore your work ... and [where] there are opportunities," the message read. That meeting led to more meetings with Geeta and TBF staff. Geeta then passed my name along to a consultant team she had hired to evaluate TBF's grants to Corridor organizations. I was offered a spot on the team shortly thereafter, giving me full access to all Corridor-related TBF documents.

A parallel dynamic led to access with nonprofit leaders. In January 2010, at the very early stages of my research, I emailed Jeanne DuBois, then-executive director of the Dorchester Bay Economic Development Corporation. I explained my research and asked if she would be willing to share any relevant information. I made no mention of Jeanne's meetings with other nonprofit coalition members in the Corridor (partially because, at the time, I didn't know about them), but in her reply, Jeanne extended an invitation: "If you want to come to a coalition ... meeting," she wrote, "please contact Joan Tighe, our coordinator."

Joan quickly emerged as a key point of contact. A white resident of Upham's Corner, she was not married and had no children. Her social life seemed partly wrapped up in community meetings and neighborhood politics—topics she liked to gossip about. She also set the schedule for meetings of the various nonprofit coalitions and sent email reminders. Access to Joan meant access to a near-complete schedule of meetings. She eventually included me in emails and would forward relevant announcements to me.[7]

When I attended meetings, people rarely questioned my presence, even if they were unclear or forgot why I was there. One instance stands out. By 2012, after I had attended dozens of meetings, I realized that taking sufficiently detailed notes by hand was impossible; I had to record and play back audio if I wanted to capture everything that was said. It was especially important for meetings of the coalition of nonprofit developers, who often used confusing acronyms and shorthand.

I made the request early that year for permission to record the meetings. I was taken aback when Gail, executive director of Codman Square Neighborhood Development Corporation, replied that she was not comfortable with audio recording because she had no idea what I was studying. I tried to joke that I didn't know either, but Gail scowled. "Before I can agree . . . I'd like to know how you're—without trying to influence it—I just would like to know what you're doing. I have no clue. Never have. And I've just gone along with the program," she said.[8] I had, in fact, told Gail and her colleagues in the coalition about my research plans during an informal presentation in 2010. I distributed a Memorandum of Understanding to each director, detailing the purpose of my study and procedures for reviewing quotes before publication. I briefed each of the directors again—Gail included—when I interviewed them individually. Still, after Gail raised her objections, I gave another presentation, no different from the one I'd given two years prior. Afterward, Gail said she was willing to "take a leap of faith" and agreed to let me audio record the coalition meetings.

Gail's reference to "[going] along with the program" sheds important light on the question of access: It is likely that I was able to attend so many private meetings partly because no one assumed the authority to question my presence or ask me to leave. I have no doubt race and gender played a role as well; while many meetings I attended included diverse groups of participants, an abundance of research suggests my presence *would* have been questioned or challenged if I were anything but a white man. Additionally, I also suspect I was never kicked out of a meeting because no one really felt like they were 100 percent in charge. When nonprofit grantees met with funders, or when government officials convened interagency meetings, there may have been a chair leading the agenda. But no one clearly dominated anyone else. Analytically, this told me quite a bit about power relations in the community development field.

Methodologically, however, Gail's comments presented a dilemma. What does it mean for informed consent when I had, in fact, informed Gail about the study and she consented to my presence but later forgot? Gail and her colleagues were a big part of my world; it was clear, however, that I was *not* a big part of theirs. In my fieldwork interactions, I always introduced myself as a researcher and explained that I was interested in understanding how decisions got made and how plans were implemented—"I want to know how the sausage gets made," I would say. I did not give regular updates, nor did I continuously refresh people's memories about my biography. In general, I practiced what ethnographers call "shallow cover": I was upfront about my identity as a researcher but did not explain the particulars of my research questions.[9] Gail made me question this approach—though I never did come up with a satisfactory solution to the problem.

Entering the field through many different doors meant that different people had different ways to make sense of my presence. I liked to pause and wait for people to try and place me in the community development field before introducing myself. City officials asked if I was a resident, residents asked if I was a city official, and foundation staff wondered if I was a nonprofit organizer. As my relationships broadened and deepened, I eventually became a go-to source of information across domains. When I was working in City Hall, Joan asked me about city government's perception of the Corridor. When I told a pair of city officials about my research, they asked me about the nonprofit leaders' perception of city government. Nonprofit directors sent Master's students and new hires to me to get an overview of community development in the Corridor. Mike, a white nonprofit developer, asked me to fill him in when he missed a public meeting. Inés, a Latina city government official, asked me to supply the official notes for a public meeting when the city's note-taker couldn't attend. Mela, a Black community organizer, deferred to me—instead of the Black nonprofit director sitting to my right—when she wanted to know more about the recipients of a particular grant. "You explain this to me!" Mela insisted. "I know you go to all these meetings and are always taking notes! I know you know what's going on!" By the end of my fieldwork, my expanding access meant that I was one of the few people who had at least some understanding of every player in the field. Access became taken for granted by the people I wanted to access.

Above all else, the strongest predictor of access was simply showing up. It was a technique that did not go unnoticed. Karen, a white city official, had a running joke about it. On Valentine's Day in 2013, I attended a meeting in City Hall about city government's support for nonprofit-led development projects in the Corridor. I sat directly facing the door, and Karen and I made eye contact as she entered the room.

"Oh no, it's him!" Karen joked. "What is *he* doing here?!?"

"I was just speaking so nicely of you on the walk over!" I said with a laugh, trying to be in on the joke, not the butt of it.

"Were you?" Karen asked rhetorically but warmly.

"He was," Mike, a nonprofit director sitting next to me responded. "Actually, to me."

As everyone turned to face us, Mike asked if anyone remembered *Zelig*, a Woody Allen movie about a man who kept popping up at various historical events. A couple of people responded yes, but Karen looked confused. "He'd show up everywhere?" Mike pushed, trying to jog Karen's memory about a movie she may never have seen. "Yes, yes, yes," Karen remembered (or pretended to remember) after pausing for a second.

"Well it's Zelig, right here," Mike said, pointing at me.

"Well, it is interesting," Karen said, speaking directly to Mike. "I'll be at DSNI [a Corridor nonprofit] and look over, and I'm like, 'There he is.'" She pointed, over and over again, as she repeated, " 'There he is.' At all these places."[10]

I was in that same conference room for a meeting the following week. "You again!" Karen exclaimed when she saw me. Everyone laughed.

Accessing so many people and places turned out to be an emotionally challenging approach to fieldwork. The people I observed often complained about one another, and each time this happened, I found myself frustrated with whomever I was observing and silently defending whoever was not present. For example, when funders criticized community organization leaders for failing to produce meaningful outcomes, I found myself annoyed with funders' arbitrary metrics of success. Community organizations in the Corridor are undeniably doing *some* good, I thought to myself, so why should they be held to such stringent standards? But when nonprofit directors grumbled about rigid funders, I found myself equally annoyed with their embellishments. Funders are *right* to hold community organizations accountable, I thought, because nonprofit leaders consistently exaggerate their impact. I had the same reaction whenever I observed government officials, consultants, or anyone else in the field: a constant state of silent annoyance with at least one actor and silent defense of another.

I did not plan for this internal conflict, but it proved analytically useful. By approaching fieldwork as ongoing dialectic of defense and critique, I avoided the tendency to create categories of "victims" and "perpetrators" or "heroes" and "villains"—common tropes in urban ethnography.[11] I had to confront my personal feelings about people in relation to my analysis of their work. That is not to say I was uniquely objective (or to argue one way or another that objectivity is possible), but rather to argue that my multi-sited approach forced me to be reflexive and consider these contradictions head-on.

Presence in the Field

Ethnographers rightly (and constantly) worry that our presence in the field influences what we observe. The concern is that people will change their behavior and therefore provide an incomplete or misleading sense of their "true" thoughts, feelings, and actions.

Ethnographers use different techniques in an effort to minimize their presence in the field. In a study of crime and police surveillance in Philadelphia, Alice Goffman tried to make her body small to become, as literally as possible, a "fly on the wall." "I came up with tests for how well I was doing," she writes. "If someone told a story about a past event and couldn't remember whether I had [been] present for it, then I knew I was doing fairly well."[12]

Several times over the course of my fieldwork people recounted events to me or to others and either forgot or failed to disclose that I had also attended. Yet when I returned to my field notes, it was clear that my presence had been felt in those moments, even if participants later forgot I was there. It suggested that this technique is less useful for testing whether you were seen as indistinguishable from other participants and more helpful for showing that people didn't necessarily remember acting any differently at the meetings you attended.

Another test I considered was to compare conversations from conference calls—where I was by definition less visible—with conversations from in-person meetings. I failed this test as well; one time, when someone made a disparaging remark about someone else not on the call, I was asked to "put [my] pen down" and not record the comment. I was not as hidden as I had thought.

A third test gave me more confidence: I compared how people in the field spoke to me with how they spoke to other researchers, journalists, or newly hired consultants. One example is illustrative. In March 2013, I attended a public meeting with another graduate student from a nearby university. The graduate student was beginning her own research project on the Fairmount Corridor and had previously interviewed Inés, one of the city officials managing the Fairmount Corridor Planning Initiative. As the graduate student and I walked into the meeting room, we stopped to talk to Inés. Our conversation included some gossip and banter about CBO leaders in the Corridor. After, the graduate student pulled me aside. She said that, compared to the interview, Inés acted "*completely* different" while speaking with me.

There were also instances when I actively tried—and failed—to influence the people I followed. One notable instance occurred in February 2012. A program officer at TBF invited me to a luncheon with visitors from Pittsburgh-based Heinz Endowments. Apparently, a senior program officer from the Barr Foundation had encouraged a program director from Heinz to visit TBF and learn more about the Fairmount Corridor. Since 2010, Heinz staff had coordinated with two other foundations as well as city government officials to fund community development projects in a neighborhood called Hazelwood. The parallels with the Fairmount Corridor were quite clear.

The meeting included TBF and Heinz staff, as well as city government officials and nonprofit grantees from the Fairmount Corridor. After introductions, Geeta, associate vice president of programs at TBF, asked Jeanne, a nonprofit grantee, to describe the history of the Fairmount Corridor. Jeanne's depiction of the Corridor's history was incorrect. Mike, another nonprofit grantee, corrected her—and in doing so, referenced a previous conversation in which Mike and I had discussed the correct historical timeline. Despite the correction, Jeanne was undeterred:

> JEANNE: We had 13 stations up and down this rail line, up until the 1950s.[13] And then, as the neighborhood started to change, investment left, they shut down stations. And there was only, but for community organizing, at the northern end of the line—
> PROGRAM OFFICER WITH HEINZ: Is it because of the ridership? The ridership was bad?
> JEANNE: No, it was white flight, and disinvestment and blockbusting that was using race—

MIKE: But let's pause there, because our doctoral student, in the corner, actually has pointed out that it did begin *before* that. The stations started closing back to the '40s, Jeremy, is that right?
JEREMY: Yeah.
MIKE: So it might be a *bit* more nuanced than clearly white flight.
JEANNE: It *is* more nuanced than, you know, just white flight and disinvestment, but those were the big things.
GEETA: The big trends.
JEANNE: Those were the big trends.

Jeanne and Geeta were incorrect and Mike prompted me to correct them. I did, but my contribution was dismissed.

There are two reasons why, on the whole, I do not think my presence impacted people's thoughts and behaviors as much as I had feared. First, some people in the field treated me like a naïve child. On four occasions, I observed the members of the CDC coalition and their consultants debate the merits of my study, as well as my presence at, and recording of, their private meetings. One director thought that publication of my research would spark positive publicity for the organizations' work, while another warned that they couldn't expect my research to paint their organizations in a positive light. A consultant acknowledged the time lag for publication and argued that by the time any quote made it to print, "sensitive" issues would be long resolved; a nonprofit director strongly disagreed. Another consultant noted that few people would read my work anyway; one director agreed, but another anticipated my work would be hugely successful and generate lots of press. All of these conversations occurred with me in the room, as if I was a small child unable to comprehend adult topics. These were infantilizing experiences, to be sure. But they did alleviate concerns that my study subjects wouldn't engage in honest and open conversations in my presence.[14]

The second reason was structural: These were busy people who had to discuss strategy and make decisions during meetings. It would have been extremely difficult, if not impossible, to *not* openly discuss topics during the meetings I attended because there was simply no other time to do so. That's not to say I observed every decision that was made. Some preceded my fieldwork, and others were hashed out over email or at meetings I missed. But it does suggest that what I saw during meetings was meaningful and that my presence could only have limited impact.

Naming Names

As I was writing this book, Alexandra Murphy and Colin Jerolmack published a series of articles arguing against the practice of masking in ethnographic research.[15] Legal scholar Steven Lubet similarly critiqued the use of pseudonyms and other strategies ethnographers use to ensure anonymity.[16] Obscuring details for the sake of anonymity, they point out, makes it difficult for readers to make informed critiques or revisit and update the ethnographer's analysis. Providing the option for disclosure, conversely, transfers power from the gatekeeping ethnographer to the people under study, allowing them to decide whether they want to remain anonymous.

I agree with the criticisms and believe ethnographic studies should, as a default, err on the side of disclosure.[17] And so, for this book, I decided to disclose the real names of people, organizations, and places, providing they gave permission. In February 2019, I contacted thirty-nine people who were quoted during private meetings or conversations.[18] I offered everyone the opportunity to review each of their quotes in writing or over the phone. If anyone thought a particular quote might cause personal or professional harm, I offered to collaboratively decide on a solution to mask their identity. I generally treated quotes from public meetings as fair game but did share some of these public quotes with those who were also quoted in private.

Of the thirty-nine people I contacted, twenty-three granted approval to use their real names for all quotes. Six did not return my calls or emails, so I masked their identities in the text. Four requested partial anonymity for some quotes. Three people asked me to edit some quotes, either for clarity or because they said something that could be interpreted as offensive or harmful. In those instances, I removed particular clauses but did not change the substance of the remarks. A few quotes in the text do not refer to people by name for reasons related to readability. In those cases, I still ran each quote by the person who said it.

Three people—one private funder and two government officials—did not approve my request to quote them in the book. I quoted the private funder briefly in two scenes in which she denied funding requests made by the directors of MCDC and SWBCDC, respectively. When I shared her quotes over email prior to scheduling a call, she responded that my description lacked context; the quotes did not sufficiently explain why her organization denied both requests, reasons that included "[the] extent to which results were accomplished via prior support," "stability of management," and "board oversight." I offered to include any and all additional context in the text and suggested times when we might discuss further over the phone. She replied one month later and asked me to remove her from the text entirely. I complied. The removal did not impede my ability to write about either scene; her comments were ancillary to those of another funder who, lucky for me, provided (and approved) the most meaningful quotes for the purpose of my analysis.[19]

With respect to the government officials, one forwarded a statement that appeared to have been written by a member of his agency's communications department. The other stated that she "would prefer" I not quote her by name because she did not remember saying the quotes and "[didn't] think they were meant to be public." This was a frustrating response from a person in power, especially considering she knew during my fieldwork that I was a researcher writing a book about the Fairmount Corridor (someone even teased her that she would "be in the middle to later chapters of the book"). One of the quotes actually came from remarks she gave over a loudspeaker to a bus full of reporters—meaning any expectation of privacy was absurd. It was clear to me that she did not review the quotes I sent her and was simply blowing me off. While I personally think her quotes are exceedingly mundane—the kinds of things she said in rooms full of people and would repeat to anyone who would listen—I nevertheless assigned her a pseudonym in the text.

As mentioned above, many of the people in this study often provide sound bites for the press. That made ethnographic observations preferable to interviews; by observing people in their regular work routines, I hoped to move beyond the frontstage of self-presentation and view the backstage of their actual work. Yet precisely because many were used to being quoted in the press, they were extremely vigilant about how their quotes would be portrayed in this book. Some would only grant permission if they were told the full context of the quote, including how I interpreted it in my own analysis (I always provided the full context). Three people consulted public relations or communications professionals as they reviewed their quotes. Another person was extremely upset with what he thought was a "poor representation" of his organization. He said my use of a single quote from him was "disrespectful at a minimum, and potentially dishonest." He invited me to "change [his] mind," and we spoke on the phone for 45 minutes. He remained upset that I was not interested in asking what he called "valid questions"—including "how innovative" his work is and how a particular program "largely accomplished [its] ambitious goals"—but he nevertheless agreed that the quote in question would not cause him or his organization harm. In his view, I committed an error of omission, not commission.

The exercise was ultimately useful, as some people corrected professional titles, organizational names, or other details. The use of real names in this book also allows other researchers to update, compare, or correct my analysis. Equally important, I think it provides readers with sufficient detail to make the most informed critiques possible.

Fieldwork Failures

Most methodological appendices detail what was done to complete a study, not what *wasn't* done. Yet fieldwork failures provide useful information. With respect to this study, I can think of at least three. In the first instance, I applied to be a Boston-based field researcher on the HUD Choice Neighborhoods evaluation team, managed by the Urban Institute. The tasks for the position included interviews and observations with the Choice Neighborhoods grantees in Boston—including city agencies and nonprofits in the Fairmount Corridor. I hoped to leverage the position into a deeper understanding of the Choice Neighborhoods grant and the role of federal policy in Corridor development. In 2011, I made it to the final round of interviews, but the job ultimately went to someone else. I never pursued the matter further and did not attempt to observe the Choice Neighborhoods implementation meetings. It's something I really regret.

In a second instance, I pushed a little harder for a role in government. I offered to help out with the BRA's Fairmount Corridor Planning Initiative as an unpaid intern. Similar to my application to the Urban Institute, I hoped to gain more insight into city government's behind-the-scenes role in the Fairmount Corridor. I went so far as to submit a formal letter of application, per the suggestion of a friendly BRA official. I never heard back. The official later told me that it related to concerns about "the book thing." An urban planning Master's student from MIT was selected instead.

The third failure relates to social position. When I reflected back on my fieldwork, it was clear that I developed more collegial relationships with the white and/or middle-class people I studied. In other words: I got closer to the people who looked and talked like me. I made it a point to seek multiple viewpoints, and I analyzed the data with these and other biases in mind. I even re-wrote portions of this book after seeking feedback from peers with distinct personal and intellectual backgrounds. One change I made was to note the race of various actors throughout the text. Problematically, I had defaulted to an assumption of whiteness in my descriptions. I explicitly remarked on the race of people of color, while omitting this information for white people. In making these and other changes, I did the best I could while acknowledging my best may not have been enough. Ultimately, I do not think this book (or any book) can be *the* story of urban governance, community development, or the Fairmount Corridor. It is *a* story, based on years of fieldwork with a specific group of people and written from a particular vantage point. Only through complementary research, conducted by people from varying backgrounds, can we get a complete picture of these important social processes.

There are ways I believe I made up for deficiencies, specifically as it relates to government access. Yet I can't help but wonder if this book would have turned out differently had I gained access to different field sites or developed deeper relationships with different people. I cannot know for sure. I leave it to the reader to decide whether these blind spots undermine the strength of my arguments. And I leave it to future researchers to learn from, and build upon, these and any other deficiencies in my fieldwork.

NOTES

Introduction

1. Dezenski (2014).

2. These ideas come from a variety of scholarly literatures, including sociology, political science, public administration, geography, urban studies, and nonprofit studies. On collaborative and networked governance, see Ansell and Gash (2008), Bingham et al. (2005), Bogason and Musso (2006), Rich and Stoker (2014), Siriani (2010), Stoker (2006), and Weir et al. (2009). On "neoliberal" and austerity urbanism, see Brenner (1999, 2004), Brenner and Theodore (2002), Mayer (2003), Mele (2013), Peck and Tickell (2002), and Peck et al. (2009). On the hollow state, third-party government, and "governance without government," see Milward and Provan (2000), Peters and Pierre (1998), Salamon (1981, 1987), and Wachhaus (2014). On consensus planning, see Booher and Innes (2002), Healey (1998), Healey (2003), Innes and Booher (1999a, 1999b). On collective impact, see Kania and Kramer (2011) and Hanleybrown et al. (2012). An alternative formulation is the idea of "post-political" cities: a rise of technocratic forms of governance and an active suppression of contentious politics; see MacLeod (2011), Legacy et al. (2018), and Swyngedouw (2009). A related but distinct conceptualization is "heterarchic" governance, described by McQuarrie (2011). We might expect political science to dominate the study of urban politics, but since the 1980s, the subfield has been marginalized from the core of the discipline (Trounstine 2009; see also Judd 2005 and Sapotichne et al. 2007). In sociology, urban poverty scholars have become increasingly interested in issues of governance; see Marwell and Morrissey (2020) for a review.

3. Conflict still occurs (see Becher 2010), but it is largely seen as taboo and unproductive by those in control of grants and other resources. See McQuarrie (2013b) for a critique of urban policy and the privileging of consensus over conflict.

4. For theoretical discussions synthesizing the disparate strands of literature related to urban governance, see da Cruz et al. (2019), Marwell and Brown (2020), and Marwell and Morrissey (2020). For an empirical application, see Marwell et al. (2020). In a related study, Chaskin (2003, p. 162) refers to the shift from government to governance as a move toward "neighborhood-based governance." While collaboration is the norm in contemporary urban governance, that doesn't mean contentious politics disappeared. See Pasotti (2020) for an analysis of the strategies urban residents from across the globe use to resist redevelopment and displacement.

5. From Kenneth Clark's series of interviews produced by WGBH in 1963, "The Negro and The American Promise." Hyra (2008) argues that there was a period of "new urban renewal" during the 1990s and 2000s that was nevertheless distinct from the old urban renewal, especially in terms of the relevant actors and consequences for inequality.

6. See Baiocchi (2005), Baiocchi and Ganuza (2016), Becher (2010), Briggs (1998), Eliasoph (2014), Fung (2004), Lederman (2019), Lee et al. (2015), Lee (2015), Levine (2017), Mansbridge (1983), Moffitt (2014), McQuarrie (2013), and Walker (2014). Social movement scholars also analyze the promise and pitfalls of participatory democracy; see Polletta (2002, 2013, 2014). See Einstein et al. (2020) for a recent critique of current practices, and an illustration of the negative consequences of public participation—as it is currently practiced—with respect to housing. See McCabe (2016) for a thorough analysis of

the relationship between homeownership and civic engagement—and in particular, how homeowners engage in a politics of exclusion.

7. Nonprofits overall grew 40% between 1995 and 2013. The number of "foundations like The Boston Foundation" refers to *community foundations*, a particular form of foundation that focuses grant-making on local communities or regions. Philanthropic foundations overall grew 33% between 2002 and 2015, whereas community foundations grew 20.3% during this same time period. I discuss differences between these foundation types in more detail in chapter 5.

8. NACEDA (2010) and Schwartz (2010). See also Bratt (2008).

9. Measured in inflation-adjusted 2015 dollars. Data come from the Foundation Center (http://data.foundationcenter.org). On the growth of community development nonprofits, see LeRoux and Feeney (2015). For more on growth in community foundations since 1980, see Salamon (2012). Government funding and contracting is the primary source of funding for the sector as a whole, but private funding is often used in planning projects, before proposals even reach the desks of public officials.

10. Eikenberry and Kluver (2004); Hwang and Powell (2009); Kirkpatrick (2007); Suárez (2010). See also Goldstein (2017) for a historical account. See INCITE! (2007) and Arena (2012) for critiques of professionalization in the nonprofit sector and arguments supporting a more radical organizing approach, rejecting the dominance of philanthropic foundations.

11. Dahl (1961, p. 86).

12. See for example Wolfinger (1973) and Polsby (1980). For more on the community power debate and subsequent theoretical development in the 1980s and 1990s, see Harding (1996).

13. Logan and Molotch (2007 [1987]). The idea of "pro-growth coalitions" first appeared in an essay by John Mollenkopf (1975) but has since become more associated with Logan and Molotch's *Urban Fortunes*. It is important to note that Logan and Molotch conflate their theory of urban growth and uneven development with an analysis of urban political power. On the one hand, the authors persuasively show how political and economic elites form coalitions and reorient urban policy toward growth, largely at the expense of the urban poor. Yet on the other hand, they also argue, "we use the term growth machine to signal our conception of just who is dominant and how they function" (p. ix). In defending this latter part of the argument against critics, the authors essentially present their theory as non-falsifiable: "It does not even matter that elites often fail to achieve their growth goal," they argue, because there is no cultural disagreement about the value of growth and no "fundamental disunity" among pro-growth elites (p. 57). Subsequent research in urban sociology has, as a result, selected cases that assume rather than question the relative power of growth coalitions in cities. My own thinking is more in line with Brenner (2009), who argues that pro-growth coalitions rule more at the national level, pushing for certain federal urban policies, rather than at the city level.

14. Stone (1989). Regime theory approaches urban governance from a productive rather than domination perspective—"*power to*, not *power over*," as Stone (p. 229) puts it. On regime typologies, see Elkin (1987), Dowding (2001), Dowding et al. (1999), Fainstein and Fainstein (1983), Mossberger and Stoker (2001), Pierre (1999), and Reed (1999). For a critique and extension of regime theory, see Ferman's (1996) conceptualization of "urban arenas." For a more recent analysis of "white racial regimes," see Seamster (2018). And for a critical extension of regime theory, see Imbroscio (2010).

15. Angelo and Wachsmuth (2015). This idea relates to thinking in critical urban studies on appreciating the role of globalization in urban governance; see Allen and Cochrane (2007), Jessop and Sum (2000), and Swyngedouw (1997).

16. Peterson (1981). See also Hyra (2008) on the effect of global economic pressures on urban politics. Pasotti (2020) shows how urban residents can take advantage of these structural circumstances, circumventing uncooperative local leadership by making alliances with more amenable state and federal officials.

17. Frug and Barron (2013), Schragger (2016). See also Self and Sugrue (2002). For more on housing and the law, see Desmond and Bell (2015).

18. On nonprofit organizations and public-private forms of governance, see Bushouse and Mosley (2018), Clemens and Guthrie (2010), Donaghy (2018), Eliasoph (2009), Ferman (1996), Finger (2018), Fyall (2016, 2017), Fyall and McGuire (2015), Galaskiewicz (1997), Goss and Berry (2018), Heil (2018), Lichterman and Eliasoph (2014), Martinez-Cosio and Rabinowitz Bussell (2012, 2013), Marwell (2004, 2007), Marwell and Brown (2020), Mosley and Galaskiewicz (2015), Mosley and Grogan (2013), McQuarrie (2013a), Newman and Lake (2006), Owens (2007), Park et al. (2018), Quinn et al. (2014), Reckhow and Tompkins-Stange (2018), Reckhow et al. (2019), Suárez et al. (2018), Thomson (2018, 2020), Walker and Febres-Cordero (2020), Weir (1999), and Yin (1998). For Swanstrom (1999), the emergence of the nonprofit community development industry reflects "the nonprofitization of housing policy." See Danley (2018) for a related study of neighborhood associations and urban governance.

19. See de Graauw (2016, pp. 47–51) for a detailed description of government restrictions on nonprofit political activity, and how restrictions vary by tax code status. See Tompkins-Stange (2016, pp. 13–14) for additional information on restrictions placed specifically on philanthropic foundations. The restrictions I refer to apply to 501(c)3 public charities, not 501(c)4 social welfare organizations, which have more latitude to engage in politics (but do not benefit from the same government incentives, such as tax-deductible contributions).

20. Hall (2006, p. 36).

21. *Walsh Commission on Industrial Relations* (1915, p. 32).

22. Bishop and Green (2010). For an excellent critique of this market-based approach to charity, see Eikenberry and Mirabella (2018).

23. Eisinger (2015). See also Callahan (2017). Zuckerberg and Chan ultimately decided against a nonprofit foundation and instead created a Limited Liability Corporation (LLC)—raising even more concerns about the relationship between private wealth, charity, and political power.

24. Smith and Lipsky (1993). See also Milward and Provan (2000) and Salamon (1981, 1987).

25. Smith and Lipsky (1993). See Mayrl and Quinn (2016) on the politics of state legibility and boundary work.

26. Montanaro (2012). See also Saward (2006, 2009). See Rubenstein (2014) for a counter-argument, Reich (2018) for an application to philanthropy, and Seamster (2018) for an application to emergency management laws.

27. In other published work, I provide a theoretical description of nonelected neighborhood representatives and compare this ideal type to three alternative conceptualizations in the literature: third-party government, interest groups, and machine politics CBOs. See Levine (2016) and chapter 4 of this book. Other research also points to local elected politicians' diminished control over resources being spent in the neighborhoods they formally represent. For instance, in a study of city council members' contracts to social service providers in New York City, Marwell et al. (2020) find that council members have increasingly allocated contracts to service providers *outside* their own neighborhoods: Whereas 55% of contracts went to council members' own neighborhoods in 2003—a surprisingly small percentage in its own right, I would argue—that figure dropped to 34% by 2012. Insofar as

controlling resources is a form of power, the findings suggest local politicians prefer to flex their muscles in places outside their own districts—leaving the door open for community-based organizations to fill the leadership vacuum in poor neighborhoods.

28. Cordelli (2020) provides a deep analysis of the privatized state from a political philosophy perspective.

29. Betancur et al. (2015, pp. 82–84). Recently, Chicago politicians have taken notable steps to weaken aldermanic power. In 2018, Alderman Ameya Pawar (47th ward) introduced an ordinance to remove aldermanic veto power with respect to affordable housing development. And in 2019, Mayor Lori Lightfoot signed an executive order banning city departments from deferring to aldermen demands (Pratt 2019).

30. Wilson (1987, 2009). In the second edition of *The Truly Disadvantaged*, Wilson includes an extensive afterword that reviews research based on his structural and cultural analysis. For more on the interplay between structure and culture in urban poverty, particularly as an alternative to "the culture of poverty," see Edin and Kafalas (2005), Harding (2010), Small et al. (2010), Smith (2006), and Young (2006).

31. Small (2006).

32. Murphy (forthcoming).

33. Marwell (2007), Vargas (2016).

34. Marwell and McQuarrie (2013, p. 133).

35. For a review, see Sampson (1999).

36. Hillery (1955).

37. Hunter and Robinson (2018).

38. See Berndt (1977), DeFilippis and Saegert (2007), Goldstein (2017), Hill and Rabig (2012), Johnson (2004), Shipp (1996), and Tabb (1979).

39. Sampson (1999, p. 242).

40. In other work, I develop a theory of "community" as a floating signifier of the common good (Levine 2017). See Joseph (2002) for a related critique of the concept from a cultural studies and critical theory perspective. Similarly, social anthropologist Anthony Cohen (1985) analyzes the symbolic construction of the concept. My complementary conception emphasizes its political use.

41. In 2013, a pilot program reduced the fare to be equivalent to rapid rail as a strategy to boost ridership. As of this writing, the reduced fare remains in place for all but one of the stations. The reason is somewhat arbitrary: The state transportation authority determines commuter rail pricing based on concentric zones around the city center. Seven of the Fairmount Line stations are currently within Zone 1A—meaning the same fare as rapid rail. The southernmost station is in Zone 2, increasing the cost of a single ride from $2.40 to $7.00. In May 2017, Congressman Michael Capuano supported free rides on Fairmount Line for two weeks, donating $53,000 from his campaign funds. Ridership increased 25% during the first week and 44% during the second week but dropped back down to normal levels when the fares returned (Gaffin 2017). In 2017, State Representative Evandro C. Carvalho introduced H 2723, a bill that would make fares at all stations equivalent to rapid rail, increase service levels, and increase marketing for a two-year pilot period. The bill failed. State Representatives Dan Cullinane and Liz Miranda, as well as State Senator Nick Collins, have each introduced similar legislation to increase service. In a July 2019 letter to the secretary of the Massachusetts Department of Transportation, Mayor Marty Walsh advocated for increased service on multiple transit lines, including the Fairmount Line. In early 2020, the MBTA Fiscal and Management Control Board approved eight new trips per day on the Fairmount Line as part of a pilot program. The fare and service levels—as well as a potential shift to electric cars—remain points of local activism.

42. Newmarket contains approximately 5,000 residents, and 90.3% of the neighborhood's land area is industrial, commercial, or tax-exempt; only 9% is residential. Readville

contains approximately 3,000 residents, and 68.9% of the neighborhood's land area is industrial, commercial, or tax-exempt; only 30.9% of land is residential.

43. See Sampson et al. (2002).

44. Statistics are based on reports from consultant Tim Davis (prepared for The Boston Foundation) and the Boston Redevelopment Authority Research Division (prepared for the Fairmount Indigo Planning Initiative).

45. See the methodological appendix for a breakdown of these projects.

46. As Desmond (2014, p. 569) argues, "Gaining entrée in one community or group is hard enough; doing so in multiple communities and groups is that much more trying. Harder still is . . . gaining access to an interconnected web of people, many of whom are bound in relationships of antagonism." Katz (1997, p. 419, n.5) similarly acknowledges the challenge of gaining access to elite political actors: "The most fundamental reason that elites pose special difficulties for ethnographic study is that by definition there are relatively few of them. If one is rebuffed in the attempt to study social life on an inner-city ghetto street corner, then there are lots of alternatives. But if one wants to study a small group that presumably governs a city, then a rebuff may be much more disturbing even if it is much less likely to occur because there is nowhere else to go."

47. These are emails sent directly to my email address, or ones in which I received a copy. See Pattillo (2007, pp. 142–143) for a similar use of email correspondence in ethnographic research.

48. For more on saturation as a goal of qualitative research, see Small (2009). I discuss access in greater detail in the methodological appendix.

49. I was not copied and did not see the actual email. The consultant told me about it before a meeting we both attended in City Hall, and then joked about it with the city official during the meeting.

50. Molotch (1976, p. 313).

51. For research on cities outside of Boston that nevertheless share some common elements with the Fairmount Corridor, see Adams (2014), BondGraham (2011), Cervero (2004), Dittmar and Ohland (2004), DeFilippis and Saegert (2007), Douglas (2010), Elkind (2014), Heil (2018), Lowe (2014), Marwell (2007), McQuarrie (2013a, 2013b), Park et al. (2018), Pieterse (2019), Pill (2018), Shelton (2017), Stone and Stoker (2015), Thomson (2018), and Vargas (2016).

Chapter 1: Slow Train Coming

1. Gans (1982, p. 327).
2. Ibid., pp. 332–333.
3. Ibid., p. 335.
4. Ibid., p. 332.
5. Ibid., p. 328.
6. Ibid., p. 338.
7. Ibid., pp. 339–340.
8. Historian Lizabeth Cohen (2019) brilliantly captures this transition through a case study of Ed Logue. Whereas Cohen interprets Logue's transition from top-down planner in New Haven, Boston, and New York State to nonprofit leader in the Bronx as a (partial) triumph of local democracy, my analysis is more critical.
9. Warner (1978).
10. For support of Snell's theory, see St. Clair (1981) and Whitt and Yago (1985). For refutations, see Adler (1991) and Slater (1997).
11. Gamm (2001, p. 11).
12. For more on the Great Migration, see Brown (2018), Grant (2020), and Wilkerson (2011).

13. See Boustan (2016), Freund (2010), Rothstein (2017), Sugrue (1996), and Trounstine (2018).

14. Often, the presence of *any* Black residents resulted in a lower grade. See Jackson (1985).

15. Vale (2002, p. 201).

16. Historians have debated the impact (and intentionality) of BBURG on racial change in Boston. See Levine and Harmon (1992), Gamm (2001), and Vale (2002). This process is an example of what Seamster and Charron-Chénier (2017) and Taylor (2019), respectively, call "predatory inclusion."

17. See Heathcott (2012), Rainwater (1970), and Venkatesh (2000). Some critics of public housing argued that the projects' modernist architecture created poor living conditions. Others argued that the buildings' residents—mostly low-income Black families—were to blame, drawing on racist notions of cultural deficiencies. Most scholars now trace poor conditions to the political economy of cities and suburbs: As cities' tax bases shrunk, public housing authorities had fewer resources for maintenance. Limited resources, combined with the stigma of public housing, caused city governments to effectively turn their backs on public housing residents.

18. Nall (2018).

19. See Hunter (2013), King (1981), Mollenkopf (1983), Small (2004), and Woodsworth (2016).

20. The South End, which is actually north of most of Boston, is just south of downtown—hence the name. The Fairmount Corridor includes a part of Roxbury, but not the part most involved in this era of activism.

21. King (1981, p. xxiii).

22. Small (2004, p. 38).

23. Ibid., p. 42.

24. See Crockett (2018) and Gakenheimer (1976). Similar activism occurred in other cities, such as Philadelphia. See Hunter (2013, pp. 115–165).

25. *Boston Transportation Planning Review Final Study Summary Report* (1973).

26. Instead of a rapid rail line, the state provided the Silver Line, a bus line with only limited right-of-way.

27. *Boston Globe* (November 10, 1987).

28. See O'Connor (1996). For more on the Ford Foundation, particularly its relationship to the Black Power Movement, see Ferguson (2013).

29. Dunning (2016, p. 99).

30. A sixth site was also selected: the state of North Carolina.

31. Nonprofit CAAs were, and remain to this day, quasi-independent. Each had a "tripartite" governing board structure: One-third elected residents, one-third elected officials, and one-third representatives from "major groups," including neighborhood businesses, churches, schools, and labor organizations. For more on CAAs, see Cazenave (2007).

32. Rubin (1969). In practice, participation was uneven and its effects varied considerably. See Greenstone and Peterson (1973).

33. For example, LISC's New Communities Program (NCP), first piloted in 1998, is a direct descendant of the "community action" approach. See also McQuarrie (2013a).

34. The Ford Foundation's actions during the 1960s were an important rationale for the Act, but they were not the *only* rationale. Congressman Wright Patman (D-Texas) had tried to limit the influence of foundations as early as 1961.

35. In 2018, New York Attorney General Barbara D. Underwood sued the Donald J. Trump Foundation for self-dealing transactions. The petition alleged that the foundation used charitable assets to pay off Donald Trump's legal obligations, promote Trump hotels and other businesses, and purchase personal items. Most salaciously, the petition alleged

that the Foundation coordinated with Trump's political staff in the days leading up to the Iowa caucus during the 2016 presidential race, distributing donations to particular charities for explicitly political purposes. In December 2018, Trump agreed to dissolve the foundation under judicial supervision.

36. Caraley (1992).

37. Wilson (1987, 1996).

38. Measured in inflation-adjusted dollars. For more on CDBG funding decreases, see de Graauw et al. (2013) and Rohe and Galster (2014). The Low-Income Housing Tax Credit (LIHTC) also provides the equivalent of $8 billion annually to state and local agencies for affordable housing development. LIHTC is limited to housing rather than community development more broadly.

39. See Vale (2002). See also Rosen (2020) on Section 8 policy.

40. The Boston Housing Authority leased nearly 3,000 units from private landlords in 1973. See Vale (2002).

41. Austen (2018).

42. See Grogan and Proscio (2000). Ten percent of LIHTC funds are earmarked for nonprofits.

43. Walker (2002), von Hoffman (2013).

44. Since 1993, the line item earmarks funding for five national intermediaries: Living Cities, LISC, Enterprise Community Partners, Habitat for Humanity International, and YouthBuild USA. The purpose is to increase the capacity of community development organizations through these intermediaries.

45. Sharkey et al. (2017).

46. See Bromley and Meyer (2017), Hwang and Powell (2009), Smith and Lipsky (1993), and Suarez (2010). For a specific discussion of nonprofits in the affordable housing sector and "cooptation by cohort replacement," see Robinson III (2020). For a brief history of city policy and community development nonprofits in Boston in the 1980s and early 1990s, see Clavel (2010).

47. GFCAC was widely acknowledged as a "grassroots" nonprofit, less professionalized than other organizations in the community development field. Nevertheless, the organization was not immune to professionalization trends; the organization's lead organizer engaged in a strategy she called "grasstops" community organizing, which involved collaboration with elites and experts rather than residents. On "grasstops" approaches to social change, see Tompkins-Stange (2016).

48. Hanchett (2002). The collaboration between Marvin and Noah should be understood within the context of 1990s transportation policy. In 1991, Congress passed the Intermodal Surface Transportation Efficiency Act (ISTEA). The legislation empowered Metropolitan Planning Organizations—regional organizations established through the Federal-Aid Highway Act of 1962—to reduce the harm caused by transportation in cities. Most important, ISTEA institutionalized public participation in regional transportation planning and required outreach to marginalized populations. Nonprofit leaders like Marvin gained newfound access to transportation policy networks (Lowe 2014, Weir et al. 2009).

49. DePasquale (2004).

50. In an unexpected twist, CLF's former president and CEO, Doug Foy, was appointed the secretary of Commonwealth Development in the Romney administration, and as a result, one of the plaintiffs of the 1990 lawsuit became one of the defendants in 2005.

51. The state also included plans for the new stations in its State Implementation Plan (SIP), the annual document required by the EPA to monitor each state's compliance with the Clean Air Act. The SIP set an original deadline of new station construction by December 2011.

52. Owens (2016), Tach and Emory (2017).

53. Geeta would not necessarily use the word "leader" to describe her role in the Corridor. She is selfless, but more important, politically savvy and quick to share credit for accomplishments. That said—and this is a key methodological point—I do not see ethnographers' role as merely repeating what people told them. At least one "warrant" of ethnography is to debunk local practices and pretenses (Katz 1997).

54. According to data from the Foundation Center, total foundation funding was $62,793,608,844 in 2015, compared to $30,174,135,261 in 2002.

55. See Horvath and Powell (2016), Reckhow (2012), Tompkins-Stange (2016).

56. For more on HOPE VI, see Graves (2010), Holin et al. (2010), Popkin et al. (2004), Tach (2009), and Tach and Emory (2017). For a more general analysis of gentrification and the implementation of mixed-income housing policy, see Chaskin and Joseph (2015).

57. Urban Institute (2013).

58. These were all Section 8 units. At the time of the redevelopment, the apartments had recently renewed their Section 8 contract for another twenty years.

Chapter 2: A Seat at the Table

1. For more on why CBOs, elected politicians, and government officials engage in interdependent partnerships, see Frasure and Jones-Correa (2010).

2. Pacewicz (2016). See Katznelson (1981) for an alternative theory on the distinctiveness of community politics. And see Pasotti (2020) for recent analysis of contentious politics and urban redevelopment.

3. This builds on Pacewicz (2016), which by contrast depicts "partner" as a static category rather than a contested identity.

4. Barley (2007).

5. Abraham (1999).

6. Squires (1991). And it wasn't just major metropolitan areas: Pacewicz (2016) depicts similar dynamics of business-led coalition dominance in two smaller cities in Iowa.

7. Walker (2013, p. 181). See also Nevarez (2000). For a recent review of research on corporate philanthropy, see Gautier and Pache (2015). Bertrand et al. (2020) find donations from corporate foundations resemble political action committee (PAC) spending and strategically target particular legislators' own nonprofits and districts.

8. Some urban geographers refer to this era of urban governance as "post-politics" or "post-political." See MacLeod (2011) and Swyngedouw (2009). See also Harvey (1989), McQuarrie (2013a), and Pacewicz (2016) on technocratic partnerships.

9. Abraham (1999). On the fragmentation of business elites, see Mizruchi (2013).

10. Drawing on case studies of six North American cities, Stone and Stoker (2015) depict a consistent shift from downtown to residential neighborhood development—what the authors call a "new era of urban politics"—beginning in the 1990s and continuing through the 2010s.

11. Chesto (2016).

12. Data come from direct observations and mentions of meetings I did not attend due to scheduling conflicts or lack of access. The meetings do not include meetings limited to specific grants, such as annual progress meetings or grant requests. This is a network of *private* meetings, not public meetings, so the organizations represented on Advisory Group for the Fairmount Corridor Planning Initiative are not necessarily included.

13. Urban, political, and organizational theorists have proposed a number of metaphors to describe similar policy networks. Using the language of Milward and Provan (2000), we might refer to this arrangement as a "hollow state": Government, to the right of the network, is hollowed out by nonprofit service providers. Barley's (2007) "asteroid belt

of organizations" is also apt: We might think of the entire left side of the network as a layer of private organizations that separates citizens from government. The idea of cooptation might also apply—and, based on my observations, I would argue it is more in line with Selznick's (1953) depiction of different interests coming to the table to negotiate, as opposed to Piven and Cloward's (1977) depiction of previously radical nonprofits "selling out" or Gamson's (1975) depiction of policymakers offering only symbolic recognition. The important thing is that each concept describes the same underlying empirical reality: Public and private organizations collaborate to produce public policy. In this book, I am less interested in proposing an alternative descriptor than in revealing the *consequences* for democratic representation and neighborhood inequality in cities.

14. For more on the distinction between thoughts and actions, particularly in qualitative research, see Jerolmack and Khan (2014) and Lamont and Swidler (2014). On "ethnographic interviews," see Rinaldo and Guhin (2019).

15. Variances are administratively determined exceptions to zoning rules. For example, a commercial project could move forward in an area zoned for residential uses if the developer receives a variance.

16. In general, the precise number of organizations involved in these overlapping coalitions was hard to pin down. Some representatives would attend meetings for a year or two, then stop when funding ran out or staffing changed. Mattapan CDC was a member of all three coalitions for the first two years of my fieldwork but left when the organization went bankrupt.

17. Members referred to the coalitions as "the Fairmount CDC Collaborative," "the Fairmount/Indigo Transit Coalition," and "the Fairmount Greenway Task Force," respectively—though these labels were subject to various shorthand and changed after my fieldwork ended.

18. The CDC coalition had a standing conference call each week in addition to a monthly in-person meeting.

19. One way to make sense of these findings theoretically is to understand the idea of authenticity. As Walker and Stepick (2020) argue, social movement organizations—similar, though distinct from the particular community-based organizations under discussion here—gain recognition from policymakers and other resources holders when they display *institutional authenticity*; that is, when they are "typical" of other organizations in the field and work in a clearly defined niche. Policymakers discredit organizations that do not display *grassroots authenticity*, or the ability to represent and mobilize a constituency without coercion. Most CBOs in the Fairmount Corridor mobilized enough residents to avoid perceptions of grassroots inauthenticity yet were highly professionalized so as to maintain institutional authenticity. When Jeanne failed to perform grassroots authenticity, she suffered the consequences.

20. The specific event that prompted Jeanne's concerns was a forum organized by the Citizens Housing and Planning Association (CHAPA). Jeanne was out of town and could not attend. She said that Mat did "really, really well" in her place. Had he performed poorly, she may not have been so worried.

21. Sociologists sometimes refer to this as "social skill." See Fligstein and McAdam (2011) and McQuarrie and Krumholz (2011).

22. For more on CCIs, see Chaskin (2003), Chaskin et al. (1997), and Martinez-Cosio and Rabinowitz Bussell (2013).

23. Four months later, State Representative Walsh was elected mayor of Boston, defeating at-large City Councilor John Connolly.

24. See Brenner (2009) and Wachsmuth (2017).

25. For examples of these high-stakes debates, see Arena (2012) and Pattillo (2007).

Chapter 3: In Search of Spatial Legibility

1. Ryan (2013).
2. See Hunter (1974) and Suttles (1972).
3. Hunter (1974, p. 193).
4. See Brown-Saracino (2015), Molotch et al. (2000), and Papachristos et al. (2013).
5. Hwang (2016) shows how different groups in a gentrifying neighborhood have different perceptions of its boundaries.
6. Rankin (2016, p. 114).
7. My thinking draws on James Scott's (1998) discussion of legibility. Legibility is the process by which modern states simplify complex local practices in order to make state intervention possible. The introduction of landownership maps, for instance, made taxation significantly more efficient. Maps produce *spatial* legibility: They standardize and rationalize geographic territory, allowing those who govern to exploit and control the governed. The idea of spatial legibility is similar to other urban processes, like place-naming or what critical urban theorist David Madden (2014) calls "spatial projects." Madden describes the creation of the Dumbo neighborhood in Brooklyn, whereby real estate agents and governments created Dumbo to be "*a* neighborhood marked by exclusivity, luxury and distinction" (p. 484, emphasis added). By contrast, my conceptualization of spatial legibility does not require new neighborhood boundaries to gain broader social acceptance or even social recognition. Indeed, unlike Dumbo, it is in the interests of players in urban governance for community boundaries to remain malleable and unfixed, such that boundaries can shift depending on political circumstances. Nor is the intended goal necessarily to increase real estate value. In this case, it was a tactic to affect resource allocation and organizational survival. The focus was more on immediate outcomes rather than broader neighborhood change.
8. I did not attend the conference. I downloaded audio and presentation slides from the conference website.
9. Rosso (2012), *Dorchester Reporter* (2012).
10. Moreover, if there were more people living in the Corridor, that meant more potential transit riders—and this "fact" could persuade transportation officials to build new stations on the line, as the coalition hoped.
11. Most official documents refer to the initiative as the Fairmount-Indigo Planning Initiative (FIPI). I generally refer to it as the Fairmount Corridor Planning Initiative or Fairmount Corridor planning process for readability reasons.
12. Diversity can be used as a powerful buzzword signifying the common good; see Bell and Hartman (2007), Berrey (2015), and Mayorga-Gallo (2014).
13. Voting rules were never discussed, and no one other than me appeared to count the exact number of votes for each station area. Some advisory group members voted twice (because there were two sites to determine); others voted three or four times. The city official who recorded meeting notes was absent, so there was no official record. After the meeting ended, Inés asked me to send her my fieldnotes, which she uploaded to the BRA's website to take the place of official notes (I sent her an edited version of my fieldnotes, limited to a basic recounting of what occurred and how many hands I saw go up for each station area). No one ever challenged the ultimate decision, which was to devote planning resources for Four Corners and Mattapan, even though it directly contradicted the voting results.
14. In private communication, a BRA official told Gail, executive director of CSNDC in Codman Square, that resources would be earmarked for a Codman Square planning process at a later date, as yet to be determined. They also told Mike, executive director of SWBCDC in Hyde Park, that Hyde Park had just undergone a rezoning process and therefore was a lower priority for station area planning.

15. Sampson (1999, p. 248).
16. Suttles (1972, p. 59).
17. Some staff assumed that lessons from the Fairmount Corridor would then be applied to other areas. It was not always immediately clear how or if that would happen.
18. For more on the potential downstream effects of gerrymandering on urban inequality, see Vargas (2016).

Chapter 4: Representing the Community

1. Berry and Arons (2005), de Graauw (2016). This applies to nonprofits classified as 501(c)3 public charities. Others, classified as 501(c)4 social welfare organizations, can engage in lobbying, but donations to these organizations are not tax deductible.
2. Smith and Lipsky (1993).
3. Berry and Arons (2005), de Graauw (2016). See also Goss et al. (2019).
4. Marwell (2004, 2007).
5. Mayhew (1974). One nonprofit director said with a straight face, "As I say, elected officials will go to an opening of an envelope."
6. In previously published work, I describe nonelected neighborhood representatives in more abstract theoretical terms. See Levine (2016).
7. Initial resources went to Four Corners and Mattapan; resources did not *immediately* go to Codman Square. Mike, executive director of SWBCDC, took a different approach. He worked closely with City Councilor Rob Consalvo to act as a go-between with the mayor, assuming that Consalvo, who represented the mayor's former City Council district, had a good relationship with the mayor. Compared to Gail's assertion of neighborhood representation, Mike's strategy failed.
8. For a longer discussion of Vito Lopez and RBSCC, see Marwell (2007).
9. MACDC staff pushed a program, called "Donuts with Delegates," in which they encouraged CDC directors to host breakfast chats with state senators and representatives.
10. State transportation officials saw it differently than advocates and other casual observers. Municipal borders are less deterministic for the state agency, and officials price based on a variety of variables, including geographic distance and demand.
11. During the summer of 2019, the 2013 election winner, Mayor Walsh, did in fact lobby the state for more frequent service on the Fairmount Line. At the time, there were significant delays on the Red Line, one of the city's busiest rapid rail lines. Mayor Walsh wrote a letter to the secretary of the Massachusetts Department of Transportation requesting more service on the Red Line and, secondarily, the Fairmount Line and the South Shore Limited to "relieve some pressure on the Red Line." In his letter, Mayor Walsh made sure to mention that the city had just passed a budget including $90 million to the MBTA—a not-so-subtle reminder that city government helps subsidize the state's transportation system. It is not clear whether *the mayoral forum* caused the mayor to lobby the state six years later, however. If so, it would nevertheless support the central argument of this chapter: Local nonprofits represented "their" neighborhoods and persuaded the mayor (rather than elected representatives) to lobby state officials on their behalf.
12. I did not attend the event. My estimation on crowd size comes from photos of the event. See also Powers (2013).
13. The fare pilot did not include Readville Station, which became a major point of contention. State transportation officials explained during a June 2013 meeting with Corridor nonprofit leaders that because other train lines also passed through Readville, it would not be feasible to reduce the fares for Fairmount riders alone.
14. Irons (2013a).
15. Powers (2013).

16. See Irons (2013b) and *Boston Globe* Editorial Board (2013). As of this writing the reduced fare is still in place.

17. My fieldwork continued for six months after the forum. I do not know if the nonprofit leaders reached out to any of the candidates after I stopped observing their meetings.

18. Race and age also may have played a factor: Henriquez was a 36-year-old Black man, and the city official was a middle-aged white man. Henriquez was well-known among nonprofit leaders in Upham's Corner; he was involved with the Dudley Street Neighborhood Initiative (DSNI) as a child and would later become president of the organization's Board of Directors. In 2014, he was sentenced to six months in jail and two years of probation for assault and battery, stemming from an altercation with his former girlfriend (he maintains his innocence). He was subsequently expelled from the Massachusetts State Legislature. After serving his sentence, he ran for the District 7 seat on the Boston City Council in 2017 (a position he had also run for—and lost—in 2009). He finished in eleventh place. He was later hired by Mayor Walsh as a consultant and then full-time government official working on an antiviolence and community engagement program but resigned in 2018 when his employment was made public by the *Boston Globe*.

19. Some, of course, do very little if anything related to city policy: A 2015 analysis by the *Boston Globe* of parking garage records and hearing attendance found city councilors who golfed, pursued law and public administration degrees, and maintained jobs as partners in downtown law firms—all while supposedly serving as full-time public servants (Ryan 2015). The councilors interviewed disputed the implications of the analysis and said they frequently met with constituents outside the office as well as on weekends and over holidays. In some cities, city councilors can award small contracts to social service providers (Marwell et al. 2020).

20. See http://web.archive.org/web/20191008234420/https://abolishthebpda.com/. As of this writing, there has not been substantive movement on the proposal. At the time, I interpreted it as Wu laying the groundwork for a future mayoral run (Wu officially announced her candidacy for mayor of Boston in September 2020). Reflecting a core argument of this chapter, the proposal would essentially allow city councilors to retain more power over development—thus illustrating the limited power they currently hold.

21. The law designated up to $1.5 million in grants for community development nonprofits in 2013; ultimately, the state provided $750,000 in grants to twenty-eight organizations. The law also stipulated up to $3 million in tax credits in 2014, and up to $6 million in tax credits annually from 2015 to 2019. In 2014 and 2015, the state allocated $8.54 million out of a possible $9 million in tax credits. In 2016, the state allocated the maximum $6 million in tax credits to forty-eight nonprofits across the state. Over the course of these four years, CDCs in the Corridor received $75,000 in grants and more than $1 million in tax credits that they used to incentivize donations. These donations were unrestricted, so the money went to operations and communications—two areas where nonprofits have the greatest funding need.

22. Pfeiffer (2014).

23. See for instance Hertel-Fernandez (2019).

24. I did not attend the event but watched video posted on MACDC's website. See https://web.archive.org/web/20200919063603/https://macdc.org/news/governor-baker-champions-cdcs-community-investment-tax-credit.

25. An alternative way to think about the diminished role of elected politicians as neighborhood representatives is to consider redistricting. In Vargas's (2016) study of a neighborhood in Chicago, some poor residents lacked connections to local elected politicians because their voting district had been carved up in such a way that neighborhood boundaries did not neatly align with district boundaries. Seamster (2016, 2018) offers another alternative interpretation in her study of Benton Harbor, Michigan, where a racialized network of predominantly white nonprofit leaders and businesspeople—what she calls the white urban

regime—used emergency management laws to circumvent Black political leadership in the small town. The white urban regime pursued its profit-motivated interests, which conflicted with the interests of Black politicians. As discussed in chapter 2, I did not observe a stable regime of decision-makers in Boston. Nor did I observe uniform interests among politicians, including (but not limited to) Black politicians. I found that elected officials of all races and ethnicities were at least somewhat marginalized in community development politics. The difference in analysis may stem from the difference in field sites: Benton Harbor is a small town anchored by a single *Fortune 500* company, while Boston is a large, multi-racial city.

26. I saw a copy of the letter and observed Gail speak to Evelyn after the meeting. I was not part of the conversation and only heard Gail describe the substance of the conversation after the fact.

27. City officials never explained the process, but I happened to be working in City Hall when the urban agriculture plans were developed. In the summer of 2010, a City Hall intern—a graduate student with Princeton University's Masters in Public Administration Program—pulled up a map of Boston and created a list of sites that fit the technical specifications for urban agriculture. She submitted that list to the city's "Food Czar," who chose four pilot sites.

28. Rosso (2013a).

29. Rosso (2012).

30. I received second-hand reports from informants about the call to Representative Holmes and the meeting in City Hall.

31. I did not observe these actions firsthand. I observed LISC's executive director discuss them with members of the Corridor's nonprofit coalition.

32. The station eventually opened in February 2019.

33. In 2010, a funding intermediary selected Mattapan as one of three neighborhoods for a multiyear neighborhood planning initiative. Those efforts continued even after MCDC's demise; the Mattapan branch of a citywide social service agency with limited connections to the neighborhood served as lead agency. But tangible achievements were limited, and funders bemoaned the lack of stable institutions in the neighborhood—especially relative to other neighborhoods in the Corridor. Today, there is a new CDC operating in Mattapan, founded in 2011: Caribbean Integration Community Development (CICD). As of this writing, the BRA has approved CICD, in partnership with the Planning Office for Urban Affairs (the nonprofit development arm of the Archdiocese of Boston), to develop approximately 140 new housing units in the neighborhood. As an organization, CICD claims to represent the Caribbean diaspora in Boston and does not appear to be involved in any Corridor-wide efforts.

34. Trojano (2019).

35. In the summer of 2020, two nonprofit housing developers, Caribbean Integration Community Development (CICD) and the Planning Office for Urban Affairs, expressed interest in the complex but did not have the estimated $40 million needed to purchase it at market value. The nonprofits hoped to take advantage of a City program that fills budget gaps when the new owner—typically a nonprofit—promises to keep rents affordable (Logan 2020). In October 2020, however, the building was sold to California-based Aventha Capital Management, LLC. City Life/Vida Urbana, a local housing advocacy nonprofit, helped residents negotiate a deal with their new landlord that would protect them from rent increases for five years.

36. Radical organizations like INCITE! (2007) refer to this system as "the nonprofit industrial complex." See also Arena (2012).

37. Montanaro (2012, p. 1098).

38. Ibid., p. 1104.

39. Page and Gilens (2017).

40. Broockman and Skovron (2018). See also Achen and Bartels (2016) and Hertel-Fernandez et al. (2019) on legislative staff.

41. Sheffer et al. (2018).
42. See for example Adams (2014), Arena (2012), and INCITE! (2007).

Chapter 5: Following the Money

1. Zunz (2012).
2. Reckhow (2012), Tompkins-Stange (2016).
3. Bartley (2007), Francis (2019).
4. Arena (2012), Kohl-Arenas (2015), Ostrander (1995).
5. With respect to the role of private funders in urban governance, one exception is McQuarrie and Krumholz (2011). Additionally, Thomson (2020) systematically analyzes foundation funding for community economic development in thirty cities. While he stresses "a danger in equating funding with power, policy influence, or governance," he finds substantial funding across cities, thus suggesting a strong *potential* for foundations to influence urban governance.
6. TBF Annual Report 2016.
7. The Ford Foundation conceived and funded the creation of LISC in 1979. LISC's Boston office was founded in 1981, with partial financial assistance from The Boston Foundation. In the eyes of nonprofit grantees, the Metropolitan Area Planning Council (MAPC) is functionally a funding intermediary. But it is actually a public agency, governed by representatives from cities and towns on the eastern side of the state.
8. Bertrand et al. (2020), Walker (2013).
9. In an interview, Geeta couldn't remember the precise date, but told me it coincided with Robert Lewis Jr. joining TBF. He was named vice president in July 2007. In a separate interview, another funder also indicated that she wasn't sure if the first meeting was in 2007 or 2008.
10. In an interview, another funder remembered representatives from Garfield, Barr, and Surdna also being involved in those early years.
11. Additional funding came from TD Bank, Bank of America, Sovereign Bank, Citizens Bank, Massachusetts Growth Capital Group, as well as federal, state, and city government agencies.
12. LISC ended up receiving enough funding to support RC/RF in three neighborhoods, two of which are in the Corridor, satisfying the requirements set by Barr and TBF.
13. After my fieldwork, LISC additionally funded a "Fairmount Network," bringing leaders from various organizations together to regularly discuss community development projects in the Corridor.
14. The program was specifically for families receiving Section 8 vouchers.
15. The organization was later recognized for reducing greenhouse gas emissions; see deBarros (2014).
16. The evidence presented in this section comes from a variety of sources, including observations of CDC coalition meetings, observations in City Hall, real-time emails and document attachments, and retrospective interviews conducted in 2013 with Geeta, a TBF staff member, and a nonprofit consultant.
17. During a private meeting in 2010, the late Mayor Thomas Menino told me that he would "blow up" all of the city's nonprofits if he could (it should go without saying, but I interpreted it as a dry joke, not an actual threat).
18. There is some empirical validity to the idea that local nonprofits tend to hoard resources within, rather than across, poor neighborhoods. See Levine (2013).
19. Other attendees at the meeting included two consultants hired by the nonprofit CDC directors; a TBF staff member; two representatives from the Metropolitan Area

Planning Council (MAPC), a regional planning agency; and the director of The American City Coalition, a nonprofit urban planning organization established in 1994 by a for-profit housing developer.

20. There was some conflict over the advisory group membership. Each CDC director wanted a seat on the advisory group, but according to city officials, the mayor rejected the idea. The official reason was that nonprofit developers may bid on future projects, and it would create an unfair advantage if they had special influence over the planning process. At the same time, the BRA included other developers in the advisory group. The BRA then offered one seat for a single director from the coalition but balked when the coalition nominated Jeanne. The official reason given was that the mayor thought Jeanne's time was better spent on other initiatives (specifically, a Choice Neighborhoods grant). Unofficially, there were rumors that the mayor sometimes saw Jeanne as an adversary—something Jeanne herself acknowledged. Neither Gail nor Mike had the time to sit on the advisory group, and both sides compromised by designating the spot for Mat, a consultant for the coalition.

21. Ina's adoption of the "partner" identity coincides with the larger logic of "partnership" in urban politics. See Pacewicz (2016).

22. Susan Ostrander's (1995) study of the Haymarket People's Fund in Boston, for instance, is an exceptional depiction of a foundation adopting this approach. See also Tompkins-Stange (2016). See Jones (2013) on the role of Black philanthropists and their diverse, complicated relationships to Black-led organizations and philanthropy as a project of racial uplift. See Ferguson (2013) on top-down racial liberalism and the historical relationship between the Ford Foundation and Black Power Movement activism.

23. Bob was not laughing at Barr's specific expectations, but the situation he found himself in, where multiple funders expected multiple outcomes of the RC/RF program.

24. The Great Neighborhoods Initiative's annual Impact Reports, for example, listed numerous Corridor projects and programs that were implemented without any MSGA funding.

25. A similar dynamic unfolded with another funder, the Metropolitan Area Planning Council (MAPC). MAPC, a quasi-public regional planning agency, received a federal grant in 2011 and redistributed a portion to nonprofits in the Fairmount Corridor. The grant did not include direct cash, but an offer to pay its in-house planners to assist the nonprofit grantees. Those grantees were not pleased with the arrangement, and in private, threatened to turn down the grant. After meeting with MAPC in early 2012, one nonprofit organizer said, "I believe we should feel strong enough to say, 'We can take this or leave it.' It was good they put Fairmount [Corridor organizations] into their proposal, because other people have been looking at [the] Fairmount [Corridor]. But if they get something out of it, we need to get something out of it." The two sides ultimately reached a compromise; see chapter 2.

26. The nonprofit directors found considerable value in the experience and hired him again in March 2013 to help resolve conflict with their regular consultants.

27. During a conversation in March 2019, Gail noted that while she did question the leadership at the organization, she was always a strong supporter of Mattapan and had, with other members of the coalition, set aside grant funding specifically for projects and organizing in that neighborhood.

28. Michelle didn't voice her agreement, but she didn't voice an objection, either. She looked off into space and frowned as the discussion unfolded.

29. While speaking with Geeta in 2013, she acknowledged that the Corridor "impacts" Hyde Park yet made no mention of the neighborhood during the rest of our ninety-minute conversation. In Geeta's telling, Hyde Park was in the Fairmount Corridor, but not a

Fairmount neighborhood. The reason related to race and class: Historically, Hyde Park was a middle-class white neighborhood. That changed during the 1990s and 2000s. Between 2000 and 2010, the neighborhood's white population dropped significantly, from 42% to 15.1%. As I conducted my fieldwork, Hyde Park was approximately 50.2% Black and 19.7% Latino. The neighborhood remained relatively affluent; its poverty rate was about half of the rest of Corridor. To Geeta and other TBF staff, Hyde Park's relative affluence and reputation as a white neighborhood made it less worthy of resources than other neighborhoods in the Corridor.

30. After nearly twenty years of planning, that project, a joint venture between SWBCDC and CSNDC including twenty-seven apartments, finally received approval in 2017. It was renamed "The Residences at Fairmount Station" and opened in 2018. Twenty-four apartments were designated for households earning at or below 60% of Area Median Income (AMI), and the remaining three apartments were designated for households earning at or below 70% AMI. The development also includes 6,000 square feet of recreational space as well as a public community room.

31. O'Connor (1996).

32. Krause (2014, pp. 28–29).

33. Simon (2001), McQuarrie (2013a). This is also part of the radical critique of the "nonprofit industrial complex" offered by INCITE! (2007) and others.

34. See Reckhow (2012), Reich (2018), Reich et al. (2016), and Tompkins-Stange (2016) for further discussion on the role of philanthropy in democratic societies.

Chapter 6: Community Power

1. Lee (2015, p. 4).

2. See for example Fung (2004), Fung and Wright (2003), and Guttman and Thompson (2004).

3. McQuarrie (2013b, p. 148). See also Einstein et al. (2020) and Silverman et al. (2020).

4. See Levine (2017, p. 1159). The term is common in policy areas beyond community development. Bell (2019, p. 197), for instance, provides an exceptional analysis of "the oft-invoked 'community'" in criminal justice research and advocacy.

5. On the relationship between social categories—particularly race and gender—and participatory democracy, see Polletta (2005) and Polletta and Chen (2013). Lichterman (1996) shows how the racial composition of groups can introduce blind spots in participatory processes.

6. I did not attend this meeting. Representative Russell Holmes and Representative Linda Dorcena Forry described it during a public meeting a few months later. Residents from Woodhaven Street were on hand and confirmed the meeting took place.

7. Consalvo later returned to work in city government as deputy director of the Boston Home Center, a homeowner's assistance agency.

8. The Greater Boston Interfaith Organizations (GBIO), for example, is a coalition of religious organizations focused on organizing around social justice issues.

9. I was not copied on Pastor Williams's email to the state officials, but at a later meeting, a state official mentioned the letter, indicating that it had been sent and received.

10. Dezenski (2014).

11. Forry (2013a).

12. Forry (2013b).

13. Rosso (2013b).

14. Rosso (2014).

15. Forry (2014).

16. Thirty-eight apartments were restricted to families earning 30%–60% of area median income, and another eight were restricted to families earning less than 30% of area median income.

17. The sixteen apartments were restricted to families earning below 70% of area median income.

18. Forty-four apartments were funded by LIHTC and reserved for families earning less than 60% of the area median income (AMI), ten apartments reserved for families earning between 61% and 80% AMI, and twenty-six apartments reserved for families earning between 81% and 110% AMI.

19. Construction was underway as I finished writing in 2020.

20. See for example Bowes and Ihlanfeldt (2001). While their property values may increase, property *taxes* may also increase, thereby creating new short-term costs alongside the potential of long-term profits.

21. Pattillo (2007).

Conclusion

1. Clark (2012). Fittingly, Clark's article was "made possible with generous support from the Ford Foundation."

2. Limited public accountability can have devastating effects on poverty and inequality. These effects are especially pronounced in the context of emergency management and municipal takeovers. See Nickels (2019), Seamster (2016, 2018), and Davis (forthcoming).

3. Horvath and Powell (2016). See also Mettler (2018).

4. See Stoecker (1997) and McQuarrie (2013a).

5. The proposal was approved by state lawmakers but held up by the governor, who wanted an amendment that required a majority vote by property owners to form a CBD (Lannan 2017).

6. See https://web.archive.org/web/20181221164036/https://ma-smartgrowth.org/wp-content/uploads/2018/07/CBD-info-packet-7-26-18-final.pdf.

7. Reich (2018) refers to this as the "discovery" and "pluralism" cases for foundations.

8. Medoff and Sklar (1994).

9. The use of this funding was notably contested during my fieldwork. High-level TBF staff were reluctant to fund operations rather than projects (as seen in the case of the project manager position funding request in chapter 5), and the directors of the CDC coalition were reluctant to use the funding for a central staff of consultants who handled operations. And so, even when operations funding was available, it was not always easy to implement.

10. See Reich (2018, pp. 137–140). Rockefeller also proposed that the time limit could be extended to 100 years if two-thirds of Congress approved, as well as additional partial public oversight over foundation operations.

11. Galaskiewicz (1985, 1997).

12. Pallotta (2016).

13. Williams (2018).

14. Berry (2016) offers an excellent critique of the use of quantifiable metrics in practice. See also Eikenberry and Mirabella (2018).

15. Reliance on metrics also incentivizes nonprofit leaders to reject potential clients or otherwise fail to adequately serve their needs (Krause 2014; Osborne 2019; Siliunas et al. 2019; Springer 2020). See Brest (2020) for a history of outcome-oriented philanthropy, based in part on the author's personal experience as former president of the Hewlett Foundation. See Teles and Schmitt (2011) for a discussion of the challenge of evaluating advocacy.

16. See https://web.archive.org/web/20200203234509/https://www.dsni.org/board/ and Medoff and Sklar (1994). Additionally, seven seats are reserved for "Nonprofit agencies

representing the Health and Human Service fields from the whole area," two seats for community development corporations, two seats for small business representatives, two seats for religious organizations, four seats for youth from the neighborhood (ages 15–17), and two seats for residents appointed by the newly elected board.

17. See Martin (2007, p. 605) and Hyra (2015).

18. Schlozman et al. (2018). With respect to unequal participation at planning board and zoning board meetings, see Einstein et al. (2019, 2020). With respect to inequality and voter turnout, see Fraga (2018). With respect to poor people's inclusion in national political parties, see Jusko (2017). For an alternative case in which residents of Black neighborhoods exhibit greater political voice, see Levine and Gershenson (2014).

19. For more information, see https://web.archive.org/web/20170511013024/https://www.ds4si.org/civic-engagement/2015/12/29/imaginary-tea-stop.

20. See Salganik and Levy (2015) for a deeper discussion and descriptions of two applications in New York City.

21. Bell (2019, p. 210). Small (2008) makes a similar point with regard to the heterogeneity of poor Black neighborhoods.

Methodological Appendix

1. Marcus (1995).

2. Those tasks included designing an education policy that was never implemented and analyzing data from the city's basic city service request system.

3. For more information on the evaluation, see Friedman (2011).

4. I only conducted a handful of these interviews personally. I used them sparingly, more as a check to verify basic facts or as a springboard to probe further. In this book, I include quotes from four interviews—but only after I cleared them with the speaker first. I also draw on my own experience working as a consultant on the evaluation team. The data in this regard were my own observations of the evaluation process, not the actual data used in the evaluation, which was confidential.

5. See Duneier (2012) on the importance of reflexively approaching one's point of entry in an ethnographic study.

6. Jerolmack and Khan (2014, p. 179).

7. I am very much indebted to Joan and her insights. She played an important gatekeeper role in this study, much like "Doc" in Whyte's *Street Corner Society* (1943) or Hakim in Duneier's *Sidewalk* (1999). Unlike other characters in ethnography (see Wynn 2011), she does not play a major role in the narrative or analysis. But she was absolutely indispensable in terms of data collection.

8. I captured this quote in my handwritten notes, which were allowed in my original agreement with Gail and her colleagues.

9. This was partly out of necessity, as my particular research questions changed over the course of my fieldwork. On "shallow cover," see Fine (1993) and Hoang (2015).

10. I never actually saw Karen at DSNI. She assumed I was there because she perceived me to be present for every conversation related to organizations in the Corridor.

11. See Rios (2015).

12. Goffman (2014, p. 235).

13. There were eleven intermediate stations between the two terminus stations, but people like Jeanne interchangeably referred to eleven or thirteen stations.

14. That said, I do not think the people I studied trusted me. Once, after two years of fieldwork, I offhandedly asked Jeanne to "trust me" with respect to some aspect of the study. "No," she responded sharply, "when someone says 'trust me' the first thing I will do is

I *won't* trust you. I like you but I'm not going to trust you completely." In *Sidewalk*, Duneier (1999) recalls a similar incident in which the street vendors he followed revealed they did not trust him. Yet in Duneier's scene, the expressions of distrust were caught on audio while he was out of the room. Jeanne told me to my face that she didn't trust me—and she wasn't the only one. Still, distrust didn't stop her from allowing me to attend meetings, supporting Duneier's (1999, p. 338) assertion that "participant observers need not be fully trusted in order to have their presence at least accepted."

15. Jerolmack and Murphy (2019). See also Reyes (2018).

16. Lubet (2017).

17. In previously published work, I relied on pseudonyms and mixed-and-matched gender, ethnicity, and organizational titles (Levine 2016). But after reading the recent studies advocating for disclosure, I came to appreciate the downsides of this approach.

18. Two additional people died over the course of my research. I use their real names in the text.

19. Situations like this are a unique frustration that comes with disclosure: For the same conversation, some people can be comfortable being quoted, while others might not be.

BIBLIOGRAPHY

Abraham, Yvonne. June 20, 1999. "A New Deal: The Vault Is Closed, and It's No Longer. Business—or Politics—as Usual." *Boston Globe Magazine.*

Achen, Christopher and Larry Bartels. 2016. *Democracy for Realists: Why Elections Do Not Produce Responsive Government.* Princeton, NJ: Princeton University Press.

Adams, Carolyn T. 2014. *From the Outside In: Suburban Elites, Third-Sector Organizations, and the Reshaping of Philadelphia.* Ithaca, NY: Cornell University Press.

Adler, Sy. 1991. "The Transformation of the Pacific Electric Railway: Bradford Snell, Roger Rabbit, and the Politics of Transportation in Los Angeles." *Urban Affairs Quarterly* 27(1): 51–86.

Allen, John and Alan Cochrane. 2007. "Beyond the Territorial Fix: Regional Assemblages, Politics and Power." *Regional Studies* 41(9): 1161–1175.

Angelo, Hillary and David Wachsmuth. 2015. "Urbanizing Urban Political Ecology: A Critique of Methodological Cityism." *International Journal of Urban and Regional Research* 39(1): 16–27.

Ansell, Chris and Alison Gash. 2008. "Collaborative Governance in Theory and Practice." *Journal of Public Administration Research and Theory* 18(4): 543–571.

Arena, John. 2012. *Driven from New Orleans: How Nonprofits Betray Public housing and Promote Privatization.* Minneapolis: University of Minnesota Press.

Austen, Ben. 2018. "The Towers Came Down, and with Them the Promise of Public Housing." *New York Times*, February 6, 2018

Baiocchi, Gianpaolo. 2005. *Militants and Citizens: The Politics of Participatory Democracy in Porto Alegre.* Stanford, CA: Stanford University Press.

Baiocchi, Gianpaolo and Ernest Ganuza. 2016. *Popular Democracy: The Paradox of Participation.* Stanford, CA: Stanford University Press.

Barley, Stephen R. 2007. "Corporations, Democracy, and the Public Good." *Journal of Management Inquiry* 16(3): 201–215.

Bartley, Tim. 2007. "How Foundations Shape Social Movements: The Construction of an Organizational Field and the Rise of Forest Certification." *Social Problems* 54(3): 229–255.

Becher, Debbie. 2010. "The Participant's Dilemma: Bringing Conflict and Representation Back In." *International Journal of Urban and Regional Research* 34(3): 496–511.

Bell, Joyce M. and Douglas Hartmann. 2007. "Diversity in Everyday Discourse: The Cultural Ambiguities and Consequences of 'Happy Talk.'" *American Sociological Review* 72(6): 895–914.

Bell, Monica. 2019. "The Community in Criminal Justice: Subordination, Consumption, Resistance, and Transformation." *Du Bois Review: Social Science Research on Race* 16(1): 197–220.

Berndt, Harry Edward. 1977. *New Rulers of the Ghetto: The Community Development Corporation and Urban Poverty.* Westport, CT: Greenwood Press.

Berrey, Ellen. 2015. *The Enigma of Diversity: The Language of Race and the Limits of Racial Justice.* Chicago: University of Chicago Press.

Berry, Jeffrey M. 2016. "Negative Returns: The Impact of Impact Investing on Power and Advocacy." *PS: Political Science & Politics* 49(3): 437–441.

Berry, Jeffrey M. with David F. Arons. 2005. *A Voice for Nonprofits*. Washington, DC: Brookings Institution.

Bertrand, Marianne, Matilde Bombardini, Raymond Fisman, and Francesco Trebbi. 2020. "Tax-Exempt Lobbying: Corporate Philanthropy as a Tool for Political Influence." *American Economic Review* 110(7): 2065-2102.

Betancur, John, Karen Mossberger, and Yue Zhang. 2015. "Standing in Two Worlds: Neighborhood Policy, the Civic Arena, and Ward Politics in Chicago." In *Urban Neighborhoods in a New Era: Revitalization Politics in the Postindustrial City*, edited by Clarence N. Stone and Robert P. Stoker, 104-140. Chicago: University of Chicago Press.

Bingham, Lisa Blomgren, Tina Nabatchi, and Rosemary O'Leary. 2005. "The New Governance: Practices and Processes for Stakeholder and Citizen Participation in the Work of Government." *Public Administration Review* 65(5): 547-558.

Bishop, Matthew and Michael Green. 2010. *Philanthrocapitalism: How Giving Can Save the World*. New York: Bloomsbury.

Bogason, Peter and Juliet A. Musso. 2006. *The Democratic Prospects of Network Governance*. Thousand Oaks, CA: Sage.

BondGraham, Darwin. 2011. "Building the New New Orleans: Foundation and NGO Power." *Review of Black Political Economy* 38(4): 279-309.

Booher, David E. and Judith E. Innes. 2002. "Network Power in Collaborative Planning." *Journal of Planning Education and Research* 21(3): 221-236.

Boustan, Leah P. 2016. *Competition in the Promised Land: Black Migrants in Northern Cities and Labor Markets*. Princeton, NJ: Princeton University Press.

Bowes, David R. and Keith R. Ihlanfeldt. 2001. "Identifying the Impacts of Rail Transit Stations on Residential Property Values." *Journal of Urban Economics* 50(1): 1-25.

Brandtner, Christof, Patricia Bromley, and Megan Tompkins-Stange. 2016. "'Walk the Line': How Institutional Influences Constrain Elites." In *How Institutions Matter! (Research in the Sociology of Organizations 48B)*, edited by Joel Gehman, Michael Lounsbry, and Royston Greenwood, 281-309. United Kingdom: Emerald Publishing.

Bratt, Rachel G. 2008. "Nonprofit and For-profit Developers of Subsidized Rental Housing: Comparative Attributes and Collaborative Opportunities." *Housing Policy Debate* 19(2): 323-365.

Bratt, Rachel G. 2012. "The Quadruple Bottom Line and Nonprofit Housing Organizations in the United States." *Housing Studies* 27(4): 438-456.

Brenner, Neil. 1999. "Globalisation as Reterritorialisation: The Re-Scaling of Urban Governance in the European Union." *Urban Studies* 36(3): 431-451.

Brenner, Neil. 2004. "Urban Governance and the Production of New State Spaces in Western Europe, 1960-2000." *Review of International Political Economy* 11(3): 447-488.

Brenner, Neil. 2009. "Is There a Politics of 'Urban' Development? Reflections on the US Case." In *The City in American Political Development*, edited by Richardson Dilworth, 121-140. New York: Routledge.

Brenner, Neil and Nik Theodore. 2002. "Cities and the Geographies of 'Actually Existing Neoliberalism.'" *Antipode* 34(3): 349-379.

Brest, Paul. 2020. "The Outcomes Movement in Philanthropy and the Nonprofit Sector." In *The Nonprofit Sector: A Research Handbook, 3rd edition*, edited by Walter W. Powell and Patricia Bromley. Palo Alto, CA: Stanford University Press.

Briggs, Xavier de Souza. 1998. "Doing Democracy Up-Close: Culture, Power, and Communication in Community Building." *Journal of Planning Education and Research* 18: 1-13.

Bromley, Patricia and John W. Meyer. 2017. "'They Are All Organizations' The Cultural Roots of Blurring Between the Nonprofit, Business, and Government Sectors." *Administration & Society* 49(7): 939-966.

Broockman, David E. and Christopher Skovron. 2018. "Bias in Perceptions of Public Opinion Among Political Elites." *American Political Science Review* 112(3): 542–563.

Brown, Karida L. 2018. *Gone Home: Race and Roots through Appalachia*. Chapel Hill: University of North Carolina Press.

Brown-Saracino, Japonica. 2013. *The Gentrification Debates: A Reader*. New York: Routledge.

Brown-Saracino, Japonica. 2015. "How Places Shape Identity: The Origins of Distinctive LBQ Identities in Four Small U.S. Cities." *American Journal of Sociology* 121(1): 1–63.

Bushouse, Brenda K. and Jennifer E. Mosley. 2018. "The Intermediary Roles of Foundations in the Policy Process: Building Coalitions of Interest." *Interest Groups & Advocacy* 7(3): 289–311.

Callahan, David, 2017. *The Givers: Wealth, Power, and Philanthropy in a New Gilded Age*. New York: Vintage.

Caraley, Demetrios. 1992. "Washington Abandons the Cities." *Political Science Quarterly* 107(1): 1–30.

Cazenave, Noel A. 2007. *Impossible Democracy: The Unlikely Success of the War on Poverty and Community Action Programs*. Albany: State University of New York Press.

Cervero, Robert (ed.). 2004. *Transit-Oriented Development in the United States: Experiences, Challenges, and Prospects* (Report No. 102). Washington, DC: Transit Cooperative Research Program.

Chaskin, Robert J. 2003. "Fostering Neighborhood Democracy: Legitimacy and Accountability within Loosely Coupled Systems." *Nonprofit and Voluntary Sector Quarterly* 32(2): 161–189.

Chaskin, Robert J. and Mark L. Joseph. 2015. *Integrating the Inner City: The Promise and Perils of Mixed-Income Public Housing Transformation*. Chicago: University of Chicago Press.

Chaskin, Robert J., Mark L. Joseph, and Selma Chipenda-Dansokho. 1997. "Implementing Comprehensive Community Development: Possibilities and Limitations." *Social Work* 42(5): 435–444.

Chesto, Jon. 2016. "Powerful Business Group Keeps Low Profile in Boston." *Boston Globe*, January 12, 2016

Clark, Anna. 2012. "Welcome to Your New Government—Can Non-Profits Run Cities?" *Next City*, July 9, 2012.

Clavel, Pierre. 2010. *Activists in City Hall: The Progressive Response to the Reagan Era in Boston and Chicago*. Ithaca, NY: Cornell University Press.

Clemens, Elisabeth and Doug Guthrie (eds.). 2010. *Politics and Partnerships: Voluntary Associations in America's Political Past and Present*. Chicago: University of Chicago Press.

Cohen, Anthony Paul. 1985. *The Symbolic Construction of Community*. London and New York: Routledge.

Cohen, Lizabeth. 2019. *Saving America's Cities: Ed Logue and the Struggle to Renew Urban America in the Suburban Age*. New York: Farrar, Straus and Giroux.

Cordelli, Chiara. 2020. *The Privatized State*. Princeton, NJ: Princeton University Press.

Cortright, Joe and Dillon Magmoudi. 2014. "Lost in Place: Why the Persistence and Spread of Concentrated Poverty—Not Gentrification—Is Our Biggest Urban Challenge." *City Observatory*. https://web.archive.org/web/20201103041425/https://cityobservatory.org/wp-content/uploads/2014/12/LostinPlace_12.4.pdf

Creswell, Jule. 2018. "Cities' Offers for Amazon Base Are Secrets Even to Many City Leaders." *New York Times*, August 15, 2018.

Crockett, Karilyn. 2018. *People Before Highways: Boston Activists, Urban Planners, and a New Movement for City Making*. Amherst: University of Massachusetts Press.

da Cruz, Nuno F., Philipp Rode, and Michael McQuarrie. 2019. "New Urban Governance: A Review of Current Themes and Future Priorities." *Journal of Urban Affairs* 41(1): 1–19.

Dahl, Robert. 2005 [1961]. *Who Governs? Democracy and Power in an American City.* New Haven, CT: Yale University Press.

Danley, Stephen. 2018. *A Neighborhood Politics of Last Resort: Post-Katrina New Orleans and the Right to the City.* Montreal: McGill-Queen's University Press.

Davis, Katrinell. Forthcoming. *Tainted Tap: The Politics of Race, Space, and Abandonment in Flint, Michigan.* Chapel Hill, NC: University of North Carolina Press.

deBarros, Rominda. 2014. "Codman Square Neighborhood Development Corporation Recognized for Greenhouse Gas Reduction." *Bay State Banner*, June 12, 2014.

DeFilippis, James and Susan Saegert. 2007. *The Community Development Reader.* New York: Routledge.

de Graauw, Els. 2016. *Making Immigrant Rights Real: Nonprofits and the Politics of Integration in San Francisco.* Ithaca, NY: Cornell University Press.

de Graauw, Els, Shannon Gleeson, and Irene Bloemraad. 2013. "Funding Immigrant Organizations: Suburban Free Riding and Local Civic Presence." *American Journal of Sociology* 119(1): 75–130.

DePasquale, Ron. 2004. "MBTA Eyes Upgrade for Dorchester Rail Line." *Boston Globe*, March 7, 2004.

Desmond, Matthew. 2014. "Relational Ethnography." *Theory and Society* 43(5): 547–579.

Desmond, Matthew. 2018. "Heavy Is the House: Rent Burden among the American Urban Poor." *International Journal of Urban and Regional Research* 42(1): 160–170.

Desmond, Matthew and Monica Bell. 2015. "Poverty, Housing, and the Law." *Annual Review of Law and Social Science* 11: 15–35.

Dezenski, Lauren. 2014. "Next Stop for Fairmount Line: Weekend Hours, Lower Fares and a New Blue Hill Avenue Station." *Dorchester Reporter*, October 16, 2014.

Dittmar, Hank and Gloria Ohland (ed.). 2004. *Transit Town: Best Practices in Transit-Oriented Development.* Washington, DC: Island Press.

Donaghy, Maureen M. 2018. *Democratizing Urban Development: Community Organizations for Housing Across the United States and Brazil.* Philadelphia, PA: Temple University Press.

Douglas, Gordon CC. 2010. "Rail Transit Identification and Neighbourhood Identity. Exploring the Potential for 'Community-Supportive Transit.'" *Journal of Urban Design* 15(2): 175–193.

Dowding, Keith. 2001. "Explaining Urban Regimes." *International Journal of Urban and Regional Research* 25(1): 7–19.

Dowding, Keith et al. 1999. "Regime Politics in London Local Government." *Urban Affairs Review* 34(4): 515–545.

Duneier, Mitchell. 1999. *Sidewalk.* New York: Farrar, Straus and Giroux.

Duneier, Mitchell. 2012. "How Not to Lie with Ethnography." *Sociological Methodology* 41(1): 1–11.

Dunning, Claire. 2016. *Outsourcing Government: Boston and the Rise of Public-Private Partnerships, 1950–2000.* PhD diss., Harvard University.

Edin, Kathryn and Maria Kefalas. 2005. *Promises I Can Keep: Why Poor Women Put Motherhood Before Marriage.* Berkeley: University of California Press.

Editorial Board. 1987. "The T's Hush-Hush Line." *Boston Globe*, November 10, 1987.

Editorial Board. 2013. "Along Fairmount Line, T Did Its Part; Now City Must Lead." *Boston Globe*, July 15, 2013

Eikenberry, Angela M. and Jodie Drapal Kluver. 2004. "The Marketization of the Nonprofit Sector: Civil Society at Risk?" *Public Administration Review* 64: 132–140.

Eikenberry, Angela M. and Roseanne Marie Mirabella. 2018. "Extreme Philanthropy: Philanthrocapitalism, Effective Altruism and the Discourse of Neoliberalism." *PS: Political Science & Politics* 51(1): 43–47.

Einstein, Katherine, David Glick, and Maxwell Palmer. 2020. *Neighborhood Defenders: Participatory Politics and America's Housing Crisis*. New York: Cambridge University Press.

Einstein, Katherine, Maxwell Palmer, and David Glick. 2019. "Who Participates in Local Government? Evidence from Meeting Minutes." *Perspectives on Politics* 17(1): 28–46.

Eisinger, Jesse. 2015. "How Mark Zuckerberg's Altruism Helps Himself." *New York Times*, December 3, 2015.

Eliasoph, Nina. 2009. "Top-Down Civic Projects Are Not Grassroots Associations: How the Differences Matter in Everyday Life." *Voluntas* 20: 291–308.

Eliasoph, Nina. 2014. "Measuring the Grassroots: Puzzles of Cultivating the Grassroots from the Top Down." *Sociological Quarterly* 55(3): 467–492.

Elkin, Stephen L. 1987. *City and Regime in the American Republic*. Chicago: University of Chicago Press.

Elkind, Ethan N. 2014. *Railtown: The Fight for the Los Angeles Metro Rail and the Future of the City*. Berkeley: University of California Press.

Ellen, Ingrid G. and Keren M. Horn. 2018. "Points for Place: Can State Governments Shape Siting Patterns of Low-Income Housing Tax Credit Developments?" *Housing Policy Debate* 28(5): 727–745.

Fainstein, Norman I. and Susan S. Fainstein. 1983. "Regime Strategies, Communal Resistance, and Economic Forces." In *Restructuring the City*, edited by Susan S. Fainstein and Norman I. Fainstein, 245–282. New York: Longman.

Ferguson, Karen. 2013. *Top Down: The Ford Foundation, Black Power, and the Reinvention of Racial Liberalism*. Philadelphia: University of Pennsylvania Press.

Ferman, Barbara. 1996. *Challenging the Growth Machine: Neighborhood Politics in Chicago and Pittsburgh*. Lawrence: University Press of Kansas.

Fine, Gary Alan. 1993. "Ten Lies of Ethnography: Moral Dilemmas of Field Research." *Journal of Contemporary Ethnography* 22(3): 267–294.

Finger, Leslie K. 2018. "Giving to Government: The Policy Goals and Giving Strategies of New and Old Foundations." *Interest Groups & Advocacy* 7(3): 312–345.

Fligstein, Neil and Doug McAdam. 2011. "Toward a General Theory of Strategic Action Fields." *Sociological Theory* 29(1): 1–26.

Forry, Bill. 2013a. "City Plans to Build Warehouse on Key Uphams Corner Parcel." *Dorchester Reporter*, July 26, 2013.

Forry, Bill. 2013b. "Mayor: Maxwell Site Should Be Used for 'Transit Oriented Development.'" *Dorchester Reporter*, July 29, 2013.

Forry, Bill. 2014. "Three Pitch City for Maxwell Site in Uphams Corner." *Dorchester Reporter*, November 12, 2014.

Foundation Center. 2014. *The Foundation Directory, 2014 Edition*. New York: Foundation Center.

Fraga, Bernard L. 2018. *The Turnout Gap: Race, Ethnicity, and Political Inequality in a Diversifying America*. New York: Cambridge University Press.

Francis, Megan Ming. 2019. "The Price of Civil Rights: Black Lives, White Funding, and Movement Capture." *Law & Society Review* 53(1): 275–309.

Frasure, Lorrie A. and Michael Jones-Correa. 2010. "The Logic of Institutional Interdependency: The Case of Day Laborer Policy in Suburbia." *Urban Affairs Review* 45(4): 451–482.

Freund, David M. 2010. *Colored Property: State Policy and White Racial Politics in Suburban America*. Chicago: University of Chicago Press.

Friedman, Donna H. 2011. "The Fairmount Initiative Quarterly Progress Report: People and Places: Understanding the Processes, Outcomes and Impacts of Interventions of the Fairmount Corridor." University of Massachusetts–Boston Center for Social Policy.

Frug, Gerald E. and David J. Barron. 2013. *City Bound: How States Stifle Urban Innovation.* Ithaca, NY: Cornell University Press.

Fung, Archon. 2004. *Empowered Participation: Reinventing Urban Democracy.* Princeton, NJ: Princeton University Press.

Fung, Archon. 2015. "Putting the Public Back into Governance: The Challenges of Citizen Participation and Its Future." *Public Administration Review* 75(4): 513–522.

Fung, Archon and Erik Olin Wright. 2003. *Deepening Democracy: Institutional Innovations in Empowered Participatory Governance.* London: Verso.

Fyall, Rachel. 2016. "The Power of Nonprofits: Mechanisms for Nonprofit Policy Influence." *Public Administration Review* 76(6): 938–948.

Fyall, Rachel. 2017. "Nonprofits as Advocates and Providers: A Conceptual Framework." *Policy Studies Journal* 45(1): 121–143.

Fyall, Rachel and Michael McGuire. 2015. "Advocating for Policy Change in Nonprofit Coalitions." *Nonprofit and Voluntary Sector Quarterly* 44(6): 1274–1291.

Gaffin, Adam. 2017. "More People Rode the Fairmount Line When It Was Free, But They Stopped When the Fares Came Back." *Universal Hub*, June 16, 2017. https://web.archive.org/web/20171015223044/https://www.universalhub.com/2017/more-people-rode-fairmount-line-when-it-was-free.

Gakenheimer, Ralph. 1976. *Transportation Policy as Response to Controversy.* Cambridge, MA: MIT Press.

Galaskiewicz, Joseph. 1997. "An Urban Grants Economy Revisited: Corporate Charitable Contributions in the Twin Cities, 1979–81, 1987–89." *Administrative Science Quarterly* 42(3): 445–471.

Galaskiewicz, Joseph. 1985. *Social Organization of an Urban Grants Economy: A Study of Business Philanthropy and Nonprofit Organizations.* Orlando, FL: Academic Press.

Gamm, Gerald. 2001. *Urban Exodus: Why the Jews Left Boston and the Catholics Stayed.* Cambridge, MA: Harvard University Press.

Gamson, William A. 1975. *The Strategy of Social Protest.* Homewood, IL: Dorsey Press.

Gans, Herbert J. 1982. *The Urban Villagers: Group and Class in the Life of Italian-Americans (Updated and Expanded Edition).* New York: Free Press.

Gautier, Arthur and Anne-Claire Pache. 2015. "Research on Corporate Philanthropy: A Review and Assessment." *Journal of Business Ethics* 126: 343–369.

Ghaziani, Amin. 2014. *There Goes the Gayborhood?* Princeton, NJ: Princeton University Press.

Goffman, Alice. 2014. *On the Run: Fugitive Life in an American City.* Chicago: University of Chicago Press.

Goldstein, Brian D. 2017. *The Roots of Urban Renaissance.* Cambridge, MA: Harvard University Press.

Goss, Kristin A. and Jeffrey M. Berry. 2018. "Foundations as Interest Groups." *Interest Groups & Advocacy* 7(3): 201–205.

Goss, Kristin A., Carolyn Barnes, and Deondra Rose. 2019. "Bringing Organizations Back In: Multilevel Feedback Effects on Individual Civic Inclusion." *Policy Studies Journal* 47(2): 451–470.

Grant, Keneshia N. 2020. *The Great Migration and the Democratic Party: Black Voters and the Realignment of American Politics in the 20th Century.* Philadelphia, PA: Temple University Press.

Graves, Erin M. 2010. "The Structuring of Urban Life in a Mixed-Income Housing 'Community.'" *City & Community* 9(1): 109–131.

Greenstone, J. David and Paul E. Peterson. 1973. *Race and Authority in Urban Politics: Community Participation and the War on Poverty*. Chicago: University of Chicago Press.

Grogan, Paul S. and Tony Proscio. 2000. *Comeback Cities. A Blueprint for Urban Neighborhood Revival*. New York: Basic Books.

Guo, Chao and Juliet A. Musso. 2007. "Representation in Nonprofit and Voluntary Organizations: A Conceptual Framework." *Nonprofit and Voluntary Sector Quarterly* 36(2): 308–326.

Guthrie, Doug and Michael McQuarrie. 2008. "Providing for the Public Good: Corporate-Community Relations in the Era of the Receding Welfare State." *City & Community* 7(2): 113–139.

Guttman, Amy and Dennis Thompson. 2004. *Why Deliberative Democracy?* Princeton, NJ: Princeton University Press.

Hall, Peter Dobkin. 2006. "A Historical Overview of Philanthropy, Voluntary Associations, and Nonprofit Organizations in the United States, 1600–2000." In *The Non-Profit Sector: A Research Handbook—Second Edition*, edited by Walter W. Powell and Richard Steinberg, 32–65. New Haven, CT: Yale University Press.

Hanchett, Doug. 2002. "T Jumps on Fairmount Upgrade; $70M Plan Will Add Stops, Stations." *Boston Herald*, September 1, 2002.

Hanleybrown, Fay, John Kania, and Mark Kramer. 2012. "Channeling Change: Making Collective Impact Work." *Stanford Social Innovation Review*. https://web.archive.org/web/20191205002554/https://ssir.org/articles/entry/channeling_change_making_collective_impact_work

Harding, Alan. 1996. "Is There a New 'Community Power' and Why Should We Need One?" *International Journal of Urban and Regional Research* 20(4): 637–655.

Harding, David J. 2010. *Living the Drama: Community, Conflict, and Culture among Inner-City Boys*. Chicago: University of Chicago Press.

Harvey, David. 1989. "From Managerialism to Entrepreneurialism: The Transformation of Urban Governance in Late Capitalism." *Geografiska Annaler* 71B: 3–17.

Healey, Patsy. 1998. "Building Institutional Capacity through Collaborative Approaches to Urban Planning." *Environment and Planning A* 30(9): 1531–1546.

Healey, Patsy. 2003. "Collaborative Planning in Perspective." *Planning Theory* 2(2): 101–123.

Heathcott, Joseph. 2012. "Planning Note: Pruitt-Igoe and the Critique of Public Housing." *Journal of the American Planning Association* 78(4): 450–451.

Heil, Melissa. 2018. "Community Development Corporations in the Right-Sizing City: Remaking the CDC Model of Urban Redevelopment." *Journal of Urban Affairs* 1–14.

Hertel-Fernandez, Alexander. 2019. *State Capture: How Conservative Activists, Big Businesses, and Wealthy Donors Reshaped the American States—and the Nation*. New York: Oxford University Press.

Hertel-Fernandez, Alexander, Matto Mildenberger, and Leah Stokes. 2019. "Legislative Staff and Representation in Congress." *American Political Science Review* 113(1): 1–18.

Hill, Lauren Warren and Julia Rabig (eds.). 2012. *The Business of Black Power: Community Development, Capitalism, and Corporate Responsibility in Postwar America*. Rochester, NY: Rochester University Press.

Hillery Jr., George A. 1955. "Definitions of Community: Areas of Agreement." *Rural Sociology* 20: 111–123.

Hoang, Kimberly. 2015. *Dealing in Desire: Asian Ascendancy, Western Decline, and the Hidden Currencies of Global Sex Work*. Oakland: University of California Press.

Holin, Mary J., Gretchen Locke, Larry Buron, and Alvaro Cortes. 2010. "Interim Assessment of the HOPE VI Program Cross-Site Report." Washington, DC: Department of Housing and Urban Development.

Horvath, Aaron and Walter W. Powell. 2016. "Contributory or Disruptive: Do New Forms of Philanthropy Erode Democracy?" In *Philanthropy in Democratic Societies*, edited by Rob Reich, Lucy Bernholz, and Chiara Cordelli, 87–122. Chicago: University of Chicago Press.

Hunter, Albert D. 1974. *Symbolic Communities: The Persistence and Change of Chicago's Local Communities*. Chicago: University of Chicago Press.

Hunter, Marcus A. 2013. *Black Citymakers: How the Philadelphia Negro Changed Urban America*. New York: Oxford University Press.

Hunter, Marcus Anthony and Zandria F. Robinson. 2018. *Chocolate Cities: The Black Map of American Life*. Oakland: University of California Press.

Hwang, Hokyu and Walter W. Powell. 2009. "The Rationalization of Charity: The Influences of Professionalism in the Nonprofit Sector." *Administrative Science Quarterly* 54(2): 268–298.

Hwang, Jackelyn. 2016. "The Social Construction of a Gentrifying Neighborhood: Reifying and Redefining Identity and Boundaries in Inequality." *Urban Affairs Review* 52(1): 98–128.

Hyra, Derek S. 2008. *The New Urban Renewal: The Economic Transformation of Harlem and Bronzeville*. Chicago: University of Chicago Press.

Hyra, Derek. 2015. "The Back-to-the-City Movement: Neighbourhood Redevelopment and Processes of Political and Cultural Displacement." *Urban Studies* 52(10): 1753–1773.

Imbroscio, David. 2010. *Urban America Reconsidered: Alternatives for Governance and Policy*. Ithaca, NY: Cornell University Press.

INCITE! Women of Color Against Violence. 2007. *The Revolution Will Not Be Funded: Beyond the Non-Profit Industrial Complex*. Cambridge, MA: South End Press.

Innes, Judith E. and David E. Booher. 1999a. "Consensus Building and Complex Adaptive Systems: A Framework for Evaluating Collaborative Planning." *Journal of the American Planning Association* 65(4): 412–423.

Innes, Judith E. and David E. Booher. 1999b. "Consensus Building as Role Playing and Bricolage: Toward a Theory of Collaborative Planning." *Journal of the American Planning Association* 65(1): 9–26.

Irons, Meghan F. 2013a. "MBTA to Open Two New Stations on Fairmount Line." *Boston Globe*, May 17, 2013.

Irons, Meghan F. 2013b. "MBTA Pilot Program to Boost New Commuter Line." *Boston Globe*, July 8, 2013.

Jackson, Kenneth T. 1985. *Crabgrass Frontier: The Suburbanization of America*. New York: Oxford University Press.

Jerolmack, Colin and Shamus Khan. 2014. "Talk Is Cheap: Ethnography and the Attitudinal Fallacy." *Sociological Methods & Research* 43(2): 178–209.

Jerolmack, Colin and Alexandra K. Murphy. 2019. "The Ethical Dilemmas and Social Scientific Trade-offs of Masking in Ethnography." *Sociological Methods & Research* 48(4): 801–827.

Jessop, Bob and Ngai-Ling Sum. 2000. "An Entrepreneurial City in Action: Hong Kong's Emerging Strategies in and for (Inter)Urban Competition." *Urban Studies* 37(12): 2287–2313.

Johnson, Kimberly. 2004. "Community Development Corporations, Participation, and Accountability: The Harlem Urban Development Corporation and the Bedford-Stuyvesant Restoration Corporation." *Annals of the American Academy of Political and Social Science* 594: 109–124.

Jones, Jane. 2013. "The Ambivalent Gift: The Diverse Giving Strategies of Black Philanthropists." *Du Bois Review: Social Science Research on Race* 10(1): 87–108.

Joseph, Miranda. 2002. *Against the Romance of Community*. Minneapolis: University of Minnesota Press.

Judd, Dennis. 2005. "Everything Is Always Going to Hell: Urban Scholars as End-Times Prophets." *Urban Affairs Review* 41(3): 119–131.

Jusko, Karen Long. 2017. *Who Speaks for the Poor? Electoral Geography, Party Entry, and Representation*. New York: Cambridge University Press.

Kania, John and Mark Kramer. 2011. "Collective Impact." *Stanford Social Innovation Review* Winter: 36–41.

Katz, Jack. 1997. "Ethnography's Warrants." *Sociological Methods & Research* 25(4): 391–423.

Katz, Michael B. 2006. *In the Shadow of the Poorhouse: A Social History of Welfare in America*. New York: Basic Books.

Katznelson, Ira. 1981. *City Trenches: Urban Politics and the Patterning of Class in the United States*. Chicago: University of Chicago Press.

Kilgannon, Maddie. 2017. "MBTA Breaks Ground on Blue Hill Avenue Station." *Boston Globe*, June 5, 2017.

King, Mel. 1981. *Chain of Change: Struggles for Black Community Development*. Boston, MA: South End Press.

Kirkpatrick, L. Owen. 2007. "The Two 'Logics' of Community Development: Neighborhoods, Markets, and Community Development Corporations." *Politics & Society* 35(2): 329–359.

Kohl-Arenas, Erica. 2015. *The Self-Help Myth: How Philanthropy Fails to Alleviate Poverty*. Berkeley: University of California Press.

Krause, Monika. 2014. *The Good Project: Humanitarian Relief NGOs and the Fragmentation of Reason*. Chicago: University of Chicago Press.

Lamont, Michèle and Ann Swidler. 2014. "Methodological Pluralism and the Possibilities and Limits of Interviewing." *Qualitative Sociology* 37(2): 153–171.

Lannan, Katie. 2017. "Housing Production Pitched as Economic Imperative at Hearing." *WBUR*, September 29, 2015.

Lederman, Jacob. 2019. "The People's Plan? Participation and Post-Politics in Flint's Master Planning Process." *Critical Sociology*. 45(1): 85–101.

Lee, Caroline. 2015. *Do-It-Yourself Democracy: The Rise of the Public Engagement Industry*. New York: Oxford University Press.

Lee, Caroline, Michael McQuarrie, and Edward Walker. 2015. *Democratizing Inequalities: Pitfalls and Unrealized Promises of the New Public Participation*. New York: NYU Press.

Legacy, Crystal, Nicole Cook, Dallas Rogers, and Kristian Ruming. 2018. "Planning the Post-Political City: Exploring Public Participation in the Contemporary Australian City." *Geographical Research* 56(2): 176–180.

LeRoux, Kelly and Mary K. Feeney. 2015. *Nonprofit Organizations and Civil Society in the United States*. New York: Routledge.

Levine, Hillel and Lawrence Harmon. 1992. *The Death of an American Jewish Community: A Tragedy of Good Intention*. New York: Free Press.

Levine, Jeremy R. 2013. "Organizational Parochialism: 'Placing' Interorganizational Network Ties." *City & Community* 12(4): 309–334.

Levine, Jeremy R. 2016. "The Privatization of Political Representation: Community-Based Organizations as Nonelected Neighborhood Representatives." *American Sociological Review* 81(6): 1251–1275.

Levine, Jeremy R. 2017. "The Paradox of Community Power: Cultural Processes and Elite Authority in Participatory Governance." *Social Forces* 95(3): 1155–1179.

Levine, Jeremy R. and Carl Gershenson. 2014. "From Political to Material Inequality: Race, Immigration, and Requests for Public Goods." *Sociological Forum* 29(3): 607–627.

Lichterman, Paul. 1996. *The Search for Political Community: American Activists Reinventing Commitment.* New York: Cambridge University Press.
Lichterman, Paul and Nina Eliasoph. 2014. "Civic Action." *American Journal of Sociology* 120(3): 798–863.
Logan, Tim. 2020. "For-Sale Sign on Affordable Apartment Building in Mattapan Raises Fears Tenants Will Be Forced Out." *Boston Globe*, July 20, 2020.
Logan, John R. and Harvey L. Molotch. 2007 [1987]. *Urban Fortunes: The Political Economy of Place.* Berkeley: University of California Press.
Lowe, Kate. 2014. "Bypassing Equity? Transit Investment and Regional Transportation Planning." *Journal of Planning Education and Research* 34(1): 30–44.
Lubet, Steven. 2017. *Interrogating Ethnography: Why Evidence Matters.* New York: Oxford University Press.
MacLeod, Gordon. 2011. "Urban Politics Reconsidered: Growth Machine to Post-Democratic City?" *Urban Studies* 48(12): 2629–2660.
Madden, David J. 2014. "Neighborhood as Spatial Project: Making the Urban Order on the Downtown Brooklyn Waterfront." *International Journal of Urban and Regional Research* 38(2): 471–497.
Mansbridge, Jane. 1983. *Beyond Adversary Democracy.* Chicago: University of Chicago Press.
Marcus, George E. 1995. "Ethnography in/of the World System: The Emergence of Multi-Sited Ethnography." *Annual Review Anthropology* 24: 95–117.
Martin, Deborah G. 2004. "Nonprofit Foundations and Grassroots Organizing: Reshaping Urban Governance." *Professional Geographer* 56(3): 394–405.
Martin, Leslie. 2007. "Fighting for Control: Political Displacement in Atlanta's Gentrifying Neighborhoods." *Urban Affairs Review* 42(5): 603–628.
Martinez-Cosio, Maria and Mirle Rabinowitz Bussell. 2012. "Private Foundations and Community Development: Differing Approaches to Community Empowerment." *Community Development* 43(4): 416–429.
Martinez-Cosio, Maria and Mirle Rabinowitz Bussell. 2013. *Catalysts for Change: Twenty-First Century Philanthropy and Community Development.* New York and London: Routledge.
Marwell, Nicole P. 2004. "Privatizing the Welfare State: Nonprofit Community-Based Organizations as Political Actors." *American Sociological Review* 69(2): 265–291.
Marwell, Nicole P. 2007. *Bargaining for Brooklyn: Community Organizations in the Entrepreneurial City.* Chicago: University of Chicago Press.
Marwell, Nicole P. and Maoz Brown. 2020. "Towards a Governance Framework for Government-Nonprofit Relations." In *The Nonprofit Sector: A Research Handbook, 3rd edition*, edited by Walter W. Powell and Patricia Bromley. Palo Alto, CA: Stanford University Press.
Marwell, Nicole P. and Aaron Gullickson. 2013. "Inequality in the Spatial Allocation of Social Services: Government Contracts to Nonprofit Organizations in New York City." *Social Service Review* 87(2): 319–353.
Marwell, Nicole P., Erez Aharon Marantz, and Delia Baldassarri. 2020. "The Micro-Relations of Urban Governance: Dynamics of Patronage and Partnership." *American Journal of Sociology* 125(6): 1559–1601.
Marwell, Nicole P. and Michael McQuarrie. 2013. "People, Place and System: Organizations and the Renewal of Urban Social Theory." *Annals of the American Academy of Political and Social Sciences* 647: 126–143.
Marwell, Nicole P. and Shannon Morrissey. 2020. "Organizations and the Governance of Urban Poverty." *Annual Review of Sociology.* 46(1): 233–250.
Mayer, Margit. 2003. "The Onward Sweep of Social Capital: Causes and Consequences for Understanding Cities, Communities and Urban Movements." *International Journal of Urban and Regional Research* 27(1): 110–132.

Mayhew, David R. 1974. *Congress: The Electoral Connection*. New Haven, CT: Yale University Press.
Mayorga-Gallo, Sarah. 2014. *Behind the White Picket Fence: Power and Privilege in a Multiethnic Neighborhood*. Chapel Hill: University of North Carolina Press.
Mayrl, Damon and Sarah Quinn. 2016. "Defining the State from Within: Boundaries, Schemas, and Associational Policymaking." *Sociological Theory* 34(1): 1–26.
McCabe, Brian J. 2016. *No Place Like Home: Wealth, Community & the Politics of Homeownership*. New York: Oxford University Press.
McQuarrie, Michael. 2011. "Nonprofits and the Reconstruction of Urban Governance: Housing Production and Community Development in Cleveland, 1975–2005." In *Politics and Partnerships: The Role of Voluntary Associations in America's Political Past and Present*, edited by Elisabeth S. Clemens and Douglas Guthrie, 237–268. Chicago: University of Chicago Press.
McQuarrie, Michael. 2013a. "Community Organizations in the Foreclosure Crisis: The Failure of Neoliberal Civil Society." *Politics and Society* 41(1): 73–101.
McQuarrie, Michael. 2013b. "No Contest: Participatory Technologies and the Transformation of Urban Authority." *Public Culture* 25(1): 143–175.
McQuarrie, Michael and Norman Krumholz. 2011. "Institutionalized Social Skill and the Rise of Mediating Organizations in Urban Governance: The Case of the Cleveland Housing Network." *Housing Policy Debate* 21(3): 421–442.
Medoff, Peter and Holly Sklar. 1994. *Streets of Hope: The Fall and Rise of an Urban Neighborhood*. Boston, MA: South End Press.
Mele, Christopher. 2013. "Neoliberalism, Race and the Redefining of Urban Redevelopment." *International Journal of Urban and Regional Research* 37(2): 598–617.
Melendez, Edwin and Lisa J. Servon. 2007. "Reassessing the Role of Housing in Community-based Urban Development." *Housing Policy Debate* 18(4): 751–783.
Mettler, Susan. 2018. *The Government-Citizen Disconnect*. New York: Russell Sage.
Milward, H. Brinton and Keith G. Provan. 2000. "Governing the Hollow State." *Journal of Public Administration Research and Theory* 10(2): 359–380.
Mizruchi, Mark. 2013. *The Fracturing of the American Corporate Elite*. Cambridge, MA: Harvard University Press.
Moffitt, Susan L. 2014. *Making Policy Public: Participatory Bureaucracy in American Democracy*. New York, NY: Cambridge University Press.
Mollenkopf, John H. 1975. "The Post-War Politics of Urban Development." *Politics & Society* 5(3): 247–295.
Mollenkopf, John H. 1983. *The Contested City*. Princeton, NJ: Princeton University Press.
Molotch, Harvey. 1976. "The City as a Growth Machine: Toward a Political Economy of Place." *America Journal of Sociology* 82(2): 309–332.
Molotch, Harvey, William Freudenberg, and Krista E. Paulsen. 2000. "History Repeats Itself, But How? City Character, Urban Tradition, and the Accomplishment of Place." *American Sociological Review* 65(6): 791–823.
Montanaro, Laura. 2012. "The Democratic Legitimacy of Self-Appointed Representatives." *Journal of Politics* 74(4): 1094–1107.
Mosley, Jennifer E. and Joseph Galaskiewicz. 2015. "The Relationship between Philanthropic Foundation Funding and State-Level Policy in the Era of Welfare Reform." *Nonprofit and Voluntary Sector Quarterly* 44(6): 1225–1254.
Mosley, Jennifer E. and Colleen M. Grogan. 2013. "Representation in Nonelected Participatory Processes: How Residents Understand the Role of Nonprofit Community-Based Organizations." *Journal of Public Administration Research and Theory* 23(4): 839–863.
Mossberger, Karen and Gerry Stoker. 2001. "The Evolution of Urban Regime Theory: The Challenge of Conceptualization." *Urban Affairs Review* 36(6): 810–835.

Murphy, Alexandra. Forthcoming. *When the Sidewalks End: Poverty in an American Suburb.* New York: Oxford University Press.

NACEDA. 2010. *Rising Above: Community Economic Development in a Changing Landscape.* Washington, DC.

Nall, Clayton. 2018. *The Road to Inequality: How the Federal Highway Program Polarized America and Undermined Cities.* New York: Cambridge University Press.

Nevarez, Leonard. 2000. "Corporate Philanthropy in the New Urban Economy: The Role of Business-Nonprofit Realignment in Regime Politics." *Urban Affairs Review* 36(2): 197–227.

Newman, Kathe and Robert W. Lake. 2006. "Democracy, Bureaucracy and Difference in US Community Development Politics since 1968." *Progress in Human Geography* 30(1): 44–61.

Nickels, Ashley E. 2019. *Power, Participation, and Protest in Flint, Michigan: Unpacking the Policy Paradox of Municipal Takeover.* Minnesota: University of Minnesota Press.

O'Connor, Alice. 1996. "Community Action, Urban Reform, and the Fight Against Poverty: The Ford Foundation's Gray Areas Program." *Journal of Urban History* 22(5): 586–625.

Osborne, Melissa. 2019. "Who Gets 'Housing First'? Determining Eligibility in an Era of Housing First Homelessness." *Journal of Contemporary Ethnography* 48(3): 402–428.

Ostrander, Susan. 1995. *Money for Change: Social Movement Philanthropy at the Haymarket People's Fund.* Philadelphia, PA: Temple University Press.

Owens, Ann. 2016. "Inequality in Children's Contexts: Income Segregation of Households with and without Children." *American Sociological Review* 81(3): 549–574.

Owens, Michael Leo. 2007. *God and Government in the Ghetto: The Politics of Church-State Collaboration in Black America.* Chicago: University of Chicago Press.

Pacewicz, Josh. 2016. *Partisans and Partners: The Politics of the Post-Keynesian Society.* Chicago, IL: University of Chicago Press.

Page, Benjamin and Martin Gilens. 2017. *Democracy in America? What Has Gone Wrong and What We Can Do about It.* Chicago: University of Chicago Press.

Pallotta, Dan. July 4, 2016. "What Foundations Are Missing About Capacity Building." *Harvard Business Review*. https://web.archive.org/web/20201009020545/https://hbr.org/2016/07/what-foundations-are-missing-about-capacity-building

Papachristos, Andrew V., David M. Hureau, and Anthony A. Braga. 2013. "The Corner and the Crew: The Influence of Geography and Social Networks on Gang Violence." *American Sociological Review* 78(3): 417–447.

Park, Sunggeun, Jennifer E. Mosley, and Colleen M. Grogan. 2018. "Do Residents of Low-Income Communities Trust Organizations to Speak on Their Behalf? Differences by Organizational Type." *Urban Affairs Review* 54(1): 137–164.

Pasotti, Eleanora. 2020. *Resisting Redevelopment: Protest in Aspiring Global Cities.* New York: Cambridge University Press.

Pattillo, Mary. 2007. *Black on the Block: The Politics of Class and Race in the City.* Chicago: University of Chicago Press.

Peck, Jamie. 2012. "Austerity Urbanism: American Cities Under Extreme Economy." *City* 16(6): 626–655.

Peck, Jamie, Nik Theodore, and Neil Brenner. 2009. "Neoliberal Urbanism: Models, Moments, Mutations." *SAIS Review of International Affairs* 29(1): 49–66.

Peck, Jamie and Adam Tickell. 2002. "Neoliberalizing Space." *Antipode* 34(3): 380–404.

Pecorella, Robert F. 1985. "Resident Participation as Agenda Setting: A Study of Neighborhood-based Development Corporations." *Journal of Urban Affairs* 7(4): 13–27.

Pendall, Rolf, Juliet Gainsborough, Kate Lowe, and Mai Nguyen. 2012. "Bringing Equity to Transit-Oriented Development: Stations, Systems, and Regional Resilience." *Building Resilient Regions: Urban and Regional Policy and Its Effects* 4:1 48–92.

Peters, B. Guy and John Pierre. 1998. "Governance without Government? Rethinking Public Administration." *Journal of Public Administration Research and Theory* 8(2): 223–243.
Peterson, Paul E. 1981. *City Limits.* Chicago: University of Chicago Press.
Pettijohn, Sarah L., Elizabeth T. Boris, Carol J. De Vita, and Saunji D. Fyffe. 2013. *Nonprofit-Government Contracts and Grants: Findings from the 2013 National Survey.* Washington, DC: Urban Institute.
Pfeiffer, Sacha. 2014. "Innovative Tax Credits Await." *Boston Globe,* December 25, 2014.
Pierre, Jon. 1999. "Models of Urban Governance: The Institutional Dimension of Urban Politics." *Urban Affairs Review* 34(3): 372–396.
Pieterse, Edgar. 2019. "Urban Governance and Spatial Transformation Ambitions in Johannesburg." *Journal of Urban Affairs* 41(1): 20–38.
Pill, Madeleine. 2018. "Philanthropic Foundations in the City Policy Process: A Perspective on Policy Capacity from the United States." In *Policy Capacity and Governance: Assessing Governmental Competences and Capabilities in Theory and Practice,* edited by Xun Wu, Michael Howlett, and M Ramesh, 313–335. Cham: Palgrave Macmillan.
Piven, Frances Fox and Richard Cloward. 1977. *Poor People's Movements: Why They Succeed, How They Fail.* New York, NY: Pantheon.
Polletta, Francesca. 2002. *Freedom Is an Endless Meeting: Democracy in American Social Movements.* Chicago: University of Chicago Press.
Polletta, Francesca. 2005. "How Participatory Democracy Became White: Culture and Organizational Choice." *Mobilization: An International Quarterly* 10(2): 271–288.
Polletta, Francesca. 2013. "Participatory Democracy in the New Millennium." *Contemporary Sociology* 42(1): 40–50.
Polletta, Francesca. 2014. "Participatory Democracy's Moment." *Journal of International Affairs* 68(1): 79–92.
Polletta, Francesca and Pang Ching Bobby Chen. 2013. "Gender and Public Talk: Accounting for Women's Variable Participation in the Public Sphere." *Sociological Theory* 31(4): 291–317.
Polsby, Nelson W. 1980. *Community Power and Political Theory: A Further Look at Problems of Evidence and Inference.* New Haven, CT: Yale University Press.
Popkin, Susan J., Diane K. Levy, Laura E. Harris, Jennifer Comey, Mary K. Cunningham, and Larry F. Buron. 2004. "The HOPE VI Program: What about the Residents?" *Housing Policy Debate* 15(2): 385–414.
Powers, Martine. 2013. "Trying to Follow—and Read—the Signs." *Boston Globe,* June 16, 2013, B5.
Pratt, Gregory. 2019. "In Her First Official Act as Chicago Mayor, Lori Lightfoot Signs Order Aimed at Limiting Aldermen's Powers." *Chicago Tribune,* May 21, 2019.
Quinn, Rand, Megan Tompkins-Stange, and Debra Meyerson. 2014. "Beyond Grantmaking: Philanthropic Foundations as Agents of Change and Institutional Entrepreneurs." *Nonprofit and Voluntary Sector Quarterly* 43(6): 950–968.
Rainwater, Lee. 1970. *Behind Ghetto Walls.* Piscataway. NJ: Transaction.
Rankin, William. 2016. *After the Map: Cartography, Navigation, and the Transformation of Territory in the Twentieth Century.* Chicago: University of Chicago Press.
Reckhow, Sarah. 2012. *Follow the Money: How Foundation Dollars Change Public School Politics.* New York: Oxford University Press.
Reckhow, Sarah, Davia Downey, and Josh Sapotichne. 2019. "Governing Without Government: Nonprofit Governance in Detroit and Flint." *Urban Affairs Review* 1–31.
Reckhow, Sarah and Megan Tompkins-Stange. 2018. "Financing the Education Policy Discourse: Philanthropic Funders as Entrepreneurs in Policy Networks." *Interest Groups & Advocacy* 7(3): 258–288.
Reed, Adolph. 1999. *Stirrings in the Jug: Black Politics in the Post-Segregation Era.* Minneapolis: University of Minnesota Press.

Reich, Rob. 2018. *Just Giving: Why Philanthropy Is Failing Democracy and How It Can Do Better*. Princeton, NJ: Princeton University Press.

Reich, Rob, Lucy Bernholz, and Chiara Cordelli. 2016. *Philanthropy in Democratic Societies*. Chicago: University of Chicago Press.

Reyes, Victoria. 2018. "Three Models of Transparency in Ethnographic Research: Naming Places, Naming People, and Sharing Data." *Ethnography* 19(2): 204–226.

Rich, Michael J. and Robert P. Stoker. 2014. *Collaborative Governance for Urban Revitalization: Lessons from Empowerment Zones*. Ithaca, NY: Cornell University Press.

Rinaldo, Rachel and Jeffrey Guhin. 2019. "How and Why Interviews Work: Ethnographic Interviews and Meso-level Public Culture." *Sociological Methods and Research*, 1–34.

Rios, Victor. 2015. "Review of *On the Run: Fugitive Life in an American City* (University of Chicago Press, 2014)." *American Journal of Sociology* 121(1): 306–308.

Robinson III, John N. 2020. "Capitalizing on Community: Affordable Housing Markets in the Age of Participation." *Politics & Society*. 48(2): 171–198.

Robinson, Tony. 1996. "Inner-City Innovator: The Non-Profit Community Development Corporation." *Urban Studies* 33(9): 1647–1670.

Rohe, William M. and George C. Galster. 2014. "The Community Development Block Grant Program Turns 40: Proposals for Program Expansion and Reform." *Housing Policy Debate* 24(1): 3–13.

Rosen, Eva. 2020. *The Voucher Promise: "Section 8" and the Fate of an American Neighborhood*. Princeton, NJ: Princeton University Press.

Rosso, Patrick. 2012. "Mattapan Housing Nonprofit Faltering." *Boston Globe*, May 14, 2012.

Rosso, Patrick. 2013a. "Ballou Avenue Lots Eyed for Community Garden and Tot Lot." *Boston .com*, October 3, 2013.

Rosso, Patrick. 2013b. "City-owned Site in Uphams Corner Eyed for Public Works Facility to Be Sold Instead." *Boston.com*, August 13, 2013.

Rosso, Patrick. 2014. "City, Residents Discuss Sale of Maxwell Property in Uphams Corner." *Boston.com*, March 7, 2014.

Rothstein, Richard. 2017. *The Color of Law: A Forgotten History of How Our Government Segregated America*. New York: W.W. Norton.

Rubenstein, Jennifer C. 2014. "The Misuse of Power, Not Bad Representation: Why It Is Beside the Point that No One Elected Oxfam." *Journal of Political Philosophy* 22(2): 204–230.

Rubin, Lillian B. 1969. "Maximum Feasible Participation: The Origins, Implications, and Present Status." *ANNALS of the American Academy of Political and Social Science* 385(1): 14–29.

Ryan, Andrew. 2013. "Officials Hope Gang Raid Results in Long Prison Terms." *Boston Globe*, January 18, 2013.

Ryan, Andrew. 2015. "For Some City Councilors, Short Days in City Hall." *Boston Globe*, October 18, 2015.

Salamon, Lester M. 1981. "Rethinking Public Management: Third-Party Government and the Changing Forms of Government Action." *Public Policy* 29(3): 255–275.

Salamon, Lester M. 1987. "Of Market Failure, Voluntary Failure, and Third-Party Government: Toward a Theory of Government-Nonprofit Relations in the Modern Welfare State." *Journal of Voluntary Action Research* 16(1–2): 29–49.

Salamon, Lester M. 2012. *The State of Nonprofit America*. Washington, DC: Brookings Institution Press.

Salganik, Mathew J. and Karen E. C. Levy. 2015. "Wiki Surveys: Open and Quantifiable Social Data Collection." *PLoS ONE* 10(5): e0123483.

Sampson, Robert J. 1999. "What 'Community' Supplies." In *Urban Problems and Community Development*, edited by Ronald F. Ferguson and William T. Dickens, 241–292. Washington, DC: Brookings Institution Press.

Sampson, Robert J., Jeffrey D. Morenoff, and Thomas Gannon-Rowley. 2002. "Assessing 'Neighborhood Effects': Social Processes and New Directions in Research." *Annual Review of Sociology* 28: 443–478.

Sapotichne, Joshua, Bryan D. Jones, and Michelle Wolfe. 2007. "Is Urban Politics a Black Hole? Analyzing the Boundary Between Political Science and Urban Politics." *Urban Affairs Review* 43(1): 76–106.

Saward, Michael. 2006. "The Representative Claim." *Contemporary Political Theory* 5(3): 297–318.

Saward, Michael. 2009. "Authorisation and Authenticity: Representation and the Unelected." *Journal of Political Philosophy* 17(1): 1–22.

Schlozman, Kay Lehman, Henry E. Brady, and Sidney Verba. 2018. *Unequal and Unrepresented: Political Inequality and the People's Voice in the New Gilded Age*. Princeton, NJ: Princeton University Press.

Schragger, Richard. 2016. *City Power: Urban Governance in a Global Age*. New York: Oxford University Press.

Schwartz, Alex F. 2010. *Housing Policy in the United States*. New York: Routledge.

Scott, James C. 1998. *Seeing Like a State: How Certain Schemes to Improve the Human Condition Have Failed*. New Haven, CT: Yale University Press.

Seamster, Louise. 2016. *Race, Power and Economic Extraction in Benton Harbor, MI*. PhD diss.,, Duke University.

Seamster, Louise. 2018. "When Democracy Disappears: Emergency Management in Benton Harbor." *Du Bois Review: Social Science Research on Race* 15(2): 295–322.

Seamster, Louise and Raphaël Charron-Chénier. 2017. "Predatory Inclusion and Education Debt: Rethinking the Racial Wealth Gap." *Social Currents* 4(3): 199–207.

Self, Robert and Thomas Sugrue. 2002. "The Power of Place: Race, Political Economy, and Identity in the Postwar Metropolis." In *A Companion to Post-1945 America*, edited by Jean-Christophe Agnew and Roy Rosenzweig, 20–43. Malden, MA: Wiley-Blackwell.

Selznick, Philip. 1953. *TVA and the Grass Roots: A Study in the Sociology of Formal Organization*. Berkeley and Los Angeles: University of California Press.

Sharkey, Patrick, Gerard Torrats-Espinosa, and Delaram Takyar. 2017. "Community and the Crime Decline: The Causal Effect of Local Nonprofits on Violent Crime." *American Sociological Review* 82(6): 1214–1240.

Sheffer, Lior, Peter John Loewen, Stuart Soroka, Stefaan Walgrave, and Tamir Sheafer. 2018. "Nonrepresentative Representatives: An Experimental Study of the Decision Making of Elected Politicians." *American Political Science Review* 112(2): 302–321.

Shelton, Kyle. 2017. *Power Moves: Transportation, Politics, and Development in Houston*. Austin: University of Texas Press.

Shipp, Sigmund C. 1996. "The Road Not Taken: Alternative Strategies for Black Economic Development in the United States." *Journal of Economic Issues* 30(1): 79–95.

Siliunas, Andreja, Mario L. Small, and Joseph Wallerstein. 2019. "We Can Help, but There's a Catch: Nonprofit Organizations and Access to Government-Funded Resources among the Poor." *Journal of Organizational Ethnography* 8(1): 109–128.

Silverman, Robert M., Henry Louis Taylor, Jr, Li Yin, Camden Miller, and Pascal Buggs. 2020. "Are We Still Going Through the Empty Ritual of Participation?: Inner-City Residents' and Other Grassroots Stakeholders' Perceptions of Public Input and Neighborhood Revitalization in Buffalo, NY." *Critical Sociology* 46(3): 413–428.

Simon, William H. 2001. *The Community Economics Development Movement: Law, Business, and the New Social Policy*. Durham, NC: Duke University Press.
Siriani, Carmen. 2010. *Investing in Democracy: Engaging Citizens in Collaborative Democracy*. Washington, DC: Brookings Institution Press.
Slater, Cliff. 1997. "General Motors and the Demise of Streetcars." *Transportation Quarterly* 51: 45–66.
Small, Mario L. 2004. *Villa Victoria: The Transformation of Social Capital in a Boston Barrio*. Chicago, IL: University of Chicago Press.
Small, Mario L. 2006. "Neighborhood Institutions as Resource Brokers: Childcare Centers, Inter-Organizational Ties, and Resource Access Among the Poor." *Social Problems* 53(2): 274–292.
Small, Mario L. 2008. "Four Reasons to Abandon the Idea of 'The Ghetto.'" *City & Community* 7(4): 389–398.
Small, Mario L. 2009. " 'How many cases do I need?' On Science and the Logic of Case Selection in Field-Based Research." *Ethnography* 10(1): 5–38.
Small, Mario L., David J. Harding, and Michéle Lamont. 2010. "Reconsidering Culture and Poverty." *Annals of the American Academy of Political and Social Science* 629: 6–27.
Smith, Sandra Susan. 2006. *Lone Pursuit: Distrust and Defensive Individualism Among the Black Poor*. New York: Russell Sage.
Smith, Steven Rathgeb, and Michael Lipsky. 1993. *Nonprofits for Hire: The Welfare State in the Age of Contracting*. Cambridge, MA: Harvard University Press.
Špringer, Emily. 2020. "Bureaucratic Tools in (Gendered) Organizations Performance Metrics and Gender Advisors in International Development." *Gender & Society* 34(1): 56–80.
Squires, Gregory. 1991. "Partnership and the Pursuit of the Private City." In *Urban Life in Transition*, edited by M. Gottdiener and Chris Pickavance. Newbury Park, CA: Sage.
St. Clair, David J. 1981. "The Motorization and Decline of Urban Public Transit, 1935–1950." *Journal of Economic History* 41(3): 579–600.
Stoecker, Randy. 1997. "The CDC Model of Urban Redevelopment: A Critique and an Alternative." *Journal of Urban Affairs* 19(1): 1–22.
Stoker, Gerry. 2006. "Public Value Management: A New Narrative for Networked Governance?" *American Review of Public Administration* 36(1): 41–57.
Stone, Clarence N. 1989. *Regime Politics: Governing Atlanta, 1946-1988*. Lawrence: University Press of Kansas.
Stone, Clarence and Robert P. Stoker. 2015. *Urban Neighborhoods in a New Era: Revitalization Politics in the Postindustrial City*. Chicago: University of Chicago Press.
Suárez, David F. 2010. "Collaboration and Professionalization: The Contours of Public Sector Funding for Nonprofit Organizations." *Journal of Public Administration Research and Theory* 21(2): 307–326.
Suárez, David F., Kelly Husted, and Andreu Casas. 2018. "Community Foundations as Advocates: Social Change Discourse in the Philanthropic Sector." *Interest Groups & Advocacy* 7(3): 206–232.
Sugrue. Thomas J. 1996. *The Origins of the Urban Crisis: Race and Inequality in Postwar Detroit*. Princeton, NJ: Princeton University Press.
Suttles, Gerald D. 1972. *The Social Construction of Communities*. Chicago: University of Chicago Press.
Swanstrom, Todd. 1999. "The Nonprofitization of United States Housing Policy: Dilemmas of Community Development." *Community Development Journal* 34(1): 28–37.
Swyngedouw, Eric. 1997. "Neither Global Nor Local: 'Glocalization' and the Politics of Scale." In *Spaces of Globalization: Reasserting the Power of the Local*, edited by K. Cox. New York: Guilford Press.

Swyngedouw, Erik. 2009. "The Antinomies of the Postpolitical City: In Search of a Democratic Politics of Environmental Production." *International Journal of Urban and Regional Research* 33(3): 601–620.
Tabb, William K. 1979. "What Happened to Black Economic Development?" *Review of Black Political Economy* 9(4): 392.
Tach, Laura M. 2009. "More than Bricks and Mortar: Neighborhood Frames, Social Processes, and the Mixed-Income Redevelopment of a Public Housing Project." *City & Community* 8(3): 269–299.
Tach, Laura M. and Allison Dwyer Emory. 2017. "Public Housing Redevelopment, Neighborhood Change, and the Restricting of Urban Inequality." *American Journal of Sociology* 123(3): 686–739.
Taylor, Keeanga-Yamahtta. 2019. *Race for Profit: How Banks and the Real Estate Industry Undermined Black Homeownership*. Chapel Hill: University of North Carolina Press.
Teles, Steven and Mark Schmitt. 2011. "The Elusive Craft of Evaluating Advocacy." *Stanford Social Innovation Review* 9(3): 40–43.
Thibault, Robert E. 2007. "Between Survival and Revolution: Another Community Development System Is Possible." *Antipode* 39(5): 874–895.
Thomson, Dale E. 2018. "Strategic Geographic Targeting in Community Development: Examining the Congruence of Political, Institutional, and Technical Factors." *Urban Affairs Review* 47(4): 564–594.
Thomson, Dale E. 2020. "Philanthropic Funding for Community and Economic Development: Exploring Potential for Influencing Policy and Governance." *Urban Affairs Review*, 1–41.
Tompkins-Stange, Megan E. 2016. *Policy Patrons. Philanthropy, Education Reform, and the Politics of Influence*. Cambridge, MA: Harvard Education Press.
Trojano, Katie. 2019. "Tenants Rally Against Rents, Conditions at Fairlawn Apartments in Mattapan." *Dorchester Reporter*, October 23, 2019.
Trounstine, Jessica. 2009. "All Politics Is Local: The Reemergence of the Study of City Politics." *Perspectives on Politics* 7(3): 611–618.
Trounstine, Jessica. 2018. *Segregation by Design: Local Politics and Inequality in American Cities*. New York: Cambridge University Press.
Urban Institute. 2013. *Developing Choice Neighborhoods: An Early Look at Implementation in Five Sites—Interim Report*. Washington, DC.
Vale, Lawrence J. 2002. *Reclaiming Public Housing: A Half Century of Struggle in Three Public Neighborhoods*. Cambridge, MA: Harvard University Press.
Vargas, Robert. 2016. *Wounded City: Violent Turf Wars in a Chicago Barrio*. New York: Oxford University Press.
Venkatesh, Sudhir. 2000. *American Project: The Rise and Fall of a Modern Ghetto*. Cambridge, MA: Harvard University Press.
von Hoffman, Alexander. 2013. "The Past, Present, and Future of Community Development." *Shelterforce*, https://web.archive.org/web/20200502153238/https://shelterforce.org/2013/07/17/the_past_present_and_future_of_community_development/
Wachhaus, Aaron. 2014. "Governance beyond Government." *Administration & Society* 46(5): 573–593.
Wachsmuth, David. 2017. "Infrastructure Alliances: Supply-Chain Expansion and Multi-City Growth Coalitions." *Economic Geography* 93(1): 44–65.
Walker, Christopher. 2002. *Community Development Corporations and Their Changing Support Systems*. Washington, DC: Brookings.
Walker, Edward T. 2013. "Signaling Responsibility, Deflecting Controversy: Strategic and Institutional Influences on the Charitable Giving of Corporate Foundations in the Health Sector." *Research in Political Sociology* 21: 181–214.

Walker, Edward T. 2014. *Grassroots for Hire: Public Affairs Consultants in American Democracy*. New York: Cambridge University Press.
Walker, Edward T. 2016. "Between Grassroots and 'Astroturf': Understanding Mobilization from the Top-Down." *SAGE Handbook of Resistance* 269.
Walker, Edward T. and Yotala Oszkay Febres-Cordero. 2020. "The Changing Face of Nonprofit Advocacy in the 21st Century: Democratizing Potentials and Risks in an Unequal Context." In *The Nonprofit Sector: A Research Handbook, 3rd edition*, edited by Walter W. Powell and Patricia Bromley. Palo Alto, CA: Stanford University Press.
Walker, Edward T. and Lina Stepick. 2020. "Valuing the Cause: A Theory of Authenticity in Social Movements." *Mobilization* 25(1):1–25.
Warner, Jr., Sam Bass. 1978. *Streetcar Suburbs: The Process of Growth in Boston, 1870–1900*. Cambridge, MA: Harvard University Press.
Weir, Margaret. 1999. "Politics, Money, and Power in Community Development." In *Urban Problems and Community Development*, edited by Ronald F. Ferguson and William T. Dickens. Washington, DC: Brookings Institution Press.
Weir, Margaret, Jane Rongerude, and Christopher K. Ansell. 2009. "Collaboration Is Not Enough: Virtuous Cycles of Reform in Transportation Policy." *Urban Affairs Review* 44(4): 455–489.
Whitt, J. Allen and Glenn Yago. 1985. "Corporate Strategies and the Decline of Transit in US Cities." *Urban Affairs Quarterly* 21(1): 37–65.
Wilkerson, Isabel. 2011. *The Warmth of Other Suns: The Epic Story of America's Great Migration*. New York: Vintage Books.
Williams, Tate. 2018. "One of the Country's Largest Foundations Is Trying to Change How Philanthropy Works." *Inside Philanthropy*, August 14, 2018.
Wilson, William J. 1987. *The Truly Disadvantaged: The Inner City, the Underclass, and Public Policy*. Chicago: University of Chicago.
Wilson, William J. 1996. *When Work Disappears: The World of the New Urban Poor*. New York: Knopf.
Wilson, William J. 2009. *More Than Just Race: Being Black and Poor in the Inner City*. New York: W. W. Norton.
Wolfinger, Raymond E. 1973. *The Politics of Progress*. Englewood Cliffs, NJ: Prentice-Hall.
Woodsworth, Michael. 2016. *Battle for Bed-Stuy*. Cambridge, MA: Harvard University Press.
Wynn, Jonathan R. 2011. "*The Hobo* to *Doormen*: The Characters of Qualitative Analysis, Past and Present." *Ethnography* 12(4): 518–542.
Yin, Jordan S. 1998. "The Community Development Industry System: A Case Study of Politics and Institutions in Cleveland, 1967–1997." *Journal of Urban Affairs* 20(2): 137–157.
Young, Alford. 2006. *The Minds of Marginalized Black Men: Making Sense of Mobility, Opportunity, and Future Life Chances*. Princeton, NJ: Princeton University Press.
Zunz, Olivier. 2012. *Philanthropy in America*. Princeton, NJ: Princeton University Press.

INDEX

Note: Page numbers in italic type indicate figures or tables.

affordable housing, 6, 43, 189. *See also* community development
African Americans: activism of, 37–38; postwar migration of, 36; urban renewal's effect on, 6, 37–38
aldermanic prerogative, 13
Alinsky, Saul, 70, 114
ArtPlace America, 53
authenticity, 9, 18, 57, 111, 132, 202, 204, 227n19

Baker, Charlie, 129
Barr Foundation, 64, 73–74, 99, 119, 140, 141, 143, 145, 150–52, 154, 155
Barros, John, 121
Berger, Noah, 47
Big Dig. *See* Central Artery/Tunnel Project
Black Power Movement, 16, 166
block-busting, 36
Blue Hill Avenue Station, 176–81, 189–90
Blue Hill Avenue trolley, 34, 35, *35*
Boston Banks Urban Renewal Group (BBURG), 36, 87
Boston Development and Planning Agency, 127. *See also* Boston Redevelopment Authority
The Boston Foundation (TBF), 4, 21, 22, 32, 44, 50, 52–53, 55, 61, 62, 75–77, 102–6, 116, 137–38, 140–49, 152–55, 157–59, 196–98, 232n7
Boston Globe (newspaper), 39, 48, 124–25
Boston Redevelopment Authority (BRA), 22, 38, 52, 55, 61–64, 68–70, 77, 83–84, 88–91, 94–95, 97, 113–14, 116–18, 127, 130, 137–38, 149–50, 173–74, 182, 188, 231n33
Boston Transportation Department, 117
BRA. *See* Boston Redevelopment Authority
Brown, Angela, 50, 141–42, 145, 155

CAAs. *See* Community Action Agencies
capacity, as funding consideration, 15–16, 26, 52, 139, 156, 160, 196–99
Caribbean Integration Community Development, 231n33, 231n35
CBOs. *See* community-based organizations
CDBG. *See* Community Development Block Grant
Central Artery/Tunnel Project (Big Dig), 48, 99
Chang-Diaz, Sonia, 126–27
Chicago School of sociology, 86–87, 106
Choice Neighborhoods, 22, 51–52, 64, 160
citizens. *See* residents
City Growers, 109–11, 130
city officials: and Fairmount Corridor, 52–53, 62–65, 68–69; funders' relationships with, 148–49; local politicians' relationships with, 127; nonprofit organizations' relationships with, 52, 64–65; and urban renewal, 31, 36, 38
Clean Air Act (1990), 99
Clean Air Act Amendments, 48
climate change, 145
Codman Square, 1–2, 21, 95–97, 113–14, 130–32, 156
Codman Square Neighborhood Development Corporation (CSNDC), 2, 15, 32, 47–48, 66, 69, 99, 112, 114, 116, 130–32, 135, 155–56, 180, 196
community: conceptions of, 16–18, 172, 203–4; constructed character of, 17, 87–88, 204; ideological and strategic significance of, 25, 32, 69, 116–17, 168–69, 172–75, 189, 203–4; maps' representation of, 86–87; membership boundaries for, 170–71, 203; performance of, 17, 69, 172
Community Action Agencies (CAAs), 41–42, 49, 194, 224n31
Community Action Programs (CAPs), 41, 166

[257]

community-based organizations (CBOs): accountability of, 13, 26, 112, 135; activities of, 6; coalitions of, 65–66, 67, 68; "community" as defined by, 18; competitive context for, 6, 10; and Fairmount Corridor, 13, 21, 65–66, 66; federal funding for, 7, 9; funders' relationship to, 13, 26, 116, 139; as gatekeepers, 112, 114–16; governance role of, 9–10, 13–16, 60; government's relationship to, 15; growth of, 6, 7, 45; place of, in macro governance structures, 14–15; political involvement of, 111, 120–26; political restrictions on, 11, 111, 122; professionalization of, 6, 10, 46, 112, 136, 225n47; representative function of, 10, 13–16, 26–27, 65, 69–70, 109–18, 130–36; resources distributed to, 130–34; strategies of, 10, 15, 113–14, 118–20

Community Benefits Districts (CBDs), 195–96

community control, 199–202

community credentials, 168–69

community development: critique of, 203; defining, 1, 16–17; federal funding for, 43; funders' influence on, 144–46, 149–50; history of, 39, 41–43; metrics for, 161; nonprofits involved in Fairmount Corridor, 45, 46; planning phase for, 4–5, 44, 53; privatization of, 43–47, 50; variety of projects constituting, 23

Community Development Block Grant (CDBG), 7, 9, 43, 53

community development corporations (CDCs), 41, 44, 47, 49, 166

Community Development Innovation Forum, 128

community foundations, 6, 8, 140

Community Investment Tax Credit (CITC), 128–29, 198, 230n21

community organizing, 3–4, 68, 70–71, 114, 179–81

community participation, 163–91; conflicts in, 176–81; and consensus, 185–90, 201, 203; critiques of, 191, 199–202; deceptive appearances of, 166–67, 172–75, 181, 189, 203; enabling marginalized voices in, 199–202; examples of, 163–65, 174–85; growth of, 41; institutionalization of, 15, 166, 199; and lighting storage facility, 181–85; and transportation issues, 174–81, 189–90. *See also* public meetings; residents

Consalvo, Rob, 176–78

Conservation Law Foundation (CLF), 48–49

consultants, 6, 71–74

Coordinating Committee (The Vault), 59–60

corporations: as funders, 141; governance role of, 59–60

corridor, defined, 19–20

Corridor Advisory Group, 117

CSNDC. *See* Codman Square Neighborhood Development Corporation

Dahl, Robert, 10–11, 14

democracy: effect of funders' policymaking involvement on, 162; effects of nonprofits' policymaking involvement on, 9–10, 14, 26, 111–12, 135, 192–94; participatory, 166, 189

Department of Public Works, 182–84

DeShields, Spencer, 66, 68, 156

Design Studio for Social Intervention (DS$_4$SI), 201, 202

DiDemenico, Sal, 128–29

Dierker, Carl, 88

Dillon, Sheila, 185, 188

donor-advised funds, 140

Dorcena Forry, Linda, 32, 127–29, 133–34

Dorchester, 34, 36, 95, 102–3

Dorchester Bay Economic Development Corporation (DBEDC), 47–48, 52, 68, 71, 112, 121, 138, 155–56, 179, 188–89

Dorchester Reporter (newspaper), 184

DuBois, Jeanne, 64, 66–74, 79–81, 112–14, 118–19, 123, 125, 136, 138, 156–57, 179–80, 183–84

Dudley Street Neighborhood Initiative (DSNI), 51, 121, 182, 185–87, 197, 200

Dukakis, Michael, 48, 176

Early, Steve, 163–64, 169

East Boston, 103, 146

Economic Opportunity Act (1964), 41, 47

Enterprise Community Partners, 44

Environmental Protection Agency (EPA), 2, 22, 51, 62, 64, 73, 134, 146, 148

Erie-Ellington Homes, Four Corners, 109

INDEX [259]

Fairmount Corridor: annexation of, 34; boundaries of, 25-26, 83-106; branding of, 93-95, 105-6; CBOs in, 13, 21; community participation in, 163-91; "corridor" concept as basis of, 19-20, 48; demographics of, 21, 35-37, 88-90; as exemplar of US urban policy, 1, 24, 51, 62; funders' role in, 139; funding for, 51, 144-45; gentrification and, 19; government agencies involved in, 62-64; groundbreaking on station for, 1-2, 32, 80-81, 125; historical context of, 31-54; housing and community development nonprofits in, 45, 46; housing in, 36-37, 48; methodology of study of, 22-25, 82, 205-18; overview of, 19-22; poverty in, 102-4; principal funders for, 140-41; private meetings on, 4-5, 55-56, 62-63; public meeting on, 3-4; significance and promise of, 50
Fairmount Corridor CDC coalition, 48, 61, 66, 67, 68-69, 118-19, 148-52, 155-58, 197
Fairmount Corridor Greenway, 64-65, 73-74, 98-102, *101*, 114-15
Fairmount Corridor Planning Initiative, 22, 52-53, 62-65, 68, 70, 77, 83, 93, 113, 116-17, 137
Fairmount Greenway Task Force, 67, 73-74, 98-102, 106
Fairmount Innovation Lab, 53
Fairmount Line: fares on, 122-25; history of, 34; map of, *20*; new stations for, 1-2, 21, 47-49, 80-81, 125, 134, 163-65, 176-81; Orange Line relocation and, 39, *40*; overview of, 19-21; population measurements centered on, 89-90; schedule of, 122-23
Fairmount Transit Coalition, 67
Family Self Sufficiency program, 144-45
Federal Aid Highway Act (1956), 37, 225n48
Federal Housing Act (1949), 37
Federal Housing Authority (FHA), 36
Federal Transportation Administration (FTA), 117
Feloney, Mike, 23, 66, 68, 72, 79, 118, 122, 123, 156-59
Fields, Barbara (HUD Regional Administrator), 75-76

Fields, Barbara (Mattapan resident), 3-4, 6, 15, 176-78, 181
Flashman, Sherry, 71-72, 119
Ford Foundation, 39, 41-42, 50, 119, 140, 145, 160, 198, 232n7
Four Corners, 21, 80-81, 95-98, 109-11, 115-16, 163-66
Friedman, Evelyn, 130
Friends of Ballou Avenue, 69
funders/foundations, 137-62; agenda setting by, 50; brokering/networking capabilities of, 75-76, 139, 146-50; capacity as funding consideration for, 15-16, 26, 52, 139, 156, 160, 196-99; CBOs' relationship to, 13, 26, 116, 139; city officials' relationships with, 148-49; coordination among, 141-46; criteria of success used by, 13, 26, 139, 152-55, 160-61, 196-98; criticisms of role of, 76-77, 140, 161-62; evaluation methods of, 152-55, 198; funding decisions made by, 156-59; grants provided by, 6, 26, 43, 50; growth of, 6; policymaking and governance roles of, 12, 13, 41-43, 74-77, 138-39; political restrictions on, 11, 42-43; pooling and packaging of funds by, 139, 150-52, 155; professionalization of, 6; projects tailored to needs/strategies of, 144-46; public policy on, 197-98. *See also* community foundations
funding intermediaries. *See* intermediaries

Garfield Foundation, 52, 140, 149
gentrification, 19, 51, 134
geography: and branding, 93-95; of community, 86-87; constructed character of, 83, 95-98, 105-6; of Fairmount Corridor, 25-26, 83-106; the greenway and, 98-102; population in relation to, 88-90; sociopolitical considerations in determining, 83-86, 90-93, 95-98, 102-6; of Upham's Corner, 84-86
gerrymandering, 106
GFCAC. *See* Greater Four Corners Action Coalition
GNI. *See* Great Neighborhoods Initiative
government: CBO funding from, 7, *9*; CBO's relationship to, 15; nonprofit

government: CBO funding from (*continued*) organizations' partnerships with, 12. *See also* city officials; politicians, state and local

grants: competitive context for, 43, 60; criteria for distribution of, 43; pooling of, 26; race as factor in, 152–53; strategies for securing, 119–20

Gray Areas program, 41, 50, 145, 160

Greater Four Corners Action Coalition (GFCAC), 46–47, 54, 99–100, 109–11, 115–16, 127, 163–65, 167, 225n47

Great Neighborhoods Initiative (GNI), 142–43, *142*, 150–52, 155

Green Amendment (1967), 42, 53, 194

greenway. *See* Fairmount Corridor Greenway

Grove Hall, 21

growth coalitions, 11, 220n13

Harnik, Peter, 73–74, 81

Hart, Jack, 176–78

Heinz Endowments, 147

Henriquez, Carlos, 126–27, 185–87, 230n18

Herman and Frieda L. Miller Foundation, 140, *141*

Holmes, Russell, 126–27, 133–34

Home Owners Loan Corporation (HOLC), 36, 87

HOPE VI program, 44, 51

housing: effect of African-American postwar migration on, 36; in Fairmount Corridor, 48; nonprofits involved in Fairmount Corridor, *45, 46*; privatization of, 43–44; segregated, 36–37; urban-renewal developments, 37. *See also* affordable housing

HUD. *See* US Department of Housing and Urban Development (HUD)

Hyams Foundation, 50, 140–43, 145, 154, 158

Hyde Park, 34, 36, 95–97, 102–3, 113, 156, 159, 162, 233n29

inequality: funders' activities as contributor to, 144, 160; governance process as contributor to, 10, 15–16, 27, 112, 139, 192–93, 196; racism as factor in, 18; theories of, 14

Innovation District, 91–93

Inquilinos Boricuas en Acción, 38, 102

intermediaries, 44, 77–80, 140

Intermodal Surface Transportation Efficiency Act (ISTEA), 225n48

international nongovernmental organizations (INGOs), 12–13

Jamaica Plain, 38–39, 102

Johnson, Lyndon, 12, 41

Joint Committee on Internal Revenue Taxation, 42

Jones, Melissa, 143, 152–55

Juvenile Delinquency and Youth Offense Control Act (1961), 41

Kennedy, John F., 41

Kennedy, Robert F., 41, 42

Knowles, Glenn, 185–86

Kriesberg, Joe, 128

land-banking, 149

Latimore, Gail, 2, 10, 15, 66, 69, 100, 114, 116, 118, 126, 128–32, 136, 145, 156–57, 180–81

legibility, in planning and governance, 26, 88, 91, 95, 100, 102, 104–5, 228n7

LIHTC. *See* Low Income Housing Tax Credit

Local Initiatives Support Corporation (LISC), 44, 50, 56, 77–78, 116, 134, 141–43, 145, 148, 152–55, 158, 198, 232n7

Logan Square, 21

Lower Roxbury, 38

Low Income Housing Tax Credit (LIHTC), 44, 47, 54, 225n38

MAPC. *See* Metropolitan Area Planning Council

maps, as political constructions, 86–87

Martin, Marvin, 21, 47, 48, 74, 99, 109–11, 115, 127, 163, 165, 167

Massachusetts Association of Community Development Corporations (MACDC), 58, 119, 121, 128, 129

Massachusetts Bay Transportation Authority (MBTA), 53

Massachusetts Smart Growth Alliance (MSGA), 141, 142–43, 150–52, 155, 195–96

Mattapan, 3, 15, 21, 34, 36, 39, 95–98, 102–3, 133–34, 156–58, 162, 176–78, 189–90, 231n33
Mattapan Community Development Corporation (MCDC), 15, 47–48, 68, 129, 132–35, 156–58, 160, 179, 196–98
Maxwell Building, Upham's Corner, 181–90, 199, 201–2
MBTA. *See* Massachusetts Bay Transportation Authority
MCDC. *See* Mattapan Community Development Corporation
McMillan, Theresa, 117
Meade, Peter, 118, 130
Melo, Mary Beth, 88
Menino, Thomas, 2, 32, 76–77, 81, 88, 90–91, 120, 124, 185
Metropolitan Area Planning Council (MAPC), 78–80, 143, 232n7, 233n25
Metropolitan Boston Housing Partnership (MBHP), 56, 144–45
Metropolitan Planning Organizations, 225n48
Murray, Timothy, 127

neighborhoods, defined, 21
neoliberal urbanism, 5
New Communities Program, 142
Newmarket, 20–21
New York Streets neighborhood, 38
nonelected neighborhood representatives, 13, 112, 135, 194–95, 221n27
nonprofit organizations: accountability of, 192–95, 197; city officials' relationships with, 52, 64–65; diversification of, 195–96; federal funding for, 41; government partnerships with, 12; growth of, 6; involved in Fairmount Corridor housing and community development, *45, 46*; policymaking and governance roles of, 9–10, 12–14, 192–95; public policy on, 197–98. *See also* community-based organizations; funders/foundations
Norris, Chris, 144–45
Not In My Backyard (NIMBY), 180

Obama, Barack, 22, 25, 49, 54, 169
Orange Line, 39, *40*

pairwise wiki surveys, 201–2
Palmarin, Inés, 55–56, 97–98, 137
participation. *See* community participation
Partnership for Sustainable Communities, 51, 62, 146, 148. *See also* Sustainable Communities program
Patrick, Deval, 2, 4, 32, 121, 124, 128, 176, 181
performance: of community, 17, 69, 172; of partnership role, 25, 58, 62, 81
philanthropists, 12. *See also* funders/foundations
Planning Office for Urban Affairs, 231n33, 231n35
political displacement, 200
politicians, state and local: city officials' relationships with, 127; legislative role of, 127–29; policymaking and governance roles of, 9, 13–14, 26, 53, 117–18, 126–29, 133–34, 221n27; representative function of, 135–36, 230n25. *See also* city officials
poverty, 102–4, 161
Pradhan, Geeta, 5, 32–33, 49–52, 55, 75–77, 81, 83, 102–5, 116, 137–38, 141–42, 144–50, 152–55, 157–59
Pressley, Ayanna, 127
private meetings: examples of, 4–5; on Fairmount Corridor, 55–56, 62–63; local politicians' absence from, 112; prior to public meetings, 5, 167
program grants, 198
Promise Neighborhoods, 22, 51, 52
public housing, 43–44, 224n17
public meetings: critiques of, 199–201; examples of, 3, 163–65, 167–69, 172–75; impact of, 26, 199; institutionalization of, 6, 10, 165–66. *See also* community participation
public transportation, 34–35, 39

race: as factor in grant evaluations, 152–53, 155; urban governance affected by, 18–19; workforce composition and, 164–65, 169, 172. *See also* African Americans
RC/RF. *See* Resilient Communities/Resilient Families
Readville, 20–21

red-lining, 36
regime theory, 11, 220n14
residents: political power of, 6, 26–27, 163–91; representation of (by CBOs vs. politicians), 10, 13, 15–16, 26–27, 65, 69–70, 109–18, 126–36; strategies of, 3. *See also* community participation
Resilient Communities/Resilient Families (RC/RF), 142, *142*, 145, 152–55
right-of-return guarantees, 37, 52
Riley Foundation, 197
Rockefeller, John D., 12, 197
Romney, Mitt, 48, 49
Rose Fitzgerald Kennedy Greenway, 99
Roxbury, 35, 39, 95, 102–3
Roxbury-Dorchester-Mattapan Transit Needs Study, 170

Salvucci, Fred P., 48
S&R Construction Company, 163–65, 169
Sargent, Francis W., 38–39
Scott, Beverly, 124–26
seats at the table, who had them and how they got them, 55–82; consultants, 71–74; funders, 74–77; government officials, 62–65; intermediaries, 77–80; networks, 60–62; nonprofit organizations, 62
Shen, Kairos, 52–53, 62–64, 118, 149
smart growth, 48
Smith, Harry, 185–88
South End, 38–39, 102
South Station, 89, 91–93
Southwest Boston Community Development Corporation (SWBCDC), 47–48, 68, 72, 122, 156, 158–60, 198
Southwest Corridor Park, 98–99
Southwest Expressway proposal, 38–39
Special Impact Program, 41
suburbanization, 36–37
Sustainable Communities program (HUD), 143–45. *See also* Partnership for Sustainable Communities
sustainable development, 15, 51, 62, 141–43

Tax Reform Act (1969), 42–43, 160, 194
Tax Reform Act (1986), 44
TBF. *See* The Boston Foundation

Thall, Mat, 71–73, 90, 92, 113–14, 119, 120, 138
Tighe, Joan, 71–72, 74, 79–80, 121–22, 151, 184–86
Tinlin, Tom, 117
TOD. *See* transit-oriented development
TPL. *See* Trust for Public Land
transit-oriented development (TOD), 47–49, 84, 88, 105–6
Transportation for Massachusetts (T_4MA), 121
Trust for Public Land (TPL), 73–74

United States Commission on Industrial Relations, 12
United States Housing Act (1954), 37
Upham's Corner, 15, 21, 39, 70, 83–87, *85*, 95, 112, 113, 138, 155, 172–73, 181–90, 199, 201–2
Upham's Corner Working Advisory Group, 83–86, 88
urban agriculture, 69, 110, 127, 130–31
urban governance: collaborative character of, 5, 57–58, 60; features of, 5; history of, 25, 57, 59; issues in, 9; public-private partnerships in, 7, 12–15, 25, 42, 52–54; race as factor in, 18–19; theories of, 10–12
urban policymaking: community-driven approach to, 39, 41–43; network model of, *61*, 226n13; Obama-era, 49–53; participatory character of, 6; paths to participation in, 55–82; people-based vs. place-based focus of, 49; perspectives on process of, 5; public-private partnerships in, 7, 33, 39, 41–43, 49–53, 62–65, 68–69, 135, 192–96; recommendations for, 193–204; residential vs. downtown focus of, 60; transit-oriented development (TOD), 47–49; urban renewal, 37–39
urban renewal, 5–6, 31, 37–39, 195
US Department of Education, 51
US Department of Housing and Urban Development (HUD), 22, 44, 51, 62, 75, 143, 159
US Department of Transportation (DOT), 22, 51, 62
US Senate Subcommittee on Antitrust and Monopoly, 34

Van Meter, Bob, 50, 141–42, 145, 148, 152, 154–55
The Vault. *See* Coordinating Committee

Walsh, Marty, 80–81, 121, 227n23
War on Poverty, 12, 41–42, 49, 53, 54, 194, 199

West End, 6, 31, 37
white flight, 36
Wilson, William Julius, 14, 16, 51
The Wire (television show), 33
Wu, Michelle, 127, 230n20

Yancey, Charles, 109–11, 127, 130–31, 132

A NOTE ON THE TYPE

THIS BOOK has been composed in Miller, a Scotch Roman typeface designed by Matthew Carter and first released by Font Bureau in 1997. It resembles Monticello, the typeface developed for The Papers of Thomas Jefferson in the 1940s by C. H. Griffith and P. J. Conkwright and reinterpreted in digital form by Carter in 2003.

Pleasant Jefferson ("P. J.") Conkwright (1905–1986) was Typographer at Princeton University Press from 1939 to 1970. He was an acclaimed book designer and AIGA Medalist.

The ornament used throughout this book was designed by Pierre Simon Fournier (1712–1768) and was a favorite of Conkwright's, used in his design of the *Princeton University Library Chronicle*.

CPSIA information can be obtained
at www.ICGtesting.com
Printed in the USA
JSHW020452150421
13598JS00002B/5